# AQUINAS'S
# *SUMMA THEOLOGIAE*

**Critical Essays on the Classics**
Series Editor: Steven M. Cahn

The volumes in this series offer insightful and accessible essays that shed light on the classics of philosophy. Each of the distinguished editors has selected outstanding work in recent scholarship to provide today's readers with a deepened understanding of the most timely issues raised in these important texts.

# AQUINAS'S
# *SUMMA THEOLOGIAE*
## Critical Essays

Edited by
Brian Davies

ROWMAN & LITTLEFIELD PUBLISHERS, INC.
*Lanham • Boulder • New York • Toronto • Oxford*

ROWMAN & LITTLEFIELD PUBLISHERS, INC.

Published in the United States of America
by Rowman & Littlefield Publishers, Inc.
A wholly owned subsidiary of The Rowman & Littlefield Publishing Group, Inc.
4501 Forbes Boulevard, Suite 200, Lanham, Maryland 20706
www.rowmanlittlefield.com

PO Box 317
Oxford
OX2 9RU, UK

British Library Cataloguing in Publication Information Available

**Library of Congress Cataloging-in-Publication Data**

Aquinas's Summa theologiae : critical essays / edited by Brian Davies.
    p. cm. — (Critical essays on the classics)
  Includes bibliographical references (p.    ).
  ISBN 0-7425-4342-0 (cloth : alk. paper) — ISBN 0-7425-4343-9 (pbk. : alk. paper)
  1. Thomas, Aquinas, Saint, 1225?-1274. Summa theologica. I. Davies, Brian, 1951- II.
Series.

BX1749.T6T46 2005
230'.2—dc22                                            2005021615

Printed in the United States of America

♾™ The paper used in this publication meets the minimum requirements of American
National Standard for Information Sciences—Permanence of Paper for Printed Library
Materials, ANSI/NISO Z39.48-1992.

# Contents

# Introduction

*Brian Davies*

THOMAS AQUINAS NEVER CALLED himself a philosopher.[1] But his contribution to philosophy is now widely viewed as outstanding. Bertrand Russell (1872–1970) claimed that "there is little of the true philosophical spirit in Aquinas."[2] Yet the philosophical climate has changed since Russell's day, and philosophers now tend to view Aquinas with considerable respect. His philosophical stature has even been emphasized by those strongly disagreeing with him in various ways. Hence, for example, Anthony Kenny can write: "Aquinas is . . . one of the dozen greatest philosophers of the western world . . . His metaphysics, his philosophical theology, his philosophy of mind, and his moral philosophy entitle him to rank with Plato and Aristotle, with Descartes and Leibniz, with Locke and Hume and Kant."[3] Books and articles on Aquinas's philosophy appear almost daily and reflect an evaluation of Aquinas quite different from that of Russell.

At one level, indeed, Russell had a point. He thought that Aquinas always presupposed the truth of Christianity. "Before he begins to philosophize," says Russell, "he already knows the truth; it is declared in the Catholic faith."[4] Now Aquinas actually *denies* that the articles of the Catholic faith (which he takes to be basically equivalent to the content of the Nicene Creed) can be *known* to be true.[5] But he *does* take Christianity to be true, and he *presupposes* its truth in all of his writings. So if a philosopher is someone who cannot write as a committed Christian, then Aquinas is no philosopher and Russell was right. Yet why should it be thought that committed Christians cannot be good philosophers? Often referred to as the "father" of modern philosophy, René Descartes (1596–1650) had strong Christian convictions. So did other famous authors whose philosophical credentials are questioned by nobody—people such as John Locke (1632–1704), G. W. Leibniz (1646–1716), and George Berkeley (1685–1753). Russell may have been thinking that Aquinas's arguments rest only on theological premises, and if that were the case then one might well conclude that Aquinas really was no philosopher. But many of Aquinas's arguments do *not* rest on theological premises.[6] Christian though he was, Aquinas often wrote with no special reliance on any religious belief.

The contexts in which Aquinas worked were certainly heavily confessional. Born around 1224, he spent most of his short adult life teaching theology at the University of Paris and at priories or centers of study belonging to the Dominicans (the religious order of which he was a member).[7] In Aquinas's day, however, the teaching of theology almost always involved a serious engagement with philosophy. Like many of his academic colleagues, Aquinas was expected to be philosophically skilled, as indeed he was. He wrote commentaries on some major philosophical texts—such as Aristotle's *On the Soul, Physics, Politics,* and *Metaphysics.* He also wrote a number of works that are not especially focused on religious themes, texts that one can only classify as purely philosophical—such as *On Being and Essence* (*De Ente et Essentia*), *On the Principles of Nature* (*De Principiis Naturae*), *On There Being Only One Intellect* (*De Unitate Intellectus*), and *On the Mixture of Elements* (*De Mixtione Elementorum*).[8] Aquinas has many theological premises, to be sure. But he is not always invoking them when trying to build his case. In spite of what its title might suggest, he is not always doing so even in his *Summa Theologiae* (*Summary of Theology*).[9]

This work's primary interests are, indeed, decidedly theological. Presented as written by a Christian for Christians, it aims to explore what Aquinas calls *sacra doctrina* (*holy teaching*)—meaning the key doctrines of Christianity, which Aquinas takes to be founded on Scripture.[10] Yet much of the *Summa Theologiae* is also concerned to ask whether any of these doctrines can be defended in a purely rational fashion. So a lot of its text is devoted to arguing without reliance on "divine revelation" for the truth of such claims as 'God exists', 'God is X, Y, or Z' (e.g., eternal, omnipotent, knowing), 'The universe is created', 'People have freedom of choice', 'People need to be virtuous', 'People need virtues X, Y, or Z' (e.g., justice, temperance, courage), and 'People are such that they could have life after death'.[11] And, though Aquinas thinks that the major doctrines of Christianity, which he usually calls "the articles of faith" (*articuli fidei*), cannot be *proved to be true* by philosophical arguments, he does not therefore conclude that they cannot be *discussed philosophically*.[12] One can *philosophically engage* with those who seek to refute what one believes even if one cannot *prove* that what one believes is true. And that is what Aquinas thinks—the result being that, in addition to the straightforward philosophical arguments mentioned above, the *Summa Theologiae* contains a lot of sustained philosophical argument even while presupposing the truth of certain religious beliefs.

Hence, in spite of its theological interests, there is a lot of philosophy in the *Summa Theologiae*. Readers of the present book will quickly begin to see that for themselves, so I shall not labor the point. Yet I should say something about the *Summa Theologiae*'s structure. For the work does not read like philosophical texts with which readers unfamiliar with medieval authors are most likely to be accustomed. It is neither a dialogue nor an extended essay or treatise.[13] Instead it takes the form of countless questions, objections, replies to objections, and resolutions of issues. The reason for this lies in the fact that the *Summa Theologiae* aims to mimic the appearance of what its first readers would have referred to as "disputations" or "disputed questions" (*quaestiones disputatae*).

Much medieval university teaching consisted of respectful analyses of texts, and some of Aquinas's teaching conformed to this pattern. Hence, for example, his first appointment at the University of Paris gave him the title of *cursor biblicus* and required him to give purely expository lectures on the Bible. Texts, however, tend to make people curious about more than exegetical issues. They invariably lead us to ask not only "What is this passage saying?" but also "Should we agree with it?" By the thirteenth century, therefore, much university teaching was devoted to non-interpretational questions and to arguments for and against conflicting answers to them. This educational strategy reached a peak in the disputed question (*quaestio disputata*), which was very much a feature of university life in Aquinas's time. It took the form of an extended debate presided over by a *Magister* (a Master, i.e., a senior professor) and frequently took place over several days. A particular question (along the lines of "Is it the case that . . . ?") would be chosen for discussion. Participants would then offer a variety of reasons favoring one conclusion or another. Finally, the Master would adjudicate, defend his own answer to the question, and reply at length to all cases made against his position.[14]

Masters frequently published accounts of disputations in which they were involved as chair (so to speak), and Aquinas was one such Master. We do not know how many disputations he chaired, or in what contexts he chaired them, but he wrote a number of texts reflecting the form of disputed questions as they took place in his lifetime.[15] They do not make for quick reading. Each of Aquinas's published disputations raises a large number of questions. Each question then poses approximately fifteen or more objections to the position that Aquinas wants to defend. Finally, each question gives arguments by Aquinas in favor of his position, and replies to every objection. Time-consuming though they may be to read through,

Aquinas's disputations are wonderful instances of discussion at work. They never reach conclusions without an extraordinary degree of attention to arguments pointing away from the positions Aquinas defends, and their basic pattern is reflected in the *Summa Theologiae*. For this work is basically a series of abbreviated disputed questions. It does not list as many arguments in defense or in criticism of answers to questions as we find in Aquinas's *quaestiones disputatae*. But it follows their intellectual characteristics. So its objectors to Aquinas get a pretty good run for their money, and positions that Aquinas wishes to support are not granted easy acceptance.

Why did Aquinas write the *Summa Theologiae*? Though it reflects the form of disputed questions, it is not the product of any formal debates. Nor does it seem to spring from lecture courses that Aquinas gave as, for example, does his commentary on the *Sentences* of Peter Lombard.[16] But a case has been made for viewing the *Summa Theologiae* as intended by Aquinas as a tool to improve the teaching of theology in his own Dominican order. Leonard Boyle, the author of the first of the following chapters, argues that this is exactly what Aquinas had in mind as he started to write it, and Boyle's views have been met with solid scholarly approval.[17]

He begins by noting (1) that the Fourth Lateran Council (1215) explicitly allied the function of hearing confessions with that of preaching, (2) that the Dominican order was founded to be an order of preachers (something completely new in the Church at that time), and (3) that in 1221 Pope Honorius III gave the Dominican order a general (and unprecedented) mandate to hear confessions—the result being that from 1221 Dominicans saw their mission as one of preaching and hearing confessions.

Boyle then reminds us of some details of Aquinas's career prior to the time when he began to write the *Summa Theologiae*. From 1256 to 1259 Aquinas was Regent Master in Theology at the University of Paris, where his students would have been relatively advanced and also from various backgrounds. Between 1261 to around 1265, however, Aquinas was working as *Lector* (person responsible for studies) in the Dominican priory at Orvieto, where his students would only have been *fratres communes*—Dominicans assigned to the Orvieto house (which was a working priory, not a formal educational establishment). His primary job was to sound forth on moral theology, on which there were some standard Dominican textbooks then available—such as Raymond of Pennafort's *Summa de Casibus* and William Peraldus's *Summa Virtutum*.

Now, Boyle goes on to note, the evidence suggests that before 1259 the Roman Dominican Province (to which Aquinas belonged) gave little priority to intellectual matters. But from 1260, when Aquinas had a voice at his province's annual chapter (the governing body of his province), we find the

Roman Dominicans starting to legislate seriously with an eye on academic affairs, and in 1265 Aquinas was deputed to establish a house of studies at Santa Sabina in Rome. It looks as though he was given carte blanche when it came to matters of curriculum, and it also seems that he did some unusual things while teaching at Santa Sabina. For example, he lectured on Lombard's *Sentences*, but instead of focusing on Book IV of that work, which deals with practical theology, and was basic reading for Dominican students at the time, he turned to Book I, dealing with God, Creation, and the Trinity. At this time also, Aquinas began to write the *Summa Theologiae*.

Boyle concludes that Aquinas started this work because he was dissatisfied with the theological education that Dominican friars were getting. Aquinas himself says that he is aiming it at newcomers to the study of "catholic truth." "The purpose we have set before us in this work," he writes, "is to convey the things which belong to the Christian religion in a style serviceable for the training of beginners."[18] Boyle suggests that the "beginners" in question are first and foremost Dominican students (friars in course of formation) and non-teaching ordained friars, whose professional reading matter hitherto had been largely confined to manuals of moral and pastoral theology. And, Boyle adds, Aquinas was trying to provide a serious framework for this theology. He was aiming to put practical theology into a full doctrinal and theological context.

As stated earlier, though, the *Summa Theologiae* is not just a work of theology. So we may also suppose that Aquinas intended it to help theological readers to appreciate how philosophy and theology connect with each other. This allows us to view the *Summa Theologiae* as an extended essay in philosophical theology, one in which philosophy is given as much attention as theology. The *Summa Theologiae*'s arrangement of topics for discussion can be schematized thus:

> The nature of *sacra doctrina*
> The existence and nature of God
> The doctrine of the Trinity
> Creation in general
> Human nature
> Human action
> Human emotions
> Sin
> Law and politics
> The difference between Old and New Testament teaching
> Christian virtues
> Christ
> Christian sacraments

This framework is transparently theological. Aquinas is starting with God, considered as the threefold source of everything other than Himself.[19] Then Aquinas turns to people, considering what they are and what they should be. Finally, he discusses what might be said about people given the truth of Christianity—his basic idea being that we are all called to a life of union with God achieved through the work of God incarnate.[20] Yet Aquinas is of the view that theological conclusions are open invitations to cross-examination. Anselm of Canterbury (c. 1033–1109) says (in a prayer addressed to God): "I do not try, Lord, to attain Your lofty heights, because my understanding is in no way equal to it. But I do desire to understand Your truth a little . . . I do not seek to understand so that I may believe; but I believe so that I may understand."[21] When it comes to believing and understanding, Aquinas is of exactly the same mind as Anselm. So the *Summa Theologiae* subjects all of its theological topics to philosophical scrutiny.

Aquinas continually asks how his beliefs fare at the bar of reason, and the essays in the present volume follow his progress.[22] Or, at least, they follow his progress so far as space allows. Much of Aquinas's philosophy in the *Summa Theologiae* emerges in its detailed discussions of specific Christian doctrines, such as the doctrine of the Trinity. The chapters herein, however, look at the philosophy in the *Summa* by focusing on sections of the work in which Aquinas is not dealing with uniquely Christian notions. Hence, for example, three of the chapters (White, Wippel, and Davies) are concerned with what Aquinas thinks can be known and said about God simply on the basis of human reasoning. Davies's chapter discusses some key philosophical notions of Aquinas as presented in the *Summa Theologiae*, while those by Pasnau, Kenny, McCabe, and Stump engage with the *Summa*'s treatment of what would today be called "philosophy of mind." The remaining essays focus on what might be loosely called the *Summa Theologiae*'s moral philosophy.

As readers of this volume shall see, Aquinas provides a great deal of food for thought, and one might therefore wonder how and from which sources his thinking developed. An obvious answer is, "He developed it from himself, for he was clearly an outstanding thinker." And that would be a fair comment. But Aquinas obviously did not work in an intellectual vacuum. There were others who influenced him, even if only by writing works with which he disagreed. The following chapters do not much explore Aquinas's sources, so it should be noted here that there were, in fact, a number of these. The first, of course, was the Bible, followed by the so-called "fathers" of the Christian church—figures such as Augustine, St. John Chrysostom (c. 347–407), St. Gregory of Nyssa (c. 330–c. 395), Pope St. Gregory I (c. 540–604), and St. Jerome (c. 345–420). Aquinas's intellectual debts are not just biblical and patristic, however. As we have seen, he knew a lot about Aristotle.[23] But he also knew (and, with various qualifications, approved of) Plato, and philosophers writing in Plato's vein (commonly referred to as Neoplatonists).[24] Aquinas also drew on Jewish and Islamic authors—notable examples being Moses Maimonides (1138–1204) and Avicenna (980–1037). Aquinas's thinking sometimes resembles that of Maimonides and Avicenna to a striking degree, and both authors are cited multiple times in the *Summa Theologiae*. This is not, of course, to say that Aquinas merely echoes his sources uncritically. He is never the slave of his philosophical forerunners, even those with whom he is most strongly in agreement.[25]

What are the key philosophical positions defended by Aquinas in the *Summa Theologiae*? The following chapters provide some detailed answers to that question. Here, therefore, I shall simply suggest that readers new to Aquinas might like to bear in mind the following points.

First, the *Summa Theologiae*, like other writings of Aquinas, basically endorses Aristotle's teaching on substance, form, accidents, matter, act, and potentiality. This teaching is not easily summarized, and I shall not attempt to expound it here.[26] Those approaching the *Summa Theologiae* for the first time, however, would be well advised to learn something about it in advance.[27]

Second, much of the *Summa Theologiae*'s philosophy can be thought of as falling under the heading "philosophy of God." Since people have understood the word "God" in very different ways, readers of the *Summa Theologiae* should pay serious attention to what Aquinas means by the term and should not allow other meanings to affect their reading of his text. In particular, they should *not* suppose that by "God" Aquinas means, as do many theists, something like a disembodied person existing alongside the universe and standing next to it as an observer who sometimes intervenes.[28] In his commentary on Aristotle's *Peri Hermeneias*, Aquinas says that God is "outside the realm of existents, as a cause from which pours forth everything that exists in all its variant forms" (*extra ordinem entium existens, velut causa quaedam profundens totum ens et omnes eius differentias*).[29] For Aquinas, God is not a person, not even a disembodied one. Indeed, says Aquinas, God is not *an* anything. And He certainly does not coexist with the universe. Aquinas's God is (1) "Subsistent Being Itself" (*Ipsum Esse Subsistens*), (2) timeless, and (3) neither an observer nor an intervener. According to Aquinas, God's knowledge is the *cause* of things, not an *effect* of them. And, Aquinas thinks, God cannot *intervene* in the universe since He is *already* creatively present to *everything* in it.[30]

Third, the *Summa Theologiae* should be approached as written by someone with a high regard for logical rigor. Almost all medieval philosophers had serious interests in logic, interests not too prevalent among philosophers from the medieval period to the emergence of modern logic around the end of the nineteenth century. Aquinas is no exception, and the *Summa Theologiae* is as good an indication of this fact as are any of his writings. It displays strong concern with questions concerning inference, reference, predication, meaning, and modality, and its readers should be aware of the fact—implying, I am sorry to say (because of the work involved), that they might do well to approach the *Summa Theologiae* with some background in medieval logic. One will never properly understand Aquinas, even at his most theological, if one does not know something about the development of logic up to and including the time in which he was writing.[31]

Fourth (and perhaps a welcome point given what I have just said), the *Summa Theologiae* is very much a "reader-friendly" text. Yes, it comes from an age long ago. And, yes, it draws on sources and ideas unknown to, or disapproved of by, many people today. Yet Aquinas in general, and the *Summa Theologiae* in particular, is relatively easy to read. Aquinas writes with great conciseness and clarity. His style is simple and fluent, and, once one has mastered some of his technical terms, his train of thought is readily apparent. He continually succeeds in making it evident where he is *coming from*, where he is *now*, and where he is *going*. As Anthony Kenny has said, "The ability to write philosophical prose easily comprehensible to the lay reader is a gift which Aquinas shares with Descartes."[32] This gift, alas, has not been given to all philosophers, but students of philosophy should be aware that Aquinas had it and that he can therefore be approached as someone able to communicate even to readers today. So one should not be afraid of confronting his texts firsthand. The present volume provides important secondary literature on Aquinas, but it will not leave you face-to-face with him. The point I am stressing now is that, regardless of how you end up evaluating his thinking, a direct encounter with Aquinas is pleasurable rather than painful. And the pleasure factor is at its peak when it comes to the *Summa Theologiae*. This is definitely one of Aquinas's most accessible writings.

Finally, prospective readers of the *Summa Theologiae* should be advised that, contrary to what they might expect, it is a surprisingly modern work. For its philosophical content contains much that makes Aquinas more of a contemporary philosopher than were many thinkers who lived between 1600 and 1900. Between those dates Western philosophy was dominated by certain epistemological views, and by certain theories concerning the nature of people. Rightly or wrongly, these views and theories came in for considerable censure in the twentieth century. Yet Aquinas embraced few of them, and he manifestly anticipates what many of their critics have said. His philosophy of mind, for instance, bears serious comparison with that of Ludwig Wittgenstein (1889–1951).[33] The same might be said of his approach to the topic of knowledge and reasonable belief. It has been claimed that philosophy disappeared between Aristotle and Descartes only to be reborn around 1641. A much more prevalent view today is that philosophy was as alive as ever from around 1100 to 1600, and those who sympathize with this position often cite Aquinas, and the *Summa Theologiae*, in its defense.[34] Aquinas, they note, stands closer to contemporary Anglo-American philosophy than does post-Renaissance thinking.[35] Their view, I think, is justified, and it is well borne out by a careful reading of the *Summa Theologiae*. Those able to work through some of Aquinas's other writings will find this view equally corroborated by them. But the *Summa Theologiae* is a good place to start when turning to Aquinas for the first time. Hence the present volume.

## NOTES

1. In Aquinas's writings the word "philosopher" (*philosophus*) is always used to refer to various ancient thinkers, all of whom Aquinas takes to be pagans. He often expresses admiration for aspects of their writings. As a Christian, however, he holds that even the best of them fall seriously short when it comes to attaining truth.

2. Bertrand Russell, *A History of Western Philosophy* (New York: Simon and Schuster, 1945), p. 463.

3. Anthony Kenny, ed., *Aquinas: A Collection of Critical Essays* (London and Melbourne: MacMillan, 1969), p. 1. For Kenny's disagreements with Aquinas, see Anthony Kenny, *The Five Ways* (London: Routledge and Kegan Paul, 1969) and Anthony Kenny, *Aquinas on Being* (Oxford: Clarendon Press, 2002).

4. Russell, *A History of Western Philosophy*, p. 463. Here Russell seems to take "Catholic" to mean "Roman Catholic" in the sense familiar since the sixteenth-century Protestant Reformation. When Aquinas uses the word "Catholic" he, being a pre-Reformation thinker, understands it to be synonymous with "Christian."

5. For more on this topic, see my *The Thought of Thomas Aquinas* (Oxford: Clarendon Press, 1992), chapter 14. See also my *Aquinas* (London and New York: Continuum, 2002), chapter 19. The Nicene Creed was drawn up at the Council of Nicaea in 325.

6. By "theological premise" I mean a premise that explicitly asserts either (1) that God exists (on some understanding of 'God'), or (2) that Christian belief is true (where "Christian belief" means, roughly, what we find in texts like the Nicene Creed).

7. The best available biography of Aquinas is Jean-Pierre Torrell, op, *Saint Thomas Aquinas: The Person and His Work* (Washington, DC: Catholic University of America Press, 1996). For an excellent brief account of Aquinas's life, see also Simon Tugwell, ed., *Albert and Thomas: Selected Writings* (New York and London: Paulist Press, 1988). For material on the Dominicans prior to the time when Aquinas joined them, see Simon Tugwell, ed., *Early Dominicans* (New York and London: Paulist Press, 1982).

8. For a list of Aquinas's writings organized by type, see Brian Davies, ed., *Thomas Aquinas: Contemporary Philosophical Perspectives* (New York: Oxford University Press,

2002), pp. 385–87. The introduction to this volume also provides a brief overview of Aquinas's main teachings.

9. Thirteenth-century manuscripts give the title *Summa Theologiae*. In printed editions, however, one sometimes encounters *Summa Theologica* (*Theological Summary*). The *Summa Theologiae* breaks down into three major parts, the second of which is divided into two. They are commonly referred to as the *Prima Pars* (which I abbreviate as 1a), the *Prima Secundae* (1a2ae), the *Secunda Secundae* (2a2ae), and the *Tertia Pars* (3a). Each part of the *Summa* is further divided in Questions and Articles. Hence, for example, we may take "*Summa Theologiae* 1a, 12" to refer to *Prima Pars*, Question 12, and we may take "*Summa Theologiae* 1a, 12, 6" to refer to *Prima Pars*, Question 12, Article 6. Note, however, that there are no established conventions for referencing texts of the *Summa Theologiae*. So, as well as finding citations like 1a, 12, 6, readers may also find ones along the lines ST I, XII, VI—and so on. Readers, by the way, should also note that the *Summa Theologiae* is an unfinished work. Aquinas died before completing the *Tertia Pars*.

10. Setting the scene for what follows, *Summa Theologiae* 1a, 1 is explicitly devoted to *sacra doctrina*. Among other things, Aquinas here asks "Do people need it?," "Is it a 'science?'" (*scientia*), and "What is its relationship to philosophical reasoning?" For a splendid account of Aquinas and *sacra doctrina*, see Per Erik Persson, *Sacra Doctrina: Reason and Revelation in Aquinas* (Philadelphia: Fortress Press, 1970).

11. For 'God exists', see *Summa Theologiae* 1a, 2; for 'God is X, Y, Z', see 1a, 3–4, 6–11, 14, 18–21, 25–26; for 'The Universe is created', see 1a, 44–47; for 'People have freedom of choice', see 1a, 82–83; for 'People need to be virtuous' and for 'People need virtues X, Y, or Z', see 1a2ae, 1–5, 18–21, 49–66, 2a2ae, 57–61, 123, 141–42; for 'People are such that they could have life after death', see 1a, 75–76. Note that I am here only drawing attention to a few of the conclusions for which the *Summa Theologiae* offers purely philosophical arguments. There are many more purely philosophical arguments in the work that could be cited.

12. See *Summa Theologiae* 1a, 1, 8 for the general point. For Aquinas arguing that a particular Christian doctrine (the doctrine of the Trinity) cannot be established philosophically, see *Summa Theologiae* 1a, 32, 1.

13. So the *Summa Theologiae* does not look at all like, for instance, Plato's writings, or texts like Descartes' *Meditations*. Note, however, that many of Aquinas's writings do take the form of what we might call an essay, treatise, or even monograph. Examples include *De Ente et Essentia* and the *Summa contra Gentiles*.

14. For more on *quaestiones disputatae*, see *Thomas Aquinas: On Evil*, trans. Richard J. Regan, ed. with an intro. and notes by Brian Davies (New York: Oxford University Press, 2003), pp. 8–12. The best available discussion of the nature of medieval disputations is Bernardo C. Bazàn, John W. Wippel, Gérard Fransen, and Danielle Jacquart, *Les Questions Disputées et les Questions Quodlibétiques dans les Facultés de Théologie, de Droit et de Médicine* (Turnhout, Belgium: Brepols, 1985).

15. Aquinas's published disputed questions include: *De Veritate* (*On Truth*), *De Potentia* (*On the Power of God*), *De Anima* (*On the Soul*), and *De Malo* (*On Evil*).

16. Lombard (1095/1100–1160) was once Bishop of Paris. His *Sententiae in Quattuor Libris Distinctae* (*Sentences Divided into Four Books*) was a standard theological textbook from the thirteenth to sixteenth centuries. Aquinas lectured on it in Paris

from 1253 to 1256. For a recent study of Lombard, see Philip W. Rosemann, *Peter Lombard* (New York: Oxford University Press, 2004).

17. For someone disagreeing with Boyle, see John I. Jenkins, *Knowledge and Faith in Thomas Aquinas* (Cambridge: Cambridge University Press, 1997), chapter 2.

18. Prologue to Part 1 of the *Summa Theologiae*. I quote from Volume 1 of the Blackfriars edition of the *Summa Theologiae* (London: Eyre and Spottiswoode; New York: McGraw-Hill Book Company, 1964), p. 3.

19. "Threefold," of course, because Aquinas believed that God is Father, Son, and Holy Spirit (the doctrine of the Trinity).

20. As M.-D. Chenu famously noted, the *Summa Theologiae* has an *exitus-reditus* framework. It deals with a coming from God (*exitus*) and a return to him (*reditus*). See M.-D. Chenu, *Toward Understanding Saint Thomas* (Chicago: Henry Regnery Company, 1964), chapter 11. Chenu's reading of the *Summa Theologiae* has been criticized. For an introduction to the criticism, see Torrell, *St Thomas Aquinas: The Person and His Work*, pp. 150–53. Note that there is nothing especially original in the order in which Aquinas treats matters in the *Summa Theologiae*. This work more or less follows the plan of Peter Lombard's *Sentences*.

21. Anselm of Canterbury, *Proslogion* 1. I quote from Brian Davies and G. R. Evans, eds., *Anselm of Canterbury: The Major Works* (Oxford: Oxford University Press, 1998), p. 87. For Anselm on God and human understanding see Brian Davies and Brian Leftow, eds., *The Cambridge Companion to Anselm* (Cambridge: Cambridge University Press, 2004). Anselm's position is foreshadowed by that of St. Augustine of Hippo (354–430). See Augustine, *De Libero Arbitrio* (*On Free Choice*), Book 2.

22. A quick way to get a sense of the philosophical content of the *Summa Theologiae* is to read through *Aquinas: A Summary of Philosophy*, translated and edited by Richard J. Regan (Indianapolis: Hackett Publishing Company, Inc., 2003). This work is a translation of various parts of the *Prima Pars* and *Prima Secundae*. Even a glance at its contents will quickly convince readers that the *Summa Theologiae* is a profoundly philosophical work (i.e., one that endeavors to explore some familiar philosophical topics without reliance on religious authorities alone).

23. Aquinas often refers to Aristotle as "the philosopher." Aquinas's use of Aristotelian ideas has led many to take him to be nothing but an Aristotelian. But his thinking significantly differs from that of Aristotle. And Aquinas has questions to ask that Aristotle never raised—a significant one being "Why is there something rather than nothing?," a query that presides over much that Aquinas writes in the *Summa Theologiae* about the relationship between God and creatures.

24. Aquinas was the first person to recognize that a work known as the *Liber de Causis* (*Book of Causes*), formerly attributed to Aristotle, was actually derived from the *Elements of Theology* by Proclus (c. 410–485), a Neoplatonic philosopher and once head of the Academy at Athens. For more on this topic, see *St. Thomas Aquinas: Commentary on the Book of Causes*, translated and annotated by Vincent A. Guagliardo, Charles Hess, and Richard Taylor (Washington, DC: The Catholic University of America Press, 1996), pp. ix–xxxii. For more on Aquinas and Neoplatonism, see W. J. Hankey, *God in Himself: Aquinas's Doctrine of God as Expounded in the "Summa Theologiae"* (Oxford: Oxford University Press, 1987).

25. An example of a favored source treated critically by Aquinas is the unknown (c. 500) author commonly called Pseudo-Dionysius or Dionysius the Areopagite. In *Summa Theologiae* 1a, 13, Dionysius is the most quoted authority. Yet Aquinas subtly corrects his teachings as he puts them to his own uses.

26. Some of this teaching is explained in this volume's chapter by Peter Geach.

27. I offer an elementary account of Aquinas on substance and other topics in chapters 3 and 4 of my *Aquinas* (London and New York: Continuum, 2002). For similar accounts, see F. C. Copleston, *Aquinas* (Harmondsworth: Penguin Books, 1955), chapter 2, and Anthony Kenny, *Aquinas* (Oxford: Oxford University Press, 1980), chapter 2.

28. I try to bring out some of the differences between Aquinas and others on the significance of the word "God" in my *An Introduction to the Philosophy of Religion*, 3rd ed. (Oxford: Oxford University Press, 2004), chapter 1.

29. Thomas Aquinas, *Expositio Libri Peri Hermeneias*, Book I, lectio 14. I quote from Timothy McDermott, ed., *Thomas Aquinas: Selected Philosophical Writings* (Oxford: Oxford University Press, 1993), pp. 282–83.

30. For more on this topic, see my *Aquinas*, chapters 7–10. See also my *The Thought of Thomas Aquinas*, chapters 3–9. In developing his account of God, Aquinas takes himself to be writing in accordance with the Bible and the Christian tradition as it came to him via patristic authors and ecclesiastical councils. He is also indebted to authors in the Jewish and Islamic traditions. For Aquinas on God with an eye to Jewish and Islamic thinkers, see David Burrell, *Knowing the Unknowable God: Ibn-Sina, Maimonides, Aquinas* (Notre Dame, IN: University of Notre Dame Press, 1986) and David Burrell, *Freedom and Creation in Three Traditions* (Notre Dame, IN: University of Notre Dame Press, 1993).

31. Two books that might help readers to understand this topic are William and Martha Kneale, *The Development of Logic* (Oxford: Clarendon Press, 1962) and D. P. Henry, *Medieval Logic and Metaphysics* (London: Hutchinson University Library, 1972). See also E. J. Ashworth, "Language and Logic," *The Cambridge Companion to Medieval Philosophy*, ed. A. S. McGrade, pp. 72–96 (Cambridge: Cambridge University Press, 2003).

32. Anthony Kenny, *Aquinas on Mind* (London and New York: Routledge, 1993), p. 10.

33. This point has been much emphasized by, among others, Anthony Kenny. See his *Aquinas on Mind*.

34. This view is reflected in the numerous recent publications on medieval philosophy aimed at students and general readers. Examples include Jorge E. Gracia and Timothy Noone, eds., *A Companion to Philosophy in the Middle Ages* (Oxford: Blackwell, 2003), Norman Kretzmann, Anthony Kenny, and Jan Pinborg, eds., *The Cambridge History of Later Medieval Philosophy* (Cambridge: Cambridge University Press, 1982), and John Marenbon, ed., *Medieval Philosophy* (London and New York: Routledge, 1998). It is also worth noting that Cambridge University Press has highlighted medieval philosophy in some of the volumes in its "Companions to . . ." series. As well as including the general volume on medieval philosophy cited in note 29 above, the series now includes volumes on Abelard (1079–1142), Anselm, Aquinas, Duns Scotus

(c. 1266–1308), and William of Ockham (c. 1285–1347). Oxford University Press has also launched a series on medieval philosophers/theologians. Called "Great Medieval Thinkers," it currently includes studies of Bernard of Clairvaux (1090–1153), Duns Scotus, John Scotus Eriugena (ninth century), Peter Lombard, and Robert Grossetteste (c. 1168–1253).

35. Those who argue in this way tend to be analytical philosophers. Contemporary continental thinkers, although clearly often interested in Aquinas, are not currently exploring him in as much depth as their analytical colleagues. For more on Aquinas and analytical philosophy, see *The Monist* 80, no. 4, (October 1997) (the topic being "Analytical Thomism") and John Haldane, ed., *Mind, Metaphysics, and Value in the Thomistic and Analytical Traditions* (Notre Dame, IN: University of Notre Dame Press, 2002).

# 1

# The Setting of the *Summa Theologiae*

*Leonard E. Boyle*

S OME TIME IN THE SECOND HALF of 1261, nearly two years after he had re-
turned from Paris to Naples as a Master in Theology, there to continue
work on his *Summa contra Gentiles,* Thomas Aquinas was appointed to the
Dominican house at Orvieto as *lector conventus.* At the age of thirty-six, he
took his place in the normal stream of the Dominican educational system in
the order's Roman Province.

By now, the Dominican order was almost fifty years old and fairly set in its
ways. It had emerged as a recognized religious order in January 1217 when the
Spaniard Dominic obtained from Pope Honorius III a mandate that turned
his small band of local preachers in the diocese of Toulouse into an Order of
Preachers-in-General. Four years later, shortly before the death of Dominic, it
was entrusted as well by Honorius with a general mission of hearing confessions. The Fourth Lateran Council in 1215 had explicitly allied the function of
hearing confessions to that of preaching in its constitution *inter caetera.* From
1221 onward the implementation of that constitution in both its facets was, in
effect, the mission of the Dominican order.[1]

Perhaps the young Order of Preachers was surprised a bit by this second
papal mandate. A general mandate to hear confessions was as new in the life
of the church as the earlier commission of the members of Dominic's Order
as Preachers-in-General. But it met the challenge at once. Within a few years
of the encyclical letter of Honorius III of 1221, and just about the time of
Thomas's birth at Roccasecca in 1224 or 1225, at least four useful manuals on
the administration of the sacrament of penance had been compiled by members of the Order at Bologna, Paris, Cologne, and Barcelona, and soon were

circulating with the Dominicans as they spread in those years between 1221 and 1225 beyond France, Italy, Spain, and the Rhineland—the confines of the order in its first flush—to Britain, Ireland, Scandinavia, Poland, Hungary, and the Near East.

These four manuals, the most celebrated of which is Raymund of Pennafort's *Summa de Casibus*, first drafted at Barcelona about 1224, represent the very first literary activity of the Dominican order, something all too readily forgotten, if ever mentioned, by historians of the order. They were the forerunners of a remarkable flow of pastoral manuals of various sizes and shapes from Dominican pens over the three centuries before the Reformation, the better-known of which, to confine ourselves to the thirteenth and fourteenth centuries, are the revised edition of Raymund's *Summa* in 1234–1235, Hugh of St. Cher's *Speculum Ecclesiae* (ca. 1240), Willelmus Peraldus's *Summa Vitiorum* (ca. 1236) and *Summa Virtutum* (ca. 1236–1249/50), Vincent of Beauvais's *Speculum Maius* (1244–1259), James of Varazze's *Legenda Aurea* (1265–1267), Hugh Ripelin of Strasbourg's *Compendium Theologicae Veritatis* (1265–1268), John of Genoa's *Catholicon* (1286), John of Freiburg's *Summa Confessorum* (1298), and John Bromyard's *Summa Praedicantium* (1326–1349).

By and large, these manuals and aids were meant for the generality of the members of the Dominican order, for the *fratres communes* generally engaged in the twin functions of the order, preaching and hearing confessions, whose "whole zeal and labor should be directed chiefly toward the advancement of souls," as Vincent of Beauvais apologetically said of himself in his *Speculum Maius*.[2] These *fratres communes*, no matter what their age, are the "juniors" (*iuniores*), "beginners" (*incipientes*), and "the simple" (*simplices*) addressed in so many Dominican prefaces. They are, on the whole, those who had not had the chance of a higher education in the manner of Albert, Thomas, Peter of Tarentaise, or other intellectual lights of the "teachable" (*docibiles*) or Lector class. It was for them, principally, that Raymund, William Peraldus, and John of Freiburg wrote. It was for them, explicitly, that Simon of Hinton, probably in the 1250s when Provincial of England composed his *Summa Iuniorum*, and Aag of Denmark, when Provincial of Scandinavia at intervals between 1254 and 1284, his *Rotolus Pugillaris* ("for the instruction of young and other Dominicans who have to engage in preaching and hearing confessions").[3]

This wide and varied pastoral output hardly needs explanation. From its very beginnings, the Dominican order was dedicated to education with a distinctly pastoral bent: "All our training," the prologue to the first constitution of 1220 states, "should principally and wholeheartedly be directed toward making us useful to the souls of our neighbors."[4] Any and every aid and possible resource was therefore pressed into the service of the "care of souls" (*cura animarum*). Preachers had to have the Bible at their fingertips, so a great alphabetical concordance, the *Concordantiae S. Iacobi*, was begun by the community of St. Jacques in Paris before 1239, probably under Hugh of St. Cher, and was perfected over the next two generations.[5] The education of youth in faith and morals was a special challenge, so William of Tournai put together his *De Instructione Puerorum*, a work commended to the whole order by the General Chapter at Paris in 1264.[6] As chess was a popular game, Jacobus de Cessolis of the Dominican house in Genoa composed a mnemonic treatise on virtues and vices in terms of a chess board and chess pieces (ca. 1290), a treatise that had an enormous general circulation and was translated before 1500 into English (by Caxton), Dutch, French, Italian, Catalan, Spanish, Swedish, and Czech.[7]

Every Dominican house, too, was geared to study in the interests of the pastoral care, and was supposed to have its own Lector to look after the instruction of the community. And even after the younger *fratres communes* had become priests and were engaged in preaching and hearing confessions, only an ad hoc dispensation could excuse them at any point from attendance at the Lector's classes. In this sense, the *fratres communes* were forever *iuniores*.

## Thomas at Orvieto

Thomas, as far as we know, had his first taste of this ordinary Dominican world of *fratres communes*, pastoral aids, and practical theology when, after a seemingly studious period of almost two years at Naples, he took on the post of Lector at Orvieto in September or October 1261.[8] He was far removed from the bubbling atmosphere of the *studia generalia* at Cologne and Paris, between which he had spent some thirteen or fourteen years in all. Although he had the local stimulus and challenge of the papal court, then at Orvieto, his main job was to be at the disposal of his own *fratres communes*, the old with the young.

As we know from Humbert of Romans, who was general of the Dominican order precisely at this time (1254–1263) and compiled an invaluable *Liber de Instructione Officialium Ordinis Praedicatorum*, Lectors were supposed to be totally at the disposition of their brethren. Their vacations were to be taken only at times when the greater part of the community was absent, during the summer, for example, or during the preaching seasons of Advent and Lent. In their lectures, they should always aim at practical and uncluttered instruction. In their periodic disputations, they should confine themselves to "useful and intelligible matters."[9]

In theory at least, Thomas was not unaware of the demands on Lectors and of the limitations of these priory schools. In June 1259, some six months before he left Paris for Naples and, eventually, Orvieto, he had been, with Albert the Great and Peter of Tarentaise, a member of a committee of five that presented a *ratio studiorum* for the whole order to the general chapter at Valenciennes, north of Paris. In their report, Thomas and his fellow masters had suggested, among other things, that each conventual Lector should have a tutor to assist him, that no one, not even the Prior of the community, was to be absent from lectures, and that priories that found themselves temporarily without Lectors should set up private classes for the brethren on the *Historia Scholastica* (of Peter Comestor), the *Summa de Casibus* (of Raymund), or some such manual, to offset any danger of idleness.[10]

Thomas himself, as Lector at Orvieto, may have lectured on the Bible as such rather than on the standard medieval work of biblical history, the *Historia Scholastica* of Peter Comestor. His literal *Expositio in Job* is probably a reworking of lectures delivered during his four-year term at Orvieto. Possibly the *Postilla super Ieremiam* and *Postilla super Threnos* come from the same stable.[11] But these are works of an exceptional Lector. In all conventual schools, practical theology—"*Collationes de moralibus*," in Humbert's terms—was the order of the day, and this was the principal function of any conventual Lector, St. Thomas not excluded. And although we do not possess any record of "*Collationes*" over which Thomas may have presided, some idea of the type of question with which a Lector might be confronted is afforded by some questions sent to Thomas at Orvieto in 1262–1263 by his fellow Lector of Santa Maria Novella in Florence, James of Viterbo, later archbishop of Taranto.

Presumably because he was unable to frame an answer from the *Summa de Casibus* of Raymund to some tricky questions on buying and selling on credit in various Tuscan merchant circles, James sent the questions from Florence to the Lector of Orvieto. Thomas, in turn, consulted with Marinus of Eboli, archbishop-elect of Capua, and with the Dominican Cardinal Hugh of St. Cher, both of whom were then at the papal curia in Orvieto. Then, with a passing glance at what Raymund of Pennafort had to say in the *Summa de Casibus*, he penned the brief, lucid reply that is now among his *Opera Omnia* as *De Emptione et Venditione ad Tempus* and upon which he later based a part of an article in the *Secunda Secundae* of his *Summa Theologiae* (IIa IIae, q. 78, a. 2, ad 7).[12]

As one may see from a collection of moral problems put together about this time by a Lector in the North of England, solving *casus* was one of the principal methods of teaching practical theology in the Dominican order.[13] Inevitably, and like any other Lector—this English Dominican, for example, or, notably, John of Freiburg—Thomas would have used Raymund's *Summa de Casibus* as his springboard for occasional *casus* and for the regular conventual "*Collationes de moralibus*." By 1261, and indeed long before that date, the *Summa* of the former General of the Dominicans (1238–1240) had become an integral part of Dominican training. William of Rennes, Lector of the house at Orléans, had written a valuable *Apparatus* to it around 1241, as well as a series of *Quaestiones Adiectae*, and Vincent of Beauvais had incorporated long extracts from both Raymund and William into Books IX and X of his *Speculum Doctrinale* between 1244 and 1259. The acts of the General Chapter at Valenciennes in 1259, echoing the commission on which St. Thomas had served, single the *Summa de Casibus* out by name, as does Humbert of Romans when speaking of conventual libraries. According to Simon of Hinton a few years earlier, it was "possessed everywhere by the brethren," and there is evidence that abbreviations of it were common within and outside of the Dominican order.[14]

Scholars allow that Thomas, who may have embarked upon his *Summa contra Gentiles* (1259–1264) at Raymund's request, probably owes many of his civil and canon law references in the *Summa* and in the *Scriptum super Sententiis* to the *Summa de Casibus*. But the dependence runs much deeper than this. Thomas had a healthy respect for Raymund as both a fine legist and an able moralist. There is a manifest reliance on Raymund in St. Thomas's treatment of matrimony in his *Scriptum super Sententiis* (1252–1256).[15] There are large and unsuspected borrowings from the *Summa de Casibus* in the one question I have examined closely in the *Summa Theologiae*, that on simony in the *Secunda Secundae*, which corresponds to the opening chapter of Raymund's *Summa*. The whole of the *Ad Quintum* in IIa IIae, q. 100, a. 1 is word for word from Raymund, as are the *Ad Sextum* in IIa IIae, q. 100, a. 2 and the long *Ad Quintum* in IIa IIae, q. 100, a. 6.[16]

A professional familiarity as Lector at Orvieto with the *Summa de Casibus* and with the system of *casus* and "*collationes morales*" certainly aided Thomas when he began composing his *Summa Theologiae*, and particularly the *Secunda Secundae*; furthermore, it enabled him to field with ease the many questions concerning pastoral care at the six *quodlibets* (I–VI) held during his second Parisian sojourn from 1268 to 1272. All the same, Thomas may have felt that practical theology was too much with the Dominican order and that the *fratres communes*, and the students in particular, both at Orvieto and in the Roman Province, as well as in the order at large, were not being allowed more than a partial view of theology. Perhaps this is why, as I shall now suggest, Thomas began a *Summa Theologiae* at Rome soon after his move there from Orvieto in 1265. Perhaps, indeed, this is precisely why he moved.

## Thomas at Santa Sabina

On or about 8 September 1265, the annual Chapter of the Roman Province to which Thomas belonged enjoined on him from Anagni, and probably in his presence as Preacher General for the house in Naples, the task of setting up a *studium* at Rome for students from various houses of the Province. The place selected, although not specified in the acts of the Chapter, was Santa Sabina on the Aventine Hill, Dominic's second Roman foundation. Thomas probably took up residence there in late September or early October of that year, remaining for three full scholastic years until posted to Paris in, probably, summer 1268 by the general of the order, John of Vercelli.[17]

During his three years at Santa Sabina, Thomas was very active. He preached, made journeys out of Rome, and held *Quaestiones Disputatae de Potentia, De Malo* (probably), and *"De Attributis Divinis"* (the latter of which he then inserted into his *Scriptum super Sententiis* as I d. 2, a. 3).[18] He also supervised and taught the students at Santa Sabina.

Just what he taught them is a little difficult to ascertain. According to Tolomeo of Lucca in 1315–1317, who, as a young Dominican, had been his friend and confessor at Naples between 1272 and 1274, Thomas "expounded almost all of the philosophical works of Aristotle, whether natural or moral, while in charge of the *studium* at Rome, and wrote his lectures up in the form of a *scriptum* or commentary on each work, particularly on the *Ethics* and *Metaphysics*."[19]

While this might suggest that Thomas taught these books to his students, Tolomeo does not say so. He confirms only that while Thomas was in charge of the *studium* at Rome, he lectured on certain aspects of Aristotle. In fact, it is highly unlikely that the immediate audience of Thomas at these lectures was his young and presumably untried bunch of students. Some of these may have been bright enough to audit without undue stress Thomas's learned and lengthy expositions of Aristotle, but the majority would likely have needed basic instruction in the fundamentals of Christian teaching.

Santa Sabina, in any case, was not an advanced *studium generale* like the five official *studia* of the order (Paris, Bologna, Cologne, Montpellier, Oxford), to which each Province was allowed to send no more than two promising students (*docibiles*) or, in the case of Paris, the senior *studium*, three. It is doubtful even that Santa Sabina was a *studium provinciale*, or half-way house between a priory school, under the control of a Lector, and a *studium generale* or *solemne*, presided over by a Regent-Master or Principal Lector. Central houses of study, or *studia provincialia* as they were later known, certainly were established in the Roman Province, at Viterbo and Naples, in 1269, but all that we know of the *studium* at Santa Sabina between 1265 and 1268 is that Thomas was ordered to set it up, that "the students there with him for the sake of study" were to have "sufficient clothing from the priories of their origin," and that Thomas was in complete charge of them, having "full authority to send them back to their respective houses" if they did not come up to scratch.[20]

Santa Sabina has the look of what I call a "*studium personale*," a *studium* set up for or by a given master. The Anagni enactment of 1265 speaks of the students as "studying with" Thomas, and makes no mention of any assistants or *Sublectores* (the term used by Humbert). It is not without interest, too, that when Thomas was transferred to Paris in the summer of 1268, the Roman *studium* seems to have died with his departure.

Perhaps the *studium* at Rome was simply an experiment to allow Thomas special scope and to expose select students from all over the Province to his influence. It may well be, indeed, that at the Chapter of Anagni in September 1265, which he as a Preacher General would have attended, a suggestion on his part that something more than mixed priory schools was necessary for the training of students in theology had been taken up by the Chapter, and that he had been given a free hand to open and conduct a personal *studium*.

On the other hand, what we may be witnessing at Anagni is simply the beginnings of a movement inspired by Thomas to improve education in his Province in the wake of the Valenciennes General Chapter of 1259, and which led not long afterwards to the establishment of *studia provincialia* for theology in Italy.

Something of the sort probably was sorely needed in Thomas's large and scattered Roman Province. Before his arrival in late 1259, studies seem not to have had any priority in the province. The first time, indeed, that a Lector as such is mentioned in the extant *Acta* of the Province is in 1259, when a house, with the constitutional "Prior and Lector," was founded at Pistoia. As for references of any kind to study, they are few and far between, apart from a prohibition, for example, of the study of astronomy and "*artes saeculares*" in 1258 at Viterbo.

Thomas was commissioned as Preacher General for Naples in September 1260. As this gave him a voice in the annual Provincial Chapter, he probably began to attend Chapters from the following September. He may not have made his presence felt at once; however, in view of the singular act in his respect of the Chapter at Anagni in 1265, that voice is hardly to be mistaken in the two Chapters that immediately preceded it. At Rome in 1263, the Chapter for the first time ever comes out openly on studies, ruling that all the brethren, the old with the young, should attend classes and "repeat" what they had learned. At Viterbo in 1264, the Chapter stated bluntly that "study in this Province is neglected." It made provision for the financial support of the three students that the Province could send to Paris. It ordered that Lectors should not drop classes at will, that Priors should compel the brethren to study, that they should see to it that weekly "*repetitiones*" were held for all, and that they should direct the Master of Students to examine everyone, and the young especially, in what had been taught during the week.[21] Perhaps this was not enough for Thomas, and as a result the Chapter at Anagni a year later gave him his head.

At all events, the *studium* at Santa Sabina probably was no more than an attempt by the Roman Province to allow select students to prepare themselves under a single master, Thomas, for the priesthood and the Dominican apostolate. Basically, the course there would have had the same pastoral orientation as that in which I presume Thomas to have been engaged for the previous four years at Orvieto.

But there was at least one great difference between Orvieto and Rome. Where in the former, Thomas would have had to divide his time between students and community, now at Santa Sabina he had the students all to himself. He was on his own, no longer tied to a basic curriculum geared to the pastoral education of the *fratres communes* at large. He was, in a word, free to devise a curriculum of his own—one that would have the *student* body as its focus. More importantly, he was now in a position to expand the students' theological education and to break out of the narrow tradition of practical theology that had hitherto marked the Dominican educational system.

One hint of a change of direction is that, according to Tolomeo, Thomas wrote on the first book of the *Sentences* while teaching at Rome. Although Tolomeo notes that a copy of this commentary existed in his home priory at Lucca, there is no trace of such a text today. But, as I suggest below, modern scholars are lucky to possess a part of a student *reportatio* of that classroom commentary that shows, among other things, that it was not at all, as has been conjectured, a reworking of his *Scriptum super Sententiis* (1252–1256) at Paris. Rather, this was an independent work in a simple, direct style not unlike that of the later *Summa*, which drew at times on the *Scriptum* itself, the *De Veritate*, and the commentary on Boethius's *De Trinitate*.[22] What is important, however, for the present argument, is not the nature of that "Roman" commentary, but the fact that this appears to be the first time that a book of the *Sentences* was taught formally to Dominican students outside of the *studia generalia*. Later on, of course, as *studia provincialia* began to be the fashion, first in the Roman Province in 1269 (possibly a result of the Roman experiment with Thomas), then generally in the order, the *Sentences* of Peter Lombard became a set text in these *studia* in each Dominican province. But there is no evidence that formal lectures on the *Sentences* were among the duties of the ordinary conventual Lectors before or after this time. On this view, it is notable that it was at Rome and not during his Lectorship at Orvieto that Thomas is reputed to have lectured on the *Sentences*.

This is not to say that Peter Lombard's work was unknown in Dominican houses. In his *Instructiones*, Humbert of Romans lists the *Sentences*, with the Bible and Comestor's *Historia*, as a text on which Lectors gave practical instruction.[23] In the summer of 1267, while Thomas was still teaching the students at Santa Sabina, the Chapter at Lucca urged the brethren in general and young priests in particular to apply themselves "more than usual" to the study of "the Bible, the *Sentences*, the *Historiae*, the writings of the saints, and the *Summa de Casibus*."[24]

But Humbert and the Lucca Chapter probably did not have the *Sentences* as a whole in mind but rather the fourth book, and this in order to supplement Raymund's *Summa* in its treatment of the sacraments. For Raymund himself, when dealing with aspects of the administration of some of the sacraments, probably set a headline for the whole Dominican order when he noted there that any of the *simplices* who wished to know more about the sacraments should read certain parts of the *Decretum* and the *Decretales* "and the fourth book of the *Sentences*."[25]

Book IV was, of course, the *locus classicus* for sacramental theology, which is the reason why, for example, John of Freiburg in his *Summa Confessorum* of 1298 cites extensively the commentaries of Albert, Thomas, and Peter of Tarentaise on that book of the *Sentences* and generally, on that book alone. Yet, significantly, it was not Book IV upon which Thomas lectured at Rome. What he taught the Dominican students at Santa Sabina was not, if both Tolomeo of Lucca and the newly identified *reportatio* prove trustworthy, the expected sacramental theology, the subject of the fourth book, upon which he had commented professionally a decade or so earlier at Paris, but rather God, Trinity, and Creation, the burden of the first book. By opting for Book I (upon which, of course, he had lectured at great length while a Bachelor at Paris), Thomas gives fair warning that he was setting a new course. By concentrating on God, Creation, Trinity, and other *dogmatic* or *systematic* areas of theology, he makes it clear that he was breaking away from the customary "practical" theology of the order to which the Valenciennes Chapter, Humbert, and, needless to say, Raymund's *Summa de Casibus*, are eloquent witnesses.

A second hint of the revolutionary character of the *studium* at Santa Sabina is the fact that it was there that Thomas began his great work "for the instruction of beginners," the *Summa Theologiae*. Since the *Prima Pars* of the *Summa* covers much the same ground as Book I of the *Sentences*, and since Thomas is not reputed to have taught at Rome on any book of the *Sentences* but the first, this suggests that the commentary which Tolomeo saw at Lucca on Book I of the *Sentences* and which now survives at second or third hand in a *reportatio* or copy thereof may well represent all or most of his teaching during Thomas's first scholastic year (October 1265–July 1266), while the *Prima Pars* of the *Summa* (with, probably, a part of the *Prima Secundae*) is the outcome of his second and third years of teaching (October 1266–July 1268).

In other words, having availed himself of the freedom of the *studium* in Rome to depart from the practical theology traditional to his order by commenting in his first year there on Book I of the *Sentences*, Thomas in his second and third year dropped the *Sentences* altogether and set out on a road of his own. It was no chance road, but one that he was determined to travel. Even when plucked out of Rome in summer 1268 for university teaching at Paris far removed from the "beginners" at Santa Sabina, he did not abandon his design. By the time he departed Paris four years later, there to embark on, although not to finish, his *Tertia Pars*, he had completed the *Prima Secundae* and had compiled the massive *Secunda Secundae*.

This persistence with the *Summa* over five heavy years at Paris and Naples (1268–1273) during which he wrote voluminously on Aristotle's *Peri-hermeneias, Analytica Posteriora, De Caelo, De Generatione et Corruptione, Me-teora, De Anima, Metaphysics, Physics, Politics,* and, possibly, *Nicomachean Ethics,* to mention only some of his writings in these years—this persistence at least suggests that, for Thomas, the *Summa* was something out of the ordinary and, indeed, meant much to him. It was, one may suggest, his legacy as a Do-minican to his order and to its system of educating the brethren in priories all over Europe. It may have been begun at Santa Sabina in Rome where the *in-cipientes* were young students of the order, but it was Orvieto and his four years of practical teaching there among the *fratres communes* that had really occasioned it. With the *Summa,* in effect, Thomas made his own personal con-tribution as a Dominican to the longstanding manualist and summist tradi-tion of the order in which he had been a participant at Orvieto (and at Valen-ciennes), and at the same time attempted to set the regular training in practical theology in the Dominican order on a more truly theological course.

## Beginning the *Summa*

What had been missing in the curriculum before Thomas's tenure at Santa Sabina was what one may term "dogmatic" or "systematic" theology. Writing roughly a decade before Thomas began his *Summa,* General of the Domini-cans Humbert of Romans noted in his *Liber de Instructione Officialium* that the librarian of each Dominican house was responsible for providing a ready-reference area containing good, legible copies of, among other books, Grat-ian's *Decretum,* Gregory IX's *Decretales,* canonist Geoffrey of Trani's *Summa super Titulis, Distinctiones Morales* (of which there were many in circulation), *Concordantiae* (probably those of the Paris Dominicans noted above), Ray-mund of Pennafort's *Summa de Casibus,* and William Peraldus's *Summa de Vi-tiis et Virtutibus,* "so that the community may always have them to hand." Humbert also lists the Bible and the *Historiae* of Peter Comestor, but if there is anything at all obvious about the professional volumes above, it is that they are wholly legal or "moral." There is not a trace, for example, of any specific *summa de sacramentis*, nor any *summa* of "*sacra doctrina*" as such. "Scientific" theology, in so far as it occurs in the list, is represented by Raymund's *Summa de Casibus* and Peraldus's *Summa de Vitiis et Virtutibus*, the two well-springs, as it happens, of Dominican practical or moral theology.[26]

This doctrinal gap in the system is precisely what Thomas attempted to fill with his *Summa*. All Dominican writers of *summae* previous to Thomas had valiantly covered various aspects of learning for their confrères in pastoral care—Raymund and his fellows for confessional practice, Peraldus for vices and virtues, Aag of Denmark for missionaries, William of Tournai for the instruction of children, James of Varazze for the lives of saints and preaching, Simon of Hinton for the practical theological needs of his English brethren. Thomas, on the other hand, went well beyond anything hitherto attempted. He provided a *summa* of general theology, a manual that dealt with God, Trinity, Creation, and Incarnation, as well as with the strengths and weaknesses of human nature.

Thomas, of course, had nothing against practical theology. After all, he had presumably taught it himself for some years, and is far from neglecting it in his *Summa*; indeed, the largest part, the *Secunda Pars*, specifically covers human beings and their acts. But he now gave that practical theology a setting not evident in Dominican circles before him. By prefacing the *Secunda* or "moral" part with a *Prima Pars* on God, Trinity, and Creation, and then rounding it off with a *Tertia Pars* on the Son of God, Incarnation, and the Sacraments, Thomas put practical theology—the study of Christian life, its virtues and vices—in a full theological context. Christian morality, once and for all, was shown to be something more than a question of straight ethical teaching of vices and virtues in isolation. Inasmuch as the person was an intelligent being who was master of himself and possessed of freedom of choice, he was in the image of God. To study human action is therefore to study the image of God and to operate on a theological plane. To study human action on a theological plane is to study it in relation to its beginning and end, God, and to the bridge between, Christ and his sacraments.

Thomas, one might add, was not alone in his dissatisfaction with the Dominican curriculum and tradition of theology. Just about the time that Thomas was beginning his *Summa*, Hugh Ripelin, Lector of Strasbourg, wrote a *Compendium Theologicae Veritatis* in seven books (God, Creation, Sin, Christ, Virtues, Sacraments, Last Things) which, with some 620 manuscripts, numerous printed editions, and translations into Armenian, Flemish, French, German, and Italian, had a huge success and might have inspired Thomas's own *Compendium Theologiae* (1269–1273).[27]

But if Thomas and Hugh Ripelin were at variance with the practical tradition of vices and virtues, *casus* and "*Collationes de moralibus*" within their order, all the same both Hugh's *Compendium* and Thomas's *Summa* very much belonged in intent and purpose to the Dominican strain of practical manuals. Like Raymund of Pennafort, Aag of Denmark, Simon of Hinton, and other Dominican manualists who had written specifically for the *iuniores* and *simplices*, and for the generality of their Dominican brethren, Thomas in particular probably had young and run-of-the-mill Dominicans primarily in mind and not a more sophisticated, perhaps university audience when in chiselled prose and in easy, logical steps he put his *Summa Theologiae* together: "My purpose," he wrote, "is so to propose the things that pertain to faith that the instruction of beginners will better be served."[28]

This, needless to say, is far from evident in the Prologue. As the Prologue stands, Thomas could be referring to any and every beginner. But given the context of the genesis of the *Summa* at Santa Sabina, and the remarkable commission given him at Anagni in 1265, the assumption is hardly out of question that his beginners are Dominican beginners first and foremost, in the manner of other Dominican colleagues of his.

There is certainly nothing in the Prologue to indicate that his sights were set on university students, although, of course, he would later release at Paris for general consumption all that he had then completed of the *Summa*. In any case, there was nothing in 1266–1267 to suggest that Thomas would ever again return to Paris or, in fact, teach in any university whatever. All that he says in the Prologue is that he found existing expositions of theology inadequate. They were a hindrance under three heads for beginners. They indulged in a multitude of useless questions, articles, and arguments. They did not give the essentials of Christian teaching in an ordered fashion but only as these came up in whatever text the writers were commenting on (*secundum quod requirebat librorum expositio*) or whenever the writers seized on a particular point and dilated on it (*vel secundum quod se praebebat occasio disputandi*). Finally, writers treated these fundamentals in so many places that the result on the part of the hearers was aversion and boredom.

It is often assumed that Thomas is here speaking of texts such as the Bible and the *Sentences*, but on the surface his plaint, rather, is against writings or commentaries on texts ("*ea quae scripta sunt a diversis*") and the procedures employed by their authors ("*secundum quod requirebat librorum expositio . . . vel se praebebat occasio disputandi*"). Père Chenu and others, however, understand the Prologue as "a reflection on the current teaching method," where the teacher was bound to the text (*librorum expositio*) and the principal in a *quaestio disputata* to "the contingent circumstances of controversy" (*occasio disputandi*).[29] Yet although the subject of this part of the Prologue is texts by various authors ("*ea quae scripta sunt a diversis*") and not authoritative texts from the tradition ("*ea quae traduntur*"), there is a possible ambiguity in the passage, as though Thomas were speaking on two levels at once. For his complaint against the longueurs and disorder in the writings on theology in question ends with a seeming reference to classrooms and teaching ("*eorumdem frequens repetitio et fastidium et confusionem generabat in animis auditorum*") rather than, as one would have expected, to reading and studying.

If, as well may be, the Prologue has this second edge, criticism on the part of Thomas of his own Dominican educational system is not to be ruled out in favor of the more obvious setting of universities and *studia generalia*—if, that is, "*expositio librorum*" also means "teaching a text" and "*occasio disputandi*" also denotes disputations and disputed questions ("*quaestiones disputatae*"). For as we know from Humbert of Romans in his *Liber* a few years earlier, "expositions" of texts (Thomas's own *Expositio in Job*, for example) and "disputations" (complete with "*opponentes*" and "*respondentes*" and even invited guests) were very much part of the Dominican curriculum.

These criticisms by Thomas may even betray a memory of some remarks of his former General there on the office of Lector. Where, for example, Humbert cautions the Lector, when teaching the Bible, the *Historiae*, and the *Sententiae*, to keep to the text, to avoid "too many divisions of the matter and frivolous expositions," and to strive always for the sake of the hearers ("*auditores*") after "useful and intelligible questions" (*quaestionum utilium intelligentiam*), Thomas notes the hazard of a multitude of "useless questions, articles, and arguments" (*inutilium quaestionum, articulorum et argumentorum*). Again, where Humbert gives advice on the care to be taken to select "useful subjects" for the regular conventual disputations, Thomas underlines the "occasional" role, with respect to the fundamentals of theology, which disputations played. Finally, and more significantly, where Humbert begs the Lector, for the good of his *auditores*, to refrain from the boring prolixity that is bound to result from too excessive repetition ("*a fastidiosa prolixitate quae accidere solet ex nimia repetitione eiusdem*"), Thomas likewise makes the point that frequent repetition of the same things tended to generate confusion in the minds of the readers ("*eorumdem frequens repetitio et fastidium et confusionem generabat in animis auditorum*").[30]

On the view, then, of both commentaries on theological texts (the primary plaint, as it seems, of the Prologue) and teaching methods (a secondary or at least implied plaint), the "beginners" there are just as likely to have been Thomas's students at Santa Sabina and his Dominican brethren in general as beginners at large or in the *studia generalia* and universities. And even if the Prologue was simply concerned with current methods of teaching theology, then these are as arguably Dominican as those described by Humbert in his *Liber* are explicitly, and would have been recognizable as such by any of Thomas's colleagues.

But probably it was the drawbacks to the commentaries and glosses in use at the time in the Dominican order that stirred him more than anything else to write his *Summa*. Remembering his own four years at Orvieto as Lector, and the pronounced summist tradition of practical theology within the order, it is therefore not at all unreasonable to suggest that the texts by various authors ("*quae a diversis scripta sunt*") that principally impeded the *novitii* and *incipientes* of his Prologue are just as likely to have been the various *summae* of Dominican authorship to which the young students and the body of *fratres communes* had to turn for their theology as the better-known or standard treatises of the universities and schools.

## The *Secunda Secundae*

How conscious Thomas was of both that summist tradition and its limitations is, to my mind, clearly to be seen in the *Secunda Secundae* of the *Summa Theologiae* and its Prologue. I base my certainty here on the fact that the *Secunda Secundae* is, in its own right, a straight *summa de virtutibus et vitiis*, a *summa* of moral theology if you wish, although not at all of the *casus* or anecdotal type hitherto in vogue in the Dominican order.

Thomas himself specifies that the first part of the *Secunda Pars* covers "moral matter" in general, while the second part or *Secunda Secundae* deals with it in particular: "After a general consideration of virtues and vices and other points pertaining to moral matter in general," he writes in the Prologue to the *Secunda Secundae*, "it is necessary to consider each of these one by one"[31] (IIa IIae, Prol.). Hence, he goes on, the best procedure will be to devote a tractate in turn to "each virtue, the gift corresponding to it, and the vices opposed to it" (ibid.).[32] In this way, he says, " the whole of moral matter is placed in the context of the virtues," and so "nothing in morals will be overlooked" (ibid.).[33]

His point of departure, and possibly the chief target of his strictures on works in this area, was, I suspect, the great and hallowed *Summa de Vitiis et Virtutibus* of his senior colleague, William Peraldus or Peyraut, the two parts of which were written over a span of thirteen or fourteen years between 1236 and 1249–1250. In Dominican circles, it clearly had the role of "speculative" companion to Raymund's *Summa de Casibus*. With Raymund's *Summa*, it is one of the volumes recommended by Humbert of Romans for a ready-reference area in houses of the order, and it is presumably the *Summa de Vitiis et Virtutibus* that is mentioned with the *Summa de Casibus* in Humbert's *Liber* as one of the sources from which Lectors could draw points for discussion at the weekly or biweekly "*Collationes de moralibus*." A Chapter of the Province of Spain at Toledo in 1250 ordered each house in the Province to inscribe its name on its copies of breviaries, Bibles, and these two *Summae*. In 1267, the two *Summae* are again mentioned in one breath at a Chapter at Carcassonne of the Province of Provence. Some five hundred manuscripts of the *Summa* of Peraldus are extant. It was translated in whole or part into French, Italian, and Flemish in, respectively, the thirteenth, fourteenth, and fifteenth centuries, and was printed repeatedly from 1469 onward.[34]

Needless to say, the *Summa* of Peraldus is looser in structure and far more discursive than the *Secunda Secundae* of St. Thomas, but the ground it covers is roughly the same. Peraldus opens with the topic "*De Virtute in Communi*"; so does Thomas, but unlike Peraldus he devotes a whole volume to it, the *Prima Secundae*. Peraldus then goes on, with a vast array of quotations from Scripture, the fathers (Augustine, Gregory, Isidore, John Damascene, in particular), classical "philosophers" such as Aristotle, Cicero, Seneca, and Ovid, and, finally, more recent authors such as Anselm, Bernard, and Guigo the Carthusian, to define and document the theological and cardinal virtues, the gifts, the beatitudes, and the seven "capital vices" or deadly sins.[35]

This, too, is exactly the range of the *Secunda Secundae*. And although there is no cogent evidence that Thomas relied on or borrowed very much from Peraldus, save, perhaps, for a quotation here and there from his battery of authorities, I am sure that Thomas was as aware of the *Summa de Vitiis et Virtutibus* as he was of Raymund's *Summa de Casibus*. His colleague Peraldus had written a thorough, learned, and valued piece of work, and Thomas appears to have made sure that nothing Peraldus had touched upon did not find a place in the *Secunda Secundae*. It is hardly by chance, for example, that when Peraldus notes immediately after his brief opening chapter on virtues in general, "We have spoken of the virtues in general. Now we will be speaking of the species of virtue" (*Dictum est de virtute in communi. Nunc dicendum est de speciebus virtutum*), Thomas marks the transition from the first to the second part of the *Secunda* in almost the same words: "After having considered the virtues and vices and other matters pertaining to morals, it is now necessary to consider specific details in each" (*Post communem considerationem de virtutibus et vitiis et aliis ad materiam moralem pertinentibus, necesse est considerare singula in speciali*) (ibid.). This sort of "bridge" can hardly be a commonplace, particularly when one remembers that the division between "the virtues in general" (*De Virtutibus in Communi*) and "special virtues" (*De Virtutibus in Speciali*) has been claimed as original to Thomas.[36]

There is, nevertheless, a world of difference between Thomas's approach to moral matters and that of Peraldus. This is not least the case because Thomas relates the gifts, beatitudes, and vices to each of the seven theological and cardinal virtues where Peraldus simply takes the virtues, vices, gifts, and beatitudes in turn, each in its own right.

Thomas seems to have been very much aware of his departure from the customary treatment of virtues and vices in *summae* and manuals and in particular, one may suggest, in this semi-official *Summa* of his own order. There is probably an oblique apology for abandoning the scheme in Peraldus's *Summa* when in the Prologue to the *Secunda Secundae*, and in terms reminiscent of the Prologue to the *Prima Pars*, Thomas notes that it is "more expeditious by far to take in turn each virtue with its corresponding gift, the vices opposed to it, and the appropriate precepts, than to take each virtue, gift, vice, and precept in isolation, for the latter course begets much repetition." Besides, he adds, this is a more logical and theological procedure, since it nicely includes all moral matter under the seven great virtues.

It is a commonplace that of all Thomas's writings, the *Summa Theologiae* "was the most widely circulated work both in manuscript and in print."[37] Yet if one examines the extant manuscripts, it soon becomes evident that "the *Summa*" as often as not means the *Secunda Secundae*, not the tripartite *Summa*. It is, in fact, rarely or relatively so that one finds all the parts of the *Summa* as a unit. Each part—and here I mean the two sections of the *Secunda Pars* as well as the *Prima Pars* and the *Tertia Pars*—seems to have circulated independently, as though each had its own identity, with the *Secunda Secundae* the clear winner. By my rough count, and out of a total of almost six hundred manuscripts examined thus far for all parts on their own of the *Summa* as Thomas wrote it, the *Tertia Pars* accounts for only 18 percent, the *Prima Secundae* for 20 percent, the *Prima Pars* for 25 percent, and the *Secunda Secundae* for 37 percent.[38]

The popularity of the *Secunda Secundae* is hardly to be wondered at. As it stands, and for all its originality and watertight Aristotelianism, the *Secunda Secundae* has the trappings of a *Summa de Virtutibus et Vitiis*, replete with dicta of Aristotle, Cicero, Macrobius, and the rest, and the Prologue quoted above does not dispel that impression. Tolomeo of Lucca, in his note on Thomas's works (ca. 1315), wrote of it that "this part of the *Summa* contains a specific treatment of all the virtues and vices, and is totally based on, and adorned with, the sayings and teachings of Philosophers and the authentic opinions of sacred doctors"—a description that is equally applicable to the *Summa* of Peraldus or any other manual of virtues and vices.[39] This is precisely how some of Thomas's contemporaries saw it, and this is surely why it outdid any other part of the *Summa* in circulation. It is not for nothing that the copy of the *Secunda Secundae* that the theologian Geoffrey of Fontaines had made for himself at Paris in the 1290s bears the following explicit, "*Summa de virtutibus et vitiis edita a fratre Thoma de Aquino.*"[40]

As for the axiomatic influence of the *Summa* as a whole within the Dominican order, the dogged effort on the part of Thomas to give a full theological direction to the pastoral preparation of Dominicans seems to have gone over the head of the generality of his brethren. Even after his canonization in 1323 and the withdrawal of the ban of 1277 on Thomas at the University of Paris, the *Summa* never became a part of the curriculum of the priory schools that, as I have suggested, really occasioned it. In these priory schools, practical theology in the old mold continued to dominate the curriculum, with Raymund and Peraldus ruling the roost, although Raymund's *Summa de Casibus* gave way in the fourteenth century to John of Freiburg's *Summa Confessorum* (1298).

In the various provincial *studia* that have come to light in the last quarter of the thirteenth century, and which may have been a result of Thomas's Roman experiment between 1265 and 1268, Peter Lombard's *Sentences*, in line with the usage of *studia generalia* and universities, became and remained throughout the Middle Ages the textbook of theology.

Thomas's own Roman Province, which in 1269 began what was to become a network of *studia provincialia*, seems never to have granted the *Summa* a place in its system. There is no sign even that any of the annual Provincial Chapters ever recommended Thomas or any of his works in the way in which, a shade unrealistically, the Chapter of 1284 at Aquila ordered that, "Lectors and others of the brethren in their lectures and disputations" should use the formulary book of papal and other letters compiled by Marinus of Eboli, lately archbishop of Capua.[41] Some bright spirits in the Province seem to have attempted to replace the *Sentences* with the *Summa* at the beginning of the fourteenth century, but they were firmly put in their places by the Chapter at Perugia in 1308: "We wish and order that all Lectors and Bachelors lecture on the *Sentences* and not on the *Summa* of Thomas."[42] However, the General Chapter of the order at Metz in 1313 was a little more accommodating. It allowed that Lectors, when teaching the *Sentences*, "should treat briefly of at least three or four articles of Brother Thomas" (presumably from his commentary on the *Sentences*), and ruled that no one was to be sent to the *studium generale* at Paris "unless he has studied diligently the teaching of Thomas for three years."[43]

The *Summa* had rather more success at another level. There were Dominicans who were aware of the "pastoral" possibilities of the work and were not slow to exploit it in that direction. Around 1290, the anonymous Dominican who added the *Speculum Morale* to Vincent of Beauvais's great *Speculum Maius* of fifty years earlier borrowed liberally from the *Secunda Secundae*.[44] A decade or so later, Albert, Lector of Brescia, who campaigned mightily for Thomas's canonization, and allegedly had a vision of Augustine and Thomas together, wrote a *Summa de Instructione Sacerdotis* in three books (virtues, vices, sacraments), drawing almost all his material from the *Secunda Secundae* and the *Tertia Pars*.[45] Between 1310 and 1314, William of Paris, of the priory of St. Jacques, composed a *Dialogus de Septem Sacramentis*, which is extant in fifty manuscripts and at least fifteen printed editions, and leans heavily on the *Tertia Pars* as well as on the commentary of Peter of Tarentaise on Book IV of the *Sentences*.[46]

Almost inevitably, given the bias of the order, it was the *Secunda Secundae* that captured the attention of Dominicans at large. Shortly before his death in 1283, General of the Dominicans John of Vercelli (the same who, recently elected, had snatched Thomas away unexpectedly from Rome and his students there in 1268, sending him to the University of Paris with Peter of Tarentaise), commissioned Galienus de Orto, probably while he was Lector at Pisa, to make an abridgement of the *Secunda Secundae*. This summary, now extant in at least five manuscripts, had no success.[47] It is schematic and perfunctory, and, in any case, another Dominican Lector of the period, John of Freiburg, took the ground from under Galienus by doing more or less the same thing in a more imaginative fashion a few years later. Where John scored over Galienus was not by engaging in any sort of precis of the *Secunda Secundae*, but rather by relating Thomas's work to the curriculum of practical theology in the priories and, specifically, to Raymund's *Summa de Casibus*, which he was then teaching as Lector in the priory at Freiburg-im-Breisgau.[48]

## John of Freiburg

"Johannes Lector," as he was known, was a remarkable man whose place in the spread of the teaching of Thomas has largely escaped historians. He had been a pupil of the Lector of Strasbourg, Ulrich Engelbert, prior to 1272; had accompanied Albert the Great to Mecklenberg in 1269; and seems to have studied at Paris for a time, perhaps between 1268 and 1272, when Peter of Tarentaise and Thomas occupied the Dominican chairs there for a second time and when Thomas held his second batch of *quodlibets*, which are so prominent in John's *Summa Confessorum*.

Posted about 1280 to the Dominican house at Freiburg-im-Breisgau as Lector, an office he held even as Prior until his death shortly before 1314, John at first occupied himself with an index to Raymund's *Summa* and to William of Rennes's *Apparatus* on it. Then, in typical Lector fashion, he began to collect "*quaestiones casuales*" for purposes of teaching. In his search for these (meaning, as he states in his preface, "useful questions which bear on the counselling of souls"), he combed councils, canonists, theologians, and, naturally, the writings of his teachers and *confrères*, Albert, Peter, Thomas, and Ulrich. On this view, both the second sextet of Thomas's Parisian *quodlibets* and the *Secunda Secundae* proved most valuable.

As a result of this intense research while lecturing on the *Summa de Casibus*, John of Freiburg was able to produce his own *Summa Confessorum* (1298)—the first manual to bear such a title—in which he totally revamped Raymund and deployed as much as possible of the material he had collected in his *Libellus Quaestionum Casualium*, notably the corpus of some twenty-two *quaestiones* from those Parisian *quodlibets* of St. Thomas, bits and pieces from the *Prima* and *Tertia partes* of the *Summa*, and passage after passage from the *Secunda Secundae*. The moral teaching of Thomas, with borrowings as well from Albert, Peter, and Ulrich, is the backbone of John's *Summa*, and sharply differentiates it in tone and content from Raymund's *Summa de Casibus*—or, for that matter, any other previous *summa* of the administration of the Sacrament of Penance. Furthermore, the *Summa Confessorum* is much broader than Raymund's, and is as much a *summa de sacramentis* as it is of penitential practice.

John's text was a resounding success. Some 160 manuscripts of it are extant, and it enjoyed three printed editions before 1500 and several afterward. In the century after its publication, it inspired in Dominican circles an abridgement (by William of Cayeux, ca. 1300), a simplified version (the *Summa Rudium*, ca. 1333), an alphabetical arrangement (which, as the *Pisanella*, after its compiler, Bartholomew of Pisa, is extant in some 600 manuscripts), and a German adaptation by Berthold of Freiburg (ante 1390).[49]

Despite the great number of manuscripts of the *Secunda Secundae* itself from 1300 through 1500, it is probably fair to state that it was largely through John of Frieburg's *Summa Confessorum*, or such derivatives as the popular *Pisanella*, that St. Thomas's moral teaching in the *Secunda Secundae* became known and respected throughout Europe in that period. Furthermore, as the *Summa Confessorum* gradually replaced Raymund's *Summa de Casibus* in the course of practical theology, Thomas's influence spread within the Dominican order itself.

In that sense at least, Thomas's legacy in the *Summa Theologiae* to beginners and to Dominicans at large had its reward. But, in the whole context of the *Summa*, this was not quite what Thomas had hoped for. Rather, it only compounded the situation that I have suggested he had attempted to correct. Where Thomas toiled to provide an integral theology for his brethren in their dedication to the *cura animarum*, the *Secunda Secundae*—a gutted *Secunda Secundae* at that—was now, through the *Summa Confessorum* of John of Freiburg, irretrievably adrift from the other parts of the *Summa*, especially the first and the third, to which St. Thomas had so carefully moored it.

But one should not place all the blame squarely on the shoulders of John of Freiburg. John had been attracted to the *Secunda Secundae* because it was, as he put it, "for the most part on morals and cases" (*pro maiori parte moralis et casualis*).[50] He had a point. The *Secunda Secundae* is indeed *casualis*, if by that one means, as John explicitly does, that it contains "useful questions bearing on the counseling of souls." And, if one is to take Thomas himself at his word in the Prologue, it is also very much *moralis*, because it considers "virtues and vices and other things pertaining to moral matter," and claims not to omit "anything related to morals." John, too, may be excused for not paying much attention to the *Prima Secundae*, which establishes the principles on which the *Secunda Secundae* rests, for Thomas himself seems to diminish the role of the *Prima* when (in the Prologue to the *Secunda*) he says, "after this general consideration [in the *Prima Secundae*] of virtues and vices and other things pertaining to moral matter, it is necessary to take these up in detail one by one. For moral teaching in the abstract is not all that useful, since what takes place in practice is with respect to particular things" (ibid.).[51]

It is hardly surprising, then, to find that far from being invariably accompanied by the *Prima Secundae*, the *Secunda Secundae* had a circulation that was almost twice that of its supposed prerequisite. One could argue, indeed, that Thomas was not particularly concerned about the circulation of these parts individually, or about the inviolability of the *Summa Theologiae* as a whole. In the list of taxes for copying university exemplars that the University of Paris issued about 1280, the *Prima Pars*, the *Prima Secundae*, and the *Secunda Secundae* (and, I may add, by these precise titles) all occur as separate items, and with separate sets of *peciae* or certified *quires*.[52] As there is no trace in this list of the *Tertia Pars*, written at Naples between 1272 and 1273, and we are sure that the *Secunda Secundae* had been finished before St. Thomas departed Paris for Naples, and probably by the spring of 1272—it is quite likely that Thomas released the three sections already completed for general copying before leaving for Naples in late 1272. This at least would explain to some extent the poor showing of the *Tertia Pars* in the circulation stakes, for it accounts for only about 18 percent of all the extant manuscripts of all the parts of the *Summa* as written by Thomas. Clearly, it never recovered from a late start.

One could argue, finally, that the relationship between the parts of the *Summa* is not as clear as it might be in the various prefaces, and that Thomas profitably could have been more forthright regarding his intentions when, in the *Summa Theologiae*, he wrote what I may now venture to call his one "Dominican" work, and made what I have suggested was his own very personal contribution to a lopsided system of theological education in the order to which he belonged.

## Notes

This chapter was previously published as Leonard Boyle, "The Setting of the Summa Theologiae—Revisited" (Pontifical Institute of Medieval Studies, Toronto, 1982; revised version in Stephen J. Pope, ed., *The Ethics of Aquinas*, Georgetown University Press, Washington, DC, 2002). Reprinted with permission from Georgetown University Press.

1. For what follows, see, in general, L. E. Boyle, "Notes on the Education of the *Fratres Communes* in the Dominican Order in the Thirteenth Century," in *Xenia Medii Aevi Historiam Illustrantia Oblata Thomae Kaeppeli O.P.*, ed. R. Creytens and P. Kunzle, 2 vols. (Rome: Storia e Letteratura, 1978), 1:249–647 at 249–51; repr. in *Pastoral Care, Clerical Education and Canon Law, 1200–1400* (London: Variorum, 1981). The present chapter is a slight reworking of *The Setting of the "Summa Theologiae" of Saint Thomas* (Toronto: Pontifical Institute, 1982), being the fifth of the Etienne Gilson Series of Lectures at the Pontifical Institute of Mediaeval Studies.

2. S. Lusignan, *Preface au Speculum maius de Vincent de Beauvais: réfraction et diffraction* (Montreal-Paris: Vrin, 1979), 138.

3. Boyle, "Notes," 254.

4. A. H. Thomas, *De oudste Constituties van de Dominicanen* (Louvain: Bibliothèque de la Revue d'histoire ecclesiastique, 1965), 311–12.

5. R. H. and M. A. Rouse, "The Verbal Concordance to the Scripture," *Archivum Fratrum Praedicatorum* 44 (1974): 5–30.

6. T. Kaeppeli, *Scriptores Ordinis Praedicatorum Medii Aevi*, XXX vols. (Rome: Ad S. Sabinae, 1975), 2:167; J. A. Corbett, ed., *The "De Instructione Puerorum" of William of Tournai O.P.* (Notre Dame, IN: University of Notre Dame Press, 1955).

7. Kaeppeli, *Scriptores*, 2:311–17; R. D. Di Lorenzo, "The Collection Form and the Art of Memory in the *Libellus super Ludo Schachorum* of Jacobus de Cessolis," *Mediaeval Studies* 35 (1973): 205–21.

8. T. Kaeppeli and A. Dondaine, eds., *Acta Capitulorum Provincialium Provinciae Romanae* (1243–1344) (Rome: Institutum Historicum Fratrum Praedicatorum, 1941), 29.

9. Humbertus de Romanis, *Opera*, ed. J. J. Berthier, 2 vols. (Rome: Befani, 1888–1889), 2:254–61.

10. *Acta Capitulorum Generalium Ordinis Praedicatorum*, vol. 1 (Rome: Typo. Polyglotta Prop. Fide, 1898), 1:99–100.

11. For these and other works, see J. A. Weisheipl, *Friar Thomas d'Aquino: His Life, Thought and Works*, 2nd ed. (Washington, DC: Catholic University of America Press, 1983), 147–95.

12. H.-F. Dondaine, ed., *De Emptione et Venditione ad Tempus*, in *Sancti Thomae de Aquino Opera Omnia Iussu Leonis XIII P.M.*, Tomus 42. Opuscula 3 (Rome: Commission Leonina, 1979), 393–94, with intro., 383–90.

13. Boyle, "Notes," 259–67.

14. A. Walz, "S. Raymundi de Penyafort Auctoritas in re Paenitentiali," *Angelicum* 12 (1935): 346–96; K. Pennington, "Summae on Raymond of Pennafort's *Summa de Casibus* in the Bayerische Staatshibliothek, Munich," *Traditio* 27 (1971): 471–80; A. Dondaine, "La Somme de Simon de Hinton," *Recherches de théologie ancienne et médiévale* 9 (1937): 5–22, 205–18.

15. J. M. Aubert, *Le droit romain dans l'oeuvre de saint Thomas* (Paris: J. Vrin, 1955), 19–23, 32, 43, 45, 60, 62, 109, 129–30.

16. Compare ST IIa IIae, q. 100, a. 1, ad 5 and *Summa de Casibus* 1.1, par. 2 (Rome: Tallini, 1603), 3a; IIa IIae, q. 100, a. 2, ad 6, ad 5 and *Summa de Casibus* 1.1, par. 16 (18a); IIa IIae, q. 100, a. 6, ad 5 and *Summa de Casibus* 1.1, par. 14 (14b).

17. *Acta Capitulorum Provincialium*, 32. The long-accepted idea (on the suggestion in passing, it appears, of P. Mandonnet) that Thomas spent 1267–1268 at Viterbo has been shown to be groundless in R. A. Gauthier, "Quelques questions à propos du commentaire de S. Thomas sur le *De Anima*," *Angelicum* 51 (1974): 419–72, 438–43.

18. See A. Dondaine, "Saint Thomas a-t-il disputé à Rome la question des attributs divins?" *Bulletin Thomiste* 10 (1953): 171–82; "Saint Thomas et la dispute des attributs divins," *Archivum Fratrum Praedicatorum* 8 (1938): 253–62.

19. A. Dondaine, ed., *Historia Ecclesiastica Nova*, bk. 22, c. 24, in "Les 'Opuscula fratris Thomae' chez Ptolomée de Lucques," *Archivum Fratrum Praedicatorum* 31 (1961): 142–203, 151, ll. 21–25.

20. "Fratri Thome de Aquino iniungimus in remissionem peccatorum quod teneat studium Rome. Et volumus quod fratribus qui stant secum ad studendum provideatur in necessariis vestimentis a conventibus de quorum predicatione traxerunt originem. Si autem illi studentes inventi fuerint negligentes in studio, damus potestatem fratri Thome quod ad conventus suos possit eos remittere" (*Acta Capitulorum Provincialium*, 32).

21. Ibid., 22 (1258); 24 (1259); 28 (1263); 29–30 (1264).

22. Dondaine, ed., *Historia Ecclesiastica Nova*, bk. 23, c. 15, 155, ll. 160–63: "Scripsit etiam eo tempore quo fuit Rome, de quo dictum est supra, iam magister existens, Primum super Sententias, quem ego vidi Luce sed inde subtractus nusquam ulterius vidi." Since Thomas probably was at the Provincial Chapter of 1267 at Lucca, then the copy of his "second" commentary on the first book of the *Sentences*, which Tolomeo saw there later, may have been one that Thomas left behind him after the Chapter. In a recent article ("'*Alia Lectura Fratris Thome*'? [*Super I Sent.*]," *Mediaeval Studies* 42 [1980]: 308–36), H.-F. Dondaine announces the discovery of a copy (probably before 1286) of the Parisian commentary of Thomas on *I Sent.* (Lincoln College, Oxford, ms. lat. 95, fols. 3r–122ra), which carries in its margins another commentary or partial commentary on *I Sent.* with references on three occasions to an "*alia lectura fratris Thome*." In a later article ("*Alia Lectura Fratris Thome*," *Mediaeval Studies* 45 [1983]: 418–29), I suggested that the "*alia lectura*" was not, as Fr. Dondaine was inclined to think, this commentary in margins of the Lincoln College manuscript, but rather the Parisian commentary of Thomas on the *Sentences* (1252–1256), and therefore that this marginal commentary could well be a copy of a *reportatio* of the Santa Sabina classroom lectures of Thomas on *I Sent.* in 1265–1266. This suggestion has been accepted by many scholars: see J. P. Torrell, *Initiation à Thomas d'Aquin: Sa personne et son oeuvre* (Fribourg-Paris: Cerf, 1993), 66–69, or, in English, Robert Royal, trans., *Saint Thomas Aquinas, I: The Person and His Work* (Washington, DC: Catholic University of America Press, 1996), 45–47.

23. Humbertus, *Opera*, 2:254.

24. *Acta Capitulorum Provincialium*, 33.

25. *Summa de Casibus*, 3, 24 (Lyons: n.p., 1603), 327b.

26. Humbertus, *Opera*, 2:265.

27. Kaeppeli, *Scriptores*, 2:260–69. For Hugh's *Compendium*, see the edition (as of Albert) in J. C. A. Borgnet, ed., *Beati Alberti Magni Opera Omnia*, vol. 33 (Paris: Vives, 1893), 1–261.

28. "Quia catholicae veritatis doctor non solum provectos debet instruere sed ad eum pertinet etiam incipientes erudire, . . . propositum nostrae intentionis in hoc opere est ea quae ad christianam religionem pertinent eo modo tradere secundum quod congruit ad eruditionem incipientium."

29. See M. D. Chenu, *Toward Understanding St. Thomas*, trans. A. M. Landry and D. Hughes (Chicago: Regnery, 1964), 300–301.

30. For Humbert see *Opera*, 2:254–56, 259–62.

31. "Post communem considerationem de virtutibus et vitiis et aliis ad materiam moralem pertinentibus, necesse est considerare singula in speciali."

32. "Erit igitur compendiosior et expeditior considerationis via si simul sub eodem tractatu consideratio procedit de virtute et dono sibi correspondente, et vitiis oppositis . . ."

33. "Sic igitur tota materia morali ad considerationem virtutum reducta . . . Et sic nihil moralium erit praetermissum."

34. Kaeppeli, *Scriptores*, 2:133–47; A. Dondaine, "Guillaume Peyraut: Vie et oeuvres," *Archivum Fratrum Praedicatorum* 18 (1948): 164–67.

35. Peraldus, *Summa Aurea de Virtutibus et Vitiis* (Venice: Paganinus de Paganinis, 1497). The proper title and order should be, of course, *Summa de Vitiis et Virutibus*.

36. T. Deman, *Aux origines de la théologie morale* (Montreal-Paris: Vrin, 1951), 105: "Aucun auteur précédant ne nous annonça rien de pareil."

37. Weisheipl, *Friar Thomas d'Aquino*, 222.

38. The percentages are based on an analysis of *Codices Manuscripti Operum Thomae de Aquino*, vol. 1, *Autographae et Bibliothecae A-F*, ed. H.-F. Dondaine and H. V. Shooner (Rome: Commission Leonina, 1967), vol. 2, *Bibliothecae Gdansk-Munster*, ed. H. V. Shooner (Rome: Commission Leonina, 1973). Two subsequent volumes do not modify these figures. Oddly, the presence of these parts of the *Summa* in the extant catalogues of medieval libraries for Austria (*Mittelalterliche Bibliothekskataloge Oesterreichs*, vol. 1, *Niederösterreich: Register*, ed. A. Goldmann [Vienna: Holzhausen, 1929], 153) works out at much the same percentage for each part: *Secunda Secundae*, 38 percent; *Prima Pars*, 29 percent; *Prima Secundae*, 15 percent; *Tertia Pars*, 13 percent; all parts of the *Summa* occur together only once, as is also the case for the two parts of the *Secunda Pars*, amounting to 5 percent in all. Again, in vol. 3 (the only one I have examined) of *Mittelalterliche Bibliothekskataloge Deutschlands und der Schweiz: Augsburg-Basel*, ed. P. Ruf (Münster: Beck, 1932), 3:1073 (Index), the percentages are *Secunda Secundae*, 43 percent; *Prima Pars*, 25 percent; *Tertia Pars*, 18 percent; *Prima Secundae*, 14 percent.

39. Dondaine, ed., *Historia Ecclesiastica Nova*, bk. 22, c. 39, 151, ll. 37–43.

40. Paris, Bibliothèque nationale, ms. lat. 15795, fol. 268r: "Explicit summa de uirtutibus et uiciis edita a fratre Thoma de Aquino, scripta sumptibus magistri Godefridi canonici Leodiensis, labore Henrici de Bavenchien." See C. Samaran and R. Marichal, eds., *Catalogue des manuscrits en écriture latine portant des indications de dates, de lieu, ou de copiste*, vol. 3 (Paris: Centre national de la recherche scientifique, 1974), 3:439

and plate LIV. Geoffrey († 1306) donated the copy to the Sorbonne, as well as a copy of the *Prima Secundae* (BN lat. 15791) written by the same scribe.

41. *Acta Capitulorum Provincialium,* 69.

42. Ibid., 169.

43. *Acta Capitulorum Generalium,* 2: 64–65.

44. Lusignan, *Préface au Speculum maius,* 87. The *Prima Secundae* is also used there.

45. Kaeppeli, *Scriptores,* 1:27–28; D. Prummer and M.-H. Laurent, *Fontes Vitae S. Thomae Aquinatis* (Toulouse: Revue Thomiste, 1912–1937), 356–58; M. Grabmann, "Albert von Brescia und sein Werk *De officio sacerdotis,*" *Mittelalterliches Geistesleben,* vol. 2 (Munich: Hueber, 1956), 2:336–38.

46. See Kaeppeli, *Scriptores,* 2:130–31.

47. Ibid., 2:6.

48. For what follows, see L. E. Boyle, "The *Summa Confessorum* of John of Freiburg and the Popularization of the Moral Teaching of St. Thomas and of some of his Contemporaries," in *St. Thomas Aquinas 1274–1974 Commemorative Studies,* ed. A. A. Maurer, vol. 2 (Toronto: Pontifical Institute of Medieval Studies, 1974), 2:245–68, and "The Quodlibets of St. Thomas and Pastoral Care," *The Thomist* 38 (1974): 232–56, both repr. in *Pastoral Care.*

49. Kaeppeli, *Scriptores,* 2:428–33, nn. 2340–45 (John of Freiburg); 94–95 (Cayeux); 1:157–65 (Bartholomew); 238–39 (Berthold); Boyle, "The *Summa Confessorum,*" 258–61.

50. *Summa Confessorum* (Lugduni: Saccon, 1517), first pref. (from the *Libellus*).

51. "Post communem considerationem de virtutibus et vitiis et aliis ad materiam moralem pertinentibus, necesse est considerare singula in speciali: sermones enim morales universales sunt minus utiles, eo quod actiones in particularibus sunt."

52. H. Denifle and E. Chatelain, eds., *Chartularium Universitatis Parisiensis,* vol. 1 (Paris: Delalain, 1889), 1:645–46. The *Prima Pars* was in 56 *peciae* at 3 *solidi* each, the *Prima Secundae* in 60 *peciae,* again at 3 *solidi,* the *Secunda Secundae* in 82 *peciae* at 4 *solidi.*

# 2

# Prelude to the Five Ways

*Victor White*

IT HAS BECOME EXTRAORDINARILY difficult to read the text of St. Thomas Aquinas as he wrote it, or as it would have been read by his contemporaries. Few even attempt to read it until they have been thoroughly initiated into later developments of Thomism with the aid of introductions and manuals, and it becomes hard to read the original except through their spectacles and without their preoccupations in mind. Those sections of the text which have a particular interest and importance of their own may all too easily be read torn out of their contexts in the closely-knit unity which is the *Summa Theologiae*; and disregard for what precedes or follows them in the original text can all too easily distort their meaning and purport. There is also the risk that we seek in the *Summa* for contributions to controversies which had not yet arisen when it was written, or answers to questions which the original context had already excluded. Our reading of the *Quinque Viae*—the so-called 'Five Ways of proving the existence of God'—in the *Summa* (I. ii. 3) is perhaps rather especially liable to be blurred in these ways. A re-examination of relevant preliminaries in the preceding pages of the *Summa* may be of some service, even though it must at times court the risk of laboring the obvious, and at others of adding to already existing complications by offering unfamiliar interpretations which may further obscure rather than elucidate the text.

In the following pages no attempt will be made to reexamine the *viae* themselves. We shall confine ourselves to consideration of their context in the *Summa Theologiae*, and especially of the prolegomena to the Five Ways as they are presented by St. Thomas himself. It will be suggested, incidentally, that some misunderstanding can be avoided and several difficulties eliminated, if

we reset the Five Ways in their original context. Too often are they read in isolation from what has gone before them in the *Summa*, with the perhaps inevitable result that more or less is read into them than they could, in St.
Thomas's own mind, contain.

Beginning with the very first page of the *Summa*, we shall *first* search the
Prologue and Question I for any presuppositions which we may find to the
Five Ways, or for anything which might be relevant to subsequent difficulties
or criticism concerning them.

*Second*, we shall examine the title of Question II, which we shall find to be
important as a statement of what the Five Ways actually set out to achieve.

*Third*, we shall turn to Articles 1 and 2 of Question II, wherein St. Thomas
expressly treats of the immediate presuppositions of the Five Ways which he
is to set out in Article 3.

### The Prologue and Question I

We risk much avoidable difficulty and misunderstanding if we are so rash as
to embark upon a study of the Five Ways in the Second Question of the
*Summa* without having first studied the First Question, in which St. Thomas
expounds the aims, scope, and method of his *Summa* as a whole.

Some consideration even of the very title and also of the Prologue of the
*Summa* will dispose of one objection which has been made to the soundness
of St. Thomas's logic in the Five Ways. This objection is to the effect that, before having even attempted to demonstrate that there is a God, he lays it down
that this can be demonstrated—and indeed that the very name *Deus* can be
derived—only from effects (*ex effectibus*) (e.g., in I. ii. 2 *corpus*, and ad 2um
and ad 3um; also I. i, 7 ad 1um). Thus, it is urged, St. Thomas begs the whole
question in advance: he assumes that given phenomena are effects, and therefore have a cause, and indeed a divine cause; the very point to be proved, and
a palpable *petitio principii*.

This objection might be valid if the *Summa* were a work of purely rational,
philosophical inquiry. But it is a *Summa Theologiae*. The Prologue makes it
quite clear for whom it is intended. It is written by and for the *doctor catholicae veritatis*, the "teacher of Catholic truth," for teaching "little ones in Christ,"
students of the Holy Teaching (the *Sacra Doctrina*): therefore for Catholics. It
is not *immediately* intended for the unbeliever or the atheist. Truly (as will become clearer in Article 8 of the First Question), it must for that very reason be
concerned to show how unbelievers are to be taught, that is to say (given St.
Thomas's understanding of what teaching is, cf. I. cxvii. 1), led from what they
do know to what they do not. But the *Summa* itself, the Prologue announces,

will follow the *via disciplinae* (i.e., the way of teaching what the teacher already knows), not the *via inventionis* (i.e., the way of discovery whereby the searcher attains conclusions he did not know). We may see this best by contrasting the Five Ways in the *Summa* with the corresponding process of thought in the *Metaphysics* of Aristotle. In Book Λ of the *Metaphysics*, we can follow Aristotle patiently examining phenomena, arguing out their implications, and *discovering*, without any foregone conclusions, that there is a Divinity and what some of its attributes must, by logical necessity, be. Not so St. Thomas in the *Summa*. Here is a Catholic writing for Catholics who already know—or anyhow believe—that there is a God. Teacher and taught take for granted that 'all things visible and invisible' are creatures or effects of God. But if the unbeliever is also to be taught this, it must be discussed in advance what method of argument is valid to lead him from what he knows to what he does not know—or perhaps doubts or denies. There is no begging of the question, no *petitio principii*, provided that this assertion that the phenomena are effects is not assumed in the line of reasoning which the teacher finally presents to the unbeliever, that is to say, in the Five Ways themselves. And in fact it is not so assumed. On the contrary the Five Ways will be concerned precisely to *show* that given agreed phenomena *are* effects which by logical necessity demand the affirmation of 'what we call God'.

This line of objection to the Five Ways is not perhaps very common or very serious. Much more common and more respectable is the objection that the 'God' which the Five Ways 'prove'—the Unmovable Mover, First Cause, Intrinsically Necessary, and the rest—has no resemblance to the God of the Bible, of revelation, or of any historical religious experience or cult. This widely-felt criticism receives its classical expression in a perhaps over-literal interpretation of Pascal's celebrated opposition between the 'God of the Philosophers' and the 'Living God of Abraham, Isaac and Jacob'. It takes many different forms, and is put forward on many different grounds. To some of them we must return, at least obliquely, before we have done. It may, however, be said at once that this line of thought is not merely a construction of captious critics or professional philosophers. It is widely felt that the Five Ways lead us at best to cold, abstract concepts which inspire little reverence, awe, or love, and with which the Biblical God of Love and Wrath has nothing to do. And let it be admitted, and indeed strongly affirmed, that the Five Ways do not, and cannot, reach to divine attributes made known only in revelation—or indeed those of any 'religious experience'—*as such*. And we shall be gravely disappointed if we look to them for anything of the sort.

It will at least clear the ground considerably for meeting this difficulty if we have read and pondered upon the first Article of the whole *Summa*. Here St. Thomas asks whether there is any need for some teaching (*doctrina*) over and

above what can be discovered by philosophical learning (*disciplinas*). Yes, he
answers, there is such need: need, namely, for a Holy Teaching, not only *about*
God but given *by* God. His reasons for this answer are familiar: God has des-
tined man for an end, a completion, which exceeds the grasp of his understanding. Since that is so, man must be made aware of it, and of how that end
is to be attained. These things only God can know (for they wholly depend on
his free gift and grace). Therefore man needs to be taught them, have them revealed to him, by God. But there is another, though secondary, reason (and it
is instructive to recall that St. Thomas has borrowed this argument for man's
need of revelation, not from any Christian Father, but from the Jewish Rabbi
Maimonides). Even though, without revelation, human reason can attain to a
certain limited knowledge about God, even *that* knowledge (which tells him
nothing of the end and the means God has ordained for man) is actually attainable only "by a few, after a long time, and with the mixture of many mistakes." We must not then, if we follow St. Thomas, expect from unaided reason any information about God, or God's relation to us, which only revelation
can supply.

But equally is it impossible to speak of the 'God of Reason' and the 'God of
Revelation' as of two Gods. Already it is implied that it is of one and the same
God that reason and revelation speak to us. In his reply to the second objection to this Article St. Thomas begins to sift out this problem more thoroughly. We may loosely translate the objection itself as follows:

> There can be no teaching about anything unless it *is*, for nothing can be known
> except it be true, and what is true is what *is*. But in the different branches of phi-
> losophy there is treatment of everything that is; even of God, hence one part of
> philosophy is called theology, or the divine science, as is clear from the Philoso-
> pher in the Sixth Book of *Metaphysics*. Therefore, there is no need for there to be
> any other kind of teaching apart from the various branches of philosophy.

(The reference, of course, is to Aristotle's description of the First Philosophy
or Metaphysics as *theologia*, in *Metaph.*, 938a, 10, cf. 1026a, 24.) To this St.
Thomas replies:

> What distinguishes the sciences from one another is a different *ratio cognoscibilis*.
> Thus the astronomer and the natural philosopher reach the same conclusion for
> instance, that the earth is round: but the astronomer reaches it by mathematical
> means, that is, by means which are abstracted from matter, while the natural
> philosopher reaches it by means observed within matter. Therefore, there is
> nothing to prevent those very same things, concerning which the philosophical
> disciplines deal to the extent that they are knowable by the light of natural rea-
> son, from being dealt with also by some other science to the extent that they are
> known in the light of divine revelation. Hence the theology which belongs to the

Holy Teaching differs in kind from that 'theology' which is said to be a part of philosophy.

*Ratio cognoscibilis* is not easily translatable. Presently, in Article 3 of this same Question, St. Thomas will render the same idea by *ratio formalis objecti*. He is saying that what distinguishes one science from another is not a difference of *things*, but different conceptions (*rationes*) of things. One and the same thing can be knowable (*cognoscibilis*) in different ways; and these different 'knowablenesses' of things are attained according as objects are viewed or reasoned about by different means or *media*. The medieval astronomer concluded that the earth was round (*not* flat!) by mathematical calculations (truly, concerning observed phenomena, but the phenomena were not the means whereby he reached his conclusion). The 'natural philosopher', however, would reach the same conclusion concerning the same earth through the observation of phenomena themselves. Faith and reason, similarly, may make the same (or they may also make different) affirmations concerning God. It cannot be concluded that they are concerned with different 'Gods'. The *media*, in the light of which they respectively make their affirmations, are quite distinct, and though they sometimes reach the same conclusions, it is consequently to other 'knowablenesses' of God they attain. Here St. Thomas goes no further than "Nihil prohibet"—"there is nothing to prevent." But it is a vitally important preliminary to understanding his identification of the 'God of Reason' and the 'God of Revelation'. It will enable him to maintain that reason can establish the reality of the selfsame God who reveals, though it cannot establish *that* he reveals or *what* he reveals. On this account only have the *viae* any place in a *theological* work.

But what, it is often asked, is the point of this rational approach to God—and of the Five Ways in particular? What need is it supposed to meet? What precise place can it occupy in what is professedly a *Summa Theologiae*? Have we not already seen that St. Thomas himself says that the 'theology' which belongs to the Holy Teaching of revelation is distinct in kind from the so-called 'theology' which is part of philosophy, and which considers 'God' solely in the light of what is discoverable by natural reason? What place can the latter have in the former? What business have 'natural theology' and the Five Ways in preaching and teaching the Gospel of salvation? These and suchlike questions haunt many besides the disciples of Karl Barth.

In his reply to the second objection to the fifth Article of this First Question, St. Thomas is quite explicit that there is no inherent necessity for the employment of reason in regard of revelation. But "this science *can* receive from the philosophical disciplines, not because it requires them of necessity, but for the greater clarification of what is delivered in this science [i.e., by revelation] . . .

The fact that it employs them is not due to any deficiency of its own, but on account of the deficiency of our own understanding."

Moreover, we should remember, St. Thomas is well aware that rational processes are not the only way in which truth concerning God is to be attained. The reply to the third objection to Article 6 is an important reminder of this. Truth, of any sort, certainly is attainable only in the judgment (or proposition) or its equivalent. But here he points out that not only study or logical argument enables us to judge correctly of Divine Things, but also 'connaturality' or 'inclination'. St. Thomas is thus careful to remind us, early in his *Summa*, that though the *Summa* itself will follow rational or 'argumentative' methods, this does not mean that affectively conditioned 'intuition' may not attain the same truths; and the judgment that 'God is' is certainly not to be excluded from its scope. (We shall see that I. ii. 1 in no way contradicts this.) Furthermore, it has already been implied in the first Article that revelation also includes truths which, though discoverable by reason, may not in fact be so discovered. The proposition that there is a God is certainly to be included among these, and is implicit in all of them.

But the questions we have posed, and of which the Barthians of our time have made us so acutely aware, remain unanswered.

For the answers we must turn again to Article 8 of the First Question. Here St. Thomas sets out in greater detail the function of proof or rational argumentation in regard of the Holy Teaching; in what ways, that is to say, logical argument can serve "the greater clarification of what is delivered" in revelation. This Article is an ingenious adaptation to the requirements of theology of the teaching of Aristotle in the Fourth Book of the *Metaphysics* on the functions of reason in the First Philosophy. First:

> As other sciences do not argue to demonstrate their own premises (*principia*) but argue *from* those premises to show other things contained within those sciences, so this Teaching does not argue in order to prove its own premises— which are articles of faith—but *from* them it proceeds to show something else, as the Apostle, in 1 Cor. xv., argues from the Resurrection of Christ to prove the General Resurrection.

The primary function of reason in any science is to draw conclusions from its premises; similarly the first task of reason in respect of revelation (summarised in articles of faith) is to draw theological conclusions; that is, to show what is contained in the potentialities of those premises, "since the whole of a science is contained in the potentiality (*virtute*) of its premises" (I. i. 7). Clearly the Five Ways, starting as they do not from articles of faith but from empirical observations,[1] are *not* an example of this way of employing reason in theology. But this is not the only function which reason can have for the *doctor catholicae veritatis*, whose business it is, just because his teaching is Catholic, to teach *all* men (see the Prologue to the *Summa* again!). St. Thomas, following and reapplying Aristotle, continues:

> But it is to be noted that, among the philosophical sciences, while the lower sciences neither prove their premises nor argue with those who deny those premises, but leave this to some higher science, the highest of all among them—namely metaphysics—does argue with those who deny its premises, given that the opponent grants anything at all. But if he grants nothing, it cannot argue with him, though it can resolve his reasons [for denying them].

What the first principles of reason are to the First Philosophy or metaphysics, that are articles of faith to theology. Neither metaphysics nor theology can demonstrate their first premises and presuppositions; for those of the former can only be intuitively acknowledged, and those of the latter can only be accepted in humble faith in God's revelation. If the opponent of the first principles of reason "will only say something," as Aristotle says (*Metaph.*, 1006a, 14) argument is still possible; there is some basis for showing him that, in the very fact of making any meaningful statement, he does in fact imply the principle of non-contradiction, and it can further be shown that denial of other principles involves denial of that. Correspondingly:

> The Holy Teaching . . . can dispute with those who deny its premises, and this by means of argument, if the opponent grants anything at all of what is received through divine revelation; thus, by the authorities of the Holy Teaching itself, we argue with heretics; and by means of one article [we argue] with those who deny another. But if the opponent believes nothing that is divinely revealed no further way lies open to prove articles of faith by using reasons; nevertheless [it does remain possible] to resolve any arguments he may bring against faith.

If the opponent of metaphysical principles, Aristotle says, will say nothing reasonable at all, no argument is possible, for "such a person is really no better than a vegetable" (*Metaph.*, 1006a, 153). If he offers arguments against them, then refutation of them remains possible, and such refutation is part of the metaphysician's task. Similarly, if the opponent of articles of faith, says St. Thomas, grants nothing in revelation, then it is impossible to argue with him on the basis of revelation. But he is not on that account a vegetable. Reason remains available; and to the extent that faulty reasoning constitutes his arguments against faith, then the "teacher of Catholic truth" can and should, on the basis of reason, set out to resolve them.

The *Summa Theologiae* is not, as is sometimes supposed, a *potpourri* of theology and philosophy; it is wholly a *Summa* of Theology concerned with the *Sacra Doctrina*, the Holy Teaching of salvation given by God's revelation. But because it is that, it can *use* philosophical argument for its own end—which is *hominis salus*—the health or salvation of man (I. i. 1). It in no way substitutes a 'natural theology' for revelation, nor does it appeal to reason for what only revelation can impart. But it is part of its own task to teach those who acknowledge no revelation at all—not indeed about the 'God of Revelation' *as such*, but at least about such presuppositions (*praeambula*), doubt or denial of which is an intellectual obstacle to faith. Such supremely is the answer to the question, *An Deus sit?*—whether there is a God at all.

The Five Ways are, quite certainly, an example (and the most important one) of this third of the tasks which St. Thomas had ascribed to reason in Question I, Article 8. Formally and intrinsically, indeed the Five Ways are 'pure philosophy'; but their end and function in the *Summa* are purely theological; or rather, to use St. Thomas's own language, they pertain to the Holy Teaching of salvation. Many of the objections to 'natural theology' from 'neoorthodox' Protestantism would perhaps be dissipated if this were more strongly emphasised.

One final point from the First Question of the *Summa* should be noted before turning to the Second, although its importance may not till then be apparent. In I. i. 7, St. Thomas establishes that the 'subject' of the Holy Teaching is God. There has been a good deal of seemingly needless mystification among some commentators as to what St. Thomas means by this, on the grounds that he has already established that the 'object' of the Holy Teaching is God. A more unsophisticated reading (confirmed, moreover, by Cajetan) suggests that St. Thomas is here simply concerned to show that the Holy Teaching is *about* God (*de Deo*)—that is to say, that the subject concerning which it makes predications is 'God'—and to answer the difficulties which this may arouse. Nor are these difficulties inconsiderable. The first objection runs:

Any science must presuppose [knowledge of] what its subject is, according to the Philosopher in the *Posterior Analytics*. But this science does not presuppose [knowledge of] what God is, for, as the Damascene says, "Of God it is impossible to say what he is." Therefore God is not the subject of this science.

In his reply St. Thomas does not (as would some later Thomists) distinguish the premisses: he knows nothing of a 'quidditative' and 'non-quidditative' knowledge of what God is. On the contrary he expressly admits the premisses, but still rejects the conclusion:

Although it is impossible to know about God 'what he is', we nevertheless employ, for those things which are studied about God in this Teaching, his effects, whether of nature or of grace, instead of a definition [of him]. So likewise in some philosophical sciences something may be proved about a cause by means of an effect, using an effect instead of a definition of the cause.

The full implication of this reply, and of the problems which it suggests, will not be threshed out until, in Questions XII and XIII, St. Thomas comes to treat of our knowledge and language about God. For our present purposes it must suffice to emphasise that for St. Thomas any 'theology', whether 'sacred' or 'natural', reaches conclusions which are made by predicates about a subject which remains essentially and intrinsically unknown. We must expect no more from the subject of the proposition with which the Five Ways finally conclude: *Deus est.* What *Deus* is remains a mystery; and indeed the Five Ways will be directed precisely to demonstrate that the mystery, which we can only even name "from effects," truly is. The Five Ways will disappoint us sorely if we look to them to establish the reality of any *a priori* conception of God, our own or another's.

### The Title of Question II: What the Proofs will Prove

The Second Question of the *Summa* is headed by the terse title: *An Deus sit.* The same title heads the third Article of this Question which contains the Five Ways themselves. Consistently and without exception throughout this Question, and indeed throughout all his works, St. Thomas states as the conclusion of his Ways the bare proposition *Deum esse* or that *Deus est.*

Yet the Five Ways are commonly known as 'proofs for the *existence of* God'. This term will nowhere be found in St. Thomas's text; nor, it may be remarked in passing, and contrary to what is sometimes asserted, do the Vatican Council Decrees or the Decree *Lamentabili* say anything about the demonstrability of the *existence* of God: indeed the term seems until very recently to have been studiously avoided in authoritative documents. It may well seem pedantic to object to so usual and hallowed a term, and rightly understood it is certainly unobjectionable. Yet experience shows that it is open to serious misunderstanding which may prejudice in advance any clear understanding of what the Five Ways do in fact set out to accomplish.

The *Oxford Concise Dictionary* may be taken to indicate to us the meanings of the verb *to exist* in current English: "have place in the domain of reality, have being under specified conditions, occur, be found." In not one of these senses can the verb *to exist* be accurately used of God. If the Five Ways lead anywhere, it is to the affirmation of that which has *no* place in the domain of reality, but which contrariwise will be found both to transcend and to include it. To 'have place in the domain of reality' implies determination and limitation, which must be precisely denied of *Actus purus*. The Ways lead, not to what 'has being under specified conditions', but precisely to what *has not* being, but *is* being, and with no specified conditions whatsoever. 'Occur' is commonly understood of a temporal, transient event: eminently inapplicable to the *ex hypothesi* Immutable and Eternal. The God to which the Five Ways lead precisely does *not* exist in any one of these accepted senses of the word. Still more obviously, *Deus est* does not mean that God is 'found', although the *viae* claim to enable us to find that he *is*.

It may be urged that, whatever dictionaries may say, scholastic authors have their own technical meaning of the verb *to exist*. This is true enough, but the fact will be of little help to our non-scholastic contemporaries to overcome their disinclination to employ the verb of God. Very often this disinclination may be attributed to a laudable reluctance to predicate of the Absolute a verb which would determine and limit it: much apparent atheism can be motivated by a genuine, if not fully conscious, appreciation of and reverence for the divine transcendence. Those untrained in analogical thinking may have a quite healthy repugnance to attributing to the Transcendent a verb which normally belongs to tables and chairs. But neither does the word existence, understood as it is in the scholastic textbooks, serve us any better. 'Existence' is there described as that *quo aliquid est extra suas causas* ("that whereby something is outside its causes"). But the God to which the Ways lead is the First Uncaused Cause—he has no causes to be outside of, and he cannot be *extra* anything. He is not 'something', *aliquid*, he is the All.

If the expression 'God exists' can thus be highly misleading, the expression 'the existence of God', as descriptive of that to which the Five Ways would lead, is still more so. God *has* not, he *is*, being. Still less has he 'existence' in any of the senses of 'exist' that we have seen.

It will reasonably be urged that in English we have no true infinitives; we have no equivalent of the Latin *esse*, and what better word can we use to translate it than the accepted word *existence*? The difficulty may be readily granted: but still the Five Ways do not, in any easily recognizable sense, prove the existence (or *esse*) of God.

St. Thomas himself is quite explicit about that, and though the point may at first strike some as difficult and subtle, it is vitally important if we would understand what the Five Ways do and do not claim to establish. In the fourth Article of the Question following upon the Five Ways (*Summa* I. iii. 4), St. Thomas sets out to show that the essence or nature of God is one and the same as his *esse*. The second objection to this thesis runs as follows:

> We are able to know *whether* God is, as has been said [i.e., in the Five Ways themselves]. But we cannot know *what* he is. Therefore the *esse* of God (*esse Dei*) is not the same as *what* he is, which is his essence or nature.

In other words: if the Divine essence is the same as the Divine *esse*, and if the Divine *esse* is proved (and therefore *known*, for a proof is *syllogismus faciens scire*, an argument which produces *knowledge* of its conclusion) by the Five Ways, then it follows that we also know the Divine Essence or nature, which, as we have seen St. Thomas shows repeatedly, we cannot in fact know this side of the Beatific Vision.

To this St. Thomas replies:

> The word *esse* is employed in a twofold way. In one way it means the act of being (*actum essendi*). In the second way it means the composition of a proposition (*compositio propositionis*) which the mind discovers by attaching a predicate to a subject.[2] In the first way of understanding *esse* we are *not* able to know the *esse* of God, any more than we are able to know his essence; but only in the second way. For what we know [i.e., by the Five Ways] is that this proposition which we construct concerning God when we say 'God is' is a true one; and this we know from his effects, as has been said above.

To know *Deum esse* (that God is) is not to know the *esse Dei* (the 'is' of God), if by this we mean his own pure act of being; the only *esse*, in the sense of act of being, that we know in the Five Ways is the *esse* of finite effects: from these we argue (and therefore *know*) that the verb 'to be' truly belongs to the subject 'God'. In the sense that this verb truly belongs to that subject we might say that we know *esse Dei* (*esse* of God): but *only* in this sense. If this is what is meant in calling the *Quinque Viae* 'proofs of the existence of God', no objection can be raised, for this perfectly reflects St. Thomas's own mind.

### The Function and Method of the Five Ways According to I. ii. 1 and 2

From our study of the First Question of the *Summa* we are already led to expect from the Five Ways not the establishment of the existence of any human preconception of 'God', no knowledge of 'what' he is, nor of his own 'existence' or *esse*, but quite simply the leading of the denying or doubting human mind to affirm an Unknown, which nevertheless we *call* Divine—or *Deus*. Indeed it may be said that the Five Ways serve, incidentally but surely, to demolish human idols and preconceptions of the Divine—the *Deus secundum opinionem* as distinct from *Deus secundum naturam* of which St. Thomas writes in I. xiii. 10. Their purpose is not to persuade the unbeliever to know *what* the Catholic already knows, but to show him the logical necessity of affirming a mystery which the Catholic already confesses. "Neither the Catholic nor the heathen knows the Nature of God as it is in itself; but both know it only according to some concept, whether of causality, of transcendence (*excellentia*) or of negation" (I. xiii. 10 ad 5). Were it otherwise, no common speech concerning the subject 'God' between the believer and the unbeliever would ever be possible. The Five Ways will precisely *show* that *omnia abeunt in mysterium*; they will therefore be quite different from Paley's argument from the watch to the Watchmaker, an already comprehensible, knowable and known cause. They will also show that this mystery is no mere ignorance in the human mind; but one of which the mind is logically compelled to affirm that it *is*. In this sense it may be said that they lead from a purely subjective to an objective agnosticism: they will show that we cannot merely say, "I do not know," but also that "there is an Unknown." It may likewise be said that they lead from an *indocta* to a *docta ignorantia*: they will show that the ground of phenomenal existence is not merely mysterious and unintelligible to us but further that both our phenomenal perceptions and all human thought are *impossible* unless the reality of that mystery be affirmed. They will show that the affirmation of this Unknown is a true and logically necessary affirmation; and it will later be shown (in Questions IV to XI) that—not because we come to know this Unknown, but because we can perceive and can reason about finite existence—certain concepts can be truly predicated concerning it, by way of inference from finite existence ('causality'), transcendence of finite existence ('excellence'), or denial of finite existence ('negation').

All this will, we think, be amply confirmed by a careful study of the Five Ways themselves and of the two Articles (I. ii. 1 and 2) with which St. Thomas prefaces them and discusses the need and manner of proving that 'God is'. To these latter we must now turn.

In the first of these Articles he asks whether the proposition 'Deus est' is *per se notum*, which we may adequately, if not quite precisely, render as 'self-evident': a term which the Article itself shows may have several different but correlated meanings. Clearly, if it is self-evident to us, and to all mankind, it is superfluous, nay impossible, to prove it: immediate perceptions are not open to discussion or argument (though one may argue about the judgments which may be made about them).

The *sed contra* to this Article appeals significantly and characteristically to a plain matter of fact. The atheist—the denier or doubter of God—in fact exists. The reality of God is in fact questioned, and is therefore open to question; while what is absolutely and universally self-evident is undeniable, unthinkable, indubitable, and unquestionable. It may be folly indeed, as the Psalmist says, to say there is no God; but it is certainly possible. The *doctor catholicae veritatis*, called to teach *all* men (see the Prologue again!), cannot ignore the fact.

As the *sed contra* draws attention to the existence (and, by implication, the need) of the atheist, so the main body of the Article meets the agnostic more than halfway. Its reasoning depends on the supposition that 'Nos non scimus de Deo quid est'—'we do not know what God is'. We cannot claim that any judgment is self-evident unless we know *what* we are talking about (the subject) and what we are saying about it (the predicate). It is a sobering thought that, when we talk about God, we do not know *what* we are talking about. This side of the Beatific Vision therefore, no statement about God can be self-evident in the sense of being amenable to direct and purely intellectual perception. This holds good of the statement *Deus est*. It is sufficient for St. Thomas's present purpose to point out that we do not know what the subject, *Deus*, is: but it is also true (see I. iii. 4 ad 2um again!) that we do not know what *est*, as predicated of God, is either. *If* the statement is to be purely intellectually known at all, it can therefore only be as a result of demonstration—'indiget demonstrari': it must be a conclusion to a process of thought, since it cannot be a first principle, an intuitively perceived datum such as are the axioms of reason which are presupposed to all thought. We say, "purely intellectually known," for St. Thomas clearly, as we have already seen, does not exclude that the statement may be accepted as true by faith or in virtue of affectively conditioned 'inclination'. Nor can we exclude *enthymeme*, a rational process or syllogism in which intermediary propositions are not expressed—"perception by way of the unconscious" is Jung's definition of intuition.

St. Thomas never suggests, as some of his exponents might sometimes seem to do, that rational proof of 'the existence of God' and other *praeambula fidei* is an indispensable prerequisite to faith for everybody; on the contrary they are intrinsically necessary only for those "who believe nothing which is divinely revealed" (I. i. 8). But though not personally necessary for everybody, the Five Ways serve also to demonstrate the logical conclusions which may be reached by unaided reason, and which stand to truths of faith as does nature to grace (cf. I. ii. 2 ad 1um, and *Expositio in Boeth. De Trin.*, II. iii). Faith presupposes, but also includes, acknowledgment that God is; and it cannot coexist with doubt or denial that he is. The Five Ways will show how unaided reason can remove the obstacles of doubt and denial, and indeed positively to affirm that he is. So St. Thomas (op. et loc. cit.) speaks of the proof that 'God is' as among those *praeambula* which are necessary to the *scientia fidei*—i.e., *knowledge* of the faith, not faith itself. For they remove the obstacles to belief precisely and only by supplying rational demonstration of those naturally attainable truths which faith presupposes and includes. Although they are necessary to the *science* of faith, part and parcel (in the way we have already seen) of the systematic 'argumentative' *sacra doctrina* (itself necessitated, not by any deficiency in revelation, but by the deficiencies of our own understanding—as we have also seen), it does not follow that their rational demonstrations are indispensable *praeambula* for each and every believer. We have seen that St.

Thomas's second argument (in the first Article of the *Summa*) for man's need for revelation makes nonsense of the idea that they are; as also the Church's practice of infant Baptism, and the fact that the need for scientifically demonstrating that there is a God seems to have been little felt in the early days of the Christian proclamation of the Gospel.

But to return to our Article. Relying on Aristotle's *Posterior Analytics*, it shows that a judgment or proposition may be intrinsically self-evident without its being so to one who does not know its subject or predicate. Such, truly enough, is the proposition *Deus est*. It can be proved, and in I. iii. 4, will be proved, that in God there can be no distinction of *essentia* and *esse*; that therefore God necessarily is. In this sense, St. Thomas already here points out, the proposition *Deus est* is *intrinsically* self-evident: in the technical language of the *Analytics* it is a *per-se-primo* necessary proposition, whose subject and predicate are mutually inclusive and indeed identical in 'what' they signify. But this requires proof: it is not, for the finite mind, an intuitively perceived *a priori* datum, for that 'what' altogether escapes its grasp. Moreover, the proof itself will be deduced from the conclusions which the Five Ways themselves reach, and cannot be presupposed to them. The thoughtful—the *sapientes*—indeed *know* that *Deus est* is an intrinsically self-evident proposition, but they know it by way of conclusion from a process of reasoning, not as something which is immediately evident to themselves.[3] That *Deus est* is intrinsically self-evident is true and demonstrable only on condition that *Deus est* is a true proposition at all, and it is this that must first be demonstrated.

The *objections* to this first Article of the Second Question are of great interest in themselves; and St. Thomas will take this opportunity to treat briefly of several previous attempts to establish that *God is* and to prepare the ground for his own approach. The first objection takes St John Damascene as a representative for the view that awareness of the Being of God (*existendi Deum*) is innate in human nature. The second is a brief but *verbatim* summary of St. Anselm's celebrated 'ontological argument', and argues that it satisfies Aristotle's conditions for self-evidence. The third is a summary of the line of thought beloved by St. Augustine (e.g., in *Contra Academicos*, III. xi. 25, cf. *Confessions*, VII. x, etc.) concerning the undeniability of truth: even the complete sceptic in his assertion of scepticism and his denial of any truth is tacitly assuming that there is some truth; if there is any truth then there is Truth—St. Augustine's favorite attribute of God.

To the first, St. Thomas replies by agreeing that some sort of knowledge of God is indeed implanted in us. God is in fact man's ultimate end and bliss; man naturally and necessarily desires his own end and bliss, and what he naturally desires he must necessarily naturally know—in some way. St. Thomas himself in the *Prima Secundae* will pursue this line of thought with great thoroughness and detail, and show that man's end and bliss can only be attained in God. But all this will need—and receive—proof. It is a fact, which St. Thomas will show over and over again, that desire for, and love of, God is implicit in every desire and every love, that there could be no good to desire or to love if there were no supreme Good: in this sense it is connatural to man and to every creature to love God above all things, for *propter quod unumquodque tale, et illud magis* (cf. I. lx. 5, I–II. cix. 3, II–II. xxiii. 3, etc.). In this sense it is a fact that, in knowing the good which we desire and the bliss which subsumes all our goods and all our desires, *that which* we know is in fact God, or at least implies God, and this knowledge is indeed part and parcel of our nature and is innate. But it does not follow that we thereby know God with an innate knowledge. Without proof that our bliss is indeed God, we do not really *know* what in fact we know. *To know* means to know that we know. St. Thomas here takes an example from ocular vision. A shape looms through the fog; the shape I see is in fact Peter, but I cannot say that I see Peter until I see *that* what I see is Peter. I see Peter only "in aliquo communi, sub quadam confusione"—"in a general way, with a certain vagueness"—and though what I see is *really* Peter, it is not until I see that what I see is in fact Peter that I *really see* Peter. Until then, my judgment of what I see may indeed be mistaken: I may suppose that it is Paul. So likewise, St. Thomas concludes, "many suppose that man's perfect good, his bliss, is wealth or sensual delight, others that it is some other thing."

The importance of this reply should not be overlooked. St. Thomas does not deny, on the contrary he expressly asserts, that some knowledge that there is a God—"in aliquo communi et sub quadam confusione"—is connatural to man. Indeed were it otherwise, we could never come to know that *God is* at all. The Five Ways will be concerned precisely to remove the vagueness and confusion from our knowledge: to analyze it and thus make explicit and actual what is in fact implicit and potential in *all* our knowledge and experience. For St. Thomas's present purpose, it is enough to give this one example in order to show that argument is needed to make clear to us the implications of our everyday knowledge.

So likewise in answering the third objection, it is enough to say that the acknowledgment of a truth does not immediately involve explicit acknowledgment of the First Truth, which we call God: though it does indeed involve a recognition of truth-in-general. St. Thomas does not repudiate St. Augustine's argument; but he points out that it is an argument and not an immediate, intuitive perception. St. Thomas himself will follow the same line of reasoning, with modifications, in his Fourth Way. It can indeed be *argued*, but it is not self-evident, that there could be no truth at all unless there were an Absolute Truth, the source and measure of all true things and of all judgments upon things; it is in this sense true that acknowledgment of God is in fact implicit in any acknowledgment of truth, real or supposed. But no more than in the vague and confused awareness of bliss, presupposed to all human desire and love, is the reality of God therein immediately evident; and here too erroneous judgment is possible and indeed frequent.

It has been questioned (for instance, by Karl Barth in his *Anselmus*) whether St. Anselm ever intended his 'ontological argument' to be a purely rational 'proof of the existence of God' as now understood. A good case can be made for the view (though also for the contrary) that this argument is covered by his general programme of *fides quaerens intellectum* and *intelligere quod credimus*. On this showing the *id quo majus cogitari non potest* ("that than which nothing greater can be thought"), which it takes as its starting point, would already be a datum received in faith, and the purpose of the 'argument' would be rather to assist in understanding what the Christian already believes than to demonstrate, from purely 'natural' premises and by purely rational processes, the reality of God. However this may be, it is still an argument, not a self-evident perception, and is presented as such.

The second part of St. Thomas's reply to this second objection—his argument against the ontological argument, which is to the effect that it is illegitimate to argue from the meaning of the name 'God' to the truth of the statement that 'God is'—has been widely commented upon and discussed. Its opening words, however, seem to have received less attention:

> Perhaps he who hears the name 'God' does *not* understand to be meant thereby something than which nothing greater can be thought, since some have believed that God is a body . . .

Here again we see at once St. Thomas's preoccupation with the needs of the unbeliever, and correspondingly with the pedagogic function of argument to conclude that *God is* as part and parcel of the Holy Teaching. Consistently with the principles which we have seen him set out in I. i. 8, he finds it necessary to find some common ground of agreement with the unbeliever that he too will accept. Anselm's argument—assuming it to be intended for such—fails precisely here: it presupposes a preconception of the meaning of the name 'God' which perhaps the unbeliever will not accept, which in fact many unbelievers do not accept. If he is to be consistent with his own criticism of Anselm, St. Thomas's own Five Ways will have to be equally free of an *a priori* preconception of the meaning of the word 'God', and cannot be made to depend for their validity on such a meaning. They must be valid even for those who suppose God to be a body; indeed they must convince him that there is a God who is precisely *not* a body.

Kantian criticism of the 'traditional proofs' has maintained that they all, at least surreptitiously, introduce the ontological argument, and that they cannot do otherwise. It is maintained that since, in any valid argument, a conclusion may contain no term which is not contained in the premises, and since the conclusion of the 'traditional arguments' is that *God is*, it must follow that some conception of the meaning of the word 'God' must be tacitly assumed in the argumentation itself, and this meaning (since it is presupposed to the proofs) must be derived from some source other than the proofs themselves. It is indeed difficult to see how this criticism can be countered if it be admitted that *any* meaning of the name 'God'—Anselm's or another's—is presupposed to the arguments; let alone if that meaning (the 'nominal definition' in scholastic parlance) be employed as the middle term (*medium demonstrationis*) of the arguments. Yet it is expressly stated by many authors that it is to be so employed, and the Five Ways themselves are frequently formulated (for instance, by Gredt) in such a way that some meaning of the word 'God' is assumed, and employed as the means whereby the conclusion is reached. It is hard to see how such a conclusion is not indeed a foregone conclusion, and one precisely which will not be accepted either by those who "crediderint Deum esse corpus" ("believe God to be a body"), or by "ponentibus Deum non esse"—("those who suppose there is no God")—whose needs St. Thomas vindicates in this reply to the Anselmian argument. But it is not lightly to be supposed that St. Thomas's own formulation of the Ways will be open to the very objection he levels at St. Anselm, or that it will fail to anticipate and avoid the criticism of Kant and his numerous successors; a criticism which, after all, should occur to the veriest novice in the rules of logic.

Against this, it will be urged, is St. Thomas's plain "necesse est accipere pro medio *quid significet nomen*" ("it is necessary to take *what the name means* for our medium of demonstration") and "accipere possumus pro medio quid significet hoc nomen *Deus*" ("we can take for our medium what this name *God* means") in the *ad secundum* of the following Article. We will examine this more closely after we have examined this second Article, 'Whether it can be proved that God is', as a whole. To it we will now turn.

The title of this second Article of the Second Question is *Utrum Deum Esse Sit Demonstrabile*: whether it can be shown that God is. From the fact that it is not self-evident to us, and so requires demonstration, it does not immediately follow that it *can* be demonstrated. Nor, it should be noted, does this Article claim to prove that it can be demonstrated without (as has been said above) a *petitio principii* for those who do not already acknowledge that phenomena are divine effects. The proof of the pudding must be in the eating, possibilities can only be fully established from actualities, demonstrabilities from demonstrations: in short, the question posed in the second Article will not be fully answered until the third, in which the *viae* must stand or fall on their own merits.

But the 'teacher of Catholic truth' can and should discuss in advance what lines or arguments will or will not be appropriate and valid, given his own assumptions, (a) that God is unknown and (b) that phenomena are dependent upon him as his effects. The first assumption will exclude any *propter quid* or *a priori* argument; from the second assumption it follows that an argument *quia*, which begins from known phenomena and shows their dependence, will establish that there is a cause on which they depend.[4]

The reply to the first objection to this Article does little more than repeat the doctrine and the *nihil prohibet* of I. i. 1 ad 2um, but in doing so emphasises its relevance to our present inquiry. Nor does the *ad tertium* bring any new light or arouse any difficulties, which we have not already touched upon. The *ad secundum* is much more problematic, and requires closer examination.

Its explicit conclusion, "accipere possumus pro medio quid significet hoc nomen *Deus*," seems to say expressly that the meaning of the noun *God* (the 'nominal definition') is the middle term in any proof that *God is*. This has, as we have said, been commonly assumed in many formulations of the 'traditional proofs'.

But this seems to run quite counter to I. i. 7 ad 1um and to I. ii. 1 ad 2um, as we have just understood them. It also seems clearly contradicted by St. Thomas's own formulation of the *viae* in which the noun God and its meaning, so far from being employed as a *medium demonstrationis*, does not occur in the course of the arguments at all. It is also contradicted by the opening words of this *ad secundum* itself, where it is clearly said, "cum demonstratur causa per effectum, necesse est uti effectu [*not* definitione nominali] loco definitionis causae" ("when a cause is demonstrated by means of an effect, it is necessary to use the effect [*not* the meaning of the name] instead of the definition of cause"). We seem up against a dilemma: either the *medium* is some effect or effects, or it is the meaning of the noun *God*. It is difficult to see how we can have it both ways.

It would be well to have the full text both of objection and reply before us. The objection may be rendered:

> The means of proof (*medium demonstrationis*) is a definition (*quod quid est*— what something is). But we cannot know what God is, but only what he is not, as the Damascene says. Therefore we cannot prove that *God is*.

It might be thought that this difficulty is fully answered in the Article itself: only in *propter quid* reasoning is it necessary to have a knowledge of what the cause is (the *quid* the conclusion is *propter*). And indeed the reply *ad secundum* does begin by recalling:

> When a cause is proved from an effect, it is necessary to use the *effect* instead of a definition of the cause [and this precisely in order] to show that there is a cause.

This is so, whether we are arguing to a fire from smoke, to Man Friday from his footprints, to sunspots from cracklings on the radio. But in these cases, we shall also have some knowledge of the causes we are talking about, as well as of the effects. They are known or knowable to us quite apart from these effects. But of the cause which we call God we have (as the objection maintains) no such knowledge, but *only* of effects. So St. Thomas continues:

> And this is supremely the case in regard to God. For to prove that anything is, we must take as our means the meaning of the name (*quid significet nomen*), but not its definition (*quod quid est*—what it is in itself), for we cannot know *what* something is until we know *that* it is (quia quaestio *quid est* sequitur quaestionem *an est*). But the names which we apply to God are themselves taken from effects, as will be shown later on. Therefore, in showing that *God is* by means of an effect, we can take as our means the meaning of the name *God.*

What is "shown later on" (in Question XIII, *passim*), is precisely that the Divine Names, and the name *Deus* itself, are all derived from creatures, all originally signify some created effect, and are attributed to God solely because divine attributes are inferred from effects. So, for St. Thomas, there is no contradiction at all in saying that our means of proof are effects *and* the *quid significet nomen* of God, for they are one and the same. By the fact that we "show that *God is* by means of an effect, we can take as our means the meaning of the name *God.*" This is what the Five Ways do. Beginning with an observation of fact, and with no mention of God, let alone the *meaning* of 'God' or a 'nominal definition', each will reach its own appropriate conclusion (*primum movens, causa efficiens prima, per se necessarium*, etc.), and the subject of each conclusion will be *called* or *understood* to be divine or 'God'.[5]

So far from some meaning of the word *God* being presupposed to the arguments, or even included in them, the meaning of *God* is precisely *discovered* by them, in and through phenomena. The meaning of Divinity, no less than its reality, is, we would maintain, precisely that to which the Five Ways lead, and the centre on which they all converge.

### Notes

This chapter was previously published as Victor White, "Prelude to the Five Ways" (chapter 4 of Victor White, *God the Unknown*, The Harvill Press, London, 1956).

1. In detail: The First Way begins *Certum est enim et sensu constat*; the Second: *Invenimus in istis sensibilibus*; the Third: *Invenimus enim in rebus*; the Fourth (*pace* those who would approximate it to an ontological argument, or present it as an argument from exemplarity independent of efficient causality): *in rebus inveniuntur*; the Fifth: *videmus.*

2. Aristotle in *Metaph.* vii (1017a, 35), on which St. Thomas bases this distinction of the meaning of *esse*, does not speak of it as meaning *compositio propositionis*, but simply "as true" (ὅτι ἀληθές). In the parallel passage in *Contra Gentiles*, I. xii, St. Thomas writes not of *compositio propositionis*, but of *compositio intellectus*. We think it is a mistake to suppose that St. Thomas considers *compositio* here to be equivalent to *copula*, or that in his mind, *est* standing alone with a subject ("secundum se") exercises a copulative rather than a predicative function: clearly it 'copulates' nothing. Rather we suggest should 'compositio' here be understood as that which formally 'composes' or constitutes the judgment (or our 'intellectus', i.e., understanding) of the truth. The solution of the question, much discussed by both scholastic and later logicians, as to whether *est* standing with a subject but no further predicate is itself a predicate must depend on our definition of a predicate. The Leonine edition gives two readings of St. Thomas's Commentary on *Perihermenias*, II. x. 2: "*est* quandoque in enunciatione praedicatur (*al.* ponitur) secundum se."

3. This is not the place to enter into the somewhat intricate discussions centred round the 'agnosticism' of St. Thomas, with which Père Sertillanges and his critics have familiarised us. But it may be noted that neither in I. iii. 4 is there any claim to know—even 'non-quidditatively'—what *essentia* or *esse* in God is. If we examine its logical structure, we see that its arguments show only that it is 'impossible' to assert a distinction of *esse* and *essentia* of that subject called 'Deus' with which the Five Ways conclude. They follow throughout the *via remotionis*: the denial of finite composition.

4. St. Thomas is not, of course, presenting in this Article a complete account of the distinction between *propter quid* and *quia* arguments, or even explaining their essential characteristics, but only such an account as serves his immediate purpose in introducing the *viae*. The distinction, as expounded by Aristotle in the *Posterior Analytics*, does not altogether coincide either with deductive and inductive reasoning, or with *a priori* and *a posteriori* argument. Still less should it be supposed that every argument *quia* concludes to a judgment of existence only. The essential characteristic of a *propter quid* (διότι) argument is that it shows *why* S is P in the conclusion; an argument *quia* (ὅτι) *that* S is P, whether the reason for asserting it is an effect or not.

5. In detail: I. *hoc omnes intelligunt Deum*; II. *quam omnes Deum nominant*; III. *quod omnes dicunt Deum*; IV and V. *et hoc dicimus Deum.*

# 3

# The Five Ways

## John Wippel

AS ANYONE WITH EVEN A CASUAL acquaintance with Aquinas's writings is aware, it is in the *Summa Theologiae* (ST) I, q. 2, a. 3 that he presents his best-known formulation of argumentation for God's existence. A number of the arguments from his earlier writings foreshadow most, if not all, of the "five ways" of the *Summa Theologiae*. These points of similarity notwithstanding, Thomas gives a personal and particular touch to each of the five ways themselves. Because of the relatively later date of this treatment (ca. 1266–1268), because of the apparently wider readership at which the *Summa Theologiae* is aimed, and because of the comprehensive way in which the five ways are fitted together, these arguments for God's existence have received more attention from Thomas's students than any of his other efforts to establish this point.[1]

At the same time, it should be remembered that the amount of space accorded to each of the five ways is relatively brief and that in certain instances, at least, familiarity with some of Thomas's most fundamental metaphysical options is presupposed by them.[2] Finally, the question has often been raised concerning whether the five ways are intended by Thomas to form one developing argument for God's existence, or five distinct and more or less independent arguments. To put this in other terms, how are these five proofs intended to fit together? Before making any attempt to answer this question, however, it will first be necessary for us to consider each of them in turn.

Question 2 of the First Part of the *Summa Theologiae* is addressed to this issue: Does God exist?[3] In a. 1 Thomas again rejects any claim that God's existence is self-evident (*per se notum*) to us, even though he continues to hold that the proposition "God exists" is self-evident in itself. Its predicate is identical

— 45 —

with its subject since God's essence is his act of being (*esse*). Because we do not know of God what he is, that he exists is not known to us *per se* but needs to be demonstrated by means of things which are better known to us, i.e., his effects. Thomas's denial that God's existence is self-evident to us also leads him to reject the Anselmian argument for God's existence.[4]

In a. 2 Thomas distinguishes between a demonstration which moves from knowledge of a cause to knowledge of its effect, that is, demonstration of the reasoned fact (*propter quid* demonstration), and demonstration which moves from knowledge of an effect to knowledge of its cause and is called demonstration of the fact (demonstration *quia*). This second kind of demonstration rests upon the fact that an effect depends upon its cause. If the effect is given, its cause must preexist. It is by means of this kind of demonstration that God's existence can be established.[5]

In replying to the second objection in this same a. 2, Thomas makes an interesting comment. According to the objection, the middle term in a demonstration is a thing's quiddity. But when it comes to God we cannot know what he is but only what he is not. Therefore we cannot demonstrate that God exists. In his response Thomas notes that when a demonstration moves from our knowledge of an effect to knowledge of its cause, we must put the effect in the place of the definition of the cause if we are to prove that the cause exists. This is especially true when we are dealing with God. In order to prove that something exists we need only use as a middle term a nominal definition of that which is to be demonstrated, not a real (or quidditative) definition. This follows, continues Thomas, because the question "What is it?" comes after the question "Is it?" But we apply names to God from what we discover in his effects. Therefore, in demonstrating his existence from an effect we may use as a middle term that which the name God signifies, that is, some purely nominal definition. Curiously, in each of the five ways, Thomas does not explicitly carry out this step for us, but leaves it for the reader to supply.[6]

### The First Way

With this we come to a. 3: "Whether God exists." Thomas begins the corpus of this article by writing that God's existence can be proved in five ways. The first and more evident (*manifestior*) way is that which is based on motion (*motus*). It is certain and evident to the senses that some things in this world are moved (*moveri*). (I shall translate this verb passively rather than intransitively.) But whatever is moved is moved by something else. In support of this claim, Thomas argues that nothing is moved except insofar as it is in potency to that to which it is moved. But something moves insofar as it is in actuality, since to move is nothing else but to reduce something from potency to act. And something can be reduced from potency to act only by some being in actuality. To illustrate this point Thomas notes that it is something which is actually hot (such as fire) which renders that which is only potentially hot (such as wood) actually hot and thereby moves and alters it. (This example is significant, for it indicates that if the argument starts from the fact of observable motion, motion itself is being taken more broadly than local motion; at the very least it also includes alteration.) Thomas now argues that it is not possible for the same thing to be in act and in potency at the same time and in the same respect but only in different respects. Thus what is actually hot cannot at the same time be potentially hot (with respect to the same degree of heat, we should understand), but it is at that time potentially cold. Therefore, it is not possible for something to be mover and to be moved in the same respect by one and the same motion, or for it to move itself (in this strict sense). Therefore, everything which is moved must be moved by something else.[7]

Thomas next turns to the second major part of the argument based on motion. If that by which something is moved is itself moved, this second mover must itself be moved by something else, and so on. But one cannot regress to infinity in moved movers. If there were no first mover, there would be no other mover, since second movers do not move unless they are moved by a first mover. Thus a stick does not move unless it is moved by a hand. Therefore we must arrive at some first mover which is moved by nothing whatsoever, and this everyone understands to be God.[8]

Keeping the two arguments from motion in *Summa contra Gentiles* (SCG) I, c. 13 in mind, we are in position to make some comments about the argument from motion in ST I, q. 2, a. 3. First of all, as we have just noted in passing, the point of departure for the argument as it is presented here now seems to be broader.[9] Motion as it is used here is not restricted to instances of local motion but, as the text explicitly indicates, is taken broadly enough so as to apply to alteration as well. Given this, one wonders whether we may apply it to any kind of motion and perhaps even to changes which are not classified by Thomas as motions in the strict sense, e.g., generation and corruption.

It should be noted that in commenting on *Physics* III, Thomas writes that in working out his definition of motion (*motus*) there Aristotle uses this term broadly so as to apply it to change (*mutatio*). Motion, therefore (meaning thereby change), is the act of that which exists in potency insofar as it is in potency. In that context Thomas speaks of motion in terms of quantity, in terms of quality, and in terms of place, as well as in terms of substance (generation and corruption).[10] In commenting on *Physics* V Thomas follows Aristotle in dividing change (*mutatio*) into three species—generation, corruption, and motion. (Again he remarks that in Book III Aristotle had taken the term "motion" broadly so as to apply it to all the kinds of change.) In Book V however, he finds Aristotle using the term "motion" more strictly so as to apply it to only one of these three species. When motion is taken in this restricted sense it may in turn be divided into motion in quality (alteration), motion in quantity (increase or decrease), and motion in place (local motion). Substantial change (whether generation or corruption) is not motion taken strictly; it is only change (*mutatio*).[11]

To return to Thomas's first way, therefore, we would seem to be justified in regarding motion taken strictly in any of its three kinds as a possible starting point for the argument, i.e., alteration, local motion, and increase or decrease in quantity. If Thomas is using the term broadly so as to equate it with change, we could even use substantial change as a possible point of departure for the first way. In fact he will explicitly appeal to generation and corruption in developing his third way.

Given all of this, I am inclined to limit motion as it appears as the starting point of the first way to some form of motion taken strictly, but to suggest that in the course of justifying the principle of motion—whatever is moved is moved by something else—Thomas uses motion broadly enough to apply to any reduction from potentiality to actuality. If this is correct, it will mean that in the second part of the argument, where he considers a possible regress to infinity, he intends to eliminate any kind of moved mover or changed changer or any series of the same as an adequate explanation for the observable motion or motions with which his argument began. He seems to have allowed for a similar broader understanding of motion at a certain stage in his second argument from motion in SCG I, c. 13, and perhaps also at one point in his first argument. Nonetheless, the starting point for both of those arguments appears to be motion taken strictly and, to be specific, local motion. Perhaps it is because the first way in the *Summa Theologiae* begins with readily observable phenomena—local motion and alteration—that Thomas describes it as the "more manifest" way.[12]

Moreover, in his effort to justify the principle that whatever is moved is moved by something else, Thomas does not mention the first two long and involved physical approaches he had used in SCG I, c. 13. He simply builds his argument on the difference between potentiality and actuality, and develops this reasoning more fully than he had done in SCG I, c. 13. If this reasoning as it appears in the *Summa contra Gentiles* already points to a broader and more metaphysical way of justifying the principle of motion, the same holds for the present context. And if Thomas's attempt to justify this principle is valid, it should apply to any reduction from potentiality to actuality or to any kind of change, not merely to motion taken in the strict sense.[13]

Almost as a matter of definition Thomas explains that something is moved only insofar as it is in potency to that toward which it is moved. In other words, that which is moved must be capable of being moved. But something moves only insofar as it is in actuality. Thomas does not mean to suggest by this that something must be or have formally that which it communicates to something else through motion. It must either be or have such formally, or else possess that characteristic virtually; this is to say, it must have the power to produce its effect. It is only with this qualification in mind that one can say of Thomas's reasoning that he means thereby that one cannot give that which one does not have (either formally or virtually).[14]

Central to Thomas's argument is the claim that something cannot be in act and in potency at the same time and in the same respect, but only in different respects. For instance, that which is actually hot cannot at the same time be potentially hot (that is, it cannot lack the same degree of heat it actually possesses); but at the same time it is potentially cold since it is capable of being cooled. This is an important part of Thomas's argument since he concludes from this that it is not possible for something to be a mover and to be moved in one and the same respect by one and the same motion, or for it to move itself (in this strict sense).[15] And if this is granted, Thomas can conclude that if something is moved, that is, if it is reduced from potentiality to actuality, this can only be because it is moved by something else. If Thomas's reasoning is valid, this principle should apply, as we have already remarked, not only to the three species of motion taken strictly, but also to change, that is, to every genuine reduction from potentiality to actuality.[16]

In the second part of the argument Thomas considers and rejects as unsatisfactory appeal to a regress to infinity in moved movers. He does so along lines which are by now familiar to us. If there is no first mover, i.e., no mover that is not moved by anything, there will be no other; for a second mover does not move except insofar as it is moved by a first mover. As before, I take this to mean not that there could not be an unending regress of moved movers but as arguing that such is irrelevant: unless there is a first mover, a mover that is not moved by anything, no other motion will be possible.[17]

Thomas's first way has generated a considerable amount of discussion in the secondary literature.[18] Many of the objections raised against the argument have to do with its claim that whatever is moved is moved by something else. Already within Thomas's century there were those who denied that this applies to all cases. Exceptions should be made, it was argued, and first and foremost for spiritual activities such as human volition. Not long after Thomas's death Henry of Ghent maintained that a freely acting agent can reduce itself from a state of not acting to acting or, as he would eventually put it, from virtual act to formal act.[19] In addition, objections were at times raised at the physical level, having to do with projectile motion, the fall of heavy bodies, and the rise of those that are light (according to the Aristotelian theory of natural place). Thus a Duns Scotus would sharply restrict the application of this motion-principle even at the purely physical level.[20] And more recently, of course, it has often been urged that the principle is rendered invalid by Newtonian physics and the principle of inertia.[21]

While detailed discussion of these points would require far more attention than space will permit here, a few remarks may be made about each of them. So far as Thomas is concerned, the principle does apply universally. Whenever we are dealing with a reduction from potentiality to actuality, appeal must be made to some distinct moving principle to account for this. If our acts of volition involve any such transition from potentiality to actuality, the same will hold for them.

In the *Summa Theologiae* I–II, q. 9, Thomas spells out some of his views concerning this. In a. 1 he is seeking to determine whether the will is moved by the intellect. He notes that something needs to be moved by something else insofar as it stands in potency to different things. He then distinguishes two ways in which a power of the soul can be in potency to different things: (1) simply with respect to acting or not acting (the exercise of an act); and (2) with respect to the particular kind of act, i.e., doing this or doing that (the order of specification). In the first case the focus is on a subject which sometimes acts and sometimes does not. In the second case the focus is on the object which serves to specify that act itself. In the order of exercise the will moves the other powers of the soul, including the intellect, to act. As Thomas puts it, we use the other powers of the soul when we will to do so. But he also recalls that since every agent acts for the sake of an end, the principle (the final cause) of the motion which is efficiently caused by the agent derives from the end (a particular good which falls under the object of the will, the good in general). But in the order of specification or determination of the act, the intellect moves the will by presenting a suitable object to it in the manner of a formal principle.[22]

Prior to this treatment in ST I–II, q. 9 (and the parallel discussion in *De Malo*, q. 6), Thomas had identified the kind of causality exercised by the intellect with respect to the will as final rather than as formal. Under that assumption, which is not Thomas's position in these two works dating ca. 1270–1271, it would still be true that neither the intellect nor the will would move and be moved under the same aspect and in the same respect. The will would move the intellect as an efficient cause and would be moved by it in the order of final causality. Even so, in our present text where he refers to the causality exercised on the will by the object as presented by the intellect as formal causality, he is still satisfied that he has not violated the motion-principle. Indeed, in a. 3 of this same q. 9 he explicitly asks whether the will moves itself. In responding he explains that the will moves itself in this sense that, because it wills an end, it moves itself to will the means to that end. This does not mean, he points out in replying to objection I, that the will moves and is moved in the same respect. It rather means that insofar as the will wills an end, it reduces itself from potency with respect to the means to that end so as to will them in actuality.[23]

As Thomas explains in a. 4, insofar as the will is moved by its object, it is moved by something external. (This, of course, is in the order of specification or determination and not in the order of efficient causality.) But, he continues, insofar as the will is moved to exercise its act of willing, we must also hold that it is moved by some external principle. That which is at times an agent in act and at times an agent in potency must be moved to act by some mover. Such is true of the will. As Thomas has indicated, the will can move itself to will the means to a given end. But this in turn presupposes an appropriate act on the part of the intellect, i.e., taking counsel. And the act of taking counsel on the part of the intellect presupposes still another act of the will which moves it to so act. Since we cannot regress to infinity by tracing one act of the will back to an act of the intellect and that back to another act of the will, etc., Thomas concludes that the will proceeds to its first motion from an impulse (*instinctus*) given it by some external mover, and finds support for this in Aristotle's *Eudemian Ethics*.[24]

In his Disputed Questions *De Malo*, q. 6, Thomas develops much of this same thinking. Here, too, he introduces the distinction between a change or motion which has to do with exercising the act of a power, and that which has to do with its specification. In dealing with the exercise of the act of the will, he observes that just as the will moves other powers, so does it move itself. He maintains that it does not follow from this that the will is in act and potency at the same time and in the same respect. Rather the will moves itself by moving the intellect to take counsel. Again he maintains that the act of choice on the part of the will presupposes an act of counsel on the part of the intellect, and that this in turn presupposes a prior act by the will. To avoid falling into an infinite regress, Thomas again concludes that the will is moved to its first motion by something external or exterior to it. He goes on to tell us more about this externally caused impulse which first moves the will to act. This impulse cannot be provided by a heavenly body, since the will is grounded in reason (the intellect), which is not a corporeal power. He concludes, therefore, developing a remark made by Aristotle in his *De Bona Fortuna* (really taken from Book VII of the *Eudemian Ethics* as he indicates in ST I–II, q. 9), that what first moves the will and the intellect must be something above them both, i.e., God. Since God moves all things in accord with their nature as movable beings—for instance, light things upward and heavy things downward—so does he move the will in accord with its condition or nature, that is to say, not in necessary fashion but as undetermined or freely.[25]

In order to place this within its broader metaphysical context we should recall that for Thomas created agents, including those that act freely, are second causes. God alone is the first cause. Nonetheless, such created agents are true causes. In the case of a human agent, Thomas has acknowledged that it can move itself in the qualified way already mentioned—by willing the means to a given end. But like all created agents, such a freely acting agent is not the first cause of its operations, including intellection and volition. As Thomas points out in q. 3, a. 7 of his *De Potentia*, God may be said to cause the actions performed by created agents in four different ways: (1) by giving to a created agent the power by means of which it acts; (2) by continuously sustaining (conserving) this created power in being; (3) by moving or applying the created operative power to its activity; (4) by serving as principal cause of that of which the created agent is an instrumental cause.[26] With respect to point 4 it should be noted that at times Thomas uses the language of first cause and second cause rather than that of principal cause and instrument to express this relationship between God and other agents.[27]

In the *Summa Theologiae* I, q. 105, a. 5, Thomas makes this same point in slightly different fashion. God works in the activities performed by created agents: (1) by serving as the final cause of such agents; (2) by acting as an efficient cause of their operations inasmuch as second causes act by reason of the first cause which moves them to act; (3) by giving to created agents the forms which are their principles of operation and by keeping these in being. As I have indicated elsewhere, we might combine into one the third and fourth ways mentioned in the text from the *De Potentia*, as Thomas himself seems to do, and view this as equivalent to the second way of the text from ST I, q. 105.[28] It is this particular form of divine causality that is of greatest interest to us here, because it shows that Thomas honors the motion principle in all cases of creaturely agency.

It is also important to note Thomas's view that if God serves as an efficient cause of creaturely operations, including human volition, he does so as the first cause. Created agents are true causes, and even true principal causes, of their appropriate operations. Moreover, although this is not our primary concern at the moment, Thomas insists that this divine causality or divine motion with respect to free human operations does not detract from their freedom. Essential to Thomas's position is the point we have just seen above—that God, the first cause, moves created agents to act in accord with their natures. If he moves natural agents to act in accord with their natures, that is, necessarily, he moves free agents to act in accord with their nature, that is, freely.[29]

My reason for introducing this discussion here is not to examine Thomas's defense of human freedom but to show that in his eyes even free human activity does not violate his conviction that whatever is moved is moved by something else. At the same time, I would not recommend that one take human volition as a point of departure for Thomas's argument from motion for God's existence. This does not seem to be the kind of starting point he has in mind for his "more manifest" way, since some philosophical effort will be required to show that motion by something else is involved in volition. Moreover, the full appreciation of Thomas's views concerning the interrelationship between divine causal activity (as the first moving cause) and free human activity presupposes that one has already demonstrated God's existence and identified him as a creating, a conserving, and the first moving cause. Only then will Thomas be in position to proceed in the other direction, as it were, and view things from the standpoint of God as the First Mover.[30]

For more detailed explanation and discussion of Thomas's application of the principle of motion to purely physical motions such as those already mentioned, the reader may consult a series of studies by J. Weisheipl. If we may quickly summarize his findings, in the case of what Thomas regarded as natural motions, i.e., the fall of a heavy body or the rising of a light body, he holds that the motion of such bodies is caused by something else, that is, by the generating agent of the bodies in question. This, therefore, and not the bodies themselves, is to be regarded as the efficient cause of such motions. As for violent motions, in many instances Thomas would regard it as evident that what is moved is moved by something else—for instance, that a stick is moved by a hand, or that a heavy object is lifted upwards by someone or something in opposition to its natural tendency to fall. In the more difficult case of projectile motion, where the apparent mover is no longer in direct contact with the object which has been thrown or hurled, Thomas still thinks that his principle applies. With Aristotle he accounts for such motion by holding that what serves as a medium—air, for instance—has now been given the power to move the projectile. Even so, such a communicated power is not to be regarded as the principal cause of the motion, but only as an instrument of the true efficient cause—the one who originally threw or hurled the object.[31]

Well and good, one may counter, but with the rise of Newtonian physics and the principle of inertia, and for that matter, already with Galileo's explanation of the motion of a body along an idealized frictionless plane, Thomas's principle of motion has been rendered invalid. And if it fails to apply in this case, one cannot claim universal validity for it or use it with any confidence in a proof for God's existence. For that matter, Aristotle's distinction between natural and violent motion also seems to have been rendered obsolete.[32]

Without attempting to enter into a full discussion of these particular questions from the standpoint of the philosophy of science or the philosophy of nature, I would recall the following points. First of all, if Thomas's explanation of natural motion is correctly understood, it does not imply that a distinct moving cause must be constantly conjoined with a body which it moves naturally. While one will hardly wish today to defend the view that light bodies tend to go up, etc., one may hold that it is because of their natures that bodies tend to behave in certain ways, for instance, to fall. If with Newton one wishes to account for this by appealing to a force exercised by another and distinct body, Thomas's general principle will not necessarily be violated. Our falling body will still be moved by something else. But as he sees things, it is the generating principle of the falling body which is the efficient cause of its tendency to fall and therefore of its actual downward motion unless it is prevented from falling by some obstacle.[33]

As for Thomas's acceptance of Aristotle's explanation of projectile motion, not too many thinkers today will be inclined to endorse their view that some moving power is communicated to the air or to some surrounding medium and that this accounts for the continuing motion of the object in question. But today's defender of Thomas's general principle of motion may still insist on searching for some efficient cause to account for the continuing motion of such a projectile, the principle of inertia notwithstanding. This point seems to have been partially recognized by Newton himself, in that he (and Descartes) acknowledged that the principle of inertia would not explain the origin of motion in the universe.[34]

For instance, one might concede a great deal to the Newtonian theory and regard motion as a state, like rest. Then one would simply appeal to an extrinsic force, and therefore to some extrinsic mover, to account for any change in the state of rest or of uniform motion enjoyed by a given body.[35] As for the body's possession of its state (rest or motion), one would again trace this back to the generating principle which produced the body with a nature such that it will remain at rest or in motion until it is acted on by some external force. I should emphasize the point, however, that this is not the way in which Thomas and Aristotle actually accounted for projectile motion.

Or one might grant considerably less to the Newtonian theory of inertia as a philosophical explanation and insist that, in spite of its ability to offer a satisfactory physico-mathematical description of uniform motion, it leaves the philosophical search for causes unanswered.[36] In attempting to offer such an explanation one might, with certain later medieval thinkers (including some Thomists, though not Thomas himself), appeal to a theory of impetus. According to this account a transitory power would be given to the moving body by the original hurler or thrower of a given projectile. This power would continue to enable the body to move after it was no longer in direct contact with the hurler, and would serve as an instrumental cause for the motion of the projectile. The original hurler would be the principal efficient cause of the motion. Some students of Aquinas—including Weisheipl—regard this explanation as in accord with Thomas's principles, even though it is not the view Thomas himself defended.[37]

Finally, various writers have argued that the principle of inertia itself has never been demonstrated.[38] This is a controversy into which I am not prepared to enter. But if this claim should prove to be correct, there would be little reason for Aquinas's students today to jettison what he regarded as a demonstrated philosophical principle—that whatever is moved is moved by another—because of seeming difficulties in reconciling it with an unproved principle of Newtonian physics and mechanics. This will be especially so for those who accept Thomas's more metaphysical justification of his principle of motion, that is, the one based on the distinction between potentiality and actuality and ultimately, therefore, on the distinction between being and nonbeing. In sum, strategies such as these are available in dealing with such alleged counterexamples for one who accepts the motion principle on philosophical and metaphysical grounds. Moreover, as at least one writer has proposed, one might, unlike Thomas, simply exclude local motion as a starting point for the argument and use another example such as alteration.[39]

This final remark brings me back to an issue already touched on: Is Thomas's first way physical or metaphysical in nature? Or to put this in different terms: Does this argument for God's existence fall under the science of being as being or under the science that studies being as mobile? As we have now seen, the argument takes as its starting point a fact that is central to physics (philosophy of nature), i.e., motion. To that extent one might argue that it is intended by Thomas to fall within the scope of physics. Moreover, it borrows heavily from Aristotle's *Physics*, especially as it is presented in the two versions in SCG I, c. 13. Nonetheless, its most convincing effort to establish that whatever is moved is moved by something else rests on a broader (and metaphysical) point, the distinction between act and potency and the impossibility that any being might be in act and potency at the same time and in the same respect. This impossibility is by no means restricted to mobile being, but applies to the full range of being as being (the subject of metaphysics). And this justification is the only one offered for the principle of motion in the first way of the *Summa Theologiae*.

Again, in presenting what appears to be primarily a physical argument from motion in SCG I, c. 13 (his second argument), Thomas has been forced to consider the possibility of a self-mover for the first heavenly sphere which is itself moved by something else in some other way, that is, in the order of desire. If such a self-mover exists, it will still be subject to his principle of motion and will depend on the unmoved mover in the order of final causality. At this point one has the impression that even this argument in SCG I, c. 13, is passing over from physics to metaphysics.

Hence my view is that the first way as it appears in ST I, q. 2, a. 3 starts from a physical fact, but that if it is to reach the absolutely unmoved mover or God, it must pass beyond this and beyond a limited and physical application of the principle of motion to a wider application that will apply to any reduction of a being from not acting to acting. In other words, the argument becomes metaphysical in its justification and application of the motion principle, and only then can it succeed in arriving at God. This means that, in its refutation of an infinite regress of moved movers as an alternative explanation, the argument concludes to a source of motion that is not itself moved in any way whatsoever and, therefore, is not reduced from potency to act in any way.

Still another way of approaching this would be to suggest that Thomas is really interested in the existence of motion from the outset and must ultimately conclude to the existence of a being that is pure actuality in order to account for the existence of the motion with which it begins. Therefore the argument would be metaphysical from beginning to end, since it would reason from the caused character of the existence of motion to an uncaused cause of the same.[40]

I would prefer to recast this suggested interpretation so that the argument would reason from the efficiently caused character of moved or changing being (rather than from the existence of motion). However, my greatest difficulty with this suggestion is historical. The argument would no longer be Thomas's first way as this appears in the text of ST I, q. 2, a. 3.

Before moving on to Thomas's second way, I should mention some additional questions about the first way which the presentation in ST I, q. 2, a. 3 seems to leave unanswered. First of all, is the argument based exclusively on motion as caused in the order of efficient (or moving) causality, or does it ultimately shift to the order of final causality? This issue can be raised both because of the apparent difference between Aristotle's procedure in *Physics* VII and VIII, on the one hand, and in *Metaphysics* XII, on the other, and because of Thomas's reference in SCG I, c. 13 to the possibility of reaching a self-moving first mover which would still be moved by something else in the order of desire and hence, we may conclude, as its final cause. In the text of the first way in ST I, q. 2, a. 3, however, there is no explicit reference to motion in the order of desire or to final causality. Moreover, the example mentioned at the very end of the argument— a stick which does not move unless it is moved by a hand—would make one think only in terms of efficient causality. Hence it is in that way that I prefer to read the argument.[41]

A second question may be raised, having to do with the concluding remark to the effect that all recognize this first unmoved mover as God. Has Thomas succeeded in establishing the point that there is only one such being at this point in his reasoning? If so, why does he argue explicitly for divine unicity (uniqueness) in ST I, q. 11, a. 3? Thomistic interpreters remain divided on this issue, but many recognize the fact that it is only in q. 11 that Thomas explicitly establishes divine unicity.[42] This procedure at least suggests that Thomas himself may have recognized that the claim that his unmoved mover is God needs to be supported and completed by additional argumentation.

In fact, at this point in Thomas's reasoning, one would not yet know whether the first mover is intelligent, or personal, or infinitely perfect, etc. So it is that Thomas will eventually develop each of these points in due course, along with others, in discussing the divine names. And there is, of course, the additional fact that Thomas is not content to offer only an argument from motion or a first way in ST I, q. 2, a. 3. All of this would seem to support the view that Thomas himself was aware that his demonstration of God's existence was not yet completed at the end of his first way.

At the same time, we should bear in mind Thomas's opening remark before he begins in question 3 and the following to take up the divine names or attributes. Once we have recognized that a given thing exists, it remains for us to determine how it exists in order that we may know of it what it is. But since we cannot know what God is but only what he is not, we must now consider the ways in which he is not. It is in the course of doing this, according to Thomas's own plan, that he establishes God's simplicity, and then his perfection, infinity, immutability, and unity. Throughout this discussion Thomas takes it as given that he has already (in his five ways) proved that God exists. With this lingering question still in mind,[43] therefore, we shall now turn to Thomas's presentation of his second argument for God's existence in ST I, q. 2, a. 3.

## The Second Way

As Thomas himself tells us, this argument is based on efficient causality. Again it takes as its point of departure something that is given to us in the world of sensible things—the fact that there is an order of efficient causes. By this Thomas means that we find that certain things efficiently cause other things, and that they depend on prior causes in order to do so. He immediately reasons that nothing can be the efficient cause of itself, for then it would be prior to itself, and this is impossible. If we may supply the reasoning that is implied, his point is that for something to cause itself efficiently, it would have to exist in order to cause (itself), and yet would not exist, insofar as it was being caused. From this he expects us to conclude that since we do experience causes that are caused, because they cannot cause themselves they must be caused by something else.[44]

If this is granted, the possibility of a series of efficient causes which are themselves caused by something else must be faced. Thomas argues that one cannot regress to infinity in ordered efficient causes. As he explains, in such an ordered series of efficient causes, the first member is the cause of the intermediary, and that in turn is the cause of the last member in the series whether there is only one intermediary cause or whether there are many. But if there were no first among efficient causes there would be no intermediary causes and therefore no last cause; for if one takes away a cause, one also eliminates the effect. In an infinite series of caused efficient causes, there will be no first efficient cause. Hence there will be no intermediary causes and no last effect. This is enough for Thomas to reject a regress to infinity as a viable alternative to a first efficient cause.[45]

While the terms in which this argument is cast differ from those for the first way, much of the same basic structure reappears. Again one begins with a fact which, for Aquinas, is based on undeniable data offered through sense experience: among the things we experience through the senses, some are causes of others, and some of these causes are ordered, that is, subordinated to others in the exercise of their causality. This confidence on Thomas's part is undoubtedly owing to his Aristotelianism, his own realistic theory of knowledge, and the high degree of credibility which he assigns to what we today often refer to as "common sense." Although he does not spell out particular examples for us in this argument, he would undoubtedly include substantial changes (generation and corruption of substances) as well as various instances of motion taken strictly which we have discussed above in connection with the first way, i.e., alteration, local motion, increase and decrease.[46]

For those who would prefer a more metaphysically grounded illustration of efficient causality at work, I would suggest an approach based on the efficiently caused character of any being in which essence and act of being (*esse*) differ as, for instance, Thomas has developed this in c. 4 of his *De Ente et Essentia*.[47] However, I hasten to add that this is not the kind of efficient causality that is immediately given to us in sense experience. In adopting such a procedure, therefore, one would now have changed the point of departure for Thomas's second way.

As I have already indicated, Thomas reasons that nothing can be its own efficient cause. Given this, by implication he is also holding that whatever is efficiently caused must be so caused by something else. This is the version of efficient causality which is at work in Thomas's second way and, as in the first way, though more briefly this time, Thomas again offers a particular justification for this within the argument itself. In other words, he does not simply assume the principle of causality as an axiom which he might apply in each and every case. For that matter, we have already seen him proceeding in similar fashion in c. 4 of the *De Ente*. There too he had judged it necessary to show that a being in which essence and *esse* differ is efficiently caused.[48]

With this we may turn to the second general step in his argument—the rejection of an infinite regress of caused causes as a viable alternative to the existence of a first cause. In reasoning which recalls that which we have already seen, Thomas makes it clear that he is dealing with what we may call essentially ordered causes (*lit.* ordered causes), that is, the case where the causal activity by a prior member of the series is required here and now for the exercise of causal activity by all subsequent members in that same series. Thomas had allowed and would continue to allow for the philosophical possibility of an infinite series of causes which are related to one another only *per accidens*, e.g., of fathers generating sons or of a carpenter replacing one hammer with another *ad infinitum*. Once again, as I read the argument, he is not concerned here with refuting the very possibility of a beginningless series of essentially ordered caused causes, but with showing that such a series is meaningless and has no explanatory power unless one also admits that there is an uncaused cause. It is in this sense that I take his usage of the term "first."[49]

As in the first way, Thomas quickly concludes to the existence of some "first efficient cause," i.e., some uncaused cause, which is named God by everyone.[50] Once more we may raise the issue of divine unicity or uniqueness: Does this argument, simply taken in itself, prove that there is only one Uncaused Cause (God)? Might it not lead to the conclusion that there are as many first causes as there are different series or at least different kinds of series of ordered caused causes? And does the argument manage to show that the first cause whose existence it establishes is intelligent, personal, all perfect, infinite, etc.? Thomas's second way tells us no more about these issues than does his first way, it would seem, although it does make it clear that in his mind the first unmoved mover of the first way and the first efficient cause of the second way are identical and also that this being exercises efficient causality.

Before leaving the second way it may be helpful for us to compare it more fully with the argumentation for God's existence presented in c. 4 of the *De Ente*. Both have in common the fact that they are based on efficient causality. Both must take into account a possible objection having to do with a regress to infinity in caused causes. But the argument in the *De Ente* begins at the level of beings in which essence and *esse* are not identical, and therefore at an explicitly metaphysical level. The second way begins with instances of causal activity which are evident to the senses, and ultimately concludes that there must be a first uncaused cause to account for such causal activity.

If, as I have suggested, the issue of divine uniqueness seems to be left unexamined by the second way, such is not true of the argument in *De Ente*, c. 4. Because that argument begins with the essence-*esse* distinction, it focuses on one instance of efficient causation, that of *esse* itself. It reasons to the existence of an uncaused cause of *esse* and therefore an uncaused being which is itself pure *esse*. This insight seems much closer to what the metaphysician seeks in attempting to understand something about God. Moreover, this argument anticipates our concern about divine unicity, since it has reasoned from the impossibility of there being more than one being in which essence and *esse* are identical. Because there can at most be one such being, essence and *esse* differ in all other beings. Such beings therefore are caused in terms of their very being. This conclusion in its turn enables Thomas to show that there is in fact only one being in which essence and *esse* are identical. From all of these perspectives, therefore, the procedure in the *De Ente* seems to be more satisfying to the metaphysician.[51]

But if all of this is so, why did Thomas not simply repeat the argumentation from the *De Ente* as his second way in ST I, q. 2, a. 3? Perhaps, we may surmise, because of its highly metaphysical character he viewed the argument of *De Ente*, c. 4 as more difficult for beginning students to grasp in its essentials. He may have realized that not all of his contemporaries, including many beginning students of theology, either understood or shared his views on the relationship between essence and *esse*. And he may not have wished to make his argumentation for God's existence dependent upon such a subtle metaphysical conclusion.

### The Third Way

With this we come to the third of Thomas's five ways, the argument based, to use his terminology, on the possible and the necessary. We find, Thomas begins, that certain things are possibles, i.e., they have the possibility of existing and not existing. His evidence for this claim is the fact that certain things are generated and corrupted and therefore can exist and not exist. But it is impossible, Thomas continues, for all things which exist to be of this kind; for that which has the possibility of not existing at some time does not exist. If, therefore, all things are capable of not existing, at some time (*aliquando*) there was nothing in reality. But if this were so, even now there would be nothing; for what does not exist does not begin to exist except through something else that exists. Given all of this, Thomas concludes that not all beings are possible beings; there must be some necessary being.[52]

At this point today's reader might assume that Thomas's argument has reached its conclusion. But if we bear in mind the distinction between possible beings and caused necessary beings which appears in his argument in SCG I, c. 15, we will not be surprised to find him adding a second and important step to the third way.[53] Every necessary being either depends on something else for its necessity or it does not. But it is not possible to proceed to infinity in necessary beings which depend upon something else for their necessity—just as, Thomas reminds us, he has already shown with respect to efficient causes (see the second way). Therefore there must be some being which is necessary of itself and which does not depend upon another cause for its necessity. This is the being which is the cause of the necessity present in other things, and it is referred to by everyone as God.[54]

Few other texts in Aquinas have occasioned so much controversy among interpreters as the first phase of this argument.[55] In an effort to understand Thomas's procedure here, we shall review the various steps in that phase and single out certain contested points. Once more Thomas takes as his point of departure something which we may derive from sense experience, that is, our awareness that certain beings are possible beings. As he uses the term "possible" here he means that they have the possibility of existing or not existing. As we see him doing in SCG I, c. 15, here again he closely associates possible beings with their capacity to be generated and corrupted. This, in fact, is the empirical evidence with which the argument begins. Because certain things which we experience are subject to generation and corruption, we may conclude that they are possible beings, not necessary beings. As Thomas sees things, such beings are composed of matter and form. It is this composition which renders them liable to corruption; and because of such composition, they naturally come into being by being generated. However, strictly speaking, Thomas need not assume at this point in his argument that such beings are composed of matter and form. The fact that they come into being through generation and cease to be through corruption is enough for him to make the point that they are possible beings.[56]

It is with the very next sentence that the difficulties in interpreting this argument begin: "It is impossible for all things which exist to be such [i.e., possibles], because what has the possibility of not existing at some time (*quandoque*) does not exist." Immediately one wonders how the expression "at some time" (*quandoque*) is to be taken: Does Thomas mean to say thereby that what is possible has been nonexistent at some time in the past, or that it will be nonexistent at some time in the future? Each reading continues to have its defenders.[57] Before attempting to answer this question, we should also note the following sentence: "If therefore all things have the possibility of not existing, at some time (*aliquando*) there was nothing in reality." From this Thomas concludes that if this were so, even now there would be nothing.[58] The fact that in the last-quoted sentence there is a reference to the past ("at some time there was nothing") strongly suggests that Thomas would have us interpret the previous sentence in the same sense. What he is asserting, therefore, is that if all things are possibles (capable of existing and of not existing), at some point in the past all things would have been nonexistent. Therefore at that point in the past there would have been nothing whatsoever and consequently there would be nothing now. Since this final supposition is contrary to fact, so is the assumption from which it follows, that is, that all things are possibles.[59]

If we take the argument this way, the question remains: How can Thomas move from the first disputed statement to the second one without being guilty of the fallacy of composition or a quantifier shift? It is one thing for him to say that what has the possibility of not existing did not exist at some time in the past. This statement makes sense if we emphasize the point that any such being—a possible—comes into existence by being generated, that is to say, after it has not existed. Unless we wish to suggest that some such being may have been produced from eternity by being created and thereby already also concede the existence of an eternal creative principle, it seems that we must grant Thomas's claim: if something has been generated, its existence was preceded by its nonexistence.[60]

But what of Thomas's next statement? If all things are possibles (capable of existing and not existing), at some point in the past nothing would have existed. This statement goes considerably farther than the previous one. If we suppose that every individual being is a possible and therefore has not existed at some point in the past, how does it follow from this that the totality of existing things will all have been nonexistent at the same point in the past? While some have defended Thomas against the charge of committing the fallacy of composition or a quantifier shift in this step, it is difficult to regard such defenses of his reasoning as successful.[61]

To expand upon this for a moment, suppose that we grant that every possible being—every being which comes into existence by generation—exists only after it has been nonexistent. Well and good, we may comment, but this admission hardly leads to the conclusion that the totality of possible beings will all have been nonexistent simultaneously at some point in the past. Why not rather suggest that one possible being has come into being after another, and that after another, extending backwards into a beginningless past? Under this supposition, some possible being or beings will have existed at any given point in time, although no single possible being will have existed from eternity. While Thomas himself does grant the philosophical possibility of an eternally created world, he does so ultimately only under the assumption that there is also an eternal creative cause. While this is true, he cannot assume the existence of such a being at this point in the third way.

One might appeal to some other form of reasoning at this step in order to show that the explanation just proposed will not of itself be enough to account for the existence of any given possible being, whether or not one posits a beginningless series of possible beings extending back into the past. Therefore, we must grant the existence of a being that is not a possible but which is necessary if we are to account for the generation of any and all possible beings.[62] This, however, would be to introduce into the third way a different kind of reasoning, based on causality, a kind which we have already seen in the first and second ways in connection with a proposed regress to infinity in moved movers or in ordered caused causes, and a kind which will reappear in the second phase of the third way itself (as applied to caused necessary beings). While such an interpretation is defensible from the metaphysical standpoint, it would entail a substantial addition to Thomas's text and a serious recasting of the first part of the third way. So true is this that one might then doubt that one was still dealing with Thomas's third way, for the temporal references in the first part would now lose their importance.[63]

In order to understand more fully Thomas's procedure in this third way, a number of recent commentators have concentrated on various possible historical sources for this argument. Aristotle, Avicenna, and Moses Maimonides have all been proposed, and not without reason. Nonetheless, careful comparison of these with the text of Thomas's third way shows that while he must have been influenced by some of them, especially by Aristotle and Maimonides, in penning his version of the argument, he has developed it in his own way.[64] In short, recourse to such earlier sources will not rescue the argument from this crucial weakness in its first stage. Why Thomas himself did not regard this as a serious flaw in his argument is something I have been unable to determine.

As for the remainder of the first phase of the argument, its conclusion follows naturally enough. If we concede that at some point in the past nothing whatsoever existed, there would be nothing now; for what does not exist cannot begin to exist except by reason of something which exists. While Kenny has expressed some reservations about this claim, and while David Hume rejected all attempts to demonstrate it, Thomas had no doubt about it: if something begins to exist, it must be brought into existence by something else which exists.[65] He had already argued for this in somewhat different terms in accounting for the origins of motion in his first way, and in terms of efficient causation in his second way. And he had made the same point with respect to existence itself in c. 4 of his *De Ente*.[66]

To repeat his reasoning in my own terms, if something begins to exist after it has not existed, this can only be owing to itself, or to nothing whatsoever, or to something else, i.e., a cause. To say that a thing is the efficient cause of its own existence is to imply that it is and yet is not at the same time and in the same respect; for it must be if it is to communicate existence (to itself) or to act as a cause, and it must not be if its existence is to be caused efficiently. To suggest that it owes its existence to nothing whatsoever is to hold that there is no explanation for its existence. Since it is not self-existent (which follows from the fact that it did not always exist but began to be), to hold that there is no explanation for its present existence is to render that existence unintelligible. For Thomas, at least, this is to fly in the face of common sense and to reject the intelligibility of being. Hence, as he sees things, only the third alternative remains. If something begins to exist after it has not existed, it must be brought into existence by something else.[67]

In the second part of the argument a line of reasoning reappears which occurs in SCG I, c. 15. If one grants that a necessary being does exist (to account for the coming into existence of the possible beings with which the argument began), such a being may or may not depend upon something else for its necessity (and, we may assume, for its existence). But one cannot regress to infinity in caused necessary beings (literally: "in necessary beings whose necessity is caused"), just as one cannot do so with efficient causes, as has been proved (see the second way). Therefore there must be an uncaused necessary being, which causes the necessity of the others, and which everyone calls God.[68]

This second phase of the argument is much less controversial and is, in my opinion, sound. Whether or not it succeeds in establishing the point that there is only one uncaused necessary being is, of course, another matter, and much of what we have said above about the conclusions of the first and second ways continues to apply. Additional reflection will be required to show that there is only one first and totally uncaused necessary being if we are to justify the claim that this being is God. One could, of course, reason that at this point in the argument Thomas is discussing beings that depend upon something else not only for their necessity but for their very existence. If so, one could then reason that their cause is an uncaused source of *esse* and therefore uncaused *esse* in and of itself. Even so, the argument will remain incomplete until it has been shown that there can only be one such being. One might do this by adopting Thomas's procedure in q. 11, or by introducing reasoning similar to that which he has presented in the *De Ente*, c. 4.[69]

In sum, the first phase of the third way strikes me as being open to serious criticisms along the lines already pointed out. In this phase it is considerably less convincing than the argumentation from SCG I, c. 15. Why Thomas introduced this particular step into his argument in ST I, q. 2, a. 3 continues to be a matter for speculation.[70] In my opinion, no completely satisfying explanation has been forthcoming. By introducing this first step he has, of course, established the third way clearly enough as a different kind of argument from either the first or second way. But one could say the same of the much less troublesome argument offered in SCG I, c. 15. There, too, he incorporates into his argumentation the distinction between possible beings, caused necessary beings, and an uncaused necessary being and there, too, he begins with possible beings and then moves on to consider caused necessary beings in order to reason to the existence of an uncaused necessary being.

## The Fourth Way

Thomas's fourth way is based on the varying degrees of perfection we find among beings. It immediately strikes the reader as being much more Platonic and Neoplatonic in inspiration than any of the other ways, even though in presenting it Thomas twice refers to a passage from Aristotle's *Metaphysics*. Foreshadowings of this kind of approach appear in his Commentary on *Sentences* I and in *Summa contra Gentiles* I, c. 13.[71] As he develops this argument in the *Summa Theologiae*, among things we find something that is more and less good, more and less true, more and less noble, and so too with respect to other perfections of this kind. But the more and less are said of different things insofar as they approach in diverse fashion something which is (such) to a maximum degree. (To illustrate this Thomas cites the example of heat: that is hotter which more closely approaches something which is hot to the maximum degree.) Therefore there is something which is truest and best and noblest and hence which is also being to the maximum degree. In support of this conclusion Thomas observes that those things which are true to the maximum degree also enjoy being to the maximum degree, and cites Book II of the *Metaphysics*.[72] He is evidently basing this on the convertible character of being and of ontological truth, a point which he had developed more fully elsewhere, especially in *De Veritate*, q. 1, a. 1.[73] With this the first part of his argument comes to an end; but rather than regard his task as completed, Thomas introduces a second stage.

In this second stage he reasons that what is said to be supremely such in a given genus is the cause of all other things which are present in that genus. (In illustration he returns to the example of fire: being hot to the maximum degree, fire is the cause of heat in all other things, as Aristotle maintains in the *Metaphysics*.) Therefore, Thomas concludes, there is something which is the cause of being (*esse*) for all other beings, as well as of their goodness and every other perfection. And this we call God.[74]

In the first stage of this argument Thomas again appeals to the world as we experience it, and goes on to apply a general principle to the same. As for the world as we experience it, we note that certain things are more and less good, true, noble, etc. By referring to things as more and less good, Thomas must have in mind their ontological goodness, that is to say, their goodness of being. In *De Veritate*, q. 1, a. 1 he had singled out goodness, along with truth and unity, as characteristics which are found wherever being itself is realized and which are convertible with being. Consequently, along with thing (*res*) and something (*aliquid*), which he also regards as coextensive with being, these are often referred to as transcendental properties of being.[75] To say that something enjoys goodness of being is to indicate that it is an object of appetite. And to say that one thing enjoys greater ontological goodness than another is to imply that it is a more desirable object in itself. Given Thomas's hierarchical view of the universe and his conviction that ontological goodness and being are really convertible, we can understand why he would view an animal as enjoying greater ontological goodness than a mere stone. The animal is endowed with life and with the power of sensation, whereas the stone is not. At the same time, an animal lacks the power of understanding which a human being enjoys and is therefore less good, ontologically speaking, than a human being.[76]

In referring to things as more and less true Thomas is thinking of truth of being or ontological truth, not of truth as it exists in the intellect (logical truth). He has in mind that quality present in any being in virtue of which it can be grasped by intellect or, to put it in other terms, the intelligibility of being. Since such truth or intelligibility is found wherever being is realized, Thomas also regards being and truth as convertible with one another. To say that one thing enjoys greater truth (of being) than another is to make the point that, viewed in itself, it is more intelligible than the other. And this in turn follows from the fact that its degree of being is greater than that present in the other. In the world as we experience it, there do seem to be varying degrees of intelligibility, or of ontological truth. Thus according to Thomas's thinking a substantial form is more intelligible than its corresponding prime matter; the essence of a human being is more intelligible than that of a rock. In sum, corresponding to the hierarchy of being is a hierarchy of ontological truth, or of intrinsic intelligibility of being.[77]

In referring to certain things as more and less noble than others, Thomas has created something of a problem for his readers. Does he intend to single out another characteristic, distinct from ontological goodness and ontological truth? If so, what does he have in mind? It is difficult to answer this question with any degree of certainty. R. Garrigou-Lagrange takes nobility as synonymous with perfection, and this suggestion may well be correct. For instance, in SCG I, c. 28 Thomas describes as universally perfect that to which no excellence (*nobilitas*) of any kind is lacking. He also indicates that a thing's excellence (*nobilitas*) follows upon its mode of being (*esse*). Accordingly, I would suggest that by this term Thomas wants to signify the varying degrees of pure ontological perfection or excellence we discover in the different beings we experience in the world about us. Just as some share more fully in ontological goodness and truth than do others, so too they may be regarded as being more perfect or more excellent, ontologically speaking, than others. Excellence (*nobilitas*) should not be regarded as a distinct transcendental.[78]

This in turn leads to another question: Does Thomas wish to restrict the starting point of the fourth way to gradation in transcendental perfections such as truth and goodness? (Interestingly enough, he does not mention ontological unity.) Or does he wish to include what we might call pure but not transcendental perfections such as life, knowledge, will, etc.? While not found wherever being is realized, such perfections also admit of degrees and, when freed from all limitation, may be applied analogically even to God, or so Thomas will maintain.[79] These perfections have the advantage of being readily recognizable in varying degrees in the world about us. But since Thomas has not explicitly singled them out in presenting the fourth way, it will be better for us not to base his argument upon them. For then one might wonder whether the general principle to which he appeals is also intended to apply to them as well as to strictly transcendental perfections. Here, therefore, I shall restrict the argument to transcendental perfections such as goodness and truth.

As Thomas expresses this principle in his text, the more and less are said of different things insofar as they approach in diverse fashion something which is such to the maximum degree. As some writers have pointed out, the example to which Thomas turns hardly proves his point. It is unnecessary for us to assume that something enjoys a maximum degree of heat in order to be aware that one kettle is hotter than another. Nonetheless, since this is only an example drawn from an outmoded medieval physics, we need not regard it as central to Thomas's argument.[80] But we may still ask: How does Thomas justify this general principle? Is it immediately evident that the more and less are said of different things only insofar as they approach something which is such to a maximum degree? Even if we restrict this principle to transcendental perfections such as those named by Thomas—goodness, truth (and nobility)—it is difficult to see how he can move so quickly from our recognition of greater and lesser degrees of these perfections to the existence of something which is such perfection to the maximum degree.

In attempting to justify this step in the argument, some commentators have maintained that it should not be interpreted as resting solely on exemplar causality. Instead, they suggest, there is an implicit appeal to efficient causality in this first stage. That which possesses goodness or truth or nobility in only a greater and lesser degree must receive such perfections from some distinct efficient cause. Therefore, one may conclude to the existence of an uncaused cause of goodness, truth, and nobility, which itself is such perfection of its essence. Confirmation for this interpretation may be sought by referring to the second stage in Thomas's text. There he reasons that what is supremely such in a given genus is the cause of everything else which belongs to that genus.[81]

Any such effort, however, runs counter to the literal text of the fourth way, or so it seems to me. The first stage of the argument concludes to the existence of something which is truest and best and noblest and hence being to the maximum degree. The final point—that it is also being to the maximum degree—is based on the convertibility of ontological truth and being, and is supported by an appeal to Aristotle's *Metaphysics*, as we have noted. But until this point in the argument no reference has been made to efficient causality. It is only in the second step, after the existence of a maximum has been established, that Thomas attempts to show that this maximum is also the cause of being, goodness, etc., for all other things.[82] Hence there seems to be no justification in Thomas's text for the claim that his proof for the existence of a maximum rests on or presupposes reasoning from efficient causation. It follows, therefore, that if we wish to present the argument as it appears in his text, it can only be based on extrinsic formal causality, i.e., on exemplar causality.

But if this argument for the existence of a maximum is free from any reference to efficient causation, is it valid? This question is more difficult to decide. Thomas makes earlier appeals in his texts to similar argumentation. In his Commentary on *Sentences* I, d. 3, he offers two arguments based on eminence. The first is taken from eminence insofar as this applies to being. The good and the better are so named in comparison to that which is the best. Since among substances a body is good and a created spirit still better, there must be some best from which the goodness present in body and spirit derives. But, Thomas offers no justification in that context for the general claim that where there is a good and a better, there must be a best.[83]

The second argument based on eminence focuses on human knowing. If we find things which are more and less beautiful, we can recognize them as such only by reason of their proximity to something which is the very principle of beauty. From this general cognitive principle Thomas quickly concludes to the existence of something from which bodies (which are beautiful) and spirits (which are more beautiful) derive their beauty. Once again, however, in the immediate context he offers no justification either for this general cognitive principle or for the ontological conclusion he draws from it.[84] While this cognitive principle makes perfect sense within an Augustinian account of human knowing, it is difficult to see how it can be granted within the terms of Thomas's own theory of knowledge and his conviction that our knowledge begins with and must in some way be derived from sense experience.[85]

Still another seeming anticipation of the fourth way is offered within this same discussion from Thomas's Commentary on *Sentences* I, an argument which Thomas describes as taken from the Dionysian way of negation (*remotionis*). Beyond everything which is imperfect there must be something which is perfect and admits of no imperfection whatsoever. Thomas goes on to apply this to bodies and then to things which are incorporeal and changeable. Beyond all of these there must be something which is completely immobile and perfect, or God.[86] Once again, however, Thomas does not see fit to justify his operative principle—that beyond that which is imperfect there must be something which is completely and totally perfect. While antecedents may be cited for such reasoning from within the Christian Neoplatonic tradition (see, for instance, Boethius's *Consolation of Philosophy* and Anselm's *Monologium*), one wonders how Thomas can justify such a claim within his own metaphysical perspective.[87]

When we return to another foreshadowing of the fourth way in *Summa contra Gentiles* I, c. 13, our perplexity remains. There Thomas reasons that if we recognize one thing as truer than another, this can only be because it comes closer to that which is true without qualification and to the maximum degree. From this he quickly draws the conclusion that there must be something which is being to the maximum degree. While this final point follows from the convertibility of ontological truth (truth of being) and of being itself, the general working principle on which the argument rests remains without justification—that the more and the less in the order of truth (and being) enables one to conclude immediately to the existence of something which is true to the maximum degree.[88]

As we return to the fourth way of the *Summa Theologiae*, we wonder whether Thomas regards this general principle as self-evident. One writer has suggested that perhaps his powers of penetration were such that he immediately saw that varying degrees of transcendental perfection require a subsisting maximum to account for their imperfect realizations in the beings we experience. Within a Platonic and Neoplatonic framework, the self-evidence of such a claim might be more readily granted. But within Thomas's distinctive metaphysical approach, even though a considerable Platonic and Neoplatonic influence must be recognized, today's reader of his text may protest: the principle in question is not self-evident to him or her.[89]

One way of supplying the missing justification is to appeal to Thomas's metaphysics of participation and to regard the fourth way as an argument based on participation. This seems to be the approach adopted by C. Fabro. As he points out, there is another and later version of such an argument in Thomas's *Lectura* on St. John's Gospel, dating ca. 1270–1272.[90] As Thomas presents this argument, it is based on the nobility (*dignitas*) of God and is the way of the "Platonists." At the same time, it is clear from the context that Thomas accepts this argument as his own. Everything which is (such) by participation is reduced to something which is such of its essence as to something first and supreme. (Thus all things which participate in fire are reduced to fire which is such of its essence.) But since all things which exist participate in *esse* and are beings through participation, there must be something at the summit of all things which is *esse* of its essence in that its essence is its *esse*. This is God, the most sufficient and noblest and most perfect cause of all *esse*, from whom all things which exist participate in *esse*.[91]

This is an interesting approach and it rests on a principle frequently employed by Thomas in other contexts. That which participates in something must be traced back to something which is that perfection of its essence. Hence, that which exists by participating in *esse* must be traced back to something which is the act of being (*esse*) of its very essence.[92] Because this argument explicitly invokes participation and deals with it in the order of *esse*, it is more satisfying from a metaphysical standpoint than that offered in *Summa Theologiae* I, q. 2, a. 3.

At the same time, we may ask whether this kind of argumentation can be justified without some implicit or explicit appeal to efficient causality. In fact, some such appeal seems to be involved at two levels within the argument. First of all, without stating this explicitly, the argument assumes that if something participates in a given characteristic, and especially in *esse*, it does not possess that characteristic of its essence or of itself. This follows from Thomas's general description of participation in his Commentary on the *De Hebdomadibus*.[93] Moreover, in various contexts he states that a participated characteristic is present in a participating subject only insofar as it is efficiently caused therein. This will follow so long as one is dealing with real or ontological participation, not merely with the logical participation of a less extended concept in one that is more extended, for instance, participation of a species in a genus.[94]

But what of participation of beings in *esse*? Thomas is convinced that this is a case of real participation. At times he reasons from the participated character of *esse* in particular entities to real distinction and composition therein of essence and *esse*.[95] In order to strengthen the claim that a participated being is efficiently caused, one might reason as follows. Because a participated being's essence differs from its *esse*, its *esse* must be received from without, i.e., it must be efficiently caused. As Thomas develops this in *Summa Theologiae* I, q. 3, a. 4, whatever is present in a thing in addition to its essence must be caused in that thing either by the principles of its essence (as is true of a proper accident), or else by something external (as heat is caused in water by fire). If the *esse* of a thing is distinct from that thing's essence, the same will apply. It must be caused either by the essential principles of that thing or by something external. But since a given thing cannot be the efficient cause of its own *esse*, the *esse* of any such thing cannot be caused by its intrinsic and essential principles. Therefore, its *esse* must be caused by something else.[96]

The argument from participation for God's existence also seems to rest on efficient causality at a second level. One must justify the claim that what exists by participation is to be traced back or reduced to that which exists of its essence. In order to do this, one should again consider and eliminate as a viable alternative to the unparticipated source appeal to a series of beings which would simply participate in other and higher participating beings and these in still others *ad infinitum*. It is true that in the first stage of the fourth way of the *Summa Theologiae* Thomas does not explicitly bring out either of these points, i.e., the proof that beings which participate in *esse* are efficiently caused, or the consideration of an infinite regress of participating beings. Nor does he bring out the second point in the argument in his *Lectura*. It seems to me, however, that this should be done if one is to view the fourth way as an argument based on participation and if one wishes to justify that argument within Thomas's metaphysics.[97]

In doing this, however, I must acknowledge that we will have reinterpreted the fourth way seriously, and even in its substance. It will no longer be based solely on exemplar causality in its first stage, as its text indicates that it was originally intended to be. It will now be equivalent to the argument offered in the *Lectura* on St. John's Gospel. But unless some such reinterpretation or substitution is introduced, it seems unlikely that the argument's first stage can be regarded as successful in its attempt to prove that a maximum actually exists.[98]

In discussions of the fourth way reference is sometimes made to Thomas's slightly earlier argumentation in *De Potentia*, q. 3, a. 5. There he is attempting to show that nothing that exists apart from God is uncreated. He offers three arguments to make this point. The first may be regarded as an argument for God's existence. The remaining two, attributed by Thomas respectively to Aristotle and to Avicenna, are less clearly so. They seem to take God's existence as already established and concentrate on showing that all beings other than God receive their *esse* from him. In these latter two arguments the theme of participation is explicitly introduced.[99]

The first argument runs as follows. If one single characteristic is common to many things, it must be caused in each of them by a single cause. This common feature cannot belong to each of the different individuals by reason of that which is proper to it as an individual; for each individual, by reason of that which it is in itself, is distinct from the others, and diversity in causes results in diverse effects. But since *esse* is common to all things and since each, when considered in itself, is distinct from the others, Thomas concludes that the *esse* realized in each must be given to it by some one cause. And this, Thomas comments, seems to be Plato's argument, since he held that before every multitude there must be some kind of unity.[100]

There is some disagreement among commentators concerning whether or not this is an argument based on participation. While Fabro concedes that the term "participation" does not appear in it, he seems to think that the notion is present therein.[101] Since the argument begins with the fact that *esse* is common to all existing things, we may, it seems to me, regard the argument as resting on the participation by the many in the perfection of *esse*. On the other hand, Van Steenberghen, while granting the argument's validity, contends that it does not start from participation but that it is based on the ontological similarity which obtains between finite beings.[102] To me this is simply another way in which Thomas makes the point that different beings merely participate in *esse* (*commune*), and that no one of them is identical with it. In any event, it is another form of argumentation based on efficient causality. By reasoning that the common perfection (*esse*) cannot be accounted for in the many which share in it by an appeal to that which is proper to and distinctive of each, Thomas is in effect showing that *esse* is efficiently caused in each of them.[103] Hence this argument can hardly be regarded as one that is based on degrees of perfection, or as an equivalent of the fourth way, although it can easily be substituted for the first stage of that argument.

As for the second stage of the argument as it stands in *Summa Theologiae* I, q. 2, a. 3, the point of this step is to prove that once we have established the existence of a maximum, we may also show that it is the efficient cause of the being, goodness, and other perfection present in other things. This part of the argument is much less troublesome than the first stage, or so it appears to me.[104] But it presupposes that one has already established the existence of the maximum in the argument's first stage, or else, as I have suggested, that one has substituted an argument based on participation in that stage to reach an unparticipated source. Enough has been said about this to enable us to move on now to the last of the five ways.

## The Fifth Way

Thomas introduces this argument by noting that it is based on the way things are governed (*ex gubernatione rerum*). We see that certain things which lack knowledge, that is to say, natural bodies, act for the sake of an end. In support of this claim Thomas reasons that it follows from the fact that they always or at least usually (*frequentius*) act in the same way in order to attain that which is best. This shows that they reach their respective end(s) not by chance but by intention. But "things which lack cognition do not tend to an end unless they are directed [to it] by some knowing and intelligent being, as an arrow is directed [to its target] by an archer." Therefore, there is some intelligent being by which all natural things are ordered to their end, and this we call God.[105]

While the fifth way is sometimes confused with an argument based on order and design and the need for a supreme designer, Thomas's text makes it clear that he really has in mind an argument based on final causality in nature. Hence it bears much greater resemblance to the argument for divine providence in *De Veritate*, q. 5, a. 2 than to the argument from design of *Summa contra Gentiles* I, c. 13.[106]

Like the other five ways, this argument begins with something which Thomas regards as evident to us from the world of everyday experience. Natural bodies, that is to say, things which are equipped with their own natures but lack the power of cognition, act for the sake of an end. Thomas knows that it is one thing for us to be aware that natural bodies act, for instance, that a heavy body tends to fall or a hot body to rise; but it is something else for us to conclude that such bodies act for an end.[107] Immediately, therefore, two possible objections come to mind. Perhaps the action of natural bodies can be accounted for merely by appealing to efficient causal activity. Or perhaps their seeming action for an end is not to be credited to the influence of any final cause but only to chance.

As regards the first objection, Thomas had learned from Aristotle about two ancient schools of thought which left no place for final causality. Some admitted of nothing but material causes; others defended the existence of efficient causes but still saw no need for final causes. Against such views Thomas had always defended the need for final causes, along with efficient, formal, and material causes, in accounting for operations in nature such as generation.[108]

For instance, in his youthful *De Principiis Naturae*, c. 3, he had reasoned that while matter, form, and privation may be regarded as principles of generation, they are not sufficient of themselves to explain this process. Something which is in potency cannot reduce itself to act. Therefore an agent is required to account for this, for instance, to reduce copper from being a statue only potentially to being such in actuality by educing the form of that statue from potentiality to actuality. The form of the statue cannot do this, since it does not actually exist until the statue itself is produced. Hence in addition to matter and form there must be some efficient or moving or agent cause. But as Aristotle states in *Metaphysics* II, what acts does so only by tending toward something. Therefore, there must also be a fourth cause or principle—that which is intended by the agent. This we call the end.[109]

In developing this final point, Thomas comments that if both natural agents and voluntary agents tend toward an end (*intendit finem*), it does not follow from this that every agent knows its end or deliberates about it. Agents whose actions are not determined, i.e., voluntary agents, must know the end if they are to determine their action to one thing rather than another. But the actions of natural agents are determined and, therefore, they need not choose means to their end. Indeed, they cannot do so, we may add. Thomas takes an example from Avicenna to show that one who plays a cithara need not deliberate about every pluck of the strings. If this were required, it would result in untimely delays and would destroy the beauty of the music. But it is surely more evident that voluntary agents deliberate than that purely natural agents do. Therefore and a fortiori, Thomas concludes that natural agents need not deliberate and that nonetheless they tend to their ends. For such an agent to tend to its end is nothing else than for it to have a natural inclination to that end, as Thomas goes on to explain.[110]

Especially important in this discussion for our immediate purpose is Thomas's claim that an agent can act only by tending toward something, i.e., an end. This applies not only to voluntary agents but to those which are determined by their natures to act in given ways. As Thomas argues in another early text (*In II Sent.*, d. 25, q. 1, a. 1), nothing acts except insofar as it is in act. Therefore every agent must be determined to one or other alternative. That which is equally open to different alternatives is, in a certain way, in potency to both, and nothing will follow from it unless it is determined to one or the other. But if an agent is to be determined to a given action, this can only be through some act of knowing which presents the end for that action.[111]

Thomas speaks in much the same vein in his considerably later *Summa Theologiae* I–II, q. 1, a. 2, while supporting his contention that every agent acts for an end. First among the causes is the final cause. Matter does not receive a form unless it is moved by an agent, since nothing can reduce itself from potency to act. An agent does not move except by tending to an end (*ex intentione finis*). To prove this he reasons that if an agent were not determined to a given effect it would not produce this effect rather than any other one. Therefore, in order for it to produce a given effect, it must be determined to something which serves as its end. In sum, Thomas's view is that unless we recognize the need for an end to influence an agent in its action, we will be unable to account for the fact that the agent produces a determined effect or, indeed, that it acts at all.[112]

To return to the text of the fifth way, suppose one grants to Thomas that the actions of natural bodies cannot be fully accounted for merely by appealing to efficient causal activity. The second objection remains. Perhaps such behavior on the part of natural bodies is owing to chance. Against this suggestion he replies briefly in the fifth way by citing the fact that natural things act always or at least usually in the same way in order to attain that which is best. In other words, mere chance cannot account for a regularly repeated pattern of behavior on the part of natural entities, and especially not when this activity achieves that which is best. Thomas had already made this same point and developed it somewhat more fully in his *De Veritate*, q. 5, a. 2.[113]

Moreover, we should note that Thomas, following Aristotle, does not regard chance as a being or as a cause *per se* but only *per accidens*. Chance is simply our way of referring to a situation in which independently operating causes intersect or collide without any of the particular agents foreseeing that this will happen. Yet each of these agents has its particular end. An illustration is offered by Boethius. A farmer discovers buried treasure while plowing a field. Both the farmer and the one who originally buried the treasure operated for their respective particular ends, and neither intended for the farmer to discover the treasure. Because this intersection of their independently intended actions was not foreseen by either, we refer to the discovery as a chance event.[114]

If one accepts this explanation of chance events, mere chance can hardly account for the regular and beneficial activity of natural agents, whether we regard that activity as beneficial only for the agents themselves, or also for nature taken as a whole.[115] Moreover, far from excluding the influence of ends upon agents, such an account really presupposes it. If we may emphasize this point, each particular agent acts for its particular end.

This is why Thomas eliminates in his fifth way any explanation based on chance. He is convinced that particular actions cannot be rendered intelligible unless one recognizes the influence of an end upon an agent. Because of this he goes on to argue that things which lack knowledge do not tend to an end except insofar as they are directed to it by some knowing and intelligent being as, for example, an arrow is directed to its target by an archer.[116]

He says the same both in his Commentary on Book II of the *Sentences* (d. 25, q. 1, a. 1) and in q. 1, a. 2 of the *Prima Secundae*. If we may fill in his reasoning a bit, his point is this. An agent does not act in a given way unless it is influenced by an end. Noncognitive agents cannot explicitly know their ends. Hence the only way of accounting for the ability of an end to influence such an agent is to appeal to an inclination which is impressed upon that agent by some intelligent being. Such an intelligent being can, of course, have in mind the end of the noncognitive agent's action.[117] This is why Thomas writes in the text from the *Prima Secundae* that agents which lack reason tend to an end through a natural inclination so as to be moved, as it were, by something else and not by themselves. Because they do not grasp the end of their action as such, they do not order themselves to that end; they are ordered to it by something else.[118]

Finally, Thomas's reference in the fifth way and in ST I–II, q. 1, a. 2 to an arrow which tends to its determined target because it is so directed by an archer might raise another question for the reader.[119] Does Thomas think that the inclination of purely natural agents to their respective ends is simply impressed on them in passing fashion, as it were, by some other intelligent being? Or does he rather have in mind a permanent inclination which is part of their very being?

The example of the archer and the arrow might lead one to believe that Thomas has in mind only the first alternative. And this would perhaps be enough for him to argue from finality in nature, though it might not be sufficient for him to show that there is only one intelligence which is responsible for such finality.

It is clear, however, from other texts that he really defends the second alternative. For instance, in the text from *In II Sent.*, d. 25, q. 1, a. 1, he had observed that the actions of natural entities are not in vain; such entities are ordered to their actions by an intellect which "constitutes" such natures. From this he goes on to conclude that the whole of nature is, in a certain fashion, the work of intelligence.[120] And on other occasions he refers to a natural body's inclination to behave in a certain way and to tend to a certain end as its natural appetite. Moreover, as he explains in ST I, q. 5, a. 5, a thing's inclination to an action follows upon its form.[121] We conclude, therefore, that what ultimately causes the form of a natural agent is also responsible for that agent's inclination to its given end. Thomas says as much in *De Veritate*, q. 25, a. 1.[122]

If one grants the validity of Thomas's reasoning up until this point, other questions may be raised about the fifth way. First of all, if he has shown that there is some intelligent being by whom all natural things are ordered to their end(s) and which we call God, can he show that there is only one such being? In other words, it seems once more that the question of the uniqueness of this supreme being must still be faced. Secondly, if such an intelligent being orders natural things to their appropriate end or ends by imposing a natural inclination upon them, is this not to say that this intelligence is also their efficient cause? If so, it would seem that the ultimate source of finality in the universe must be identified with the supreme efficient cause of all such beings. Thirdly and finally, this brings up the issue of the unity of the five ways themselves: Are they viewed by Thomas as five distinct arguments, each of which leads to God's existence? Or are they rather thought of as different steps in one longer and more involved argumentation for this conclusion?

## The Uniqueness of God

In taking up the first of these questions we return to a broader issue which may be raised about each of the five ways. Do Thomas's arguments really succeed in showing that there is only one first and unmoved mover, or first efficient cause, or uncaused necessary being, or absolute maximum or, in the case of the fifth way, one supreme intelligence which is responsible for the fact that all natural agents act for an end? Or do they leave open the possibility that there might be more than one of at least some of these—for instance, more than one unmoved mover or uncaused cause? Moreover, does his argumentation show that the unmoved mover is identical with the uncaused cause, the absolutely necessary being, the supremely perfect being, and the supreme intelligence?

One may doubt whether any of these arguments, as they stand in the text of *Summa Theologiae* I, q. 2, a. 3, fully establishes divine uniqueness, i.e., that there is one God and only one God. Our doubt concerning this is strengthened by the fact that in ST I, q. 11, a. 3, Thomas explicitly addresses himself to this issue. It might have been less confusing for the reader if Thomas had clearly indicated in the course of presenting the various five ways that he would eventually complete them by establishing divine uniqueness.[123] Be that as it may, it remains for us now to turn to his discussion of this in q. 11, and then to certain other works where he also explicitly takes up this issue.

Question 11 is addressed to the topic of divine unity. Articles 1, 2, and 4 deal with the issue of unity taken in the sense of ontological unity or the transcendental one, i.e., the undividedness of being from itself. For Thomas, since this characteristic of being is found wherever being itself is realized, it must also be present in God. But it is only in a. 3 that the question of divine uniqueness—the claim that there is only one God—is taken up explicitly.[124]

In a. 3 Thomas offers three arguments to show that there is only one God. The first of these is based on God's simplicity. That by reason of which an individual is this individual cannot be communicated to many. For example, that by reason of which Socrates is man can be communicated to many; but that by reason of which he is this man cannot be so communicated. Otherwise, just as there cannot be many Socrateses, so too there could not be many men. Because God is identical with his very nature, that by reason of which he is God and that by reason of which he is this God are one and the same. Therefore there cannot be many Gods.[125]

In order to do justice to this argumentation, one should turn back to earlier articles in the *Summa Theologiae* on which it is based, that is to say, to Thomas's efforts to show that God is simple and in particular that God is identical with his nature. Thomas had devoted the whole of q. 3 to divine simplicity. As we have remarked above, he had introduced q. 3 by noting that this discussion is part of his effort to show how God is not. In this particular case he does so by arguing that all composition is to be denied of God.[126]

Thus in the opening articles of q. 3 Thomas shows first that God is not a body (a. 1); secondly that there is no matter-form composition in him (a. 2); and then in a. 3 that there is no composition in God of quiddity or essence or nature, on the one hand, and the subject which subsists (*suppositum*), on the other—or, as Thomas also puts it, that God is identical with his essence or nature.[127]

Thomas develops the last-mentioned point by drawing upon his theory of the individuation of material substances and his views on the relationship between nature and the subsisting subject (*supposit*). In things composed of matter and form, essence or nature differs from the subject which exists (*supposit*). This is because essence or nature includes in itself only those things which fall within the definition of the species (as humanity includes only that which falls under the definition of human being). But individual matter and the accidents which serve to individuate it are not included within the definition of the species. For instance, this flesh and these bones and the accidents which designate this matter are not included within humanity, though they do fall under that which this human being is. Hence a human being, meaning this human being, and humanity are not completely identical; humanity is signified as a formal part of a human being. A human being (this subsisting subject) includes something which humanity considered in itself does not.[128]

In things which are not composed of matter and form and which are not rendered individuals by individual matter, forms are individuated of themselves. Hence these forms are subsisting subjects (*supposits*). Given this, in such beings there is no (real) distinction between nature and the subsisting subject (*supposit*). Therefore, since God is not composed of matter and form, concludes Thomas, it follows that God is identical with his deity, his life, and whatever else may be predicated of him. In other words, God, taken as a subsisting subject, is identical with his essence or nature.[129] If one grants this, it will of course follow that there can only be one God; for that by which deity is deity is identical with that by which deity is God.

One point remains to be examined in this argumentation. This is the assertion that in God there can be no composition of matter and form. Thomas had considered this in a. 2. In brief he had rejected matter-form composition in God: (1) because God as pure actuality excludes matter which is potentiality; (2) because every composite of matter and form is perfected by its form and is good through its form and, therefore, good only by participation, something which cannot be said of God, the first and best being; (3) because every agent acts through its form. Hence that which is the first and *per se* agent must be form primarily and *per se*. Because God is the first efficient cause, such is true of him. Being form of his essence, therefore, God is not composed of matter and form. In sum, these arguments against matter-form composition in God follow from the conclusions of the first way, i.e., that God is pure act (argument one); the second way, that God is the first efficient cause (argument three); and presumably the fourth way, that God is the first and best being (argument two).[130]

To return now to Thomas's defense of divine uniqueness in q. 11, a. 3, there he builds a second argument upon the infinity of divine perfection. He notes that he has already shown that God includes within himself the total perfection of being. If there were many Gods, they would have to differ from one another. Therefore something would have to belong to one which did not belong to another. If this were a privation, the God to whom it belonged would not be perfect. And if it were a perfection, that perfection would be lacking to the other God(s). Therefore there cannot be many Gods.[131]

In order to appreciate this argument we shall again have to turn back to earlier articles in the *Summa* on which it is based. Before doing this, we should mention Thomas's third argument for divine uniqueness in q. 11, a. 3. This argument appeals to the unity of the world, a unity which is manifested by the fact that different things in the world are ordered to and subordinated to one another. But if things which differ are united to form one order, they must be so united by some ordering principle. Many things are better reduced to a single order by one ordering principle than by many; for one thing is a *per se* cause of that which is one, whereas many things do not cause that which is one except *per accidens*. Since that which is first is most perfect and is such *per se* and not merely *per accidens*, the first principle which reduces the different things in the world to a single order must be one rather than many. This is God.[132]

This argument is not quite so metaphysical as the previous two and, in my judgment, not so convincing within the context of Thomas's metaphysics. It has more of an empirical base, i.e., the order we discover in the universe. If one grants that such a universal order is present, the validity of the argument rests both upon our discovery of that order and upon our inability to account for it in any other way except by appealing to one supreme ordering principle. It reminds one of an argument for God's existence based on order and design. And it strikes me as being more of an argument from fittingness than a convincing demonstration.

With this we may return to the background for the most interesting of these three arguments for divine uniqueness, the second one, which is based on the impossibility of there being more than one infinitely perfect being. Presupposed by this argument, of course, is the claim that God is infinitely perfect or, as Thomas also puts it, that God includes within himself the total perfection of being.[133]

In q. 4, a. 1 Thomas had built his case for divine perfection upon his previously established conclusion that God is the first efficient cause and presumably, therefore, on the conclusion of the second way. The first efficient cause, Thomas reasons, must be most perfect. Just as matter insofar as it is matter is in potency, so too, an agent insofar as it is an agent is in act. Therefore the first active principle, i.e., the first efficient cause, must be in act to the maximum degree, and therefore perfect to the maximum degree. In support of this final point Thomas reasons that something is said to be perfect insofar as it is in act; by the perfect we mean that to which nothing of its appropriate perfection is lacking.[134]

In replying to objection 3 Thomas develops this final point. The objection points out that Thomas has already argued that God's essence is identical with his *esse* (see q. 3, a. 4). But *esse* seems to be most imperfect, since it is most universal (*communissimum*) and admits of additions. In reply Thomas counters that *esse* itself is the most perfect of all; for it is related to all things as their act. And nothing enjoys actuality except insofar as it exists. Therefore *esse* itself is the actuality of all things, including forms themselves. Hence it is related to other things not as that which receives is related to that which is received, but rather as that which is received to that which receives it. When one speaks of the *esse* of a human being or of a horse, Thomas goes on to explain, *esse* is taken as that which is formal and received. Against the objection, therefore, he maintains that *esse* is the most perfect of all. If God is self-subsisting *esse*, we can easily see why Thomas regards God as perfect.[135]

If Thomas has connected perfection with actuality in the corpus of this article, in replying to objection 3 he has now just as clearly grounded actuality and therefore perfection in *esse*. As he uses the term *esse* in this discussion, he has in mind the intrinsic act of being (*actus essendi*). It is this which is the most perfect of all, which accounts for the fact that things exist, and which is related to a creature's essence as that which is formal and received. To repeat a point just made, if God is self-subsisting *esse*, he must be self-subsisting perfection.

In q. 4, a. 2, Thomas goes on to show that the perfections of all other things are present in God, either formally or virtually, we should add. As Thomas explains, this means that God is universally perfect in the sense that no excellence of any kind is lacking to him. He offers two arguments to establish this. The first is based on the fact that whatever degree of perfection is present in an effect must be found in its efficient cause, either in the same way if we are dealing with causes and effects of the same kind (univocal causes, as Thomas sometimes describes them), or in more eminent fashion if the cause differs in kind from and is more perfect than the effect (equivocal causes, in Thomas's terminology). In proof he reasons that it is evident that an effect preexists virtually in its efficient cause. This is simply to say that the agent has the power to produce the effect. But this is for an effect to preexist not in less perfect fashion but in a more perfect way. An agent insofar as it is an agent is perfect. Because God is the first efficient cause, the perfections of all things must preexist in him in preeminent fashion.[136]

In his second argument to show that the perfections of all things are in God, Thomas recalls his earlier proof that God is self-subsisting *esse*. It follows from this that God must contain the full perfection of being within himself. For instance, if there could be such a thing as subsisting heat, nothing of the perfection of heat could be lacking to it. Because God is subsisting being (*esse*) itself, nothing of the perfection of being can be lacking to him. Given this, it follows that the perfections of all things belong to God; for the perfections of all things pertain to the perfection of being. Thomas supports this final point by reminding us once again that things are perfect insofar as they enjoy the act of being (*esse*) in some fashion.[137]

Since Thomas has explicitly referred back to his earlier proof that God is identical with his act of being (*esse*), it will be useful now for us to turn to his discussion of this in q. 3, a. 4. In order to establish this, Thomas offers three arguments.[138] First of all, as we have already seen above in discussing a way of strengthening the fourth way, he reasons that whatever is present in a given thing in addition to its essence must be caused either by the principles of that thing's essence (as is true of proper accidents, such as the ability to laugh in a human being), or else by some external principle. Therefore, if the act of being (*esse*) of a thing differs from its essence, its act of being must be caused either by some external principle or else by that thing's essential principles. But it is not possible for a thing's act of being to be caused merely by its essential principles, since nothing can be the cause of its own act of being (*esse*), if indeed its act of being is caused. Therefore, if the act of being of a given thing differs from its essence, its act of being (*esse*) must be caused by something else. But in his second way Thomas has already shown that God is the first efficient cause and, therefore, that his act of being is not caused. From this it follows simply by denying the consequent that essence and act of being do not differ in God.[139]

As a second argument Thomas reasons that God must be identical with his act of being (*esse*) because *esse* is the actuality of every form or nature. For instance, goodness or humanity is not said to be realized in actuality except insofar as it exists. Hence an act of being (*esse*) must be related to an essence which differs from it as act to potency. Since there can be no (passive) potentiality in God, in him essence and act of being (*esse*) do not differ. We may presume that the point that there is no potentiality in God follows for Thomas from the conclusion of the first way and also, as he indicates in q. 3, a. 1, from the fact that God is the first being.[140]

As a third argument for the identity of God with his act of being, Thomas reasons that if something merely has *esse* but is not identical with its *esse*, it is a being only by participation. If God were not identical with his act of being (*esse*), he would be a being only by participation. He would not be the first being.[141] It is for these three reasons, therefore, that Thomas holds that essence and act of being (*esse*) are identical in God and as a consequence, that God is subsisting *esse*.

Finally, since Thomas has built his second major argument for divine uniqueness upon the infinity of divine perfection, we may ask how he establishes the infinity of God. Although Thomas develops this point on many occasions in his writings, in the *Summa Theologiae* I his explicit discussion appears in q. 7, a. 1. There he distinguishes between the kind of infinity which may be ascribed to matter, and the kind attributed to form. Matter is said to be infinite (we might substitute the term "indefinite") in the sense that it can receive many forms. Because it is determined and perfected by the form it receives, the infinity assigned to matter falls on the side of imperfection. The infinity which Thomas ascribes to form is a mark of perfection. It refers to the fact that form, insofar as it is form, is common to many and is not perfected by the matter which receives it. Rather it is limited thereby in that its fullness is contracted by the matter that receives it.[142]

Thomas next recalls that the act of being (*esse*) is the most formal of all. He has shown that the divine act of being is not received by anything else and that God is identical with his act of being (*esse*). From this he now draws the conclusion that God is infinite and perfect. In other words, in this argument Thomas appeals to his understanding of *esse* as that which is most formal and actual and by implication to his axiom that unreceived act (in this case, the act of being) is unlimited. Because God's *esse* is unreceived by anything else, it is unlimited. Therefore God himself is infinite and perfect.[143]

If we may briefly summarize this somewhat complicated background for Thomas's second argument for the uniqueness of God, it rests upon the following points. According to q. 3, a. 4, God is identical with his act of being. According to q. 4, a. 1, as the first efficient cause God must be in act to the maximum degree and, therefore, perfect to the maximum degree. Hence, according to q. 4, a. 2 the perfections of all other things must be present in God either formally or virtually. Finally, according to q. 7, a. 1, because the divine act of being is not received and therefore limited by anything else and because God is identical with his act of being, God's act of being is unlimited or infinite. Therefore God is infinite. Given all of this, in q. 11, a. 3 Thomas can reason that because God includes within himself the total perfection of being and because there cannot be many infinitely perfect beings, there cannot be many Gods. Therefore there is only one God.

At this juncture it may be helpful for us to consider some arguments for divine uniqueness which Thomas offers in other contexts. There is a long discussion of this in the SCG I, c. 42. Since not all of the arguments offered there are equally convincing and since they are quite numerous, here I shall single out one which strikes me as being of considerable interest. This, the second argument offered there, reminds one of a principle used again by Thomas in his second argument in ST I, q. 11, a. 3. The argument in SCG I, c. 42 is based on divine perfection. Thomas begins by recalling that he has already shown that God is totally perfect. Therefore, if there were many Gods, there would have to be many beings which are completely and totally perfect. But this is impossible. For if no perfection is lacking to any one of them, and if no imperfection is found in any of them, there will be no way in which they can be distinguished from one another. Therefore there cannot be many such beings.[144] Again we see Thomas accepting as proved the point that God is totally perfect, and reasoning that two completely perfect beings could not be distinguished from one another and therefore cannot exist.

Since Thomas introduces this particular argument by recalling that he has already shown that God is completely perfect, we may now turn briefly to his discussion of divine perfection in SCG I, c. 28. There he offers a series of arguments to make his point. He begins by observing that God, who is identical with his act of being (*esse*), is a perfect being in every way or, to translate literally, universally perfect. As Thomas explains, this means that no excellence (*nobilitas*) of any kind can be lacking to God.[145]

In his first full argument for divine perfection, Thomas reasons that a thing's excellence belongs to it in accord with its act of being (*esse*). For instance, no excellence would be present in a man by reason of his wisdom unless it were through wisdom that he is indeed wise. Thus a thing's excellence is in accord with the way (mode) in which it enjoys *esse*. If a thing's *esse* is restricted to some greater or lesser specific mode of excellence, that thing is accordingly said to be more or less excellent. And if there is something to which the total power of being (*virtus essendi*) belongs, no excellence which can pertain to any thing can be lacking to it. But a thing which is identical with its act of being (*esse*) enjoys the act of being according to the total power of being. (Thomas illustrates this by calling upon one of his favorite examples. If there were a subsisting whiteness, nothing of the power of whiteness would be lacking to it because of any deficiency on the part of a receiving subject. In other words, precisely because it was a subsisting whiteness, it would not be received by any distinct subject and could not be limited thereby.) But, as Thomas reminds us, he has already shown above (in c. 22) that God is identical with his act of being. Therefore God possesses *esse* according to the total power of being (*esse*) itself. Consequently, no possible excellence can be lacking to God.[146]

Thomas builds another argument for divine perfection upon his previously established conclusion that God is pure actuality (see c. 16). But that which is in potency in no way whatsoever and which is pure actuality must be most perfect; for a thing is perfect insofar as it is in act. As pure actuality, therefore, God is most perfect.[147]

With respect to Thomas's explicit argumentation for divine uniqueness in SCG I, c. 42, we should note that he does not yet assume there that God is infinite. In fact he will take up divine infinity in the immediately following chapter 43. In this respect, therefore, his procedure in the *Summa contra Gentiles* differs from that which he would later follow in the *Summa Theologiae*. Having already established divine infinity in ST I, q. 7, he can there justifiably rest part of his argumentation for divine uniqueness upon divine infinity when he takes this up in q. 11.

Nonetheless, within a very different context in the *Summa contra Gentiles*, that is, in Book II, c. 52, Thomas does offer an interesting argument for divine unicity which is based upon divine infinity. There Thomas is attempting to show that in created intellectual substances *esse* (the act of being) and "that which is" (essence) differ. His first three arguments attempt to show that there can only be one being which is identical with its act of being and, therefore, that in all others essence and act of being (*esse*) differ.[148]

According to the third argument, it is impossible for there to be two completely infinite instances of the act of being (*esse*). This follows because completely infinite *esse* embraces the total perfection of being. If such infinity were present in two different things, there would be no way in which one could be distinguished from the other. But subsisting *esse* must be infinite, since it is not limited by any receiving principle. Therefore it is impossible for there to be any other case of subsisting existence (*esse*) apart from the first being.[149]

This argument ultimately rests on a by now familiar central axiom of Thomas's metaphysics: unreceived *esse* is unlimited. Thomas joins this with the point that there would be no way in which completely unlimited or infinite instances of *esse* could be differentiated from one another. At the same time, this argument's location within this particular chapter of the *Summa contra Gentiles* reminds us that other arguments offered there and elsewhere by Aquinas to show that there can only be one instance of self-subsisting *esse* may also be regarded as arguments for divine uniqueness.[150]

We shall conclude our consideration of Thomas's argumentation for divine uniqueness by turning to his presentation in the *Compendium Theologiae* I, c. 15 (ca. 1265–1267), which probably precedes the discussion in ST I, q. 11 by a year or so. There he offers two major metaphysical arguments. The first reminds us of his first argument in ST I, q. 11, a. 3. That whereby a common essence is rendered individual cannot be communicated to many. Thus, while there can be many human beings, it is not possible for this individual human being to be more than one. If an essence is individuated of itself and not by reason of anything else, it cannot belong to many subjects. But the divine essence is individuated of itself, since in God there is no distinction between his essence and the subject which exists *(essentia et quod est)*. In support of this Thomas harks back to his proof in c. 10 that God is identical with his essence. Therefore there can only be one God.[151]

The second argument in c. 15 is still more interesting. Thomas now maintains that there are two ways in which a form may be multiplied: either by reason of differences (as when a generic form is so divided), or by being received in different subjects. But if there is a form which cannot be multiplied in the first way, i.e., through differences, and which does not exist in a distinct subject, it cannot be multiplied at all. For instance, writes Thomas as he appeals again to his familiar example, if whiteness could subsist apart from any receiving subject, it could only be one. But the divine essence is identical with the divine act of being *(esse)*, as Thomas has shown in c. 11. Therefore, since the divine *esse* is, as it were, a form that subsists in itself, it can only be one.[152]

Notwithstanding the fact that Thomas had offered argumentation for God's existence in c. 3 of the *Compendium* and additional argumentation to show that he is unmovable, eternal, and necessary of himself (cc. 4–6), he has judged it necessary to devote a separate treatment in c. 15 to show that God is unique. This parallels his procedure in SCG I and in ST I, and also confirms our judgment that he realized that without this additional argumentation his proof that God exists would not be complete. At the same time, as we have remarked before, this additional step was not necessary in his presentation in *De Ente*, c. 4, because there his proof that there could at most be one subsisting *esse* is a necessary step in his argument for distinction between essence and act of being in everything else and also, therefore, for his metaphysical argument for God's existence.

Having now considered a number of Thomas's explicit arguments for divine uniqueness, we may ask whether they are also sufficient to show that the one uncaused efficient cause of all other being must itself be identified with the ultimate source of finality in the universe. (It can more easily be granted that the unmoved mover, the being that is necessary *per se*, and even the maximum being of the fourth way may be identified with the first efficient cause of the second way.) Thomas clearly intends this. Thus he has identified as one and the same God the first efficient cause and the ultimate source of finality in the universe, i.e., the intelligent being which is responsible for the presence of finality in purely natural agents. But has he proved this point?[153]

That this is not an idle question is suggested by his earlier recognition in *Summa contra Gentiles* I, c. 13 that if by arguing from motion one arrives at a mover which is responsible for the motion in the universe, one may still ask whether that mover acts for an end beyond itself. As the reader will recall, Thomas there reasoned that one must ultimately conclude to the existence of an unmoved mover which does not move for the sake of an end beyond itself. In that context he seems to have combined an argument based on efficient causation of motion with one grounded on the need for an unmoved mover in the absolute sense—that is, one that does not depend upon anything other than itself even in the order of final causality.[154]

Within the context of the fifth way and its parallels, however, Thomas's procedure is different. Here he reasons to the existence of some intelligent being in order to account for the fact that noncognitive agents act for an end. If this end is to influence them in their activity and if by definition they themselves are incapable of knowing such an end, it must preexist in cognitive fashion in some intelligence which efficiently causes such natures and imposes upon them their inclinations to their respective ends.[155] In other words, this intelligent being is also the first efficient cause of such natures. And if Thomas has successfully shown that there can be only one first uncaused efficient cause of all other things and that this being is intelligent, it will follow that there is also one supreme intelligent source responsible for the finality of natural agents precisely because the two are one and the same.[156]

Thomas offers explicit argumentation to show that God is intelligent. It will suffice here to mention ST I, q. 14, a. 1. There he reasons that the immateriality of a thing determines if and to what extent it is capable of knowing. This follows from his (and Aristotle's) view that a thing is capable of knowing to the extent that it can grasp the form of some other thing in immaterial fashion. Because God is supremely immaterial, as Thomas has argued above in q. 7, a. 1, he now concludes that God is capable of knowing to the maximum degree.[157]

Moreover, as Thomas explains in replying to the first objection in q. 14, a. 1, perfections as realized in creatures are attributed to God in more perfect fashion. Therefore, when a name taken from a perfection found in a creature is assigned to God, we must negate of it all that follows from the imperfect manner in which it is realized in the creature.[158] We may presume, therefore, that Thomas would permit us to argue in this fashion as well for the presence of intelligence in God. Underlying this reasoning is Thomas's conviction that there is some kind of similarity, in spite of great diversity, between an effect and its first cause.[159]

## The Unity of the Five Ways

In concluding this discussion of Thomas's five ways, I would like to return to the third issue already mentioned at the end of section 5: Does Thomas regard the five ways as five distinct arguments for God's existence, or rather as five different versions or perhaps steps of one and the same argument? From our examination of each of them, the answer to this should now be clear. It is true that there is considerable similarity between the five ways, in that each begins with some datum based on sense experience and each, by reasoning from effect to cause, concludes to the existence of a first and uncaused cause in order to account for the effect that served as the starting point. Nonetheless, because each way begins with a different starting point and because reasoning from effect to cause is applied in different ways in each of them, each should be regarded as a distinct argument. If one grants this, however, a related question remains: Has Thomas presented the five ways in accord with some systematic organizing principle and, if so, does he regard them as the only valid ways in which God's existence can be demonstrated? There is considerable diversity of opinion among Thomistic interpreters concerning these two questions.[160]

One approach, developed by A.-R. Motte among others, holds that the grouping of the five ways is first and foremost empirical (i.e., historical) in origin. It results from Thomas's reflection upon and usage of the different historical sources he had available. He drew upon various approaches in the previous philosophical and Christian tradition which he found most suitable for his purposes. He never claimed that the five ways can be reduced to a single logical scheme or that they are the only valid ways of proving God's existence.[161]

Others have tried to reduce the five ways to a single logical scheme and/or to claim that in Thomas's mind they exclude other possible ways in which one can reason to God's existence.[162] Our examination in *The Metaphysical Thought of Thomas Aquinas* of other forms of arguments for God's existence in Thomas's texts, including that offered in *De Ente*, c. 4, to cite one of the most important, should make it unnecessary for us to devote more attention to the last-mentioned claim. The fact that he developed other arguments in other texts does not support the claim that he regarded the five ways as the only valid ways of proving God's existence. Nor do we have any textual evidence from the *Summa Theologiae* or elsewhere to suggest that he later rejected those other approaches.

As for the former suggestion, that the five ways can be reduced to some single logical scheme, some have attempted to reduce all five of them in some way to the four causes.[163] Such attempts strike me as being forced.

First of all, there is the obvious point that there are five ways but only four supreme kinds of causes. Moreover, as just mentioned above, it is clear that all of the five ways in some way reason from an effect, presumably one that is given to us in the world of sense experience, to an uncaused cause of the same. Common to the first three ways is an appeal to some form of efficient causation, whether in the order of motion (the first way), or in the order of caused causes (the second way), or in the order of beings subject to generation and corruption and then of beings which are not subject to generation and corruption but which are still caused (the third way). The fourth way stands out because of its different point of departure—varying degrees of perfection in the observable universe. While its first stage seems to rely exclusively on formal exemplar causality, I have suggested above that if this argument is to be regarded as valid, the participated and therefore efficiently caused character of beings which enjoy limited degrees of perfection must also be introduced in that stage. Thomas himself does not explicitly do this in the argument's first stage, but he does introduce efficient causality in its second stage. As we have also seen, the fifth way is based on final causality in purely natural entities, a phenomenon which in Thomas's judgment points to the existence of a first intelligence which efficiently causes such agents together with their inclinations to act for ends. Finally, efforts to reduce the five ways to the four causes all founder, at least in my judgment, when they attempt to reduce one or another argument to the order of material causality.

In dealing with this issue it is enough for us to acknowledge these points along with our recognition of the fact that Thomas sees fit to complete these arguments in various ways in his discussion of the divine attributes. To impose upon the five ways some overriding logical plan which would account for their supposed interlocking symmetry is to go far beyond Thomas's text, and to risk distorting his thought. And as I have already indicated, to regard the five ways as excluding in Thomas's mind all other possible ways of arguing for God's existence runs counter to his procedure in other passages. Some, H. J. Johnson, for instance, have emphasized the point that in ST I, q. 2, a. 3 Thomas explicitly states that it can be proved in five ways that God exists.[164] To me this does not indicate that Thomas therefore regarded the number five as exhaustive and/or that he must have had in mind a systematic organizing plan such as the four causes in making this selection. I would simply note that his text does not state that God's existence can be proved in only five ways.

On a more positive note, however, I would conclude by observing that each of the five ways does contribute something to our understanding of God, although the different perspectives which they offer do not, of course, point to any real distinctions within God himself. From our standpoint, however, to recognize God as the unmoved mover, the uncaused cause, the absolutely necessary being, the maximumly perfect being, and the source of finality within the universe enriches our effort to arrive at some fuller understanding of him. And this, together with the historical sources which were available to Thomas, his critical evaluation of their philosophical power, and his customary method of offering more than one argument for a given conclusion, should suffice to explain why he offered more than one way in ST I, q. 2, a. 3, and, for that matter, more than one argument for God's existence elsewhere in his writings.

## Notes

This chapter was previously published as John Wippel, "The Five Ways" (chapter 12 of John Wippel, *The Metaphysical Thought of Thomas Aquinas*, The Catholic University of America Press, Washington, DC, 2000). Used with permission of The Catholic University of America Press.

1. On Thomas's intention to write the *Summa* for beginners (in theology) see John F. Wippel, *The Metaphysical Thought of Thomas Aquinas* (Washington, DC, 2000), chapter 10, n. 50, and the references there to Boyle, Torrell, and O'Meara. Also see James A. Weisheipl, *Friar Thomas D'Aquino* (Washington, DC, 1983), pp. 218–19; M.-D. Chenu, *Introduction à l'étude de saint Thomas d'Aquin*, 2nd ed. (Montréal-Paris, 1954), pp. 255–58. Weisheipl also observes that while Thomas managed to carry out his purpose of addressing beginning students in theology in the first part of his work, the second and third parts "are far from being a simple introduction" (pp. 222–23).

2. Some of this background is provided in chapter 2 of my *The Metaphysical Thought of Thomas Aquinas*. It is good to bear in mind that Thomas himself sets his five ways within the background of his own philosophy and metaphysics. This in turn suggests that it is a highly questionable procedure simply to extract the five ways from their broader setting within Thomistic metaphysics and to expect them to, as it were, "stand on their own."

3. "Circa essentiam vero divinam, primo considerandum est an Deus sit . . ." (Leon. 4.27).

4. See Leon. 4.27–28, and the text cited in my *Metaphysical Thought of Thomas Aquinas*, chapter 10, n. 32. For his rejection of the Anselmian argumentation see ad 2 (p. 28).

5. Leon. 4.30. Note in particular: "Ex quolibet autem effectu potest demonstrari propriam causam eius esse . . . : quia, cum effectus dependeant a causa, posito effectu necesse est causam praeexistere. Unde Deum esse, secundum quod non est per se notum quoad nos, demonstrabile est per effectus nobis notos."

6. Leon. 4.30. If we may anticipate the first way for the sake of illustration, it begins with an effect, the fact that things are moved. By using the principle that whatever is moved is moved by something else, and by eliminating appeal to an infinite regress of moved movers as an adequate explanation, it concludes to the existence of a first and unmoved mover, or God. Here the effect—motion (the fact that things are moved)—serves as the middle term in the argument as Thomas presents it. However, in order for the argument to conclude explicitly to God's existence we must supply another syllogism such as this as suggested by Van Steenberghen: By the term "God" one means a being which is the First Mover of all motions which occur in this world. But such a First Mover exists. Therefore God exists (*Le problème de l'existence de Dieu dans les écrits de S. Thomas D'Aquin* (Louvain-La-Neuve, 1980), pp. 171–72; cf. p. 164). This syllogism uses a nominal definition, "First Mover," as one would expect from Thomas's reply to objection 2. But it is not this nominal definition which serves as a middle term in the first way as Thomas actually presents it, but rather an observable effect, i.e., that things are moved. Thomas's first way is really directed to establishing the minor of our supplied syllogism.

7. "Prima autem et manifestior via est, quae sumitur ex parte motus. Certum est enim, et sensu constat, aliqua moveri in hoc mundo. Omne autem quod movetur, ab alio movetur. Nihil enim movetur, nisi secundum quod est in potentia ad illud ad quod movetur: movet autem aliquid secundum quod est actu. Movere enim nihil aliud est quam educere aliquid de potentia in actum: de potentia autem non potest aliquid reduci in actum, nisi per aliquod ens in actu: sicut calidum in actu, ut ignis, facit lignum, quod est calidum in potentia, esse actu calidum, et per hoc movet et alterat ipsum. Non autem est possibile ut idem sit simul in actu et potentia secundum idem, sed solum secundum diversa: quod enim est calidum in actu, non potest simul esse calidum in potentia, sed est simul frigidum in potentia. Impossibile est ergo quod, secundum idem et eodem motu [for: *modo*], aliquid sit movens et motum, vel quod moveat seipsum. Omne ergo quod movetur, oporter ab alio moveri" (Leon. 4.31). Along with Van Steenberghen (op. cit., p. 167); Anthony Kenny, *The Five Ways*, p. 7, n. I; and *Summa Theologiae*, Vol. 2: Existence and Nature of God (New York-London, 1964), (London, 1969), p. 12, I have substituted *motu* for *modo* in this text. However retention of the reading *modo* will not change the argument.

8. "Si ergo id a quo movetur, moveatur, oportet et ipsum ab alio moveri; et illud ab alio. Hic autem non est procedere in infinitum: quia sic non esset aliquod primum movens; et per consequens nec aliquod aliud movens, quia moventia secunda non movent nisi per hoc quod sunt mota a primo movente, sicut baculus non movet nisi per hoc quod est motus a manu. Ergo necesse est devenire ad aliquod primum movens, quod a nullo movetur: et hoc omnes intelligunt Deum" (Leon. 4.31).

9. For the texts from (SCG) I, c. 13, see Leonine Manual edition pp. 10–11 (cited in my *Metaphysical Thought of Thomas Aquinas*, chapter 11, n. 40 [for the first argument from motion]), and p. 12 (for the second argument).

10. *In III Phys.*, lect. 2 (Marietti ed.), pp. 144–45, nn. 285–86. Note in particular: "Unde convenientissime Philosophus definit motum, dicens quod motus est *entelechia*, idest *actus existentis in potentia secundum quod huiusmodi*" (n. 285); "Accipit enim hic motum communiter pro mutatione, non autem stricte secundum quod dividitur contra generationem et corruptionem, ut dicetur in quinto" (n. 286).

11. *In V Phys.*, lect. 2, p. 322, n. 649: "Ubi considerandum est quod Aristoteles supra in tertio ubi motum definivit, accepit nomen *motus* secundum quod est commune omnibus speciebus mutationis. Et hoc modo accipit hic nomen *mutationis: motum* autem accipit magis stricte, pro quadam mutationis specie." See lect. 3, n. 661 (there are only three species of *motus*), n. 662 (there is no *motus* in the genus substance because motion taken strictly is between contraries, and there is no contrariety in the genus substance); lect. 4 (on the three kinds of *motus* taken strictly).

12. See my discussion in *The Metaphysical Thought of Thomas Aquinas*, chapter 11, n. 54, and the texts quoted in n. 58 (from the first argument in SCG I, c. 13, and its third way of justifying the claim that whatever is moved is moved by something else); n. 76 (from the second argument in SCG I, c. 13, and its attempt to show that a perpetual self-mover of the outermost heavenly sphere, as apparently proposed by Aristotle, must still be moved in the order of final causality by a completely unmoved mover or God).

13. See *The Metaphysical Thought of Thomas Aquinas*, chapter 11, nn. 58 and 59 and the corresponding part of my text.

14. See ibid., chapter 11, n. 59. Cf. Scott MacDonald, "Aquinas's Parasitic Cosmological Argument," *Medieval Philosophy and Theology* I (1991), pp. 133–35.

15. As Thomas puts it: something cannot be reduced from potentiality to actuality except by some being in actuality (*ens in actu*). Insofar as a thing is in potency to a given act, it is not yet that act. See n. 7 above.

16. Some, Van Steenberghen for instance, would take *moveri* more broadly so as to apply to *motus* in the strict sense and to generation and corruption, i.e., to change in all its forms, and apparently even at the beginning of the argument. See *Le problème*, pp. 169–70.

17. See my discussion of this with reference to SCG I, c. 13 in my *Metaphysical Thought of Thomas Aquinas*, chapter 11, nn. 62–64. Also see W. L. Rowe, *The Cosmological Argument* (Princeton, 1975), pp. 18–19, 32–38, where he reformulates and attempts to salvage what he regards as Thomas's question-begging formulation in the first and second ways. On the relation between God, the ultimate principal cause, and other causes see the interesting remarks by Gilson in his "Prolégomènes à la *prima via*," *Archives d'Histoire Doctrinale et Littéraire du Moyen Âge* 30 (1964), pp. 64–65. In reading this one should bear in mind the two ways in which Thomas uses the notion of instrument. See my *Metaphysical Thought of Thomas Aquinas*, chapter 11, n. 65.

18. See Van Steenberghen, *Le problème*, p. 180, n. 28. Others will be cited below.

19. For Henry see his Quodlibet 9, q. 5 ("Utrum voluntas moveat se ipsam"), R. Macken, ed. (Leuven, 1983), pp. 99–139; Quodlibet 10, q. 9, R. Macken, ed. (Leuven, 1981), pp. 250–55 ("Utrum subiectum per se possit esse causa sufficiens sui accidentis"). These date from Easter (i.e., during Lent) and Christmas (i.e., during Advent) of 1286. See Macken's edition of Henry's Quodlibet I (Leuven-Leiden, 1979), p. xvii. Henry seems to have developed his theory of virtual vs. formal willing in Quodlibet 10, or by that time. For discussion of Henry's views see Macken, "La volonté humaine, faculté plus élevée que l'intelligence selon Henri de Gand," in: *Recherches de Théologie ancienne et médiévale* 42 (1975), pp. 5–51; "Heinrich von Gent im Gespräch mit seinen Zeitgenossen über die menschliche Freiheit," in: *Franziskanische Studien* 59 (1977), pp. 125–82, especially pp. 141–58; R. Effler, *John Duns Scotus and the Principle "Omne quod movetur ab alio movetur,"* pp. 15, 64–66 (St. Bonaventure, NY, 1962); Wippel, *The Metaphysical Thought of Godfrey of Fontaines*, pp. 180–81, 190–91.

20. See Effler, op. cit., pp. 16–17, and throughout the rest of his study. It should be noted, however, that with Duns Scotus, Effler interprets the subject of the principle of motion to mean "everything which is in motion" rather than "whatever is moved." See pp. 33–35. This, of course, runs counter to Thomas's understanding of the principle as I read him.

21. For a helpful survey see J. Weisheipl, "Galileo and the Principle of Inertia," chapter 3 of his *Nature and Motion in the Middle Ages* (Washington, DC, 1985), pp. 49–63. In particular Weisheipl considers the views of William Whewell, Ernst Mach, Pierre Duhem, Alexandre Koyré, Anneliese Maier, and Stillman Drake. Each of these thinkers also assigns a greater or lesser role (considerably lesser according to Koyré) to Galileo in discovering the principle of inertia. As Weisheipl sums up his survey: ". . . all of these historians are unanimous in seeing a radical incompatibility between Aristotle's demand for causes of motion and Galileo's (and modern science's) rejection of efficient

causes. From the philosophical point of view perhaps Anneliese Maier's statement of the problem is typical: "Aristotle's principle 'Everything that is moved, is moved by another' had to be rejected to allow for the modern principle of inertia" (pp. 62–63).

22. Art. 1 is directed to this question: "Utrum voluntas moveatur ab intellectu." See Leon. 6.74–75. From this discussion note in particular: "Motio autem ipsius subjecti est ex agente aliquo . . . Et ideo ex hac parte voluntas movet alias potentias animae ad suos actus . . . Sed objectum movet, determinando actum, ad modum principii formalis . . . Et ideo isto modo motionis intellectus movet voluntatem, sicut praesentans ei obiectum suum." Also see ad 3: ". . . dicendum quod voluntas movet intellectum quantum ad exercitium actus . . . Sed quantum ad determinationem actus, quae est ex parte obiecti, intellectus movet voluntatem . . . Et sic patet quod non est idem movens et motum secundum idem." On Thomas's distinction between the exercise and the specification of an act see D. Gallagher, "Free Choice and Free Judgment in Thomas Aquinas," *Archiv für Geschichte der Philosophie* 76 (1994), pp. 262–70.

23. On the development in Thomas's thinking on the causality exercised by the intellect and its object on the will, see O. Lottin, *Psychologie et morale aux XIIe et XIIIe siècles,* Vol. 1 (Louvain-Gembloux, 1942), pp. 226–43 (on earlier writings), 252–62. For additional references concerning this see Gallagher, "Free Choice," p. 250, n. 10. Torrell dates ST I–II in 1271 and *De malo,* q. 6 around 1270. Whether one can establish the chronological priority of either of these sources over the other on the grounds of internal evidence is doubtful, in my judgment, although some have attempted this. See Gallagher, p. 261, n. 40 for references. For our purposes the teaching of these two sources is the same, but different from earlier discussions in *De veritate,* SCG, and ST I. ST I–II, q. 9, a. 3 is explicitly directed to this question: "Utrum voluntas moveat seipsam." In developing his answer Thomas draws an analogy between the will and the intellect. In knowing principles the intellect can reduce itself from potency to act as regards its knowledge of conclusions that follow from those principles. In like fashion the will, in that it wills an end, moves itself to will the means to that end. See his reply to objection I: ". . . dicendum quod voluntas non secundum idem movet et movetur. Unde nec secundum idem est in actu et in potentia, Sed inquantum actu vult finem, reducit se de potentia in actum respectu eorum quae sunt ad finem, ut scilicet actu ea velit" (Leon. 4.78).

24. Leon. 6.78–79. Note in particular: "Sed eo modo quo movetur quantum ad exercitium actus, adhuc necesse est ponere voluntatem ab aliquo principio exteriori moveri. Omne enim quod quandoque est agens in actu et quandoque in potentia, indiget moveri ab aliquo movente. Manifestum est autem quod voluntas incipit velle aliquid, cum hoc prius non vellet. Necesse est ergo quod ab aliquo moveatur ad volendum . . . Unde necesse est ponere quod in primum motum voluntatis voluntas prodeat ex instinctu alicuius exterioris moventis, ut Aristoteles concludit in quodam capitulo *Ethicae Eudemicae.*" For Aristotle see *Eudemian Ethics,* Book VII, c. 14 (1248a 25–32). Also see Thomas, ibid., ad I, ad 3.

25. See *Quaestiones disputatae De malo,* q. 6 (Leon. 23.148:308–149:415). Note in particular: "Sed cum voluntas non semper voluerit consiliari, necesse est quod ab aliquo moveatur ad hoc quod velit consiliari; et si quidem a se ipsa, necesse est iterum quod motum voluntatis praecedat consilium et consilium praecedat actus voluntatis;

et cum hoc in infinitum procedere non possit, necesse est ponere quod quantum ad primum motum voluntatis moveatur voluntas cuiuscumque non semper actu volentis ab aliquo exteriori, cuius instinctu voluntas velle incipiat." After concluding that it is God who first moves the will and intellect, Thomas comments: "Qui cum omnia moveat secundum rationem mobilium, ut levia sursum et gravia deorsum, etiam voluntatem movet secundum eius conditionem, non ex necessitate sed ut indeterminate se habentem ad multa" (p. 149:410–415). Also see ad 3 for this final point (p. 150:498–511).

26. Thomas introduces this particular part of his discussion by observing that God does not operate in natural things in such fashion that the natural thing itself would do nothing. In order to explain just how it is that God operates in the operations performed either by a natural agent or by a created will, he then introduces the fourfold way indicated in our text. See Marietti ed., pp. 57–58. In summing this up again at the end of the corpus of this same article, he makes it clear that he is applying this fourfold way in which God is the cause of created agents to volitions as well: ". . . sequetur quod ipse in quolibet operante immediate operetur, non exclusa operatione voluntatis et naturae" (p. 58).

27. Cf. the text from ST I, q. 105, a. 5, cited in n. 28. Cf. *De Veritate*, q. 24, a. 1, ad 5, cited in my *Metaphysical Thought of Thomas Aquinas*, chapter 11, n. 65.

28. See ST I, q. 105, a. 5 (Leon. 5.476). Cf. ad 3. Here Thomas is developing his answer to the question: "Utrum Deus operetur in omni operante." See my *Metaphysical Themes in Thomas Aquinas* (Washington, DC, 1984), p. 260. Also see my remark there in n. 56 about Thomas's views concerning God as the proper cause of *esse*.

29. For other texts on this correlation between created agents and God see, for instance, SCG III, c. 70 (ed. cit., p. 306). This does not mean that one part of the effect is caused by God and another by the created agent, but rather that the entire effect is to be assigned to God (as principal cause) and to the created natural agent (as an instrument). For additional texts where Thomas applies this to freely acting created agents, see SCG I, c. 68 (p. 64); SCG III, cc. 88, 89 (pp. 331–32). Note that Thomas concludes his discussion in c. 89 by appealing to the text from the *Eudemian Ethics* VII, c. 14. For texts where Thomas attempts to reconcile this theory of divine agency with human freedom see, for instance, *De Potentia*, q. 3, a. 7, ad 13; ad 14 (ed. cit., p. 59); ST I, q. 19, a. 8, and ad 3 (Leon. 4.244); ST I, q. 83, a. 1, ad 3 (Leon. 5.307); ST I–II, q. 10, a. 4, and ad 1 (Leon. 6.89); *De Malo*, q. 6 (as cited above in n. 25). For discussion see my *Metaphysical Themes*, pp. 258–63.

30. R. Garrigou-Lagrange seems to be of another opinion concerning this. In his *God: His Existence and His Nature* (St. Louis-London, 1949), Vol. 1, p. 268, after presenting Thomas's proof from motion, he comments: "This proof from motion may be exemplified in another way by considering motions of the spiritual order, as St. Thomas has done in the article of his *Summa* entitled, 'Whether the Will is Moved by any External Principle?' (Ia IIae, q. 9, a. 4)." However, Thomas does not present this kind of motion in that context as the starting point for his proof for God's existence. On the other hand, Garrigou-Lagrange makes some interesting points in his discussion of objections to the argument from motion (see pp. 270–87), although his treatment is not primarily historical.

31. Especially helpful with reference to this is Weisheipl's "The Principle *Omne Quod Movetur*," in his *Nature and Motion*, chapter 4, pp. 75–97. Also see there chapter 2 ("Natural and Compulsory Movement"); chapter 5 ("The Specter of *motor coniunctus* in Medieval Physics"). For Thomas's views on the generating principle as the moving principle or cause of the natural motions of physical bodies see pp. 90–93. Among the various passages he cites from Thomas note: *In VIII Phys.*, lect. 8 (Maggiòlo ed.), p. 542, n. 1036 (an excellent summarizing passage on which also see my *Metaphysical Thought of Thomas Aquinas*, chapter 11, n. 57); *In II Phys.*, lect. 1, p. 74, n. 144 (for further discussion see Weisheipl, p. 19, n. 78); *De Potentia*, q. 3, a. 7 (ed. cit., p. 57). For an interesting critique of Weisheipl's interpretation of Thomas's explanation of the natural motions of physical bodies see D. B. Twetten, "Back to Nature in Aquinas," *Medieval Philosophy and Theology* 5 (1996), pp. 205–43. On Thomas's acceptance of Aristotle's account of the motion of projectiles see Weisheipl, *Nature and Motion*, p. 31, n. 30; pp. 64–66. For Thomas see *In VIII Phys.*, lect. 22, pp. 621–22, nn. 1161–63; *In III De Caelo*, lect. 7 (Marietti ed.), p. 305, n. 591. For another succinct summarizing text see *De Potentia*, q. 3, a. 11 (ed. cit., p. 75).

32. See n. 21 above.

33. In connection with this Kenny comments that to explain the fall of such a body by the gravitational pull of the earth (with Newton) "would seem to be more favourable to Aristotle's principle than his own mechanics are" (*The Five Ways*, p. 16, n. 1). However, this seeming support from Newtonian mechanics for the Aristotelian-Thomistic principle proves to be a mixed blessing, as Kenny also points out: "For the gravitational attraction of two bodies is mutual, whereas the Aristotelian relation of 'moving' must be an asymmetrical one if it is to lead to an unmoved mover" (p. 30). Hence it seems better, if one would defend Thomas's principle of motion, to interpret it in the case of falling bodies as he did by applying it to the generating principle and by regarding this as the mover. For another succinct exposition of Thomas's theory as applied to natural and violent motion see A. Moreno, "The Law of Inertia and the Principle *Quidquid Movetur ab Alio Movetur*," *The Thomist* 38 (1974), pp. 316–25.

34. See Newton, *Optics*, Book III, Part I (in Great Books of the Western World, Vol. 34, p. 540): "By this principle [*vis inertiae*] alone there never could have been any motion in the world. Some other principle was necessary for putting bodies into motion; and now they are in motion, some other principle is necessary for conserving the motion." Cited by William Wallace, "Newtonian Antinomies against the *Prima Via*," *The Thomist* 19 (1956), p. 185; and by Kenny, *The Five Ways*, p. 28. For Descartes see his *Principles of Philosophy*, II, 36: "As far as the general (and first) cause is concerned, it seems obvious to me that this is none other than God Himself, who, (being all-powerful) in the beginning created matter with both movement and rest; and now maintains in the sum total of matter, by his normal participation, the same quantity of motion and rest as He placed in it at that time" (trans. and notes by V. Rodger Miller and R. P. Miller [Dordrecht-Boston-London, 1983], p. 58). In the immediately following context, Descartes argues for this from God's immutability and constancy. See II, 37 for his "first law of nature": "that each thing, as far as is in its power, always remains in the same state; and that consequently, when it is once moved, it always continues to move"

(p. 59). See II, 38 for his application of this to projectile motion (pp. 59–60). By seeking for some causal explanation for the continuation of such motion, today's defender of the Thomistic principle will be asking for a cause to account for more than the beginning of that motion.

35. For such a suggestion see J. Maritain, *Approaches to God* (London, 1955), pp. 24–27. Maritain reasons that if we do take the principle of inertia as established and if hypothetically we grant "it a meaning beyond the mere empiriological analysis of phenomena," it will be enough to take it as indicating that "Every body which undergoes a change *in regard to its state of rest or motion* changes under the action of another thing" (p. 26). For him this will suffice to preserve Thomas's principle that whatever is moved is moved by something else.

36. See Wallace, "Newtonian Antinomies against the *Prima Via*," pp. 173–86, especially p. 180.

37. See Weisheipl, *Nature and Motion*, pp. 31–33 (though it was first developed by the Franciscan Francis de Marchia, and then by Jean Buridan, presumably working independently. Thomists such as Capreolus and Domingo de Soto claimed that the impetus theory of motion was also Thomas's position); pp. 66–69, 95–96.

38. See Weisheipl, op. cit., pp. 36–42, 48, 49, 269; Moreno, "The Law of Inertia," pp. 307–13; Wallace, "Newtonian Antinomies against the *Prima Via*," pp. 178–80. Also cf. Kenny's presentation and discussion of what he describes as the "counter-attack with Mach" (op. cit., pp. 29–31).

39. Cf. E. Gilson, *Elements of Christian Philosophy* (Garden City, NY, 1960), p. 63: "To be both in act and in potency in the same respect would amount to being and not being in the same respect and at the same time." For an effort to free Thomas's argument from motion from an outmoded physical theory see MacDonald, "Aquinas's Parasitic Argument," pp. 135–38, where he overcomes projectile motion as a counterexample to the motion principle by restricting motion as used in the argument to alteration and increase and decrease in quantity. While this approach is philosophically defensible, it may grant more than is necessary to the alleged counterexample.

40. See Owens, "Immobility and Existence for Aquinas," in *St. Thomas Aquinas on the Existence of God* (Albany, 1980), pp. 219–20; "The Conclusion of the *Prima Via*," in ibid., pp. 148, 158–60, 166–68. Cf. chapter 11, n. 79 of my *Metaphysical Thought of Thomas Aquinas*. Also see the discussion concerning this occasioned by T. Kondoleon's review of Knasas's *The Preface to Thomistic Metaphysics* in his "The Start of Metaphysics," *The Thomist* 58 (1994), pp. 121–30; followed by Knasas, "Thomistic Existentialism and the Proofs *Ex Motu* at *Contra Gentiles* I, c. 13," *The Thomist* 59 (1995), pp. 591–615; and Kondoleon, "The Argument from Motion and the Argument for Angels: A Reply to John F. X. Knasas," *The Thomist* 62 (1998), pp. 269–90. Knasas defends and develops Owens's position on this. For a review and critique both of what he calls the "Physical" and the "Existential" readings of the first way see D. B. Twetten's "Clearing a Way for Aquinas: How the Proof from Motion Concludes to God," in *Proceedings of the American Catholic Philosophical Association* 70 (1996), pp. 260–64. See pp. 267–71 for his proposed "Metaphysical" reading, which in various respects is close to what I am proposing here.

41. See n. 8 above.

42. For discussion and reference to others such as Cajetan, S. Vanni Rovighi, Garrigou-Lagrange, and M. Cocci, see Van Steenberghen, *Le problème*, pp. 178–80. Also see MacDonald, "Aquinas's Parasitic Argument," pp. 146–55, who is struck by the fact that the first way establishes the existence of an unmoved mover, but not an immovable mover. To achieve this he believes it must be completed by other ways, such as the third and the fifth.

43. For Thomas see ST I, q. 3: "Cognito de aliquo an sit, inquirendum restat quomodo sit, ut sciatur de eo quid sit. Sed quia de Deo scire non possumus quid sit, sed quid non sit, non possumus considerare de Deo quomodo sit, sed potius quomodo non sit. Primo ergo considerandum est quomodo non sit; secundo, quomodo a nobis cognoscatur; tertio, quomodo nominetur" (Leon. 4.35). The lingering question is this: At this point in ST I, that is, after completing his five ways, does Thomas think that he has already demonstrated that only one God exists?

44. "Secunda via est ex ratione causae efficientis. Invenimus enim in istis sensibilibus esse ordinem causarum efficientium: nec tamen invenitur, nec est possibile, quod aliquid sit causa efficiens sui ipsius; quia sic esset prius seipso, quod est impossibile" (Leon. 4.31).

45. "Non autem est possibile quod in causis efficientibus procedatur in infinitum. Quia in omnibus causis efficientibus ordinatis, primum est causa medii, et medium est causa ultimi, sive media sint plura sive unum tantum: remota autem causa, removetur effectus: ergo, si non fuerit primum in causis efficientibus, non erit ultimum nec medium. Sed si procedatur in infinitum in causis efficientibus, non erit prima causa efficiens: et sic non erit nec effectus ultimus, nec causae efficientes mediae; quod patet esse falsum. Ergo est necesse ponere aliquam causam efficientem primam: quam omnes Deum nominant" (Leon 4.31).

46. See nn. 10, 11 above for references. Cf. Van Steenberghen, op. cit., p. 185.

47. For discussion of this see my *Metaphysical Thought of Thomas Aquinas*, chapter 11, section 2.

48. In the second way, however, from the very beginning of the argument the focus is on causes that are caused rather than on effects (as in *De Ente*, c. 4) or on things that are moved (as in the first way). In those two arguments Thomas subsequently shifts the focus to caused causes or to moved movers when he deals with the issue of an infinite regress.

49. See the remarks in my *Metaphysical Thought of Thomas Aquinas*, chapter 11, section 2 (*De Ente*, c. 4); chapter 11 section 4 (first argument, from motion, second and third arguments, against infinite regress); and chapter 12, section I (first way).

50. See the final part of the text as quoted above in n. 45.

51. In this discussion I am assuming that my way of interpreting the general procedure in c. 4 of the *De Ente* is correct. See my *Metaphysical Thought of Thomas Aquinas*, chapter 5, section I.

52. "Tertia via est sumpta ex possibili et necessario: quae talis est. Invenimus enim in rebus quaedam quae sunt possibilia esse et non esse: cum quaedam inveniantur generari et corrumpi, et per consequens possibilia esse et non esse. Impossibile est autem omnia quae sunt, talia [omit: semper] esse: quia quod possibile est non esse, quandoque non est. Si igitur omnia sunt possibilia non esse, aliquando nihil fuit in

rebus. Sed si hoc est [Van Steenberghen: esset] verum, etiam nunc nihil esset: quia quod non est, non incipit esse nisi per aliquid quod est; si igitur nihil fuit ens, impossibile fuit quod aliquid inciperet esse, et sic modo nihil esset: quod patet esse falsum. Non ergo omnia entia sunt possibilia: sed oportet aliquid esse necessarium in rebus" (Leon. 4.31). On the omission of *semper* from the text in accord with the majority of manuscripts see Van Steenberghen, *Le problème*, pp. 188–89; T. O'Brien, *Metaphysics and the Existence of God*, (Washington, D.C., 1960), pp. 226–27, n. 83; J. F. K. Knasas, "Making Sense of the *Tertia Via*," *New Scholasticism* 54 (1980), pp. 488–89; Kenny, *The Five Ways*, p. 55. With Van Steenberghen and O'Brien, I think it should be omitted. So, too, did Godfrey of Fontaines, if one may judge from the *abbreviatio* of the third way which he himself transcribed in the margin of a manuscript in his personal library, Paris, Bibl. Nat. 15.819, fol. 226r: "Impossibile est enim omnia possibilia esse, quia quod possibile est non esse, quandoque non est."

53. See my *Metaphysical Thought of Thomas Aquinas*, chapter 11, nn. 96, 97.

54. "Omne autem necessarium vel habet causam suae necessitatis aliunde, vel non habet. Non est autem possibile quod procedatur in infinitum in necessariis quae habent causam suae necessitatis, sicut nec in causis efficientibus, ut probatum est. Ergo necesse est ponere aliquid quod sit per se necessarium, non habens causam necessitatis aliunde, sed quod est causa necessitatis aliis: quod omnes dicunt Deum" (Leon. 4.31).

55. For references to many of these see J. Owens, "*Quandoque* and *Aliquando* in Aquinas's *Tertia Via*," *New Scholasticism* 54 (1980), pp. 447–75; Knasas, "Making Sense of the *Tertia Via*," pp. 476–511; Van Steenberghen, *Le problème*, p. 205, n. 37. Cf. my *Metaphysical Thought of Thomas Aquinas*, chapter 11, nn. 100, 102, 104. See T. K. Connolly, "The Basis of the Third Proof for the Existence of God," *The Thomist* 17 (1954), pp. 281–349, especially pp. 281–99, for a survey of much of the earlier literature concerning this.

56. On this see T. Miyakawa, "The Value and the Meaning of the 'Tertia Via' of St. Thomas Aquinas," *Aquinas* 6 (1963), pp. 250–51.

57. Though I have already cited the troublesome text above in n. 52, I will repeat the two troublesome sentences here and in n. 58. The first one reads: "Impossibile est autem omnia quae sunt, talia esse: quia quod possibile est non esse, quandoque non est." For some who hold that Thomas means to say that such a possible will be nonexistent at some point of time in the future see U. Degl'Innocenti, "La validità della 'terza via'," *Doctor Communis* 7 (1954), pp. 41–70, especially 51–56; Kenny, *The Five Ways*, pp. 57–58; Gilson, *The Christian Philosophy of St. Thomas Aquinas* (New York, 1956), p. 69. For some who take Thomas as wishing to say that any such possible being must have been nonexistent before it began to exist and who therefore see his statement as referring to the past see L. Chambat, "La 'Tertia Via' dans saint Thomas et Aristote," *Revue thomiste*, n. s. 10 (1927), pp. 334–38, especially 335; J. Bobik, "The First Part of the Third Way," *Philosophical Studies* (Maynooth) 17 (1968), pp. 142–60, esp. pp. 144–45; Owens, "*Quandoque* and *Aliquando* in Aquinas' *Tertia Via*," *New Scholasticism* 54 (1980), pp. 457–59; Van Steenberghen, *Le problème*, pp. 192–98. Still others give a nontemporal reading to *quandoque* and *aliquando* (see the following sentence in Thomas's text), meaning thereby that his purpose is rather to show that any possible being, if left to its

own devices, would be incapable of existing and therefore nonexistent. See, for instance, H. Holstein, "L'origine aristotélicienne de la 'tertia via' de saint Thomas," *Revue philosophique de Louvain* 48 (1950), pp. 366–67; Knasas, "Making Sense of the *Tertia Via*," pp. 486–89.

58. "Si igitur omnia sunt possibilia non esse, aliquando nihil fuit in rebus" (as cited in n. 52 above).

59. For some who would read the argument this way see Bobik, Owens, and Van Steenberghen as cited above in n. 57.

60. This point is brought out effectively by Bobik in his "The First Part of the Third Way," pp. 157–58. If a possible as Thomas here uses it is "a thing such by its nature that its non-existence both *precedes* and *follows* its existence," it is the period of preceding nonexistence which is essential for this step in the third way. Here the expression *quandoque* cannot mean "after," since the proof uses as its point of departure actually existing things which are capable of existing and not existing. "By elimination, therefore, 'quandoque' must mean *before*." Also see Owens, "*Quandoque* and *Aliquando* in Aquinas' *Tertia Via*," pp. 457–58, 472–73, n. 38.

61. See, for instance, Owens, "*Quandoque* and *Aliquando*," especially pp. 461–64, and p. 463, n. 26, for a defense and for references to other recent discussions of this. Also see L. Dewan, "The Distinctiveness of St. Thomas' 'Third Way'," *Dialogue* 19 (1980), 201–18.

62. Owens appeals to the Aristotelian procedure in *Metaphysics* XII, c. 6, according to which eternal motion and time are not destructible and presuppose the existence of separate substances. "The suicidal supposition that all things are possibles excludes *ipso facto* any eternal succession" (p. 461). "In the Aristotelian series no series can go backward eternally, if all things are possibles" (p. 462). In his effort to defend the argument against the charge of a quantifier shift, he contends that the argument does not reason that because "*each* possible was non-existent at one time, therefore all things if possibles were together non-existent at one time." Rather it reasons that "universal possibility ('all have the possibility for non-existence') entails universal non-existence" (p. 464). But how is this point demonstrated? Owens argues that to propose an infinite regress in time of possible beings would presume granting the reality of something necessary. In order to establish this, however, he is introducing a different kind of reasoning which in fact leads him to view this reasoning as essentially the same as that in SCG I, c. 15 (see pp. 464–66). In my judgment, however, this reasoning is missing from the text of the third way.

63. In fact, the reformulation is so pronounced that the third way will no longer be the third way of ST I, q. 2, a. 3. Moreover, unlike Owens (pp. 465–66), I do not regard the third way as it stands in ST I, q. 2, a. 3 as essentially the same argument as that presented in SCG I, c. 15. The presence of the temporal references in the first part of the third way and their absence from the first part of the argument in SCG I, c. 15 indicate an essential distinction between the two. For additional discussion of this difficulty with the third way, i.e., an apparent quantifier shift as he describes it, see Kenny, *The Five Ways*, pp. 63–65. While I have differed with Kenny's view that *quando* should be taken as referring to some time in the future rather than to the past, his criticisms of the passage now under consideration must be taken seriously. For some others who reject the validity of this step in Thomas's procedure see Bobik, "The First Part of the

Third Way," pp. 158–59; T. Pater, "The Question of the Validity of the *Tertia Via*," in Vol. 2 of *Studies in Philosophy and the History of Philosophy* (Washington, D.C., 1963), pp. 137–77 (for an extended critique of both of the difficult statements in the argument in light of the defenses offered by Connolly and Degl'Innocenti). On the other hand, D. O'Donoghue seems to be oblivious to this difficulty. See his "An Analysis of the *Tertia Via* of St. Thomas," *The Irish Theological Quarterly* 20 (1953), pp. 129–52.

64. For a brief resume of earlier twentieth-century scholarship concerning Aquinas's sources for his third way see Knasas, "Making Sense of the *Tertia Via*," pp. 477–80. For some who would see Maimonides as the major source see P. Gény, "À propos des preuves thomistes de l'existence de Dieu," *Revue de philosophie* 24 (1931), pp. 575–601, esp. 586–87; Gilson, *Le thomisme*, 6th ed. (Paris, 1965), pp. 79–81, apparently agreeing with C. Baeumker that here Thomas follows Maimonides step by step. For Baeumker see his *Witelo, Ein Philosoph und Naturforscher des XIII. Jahrhunderts* (Beitrgäe zur Geschichte der Philosophie des Mittelalters, III-2 [Münster, 1908]), p. 338. For Maimonides see *The Guide of the Perplexed*, S. Pines, trans. (Chicago, 1963), Book II, c. 1, pp. 247–48; *Dux seu Director Dubitantium aut Perplexorum*, (Paris, 1520; repr. Frankfurt, 1964), Book II, c. 2, fol. 40v. While there are similarities between Maimonides' presentation of this argument and that found in Aquinas, there are also significant differences between the two versions. Hence other writers have rightly concluded that Thomas's argument is not reducible to that of Maimonides. See, for instance, Chambat, "La 'Tertia Via'," pp. 334, 338; Holstein, "L'origine aristotélicienne de la 'tertia via'," p. 361. Some have singled out Aristotle's *De Caelo*, I, c. 12 as Thomas's source. See Connolly, "The Basis of the Third Proof," pp. 312–49, with special emphasis on Thomas's procedure in his Commentary on *De Caelo* I (*lectiones* 22–29); O'Donoghue, "An Analysis of the *Tertia Via* of St. Thomas," pp. 129–51 (*De Caelo* along with some other Aristotelian texts). For criticism of this effort to interpret the third way by means of Thomas's Commentary on *De Caelo* I see Knasas, "Making Sense of the *Tertia Via*," pp. 48–89. Still others single out *Metaphysics* XII, c. 6. See Chambat, pp. 335–38; Holstein, pp. 361–67; Knasas, p. 489. Yet, the parallelism is by no means perfect. Hence it seems best to acknowledge that while Aristotle is surely a source, Thomas is not simply repeating either his text or that of Maimonides (or Avicenna). See Owens, "*Quandoque* and *Aliquando*," p. 469; and n. 31 on Avicenna. In his "The Distinctiveness of St. Thomas' 'Third Way'," p. 213, n. 5, Dewan has proposed a text from Albert the Great's Commentary on the *Metaphysics* as another possible source for Thomas. See *Metaphysica* II.2 (Cologne, ed., 16.2, p. 482:40–71). While this is possible, the similarities between Thomas's text and Albert's can just as likely be traced back to their common sources, especially Aristotle and Maimonides.

65. For Kenny see *The Five Ways*, p. 67, and his discussion of Hume's critique in his *Treatise*. For the latter see *A Treatise of Human Nature*, L. A. Selby-Bigge, ed., 2nd rev. edition by P. H. Nidditch (Oxford, 1978), Book I, Pt. III, section 3 (pp. 78–80).

66. See my *Metaphysical Thought of Thomas Aquinas*, chapter 11, nn. 17, 18. Cf. n. 19.

67. In the argumentation in *De Ente*, c. 4 Thomas has already established real distinction of essence and *esse* in the beings with which he is concerned. In the third way he does not presuppose this point. For Thomas's own version of the first step in SCG I, c. 15, see chapter 11, section 4, n. 95.

68. See the text as cited above in n. 54.

69. Thomas's procedure in q. 11 indicates that he was fully aware of this.

70. For a listing of various suggested explanations of this and for discussion see Van Steenberghen, *Le problème*, pp. 203–5.

71. See my *Metaphysical Thought of Thomas Aquinas*, chapter 11, section 1 and section 4 (n. 87).

72. "Quarta via sumitur ex gradibus qui in rebus inveniuntur. Invenitur enim in rebus aliquid magis et minus bonum, et verum, et nobile: et sic de aliis huiusmodi. Sed *magis et minus* dicuntur de diversis secundum quod appropinquant diversimode ad aliquid quod maxime est: sicut magis calidum est, quod magis approximant maxime calido. Est igitur aliquid quod est verissimum, et optimum, et nobilissimum, et per consequens maxime ens: nam quae sunt maxime vera, sunt maxime entia, ut dicitur II *Metaphy.*" (Leon. 4.32). I have followed a suggestion by Van Steenberghen by assuming that the term *tale* is to be understood after *maxime est* in the third sentence. The logic of the argument demands this ("But more and less are said of different things insofar as they approach in different fashion something which is [such: inserted] to a maximum degree"). See *Le problème*, p. 213. For the text from Aristotle see his *Metaphysics* II, c. I (993b 30–31). Fabro notes that both here and in the reference to Aristotle's *Metaphysics* in the second stage of the argument Thomas has in mind this same general passage from *Metaphysics* II (see 993b 25–31); but in the earlier version which appears in SCG I, c. 13, Thomas had referred not only to this text in Aristotle but to another from *Metaphysics* IV, c. 4 (1008b 31–1009a 2). For Fabro see his "Sviluppo, significato e valore della 'IV Via,'" *Doctor Communis* 7 (1954), p. 78; cf. p. 75, n. 5. In citing Aristotle's *Metaphysics* (993b 30–31) Thomas has converted the references to *vera* and *entia*, but legitimately so in light of the convertibility of ontological truth and being.

73. Leon. 22.1.5:161–6:200. Cf. Thomas's reply to objection 4: ". . . dicendum quod verum est dispositio entis non quasi addens aliquam naturam nec quasi exprimens aliquem specialem modum entis sed aliquid quod generaliter invenitur in omni ente, quod tamen nomine entis non exprimitur . . ." (p. 7:229–234). Cf. ad 6. Cf. J. A. Aertsen, *Medieval Philosophy and the Transcendentals* (Aertsen: Leiden-New York-Cologne, 1996), c. 6 (pp. 243–89); Wippel, "Truth in Thomas Aquinas," *Review of Metaphysics* 43 (1989), pp. 307–21.

74. "Quod autem dicitur maxime tale in aliquo genere, est causa omnium quae sunt illius generis: sicut ignis, qui est maxime calidus, est causa omnium calidorum, ut in eodem libro dicitur. Ergo est aliquid quod omnibus entibus est causa esse, et bonitatis, et cuiuslibet perfectionis: et hoc dicimus Deum" (Leon. 4 32). For Aristotle see n. 72 above.

75. On Thomas's derivation of the transcendentals see my *Metaphysical Thought of Thomas Aquinas*, chapter 6, section 5. Goodness expresses the agreement of being with the appetitive power of the soul in that the good is that which all things desire (Leon. 22.1.5:156–159). On the transcendental character of goodness also see ST I, q. 5, a. 1 (*bonum* and *ens* are the same in reality though they differ according to reason); a. 2 (in terms of its intelligible content being [ens] is prior to goodness); a. 3 (every being insofar as it is being is good). On this final point also see Thomas's *In De Hebdomadibus*,

lect. 3 (Leon. 50.275:40–277:143); lect. 4 (pp. 279:111–280:160). Cf. Thomas's *De Malo*, q. 1, a. 1 (Leon. 23.5–6) and a. 2 (pp. 10:130–11:195); *De Veritate*, q. 21, a. 1 (Leon, 22.3.592:89–594:244); a. 2 (p. 596:61–96). The whole of q. 21 is highly recommended to the reader. Also see Aertsen, *Medieval Philosophy and the Transcendentals*, c. 7, esp. pp. 299–319.

76. For discussion of Thomas's hierarchical view of the universe of created being see, for instance, Gilson, *The Christian Philosophy of St. Thomas Aquinas*, Part Two (London, 1961), pp. 147–248; J. de Finance, *Être et agir*, 2nd ed. (Rome, 1960), pp. 31–55; J. Legrand, *L'univers et l'homme dans la philosophie de saint Thomas*, Vol. I (Brussels, 1946); J. H. Wright, *The Order of the Universe in the Theology of St. Thomas Aquinas* (Rome, 1957); O. Blanchette, *The Perfection of the Universe according to Aquinas* (University Park, PA, 1992).

77. On the convertibility of truth and being see *De Veritate*, q. 1, a. 1 and ad 4 (cited in n. 73 above). Also see his reply to objection 5: ". . . concludit Philosophus quod idem est ordo alicui rei in esse et veritate, ita scilicet quod ubi invenitur quod est maxime ens, est maxime verum" (Leon. 22.1.7:242–245). For Aristotle see *Metaphysics* II, c. I (cited in n. 72 above). Here Thomas has not converted *ens* and *verum*. He distinguishes truth as it exists in the intellect (what we may refer to as "logical" truth) from truth of being ("ontological" truth). In addition to *De Veritate*, q. 1, a. 1, see a. 2 (Leon. 22.1.9); *In I Sent*, d. 19, q. 5, a. 1 (note in particular: ". . . verum per prius dicitur de veritate intellectus, et de enuntiatione dicitur inquantum est signum illius veritatis; de re autem dicitur, inquantum est causa . . ." [Mandonnet ed., Vol. 1, p. 486]); SCG I, c. 60; ST I, q. 16, a. 2. See a. 3 and ad 1 on the convertible character of *verum* and *ens*. For fuller discussion see J. Vande Wiele, "Le problème de la vérité ontologique dans la philosophie de saint Thomas," *Revue philosophique de Louvain* 52 (1954), pp. 521–71, esp. 545–54; F. Ruello, *La notion de vérité chez Saint Albert le Grand et Saint Thomas d'Aquin de 1243 à 1254* (Louvain-Paris, 1969), pp. 179–227 (on *In I Sent.*, d. 19, q. 5. a. 1); Aertsen and Wippel as cited above in n. 73.

78. For brief discussions of this see Garrigou-Lagrange, *God: His Existence and His Nature*, Vol. I, p. 306; Van Steenberghen, *Le problème*, pp. 209, 216. For SCG I, c. 28, see ed. cit., p. 29 ("Et dico universaliter"). Note that in this context Thomas also applies *nobilitas* to wisdom. While granting this, for the sake of simplicity I will restrict it within the context of the fourth way to transcendental perfections. Also see M. Wagner, *Die philosophischen Implikate der "Quarta Via." Eine Untersuchung zum Vierten Gottesbeweis bei Thomas von Aquin (S.Th. I, 2, 3c)* (Leiden, 1989), pp. 95–97. He considers and rightly rejects identifying the *nobile* with the beautiful.

79. See Thomas's discussion of God's *scientia, vita, et voluntas* in ST I, qq. 14, 15, 18, and 19.

80. See Fabro, "Sviluppo, significato et valore," pp. 101–2; Van Steenberghen, *Le problème*, pp. 215–16. As Van Steenberghen points out, for Aristotle and his medieval followers, fire is hot of its essence and to the maximum degree. While they regarded the sun as the cause of heat in earthly things, they did not regard it as hot in itself (see n. 20, where he corrects Fabro on this detail). For fuller discussion see Wagner, *Die philosophischen Implikate*, pp. 115–21. While he concludes that this example would have been illuminating for Thomas's contemporaries who shared his world-view,

Wagner denies that the controlling principle of the first part of the fourth way rests upon the example for its justification (p. 120).

81. For Thomas's text see n. 74 above. See M. Corvez, "La quatrième voie vers l'existence de Dieu selon saint Thomas," in *Quinque sunt viae*, L. J. Elders, ed. (Vatican City, 1980), pp. 75–83, esp. pp. 77–78 (he reasons from diversity of beings in the world to the distinction of essence and existence in such beings, and from this to their efficiently caused character); Garrigou-Lagrange, *God: His Existence and His Nature*, Vol. I, pp. 301–17. Cf. Wagner, op. cit., pp. 18–25 (on Garrigou-Lagrange's approach). For a helpful summary of some other recent approaches see J. Bobik, "Aquinas's Fourth Way and the Approximating Relation," *The Thomist* 51 (1987), pp. 17–36.

82. For the text see n. 74 above. For others who agree that in its first stage the argument is based solely on exemplar causality and is intended by Thomas to establish the existence of a really existing Maximum (or God) see L. Charlier, "Les cinq voies de saint Thomas," in *L'existence de Dieu* (Tournai-Paris, 1961), pp. 181–227, especially pp. 208–11; Van Steenberghen, *Le problème*, p. 211; A. Little, *The Platonic Heritage of Thomism* (Dublin, 1949), pp. 62–68, 80, and c. VII (passim); Bobik, "Aquinas's Fourth Way," pp. 33–36 (along with other authors cited in this article). Cf. J.-P. Planty-Bonjour, "Die Struktur des Gottesbeweises aus den Seinsstufen," *Philosophisches Jahrbuch* 69 (1962), pp. 282–97, who rather sees the entire proof as resting solely on what he calls the principle of participation through formal hierarchy, without relying on efficient causality. For discussion see Wagner, *Die philosophischen Implikate*, pp. 29–37.

83. For this text see my *Metaphysical Thought of Thomas Aquinas*, chapter 11, n. 10.

84. See ibid., n. 11.

85. According to Augustine, if I am to recognize any number, or the laws of number, this can only be because the notion of number is already "impressed" on my mind. So too, if I am to recognize immutable truths such as that all men desire happiness or seek to be wise, these notions too must in some way already be impressed on my mind, presumably through divine illumination. See his *De Libero Arbitrio*, Book II, c. 8 and c. 9; (CCSL Vol. 29, pp. 250–52, 254).

86. For the text see my *Metaphysical Thought of Thomas Aquinas*, chapter 11, n. 8.

87. For Boethius see his *Consolation of Philosophy*, Book III, pr. 10 in *Boethius: The Theological Tractates. The Consolation of Philosophy*, H. F. Stewart, E. K. Rand, S. J. Tester (Cambridge, MA, 1978), p. 274:9–15: "Omne enim quod inperfectum esse dicitur, id inminutione perfecti inperfectum esse perhibetur. Quo fit, ut si in quolibet genere inperfectum quid esse videatur, in eo perfectum quoque aliquid esse necesse sit. Etenim perfectione sublata, unde illud quod inperfectum perhibetur exstiterit ne fingi quidem potest." For Anselm see his *Monologium*, cc. 1, 4 (Schmitt ed., Vol. I, pp. 14–15, 17–18).

88. Ed. cit., p. 14. For this text see chapter 11 of my *Metaphysical Thought of Thomas Aquinas*, n. 87 and my discussion there.

89. See Little, *The Platonic Heritage of Thomism*, p. 100: "But though St. Thomas obviously considers that his statement needs no proof, philosophers of lower but yet good intelligence do not find the statement in the sense just explained self-evident . . ." Also see Van Steenberghen, *Le problème*, who notes that Thomas presents the princi-

ple as immediately evident or as *per se notum*; he does not demonstrate it. See pp. 209–10. Cf. Maritain, *Approaches to God*, pp. 40–43.

90. "Sviluppo, significato e valore," pp. 81 (for the text); 82 (on the privileged character of this presentation); 89–102 (interpretation of the argument). On the date, see Jean-Pierre Torrell, *Saint Thomas Aquinas: The Person and His Work* (Washington, DC, 1996), p. 339.

91. See *Lectura super evangelium Johannis*, Busa ed., Vol. 6, p.227: "Quidam autem venerunt in cognitionem dei ex dignitate ipsius dei: et isti fuerunt platonici. Consideraverunt enim quod omne illud quod est secundum participationem, reducitur ad aliquid quod sit illud per suam essentiam, sicut ad primum et ad summum; sicut omnia ignita per participationem reducuntur ad ignem, qui est per essentiam suam talis. Cum ergo omnia quae sunt, participent esse, et sint per participationem entia, necesse est esse aliquid in cacumine omnium rerum, quod sit ipsum ipsum esse per suam essentiam, idest quod sua essentia sit suum esse: et hoc est deus, qui est sufficientissima, et dignissima, et perfectissima causa totius esse, a quo omnia quae sunt, participant esse." Note that this is one of four ways (*modi*) in which Thomas here remarks that the ancient philosophers came to knowledge of God. For all four see Fabro, "Sviluppo, significato et valore," pp. 79–82.

92. For some other texts see, for instance, ST I, q. 44, a. 1: "Si enim aliquid invenitur in aliquo per participationem, necesse est quod causetur in ipso ab eo cui essentialiter convenit; sicut ferrum fit ignitum ab igne." Cf. the reply to obj. 1: "... quia ex hoc quod aliquid per participationem est ens, sequitur quod sit causatum ab alio. Unde huiusmodi ens non potest esse, quin sit causatum..." (Leon. 4.455). See *De Substantiis Separatis*, c. 3, where Thomas is attempting to bring out points of agreement between Plato and Aristotle. After referring to Plato's theory of participation he comments: "... omne autem participans aliquid accipit id quod participat ab eo a quo participat, et quantum ad hoc id a quo participat est causa ipsius: sicut aër habet lumen participatum a sole, quae est causa illuminationis ipsius" (Leon. 40.D46:11–15). Also see *Compendium Theologiae*, c. 68: "... omne quod habet aliquid per participationem reducitur in id quod habet illud per essentiam sicut in principium et causam, sicut ferrum ignitum participat igneitatem ab eo quod est ignis per essentiam suam" (Leon. 42.103:18–22). Cf c. 123: "Item, ea quae sunt per participationem reducuntur in id quod est per essentiam sicut in causam: omnia enim ignita suae ignitionis ignem causam habent aliquo modo," (Leon. 42.127:27–30). Cf. Wagner, *Die philosophischen Implikate*, pp. 103–5.

93. See my *Metaphysical Thought of Thomas Aquinas*, chapter 4, n. 7 for the "definition" of participation offered by Thomas in his Commentary on the *De Hebdomadibus*: when something receives in particular fashion that which belongs to another in universal (total) fashion, it is said to participate in it. See n. 8 there for the third kind of participation—that whereby an effect participates in its cause. It is under this third kind, as we have seen, that participation of beings in *esse* is to be placed.

94. See the texts cited in n. 92 above on the connection between being participated and (efficiently) caused. Also see *Metaphysical Thought of Thomas Aquinas*, chapter 5, section 4, for texts where Thomas reasons directly from the participated character of

*esse* in particular beings to real distinction and composition of essence and *esse* therein. A merely conceptual distinction between essence and act of being will not suffice to account for the fact that given beings really do participate in *esse*. See, for instance, the text from Quodlibet 2, q. 2, a. 1, cited in *Metaphysical Thought of Thomas Aquinas*, chapter 5, n. 98. This is why he can reason from the participated character of such beings to the composition of essence and *esse* within them, and thus to their being efficiently caused.

95. See *Metaphysical Thought of Thomas Aquinas*, chapter 5, section 4.

96. Leon. 4.42. Note in particular: "Si igitur ipsum esse rei sit aliud ab eius essentia, necesse est quod esse illius rei vel sit causatum ab aliquo exteriori, vel a principiis essentialibus eiusdem rei. Impossibile est autem quod esse sit causatum tantum ex principiis essentialibus rei: quia nulla res sufficit quod sit sibi causa essendi, si habeat esse causatum. Oportet ergo quod illud cuius esse est aliud ab essentia sua, habeat esse causatum ab alio." Since this cannot be said of God, Thomas concludes that in him essence and act of being cannot differ.

97. The question may be raised concerning whether he regarded these points as necessary but as implied by his texts, or whether he did not even regard them as essential for an argument based on participation. While this is difficult to determine on purely historical grounds, they seem to me to be necessary for such an argument on philosophical grounds.

98. On the other hand, if one grants that this stage succeeds in establishing the existence of a maximum in the order of ontological truth, goodness, and nobility, one should also grant its inference that a maximum exists in the order of being.

99. For this text see ed. cit., p. 49. Fabro seems to regard all three arguments as proofs for God's existence. See his "Sviluppo, significato et valore," pp. 75–78. On these texts also see Van Steenberghen, *Le problème*, pp. 140–43, who regards only the first as an argument for God's existence.

100. Ed. cit., p. 49. Note especially: "Oportet enim, si aliquid unum communiter in pluribus invenitur, quod ab aliqua una causa in illis causetur; non enim potest esse quod illud commune utrique ex se ipso conveniat, cum utrumque, secundum quod ipsum est, ab altero distinguatur; et diversitas causarum diversos effectus producit."

101. "Sviluppo, significato et valore," p. 77.

102. *Le problème*, p. 221. Cf. p. 140.

103. Van Steenberghen also regards this as a way of showing that *esse* is efficiently caused in finite beings by an infinite being. See *Le problème*, p. 221, n. 1.

104. For the text, see n. 74 above. This part of the proof hardly seems to be crucial if one appeals to efficient causality (or to participation) in the argument's first stage, although it will still serve to complete the overall argumentation.

105. "Quinta via sumitur ex gubernatione rerum. Videmus enim quod aliqua quae cognitione carent, scilicet corpora naturalia, operantur propter finem: quod apparet ex hoc quod semper aut frequentius eodem modo operantur, ut consequantur id quod est optimum; unde patet quod non a casu, sed ex intentione perveniunt ad finem. Ea autem quae non habent cognitionem, non tendunt in finem nisi directa ab aliquo cognoscente et intelligente, sicut sagitta a sagittante. Ergo est aliquid intelligens, a quo omnes res naturales ordinantur ad finem: et hoc dicimus Deum" (Leon: 4.32).

106. For these see *The Metaphysical Thought of Thomas Aquinas*, chapter 11, section 3 (and nn. 33, 34); section 4 (n. 90), and my discussion there.

107. That Thomas is aware of this distinction is indicated by the fact that he immediately offers some argumentation to show that natural bodies act for an end, i.e., the fact that they always or at least more frequently act in the same way in order to obtain that which is best.

108. See *De Veritate*, q. 5, a. 2; Leon. 22.1.143:141–148 (cited in my *Metaphysical Thought of Thomas Aquinas*, chapter 11, n. 31).

109. Leon. 43.41:120–42:19. For Aristotle see *Metaphysics* II, c. 2 (994b 13–16).

110. Leon. 43.42:19–41. For Avicenna see his *Sufficientia*, I, c. 14 (Venice, 1508), fol. 22rb.

111. See Mandonnet ed., Vol. 2, p. 645 (where Thomas is defending the presence of free will in God). Note from his response: "Determinatio autem agentis ad aliquam actionem, oportet quod sit ab aliqua cognitione praestituente finem illi actioni."

112. Leon. 6.9. Note Thomas's comment regarding this determination to an end: "Haec autem determinatio, sicut in rationali natura fit per rationalem appetitum, qui dicitur voluntas; et in aliis fit per inclinationem naturalem, quae dicitur appetitus naturalis." For discussion see J. Maritain, *A Preface to Metaphysics* (New York, 1948), pp. 124ff.; C. A. Hart, *Thomistic Metaphysics: An Inquiry into the Act of Existing* (Englewood Cliffs, NJ, 1959), pp. 65–66, 298; G. Klubertanz, "St. Thomas' Treatment of the Axiom, *Omne Agens Agit Propter Finem*," in *An Etienne Gilson Tribute*, C. J. O'Neil, ed. (Milwaukee, 1959), pp. 104–5. For this same kind of argumentation also see SCG III, c. 2, where it appears within a series of arguments intended to show that "omne agens in agendo intendit aliquem finem." Some of these are, in fact, rather aimed at showing that one cannot regress to infinity in actions. For criticism of a number of them see Kenny, *The Five Ways*, pp. 98–103. Curiously, however, Kenny omits the argument just mentioned which is, in my judgment, the most effective one offered there or elsewhere by Thomas. As it runs in the *Summa contra Gentiles*: "Item. Si agens non tenderet ad aliquem effectum determinatum, omnes effectus essent ei indifferentes. Quod autem indifferenter se habet ad multa, non magis unum eorum operatur quam aliud: unde a contingente ad utrumque non sequitur aliquis effectus nisi per aliquid determinetur ad unum. Impossibile igitur esset quod ageret. Omne igitur agens tendit ad aliquem determinatum effectum, quod dicitur finis eius" (ed. cit., p. 228).

113. See *The Metaphysical Thought of Thomas Aquinas*, chapter 11, nn. 30, 31. For similar reasoning see SCG III, c. 3, where Thomas presents a series of arguments to show that "omne agens agit propter bonum." See the third argument beginning with "Adhuc." Note especially: "Videmus autem in operibus naturae accidere vel semper vel frequentius quod melius est . . . Si igitur hoc evenit praeter intentionem naturalis agentis, hoc erit a casu vel fortuna. Sed hoc est impossibile: nam ea quae accidunt semper vel frequenter, non sunt casualia neque fortuita, sed quae accidunt in paucioribus . . . Naturale igitur agens intendit ad id quod melius est . . ." (ed. cit., 229).

114. For Aristotle see *Physics* II, c. 5, passim. For Boethius see his *Consolation of Philosophy*, Book V, pr. I. Note in particular his definition of chance: "Licet igitur definire casum esse inopinatum ex confluentibus causis in his quae ob aliquid geruntur eventum" (*The Theological Tractates . . . The Consolation of Philosophy*, ed. cit., pp. 386–88).

115. See Thomas's Commentary on Aristotle's discussion of chance in the *Physics*, especially *In II Phys.* lect. 8, pp. 105–6, nn. 214–15. The text of the fifth way seems to leave the last point mentioned in my text unclear: Is Thomas there holding that natural agents act so as to reach that which is best for themselves, or that which is best for the whole of nature? The first alternative would be enough to support his claim that since such agents act to attain that which is best for them always or at least in the greater number of cases, such action cannot be owing to chance. The second alternative seems to be suggested by Thomas's conclusion from the fifth way that there is one intelligent being by which all natural things are ordered to their end. Hence it seems that Thomas would defend both alternatives and that they are not mutually exclusive. Cf. Van Steenberghen, *Le problème*, p. 231. But this again raises the question whether this argument succeeds in proving that there is one supreme intelligence.

116. For the text see above, n. 105.

117. For the text from *In II Sent.*, d. 25, q. 1, a. 1, see Mandonnet ed., Vol. 2, p. 645 (cf n. 111 above). Note: ". . . nec aliquod agens finem sibi praestituere potest nisi rationem finis cognoscat et ordinem ejus quod est ad finem ipsum, quod solum in habentibus intellectum est . . ."

118. See n. 112 above for ST I–II, q. 1, a. 2. The text continues: "Illa vero quae ratione carent, tendunt in finem per naturalem inclinationem, quasi ab alio mota, non autem a seipsis: cum non cognoscant rationem finis, et ideo nihil in finem ordinare possunt, sed solum in finem ab alio ordinantur" (Leon. 6.9). For a fuller discussion of natural appetite, sensitive appetite, and rational appetite (will) see *De Veritate*, q. 25, a. 1. In describing natural appetite Thomas comments: ". . . nihil enim est aliud appetitus naturalis quam quaedam inclinatio rei et ordo ad aliquam rem sibi convenientem, sicut lapidis ad locum deorsum" (Leon. 22.3.729: 131–36).

119. For the text from ST I–II, q. 1, a. 2, see Leon. 6.9.

120. Mandonnet ed., Vol. 2, p. 645.

121. "Ad formam autem consequitur inclinatio ad finem, aut ad actionem, aut aliquid huiusmodi: quia unumquodque, inquantum est actu, agit, et tendit in id quod sibi convenit secundum suam formam" (Leon. 4.63).

122. See Leon, 22.3.729:141–44: "Sed haec apprehensio praeexigitur in instituente naturam, qui unicuique naturae dedit inclinationem propriam sibi convenientem."

123. According to Van Steenberghen, none of the five ways, with the exception of the fourth, establishes the uniqueness of God. And as he sees things, the fourth way is invalid as it is presented in ST I, q. 2. a. 3. See *Le problème*, pp. 235–36, 297. However, if one recasts the fourth way as I have proposed above in order to defend its validity, one may still raise the issue of divine unicity at its conclusion.

124. In a. 1 Thomas asks whether unity adds anything to being. As he explains, unity does not add any real thing to being but only the negation of division of being from itself; because of this it follows that unity is convertible with being. In a. 2 he distinguishes the way in which numerical unity is opposed to numerical multiplicity from the way in which unity of being is opposed to multitude. In a. 4, while showing that God is supremely one (*maxime unus*), he concentrates on ontological unity rather than on divine uniqueness. God is supremely one because he is supremely undivided from himself; this follows from the fact that he is perfectly simple. On the transcendental one see Aertsen, *Medieval Philosophy and the Transcendentals*, pp. 201–42.

125. Leon. 4.111. Note in particular: "Manifestum est enim quod illud unde aliquod singulare est *hoc aliquid*, nullo modo est multis communicabile . . . Hoc autem convenit Deo: nam ipse Deus est sua natura, ut supra ostensum est. Secundum igitur idem est Deus, et hic Deus. Impossibile est igitur esse plures Deos."

126. Leon. 4.35. Cf. n. 43 above.

127. See Thomas's general introduction to q. 3: "Tertio: utrum sit in eo compositio quidditatis, sive essentiae, vel naturae, et subiecti" (p. 35). In a. 3 itself Thomas begins his response this way: "Respondeo dicendum quod Deus est idem quod sua essentia vel natura" (p. 39).

128. ST I, q. 3, a. 3 (Leon. 4.39–40. Note in particular: ". . . sciendum est, quod in rebus compositis ex materia et forma, necesse est quod differant natura vel essentia et suppositum . . . unde id quod est homo, habet in se aliquid quod non habet humanitas." For fuller discussion of the relationship between nature and supposit see my *Metaphysical Thought of Thomas Aquinas*, chapter 8, section I.

129. Leon. 4.40.

130. ST I, q. 3, a. 2 (Leon. 4.37–38).

131. Leon. 4.111. Note especially: "Secundo vero, ex infinitate eius perfectionis. Ostensum est enim supra quod Deus comprehendit in se totam perfectionem essendi. Si ergo essent plures dii, oporteret eos differre. Aliquid ergo conveniret uni, quod non alteri."

132. Ibid.

133. See n. 131 above.

134. Leon. 4.50. Note: "Deus autem ponitur primum principium, non materiale, sed in genere causae efficientis: et hoc oportet esse perfectissimum . . . Secundum hoc enim dicitur aliquid esse perfectum, secundum quod est actu: nam perfectum dicitur, cui nihil deest secundum modum suae perfectionis."

135. Ibid. ". . . ipsum esse est perfectissimum omnium: comparatur enim ad omnia ut actus. Nihil enim habet actualitatem, nisi inquantum est: unde ipsum esse est actualitas omnium rerum, et etiam ipsarum formarum."

136. Leon. 4.51–52. Note that if Thomas holds that an effect preexists in a more perfect efficient cause in more perfect fashion, such is not true of the way an effect preexists in the potency of its material cause. There it preexists more imperfectly.

137. Leon. 4.52. Note: "Omnium autem perfectiones pertinent ad perfectionem essendi: secundum hoc enim aliqua perfecta sunt, quod aliquo modo esse habent. Unde sequitur quod nullius rei perfectio Deo desit."

138. As Thomas introduces his reply: "Respondeo dicendum quod Deus non solum est sua essentia, ut ostensum est, sed etiam suum esse" (Leon. 4.42).

139. Ibid. See n. 96 above.

140. Leon. 4.42. In q. 3, a. 1 see corpus, arg. 2 (Leon. 4.35–36).

141. Leon. 4.42.

142. Leon. 4.72. Cf. chapter 9 of my *Metaphysical Thought of Thomas Aquinas*, nn. 41, 42, 43, 44, 48 on form or act as limited by matter as a potency that receives it, and the application of the axiom that unreceived act is unlimited to the issue of divine infinity.

143. Leon. 4.72. Note: "Cum igitur esse divinum non sit esse receptum in aliquo, sed ipse sit suum esse subsistens . . . ; manifestum est quod ipse Deus sit infinitus et perfectus." Central to this argument is the assumption that unreceived *esse* is unlimited. Thomas often appeals to this axiom in order to establish divine infinity. See, for

instance, *In I Sent.*, d. 8, q. 2, a. 1 (Mandonnet ed., Vol. 1, p. 202); *In I Sent.*, d. 43, q. 1 a. 1 (p. 1003); SCG I, c. 43 (ed. cit., p. 41); SCG II, c. 52 (for which see n. 149 below); *Compendium Theologiae*, c. 18 (Leon. 42.88:7–8).

144. Ed. cit., p. 38 ("Praeterea"). Kretzmann rejects this argument on the grounds that it implicitly assumes "that every characteristic must count either as a perfection or as an imperfection," which strikes him as false. I assume he envisions the possibility of a distinguishing characteric in one all-perfect being which would distinguish it from another without itself being a perfection or an imperfection. For Thomas, however, to the extent that such a characteristic is actual (there could be no passive potentiality in an all-perfect being), it must be a perfection. And if it is a privation or negation of something positive present in another all-perfect being, it would have to be counted as a lack of perfection in the first all-perfect being, i.e., an imperfection. For Kretzmann see *The Metaphysics of Theism* (Oxford, 1997), p. 160. For his presentation and defense of another more extensive argument for God's uniqueness in c. 42 based on Thomas's earlier conclusion that God is a necessary being *per se*, see pp. 161–65.

145. ". . . Deus tamen, qui non est aliud quam suum esse, est universaliter ens perfectum. Et dico universaliter perfectum, cui non deest alicuius generis nobilitas" (ed. cit., 29).

146. Ed. cit., pp. 29–30, cited in my *Metaphysical Thought of Thomas Aquinas*, chapter 5, n. 109. See my comments in chapter 5, section 5 on Thomas's references to a "power of being" in this text and elsewhere. On this particular text also see Kretzmann, op. cit., pp. 133–38.

147. Ed. cit., p. 30: "Amplius. Unumquodque perfectum est inquantum est actu; imperfectum autem secundum quod est potentia cum privatione actus. Id igitur quod nullo modo est in potentia sed est actus purus, oportet perfectissimum esse."

148. Ed. cit., p. 145. For discussion of the first three arguments see my *Metaphysical Thought of Thomas Aquinas*, chapter 5, section 2, and nn. 51–54.

149. Ed. cit., p. 145: ". . . esse enim quod omnino est infinitum, omnem perfectionem essendi comprehendit; et sic, si de duobus talis adesset infinitas, non inveniretur quo unum ab altero differret."

150. For a number of these see *The Metaphysical Thought of Thomas Aquinas*, chapter 5, section 2.

151. Note that this argument is preceded by another less persuasive one which reasons that if the term "god" is applied equivocally, to say "there are many gods" will not be to the point. If it is applied univocally, the many gods would have to agree in genus or in species. But he has shown that God cannot be a genus or species (Leon. 42.87:1–10). For the argument analyzed in our text see p. 87:11–21. Cf. n. 125 above for ST I, q. 11, a. 3.

152. Leon. 42.87:22–35. In *De Ente*, c. 4. Thomas had also mentioned reception of a form in matter as another possible way of multiplying specific forms in individuals, and rejected this as not applicable to subsisting *esse*. See Leon. 43:376:105–377:121.

153. Indeed, the conclusion established by each of the five ways he has identified with God. Compare the conclusion of the second way (and of the first and third, for that matter) with the conclusion of the fifth way.

154. See my *Metaphysical Thought of Thomas Aquinas*, chapter 11, n. 76 for the text and discussion of the same.

155. Cf. *In II Sent.*, d. 25, q. 1, a. 1 (Mandonnet ed., Vol. 2, p. 645); *De Veritate*, q. 25, a. 1 (Leon. 22.3.729:141–44), cited above in n. 122.

156. I am assuming here that for Thomas the ultimate efficient cause of a finite nature is the cause both of its essence and its act of being (*esse*). See, for instance, *De Potentia*, q. 3, a. 5, ad 2 (ed. cit., p. 49).

157. Leon. 4.166. For more on Thomas's view that knowledge involves possessing the form of a thing in immaterial fashion see ST I, q. 84, aa. 1–2.

158. Leon. 4.166–67.

159. See ST I, q. 13, a. 5: "Et sic, quidquid dicitur de Deo et creaturis, dicitur secundum quod est aliquis ordo creaturae ad Deum, ut ad principium et causam, in qua praeexistunt excellenter omnes rerum perfectiones" (Leon. 4.147).

160. For a helpful review of a number of these competing interpretations, see Van Steenberghen, *Le problème*, pp. 238–41.

161. See his "A propos des 'Cinq voies,'" *Revue des sciences philosophiques et théologiques* 27 (1938), pp. 577–82. To support his case Motte cites the dependency of the five ways as they are presented in the *Summa Theologiae* upon Thomas's argumentation in SCG I, cc. 13 and 15, and the explicit references in SCG to historical sources, that is, to the arguments by which philosophers and *doctores Catholici* have proved that God exists (SCG I, c. 13, ed. cit., p. 10). Thomas there goes on to offer two detailed arguments based on motion, each of which he assigns to Aristotle, another argument taken from Aristotle's *Metaphysics* II (to refute appeal to an infinite regress of efficient causes), one taken from both *Metaphysics* II and IV (based on degrees of truth), and one explicitly assigned to John Damascene (the argument from the way things are governed). One of the arguments offered for divine eternity in SCG 1, c. 15 strongly foreshadows the third way. However, Motte (pp. 579–80) does not bring out sufficiently the differences between the argument from divine governance in SCG I, c. 13 and the fifth way, and between the argument based on possible and necessary being of SCG I, c. 15 and the third way. See p. 580 for his still sound conclusion that no systematic idea or scheme predetermined either the organization or the number of the five ways.

162. L. Charlier rejects the first effort (to reduce the five ways to a single proof; though they complement one another, each is a distinct proof), but supports the second claim (Thomas thought that all other valid proofs could be reduced to the five ways). See his "Les cinq voies de saint Thomas," pp. 189–90. In addition to Motte's critique of efforts to reduce the five ways to complementary aspects of a single proof (p. 577), see Van Steenberghen, *Le problème*, pp. 238–41 (especially for his résumé and critique of more recent efforts to reduce the five ways to a single organizing principle or scheme). Owens comments: "The impression that the five ways are the only ones recognized by Aquinas, and that all other variations have to be reduced in one way or another to their forms, stems from the Neoscholastic manuals." See his "Aquinas and the Five Ways," in *St. Thomas Aquinas on the Existence of God*, p. 257, n. 1.

163. See, for instance, L. Elders, "Justification des 'cinq voies,'" *Revue thomiste* 61 (1961), pp. 207–25 (most surprising is his attempt to base the first way on material causality); H. Johnson, "Why Five Ways? A Thesis and Some Alternatives," in *Actes du quatrième congrès international de philosophie médiévale* (Montreal, 1969), pp. 1143–54,

especially pp. 1143–45 (who would base the third way on material causality). For Elders's more recent thought concerning this see his "Les cinq voies et leur place dans la philosophie de saint Thomas," in *Quinque sunt viae*, L.J. Elders, ed., Studi tomistici 9 (Vatican city, 1980), pp. 133–46. Here he continues to reduce the five ways to the four kinds of causality, again basing the first way on material causality and basing the third way on a fifth kind of causality, God's communication of *esse* to other things (pp. 138–39). See p. 141 (for his critique of efforts by A. Kenny to link the third way to material causality); p. 145 (for his conclusion that because of the close bond between the five ways and the kinds of causality, a new proof for God's existence which would differ fundamentally from the five ways is not possible). Now also see his *The Philosophical Theology of St. Thomas Aquinas* (Leiden, 1990), pp. 85–88. For Kenny see *The Five Ways*, pp. 35–37. Also see Maritain, *Approaches to God*, pp. 18–19, for the view that because the various ways start from different facts based on experience, they are specifically distinct proofs. Also see M. F. Johnson, "Why Five Ways?" in *Proceedings of the American Catholic Philosophical Association* 65 (1991), pp. 107–21, who, unsuccessfully, in my opinion, proposes still another organizing principle for the first four ways based on Aristotle's discussion of actuality and potentiality in *Metaphysics* IX, while the fifth way would attain to God as the source of directed motion. He rightly regards the five ways as formally distinct proofs (pp. 110, 115). For an earlier attempt to find a key to the organization of the first four ways in Aristotle's discussion of actuality and potentiality in *Metaphysics* IX see L. Dewan, "The Number and Order of St. Thomas's Five Ways," *Downside Review* 92 (1974), pp. 1–18.

164. H. J. Johnson, op. cit., p. 1151.

# 4

# Form and Existence

## *Peter Geach*

H ERE I SHALL DISCUSS WHAT AQUINAS meant by his term *esse*, or *actus essendi*, act of 'existing'. Another synonym that he uses, *quo aliquid est*, 'that by which a thing is (or: exists)' suggests a convenient division of the subject: we can first discuss Aquinas's philosophical use of *quo*, 'that by which', and then consider which sense of *est*, which sort of existential proposition may be relevant to Aquinas's doctrine of *esse*. But we shall see that, having got thus far, we cannot arrive at the meaning of the whole phrase, *quo aliquid est*, or the reasons for the way Aquinas uses it, simply by combining our separate considerations about *quo* and *est*.

## I

Beginning with Aquinas's use of *quo* brings a great immediate advantage. The predicate *est*, 'is' or 'exists', is at least a peculiar one, and many people would deny that it is properly a predicate at all; but Aquinas uses *quo* not only with *est* but also with unexceptionable predicates. In this use, *quo* followed by a noun subject and an (ordinary) predicate is synonymous with the phrase formed by the abstract noun answering to the predicate followed by the genitive of the noun that was subject; *quo Socrates albus est* ('that by which Socrates is white') is synonymous with *albedo Socratis* ('the whiteness of Socrates') and so on. Either kind of phrase is thus used in order to designate what Aquinas calls Forms; to understand his use of *quo* we must examine his notion of forms, which moreover is intimately connected in other ways with his doctrine of *esse*.

For Aquinas, the real distinction between a form and the self-subsistent individual (*suppositum*) whose form it is comes out in the logical distinction between subject and predicate (Ia. q.13 art.12; q.85 art.5 ad 3 um). I think this is the way to introduce his notion of form to modern philosophers. There are, however, strong prejudices against allowing that this logical distinction answers to *any* real distinction. One such obstacle is the old two-name or identity theory of predication, which flourished in the Middle Ages, and still keeps on appearing in new guises: the theory that a true predication is effected by joining different names of the same thing or things, the copula being a sign of this real identity. I shall not waste time on this logically worthless theory. Anybody who is tempted by it may try his hand at explaining in terms of it how we can fit together the three terms 'David', 'father', and 'Solomon' (which on this theory are three *names*) to form the true predication 'David is the father of Solomon'.

The futility of the two-name theory comes out clearly at the beginning of Lewis Carroll's *Game of Logic*. Lewis Carroll professes to find a difficulty over saying 'some pigs are pink'; as it stands, this suggests an impossible identity between certain things (pigs) and a certain attribute (signified by 'pink')! He seeks to remove this difficulty by expounding the proposition as meaning 'some pigs are pink pigs,' where 'are' signifies real identity. But 'pink pigs' means 'pigs that are pink,' and there is as much or as little difficulty about this phrase as about the predication 'pigs are pink' at which he stumbles.

If noun-phrases like 'thing that runs' can properly be regarded as names (a difficult problem of logical theory that cannot be discussed here), then it *is* possible to state the truth-condition of an affirmative predication as an identity of reference between two names; 'a man runs', let us say, is true if and only if 'man' and 'thing that runs' are two names of the same individual. Aquinas uses this way of stating truth-conditions quite often, and has in consequence been wrongly regarded as holding the two-name theory. But it is not the name 'thing that runs' that is used in the sentence 'a man runs,' but the predicate 'runs' from which this name is formed; and 'runs' and 'thing that runs' are by no means synonymous; the relation between their ways of signifying in fact raises over again the same problem as the relation of subject and predicate, a problem that is thus merely shifted by expressing the truth-conditions of predication in terms of identity of reference.

Modern philosophers have pretty generally abandoned the two-name theory; at least to the extent of admitting that a logical subject and a predicate have radically different ways of signifying. But need we admit also a difference of type as regards the realities signified? Surely what distinguishes a predicate from a name is just the fact that it does not *name* anything, but is rather true or false *of* things; a true predication is one in which the predicate *is true of* what the subject names. Are we not blurring this distinction if we say that predicates stand for (why not, that they *name*?) a type of entity other than that which names stand for? Have not philosophers said the queerest things about the entities that predicates are supposed to stand for? No wonder; such paradoxes are bound to arise if you treat as a name what is not a name; like the paradoxes about Nobody in *Through the Looking-glass.*

But, whatever difficulties it may involve, I think we have to allow that logical predicates do stand for something, as well as being true or false *of* things. For when a question *how many* is asked and answered, we can surely ask: To what is this manyness being ascribed? And in any concrete instance we shall find that in asserting manyness we use a logically predicative word or phrase, and are ascribing manyness to what this stands for. 'How many ducks are swimming in the Chamberlain Fountain?' 'Three'. If this answer were true, there would be objects of which 'duck swimming in the Chamberlain Fountain' could truly be predicated; and my number-statement is about what this predicate stands for. You cannot say my statement ascribes a property (threeness) to a certain set of individuals—the ducks swimming in the Chamberlain Fountain. So far as I know no ducks are swimming there; and it makes no difference whether there are any or not; for the sense of the question how many such ducks there are cannot depend on what the right answer to the question is. Now the answer 'three' cannot be taken as a predication about a set of ducks unless the question answered is a question about them; but the question how many such ducks there are *admits* of the answer '0'; and noughtishness certainly is not here being taken as a property of any set of ducks. You may indeed rightly say that my proposition is about *ducks* (not: *the* ducks) swimming in the Chamberlain Fountain. The omission of the definite article is here significant. A proposition that could rightly be called 'a proposition about *the* ducks (etc.)' *would* have to refer (or at least profess to refer) to a certain set of ducks; but in speaking of 'a proposition about ducks (etc.)' I am not implying that the proposition mentions any individual ducks, but on the contrary that it is about what the predicate 'duck swimming in the Chamberlain Fountain' stands for.

It is only to what such a predicative expression stands for that we can even falsely ascribe manyness. It is nonsense, unintelligible, not just false, to ascribe manyness to an individual; what can be repeated must be a common nature. *Non enim potest nec in apprehensione cadere pluralitas huius individui* (Ia. q.13 art.9). Because, for Aquinas, forms are what answer *in rebus* to logical predicates, it is consistent for him to say that forms are as such multipliable (Ia. q.3 art.2 ad 3 um; q.7 art.1).

I cannot help being reminded here of the very similar language that we find in Frege. Frege, like Aquinas, held that there was a fundamental distinction *in rebus* answering to the logical distinction between subject and predicate—the distinction between *Gegenstand* (object) and *Begriff* (concept). (In using *Be-*

*griff* as a term for what logical predicates represent, Frege was not accepting any form of conceptualism; on the contrary, he explicitly denies that the *Begriff* is any creature of the human mind—it is, he says, 'objective'.) And for Frege the *Begriff*, and it alone, admits of repetition and manyness; an object cannot be repeated—*kommt nie widerholt vor.*

Understood in this way, the distinction between individual and form is absolutely sharp and rigid; what can sensibly be said of one becomes nonsense if we try to say it of the other. (Aquinas's 'subsistent forms' might seem to bridge the gulf; but, as we shall presently see, they do not, nor did Aquinas really think they do.) Just because of this sharp distinction, we must reject the Platonic doctrine that what a predicate stands for is some single entity over against its many instances, *hen epi pollôn.* On the contrary: the common nature that the predicate 'man' (say) stands for can be indifferently one or many, and neither oneness nor manyness is a mark or note of human nature itself. This point is very clearly made by Aquinas in *De Ente et Essentia.* Again we find Frege echoing Aquinas; Frege counts oneness or manyness (as the case may be) among the properties (*Eigenschaften*) of a concept, which means that it cannot at the same time be one of the marks or notes (*Merkmalen*) of that concept. (Frege's choice of words is here unfortunate; his saying that it is an *Eigenschaft*, e.g., of human nature to be found in many individuals has led people to suppose that he regards this as a *proprium* of human nature—although so to read him makes complete nonsense of his distinction. Aquinas's saying that oneness or manyness is incidental, *accidit*, to human nature is a much clearer expression.)

The Platonic mistake about the nature of forms goes with a liberal use of what we may class together as abstract-singular expressions like 'X-ness' or 'the attribute of being X'; these expressions are not just grammatically but also logically, argumentatively, handled as though they were proper names. I do not say that such abstract expressions looking like proper names should be totally banned; it would make things very difficult for philosophers. (I myself used 'human nature' in this way in the last paragraph.) But I do say that anyone who uses them ought to be ready to replace them on demand by use of the concrete predicates from which they are derived. (Thus: for 'neither oneness nor manyness is a mark of human nature itself' read 'whether there is one man or many men is irrelevant to what X must be if X is a man', or something like that.) Sometimes this replacement is stylistically better, sometimes not. But it must be possible; a sentence with an *irreducible* abstract 'proper name' in it (say: 'Redness is an eternal object') is nonsense.

All the same, Platonism of this sort is a very great temptation; and I think it is instructive to watch Frege's unsuccessful struggles against temptation in his paper *Ueber Begriff und Gegenstand* ("On Concept and Object"). I quote (op. cit., p. 197):

In logical discussions one quite often needs to assert something about a concept, and to express this in the form usual for such assertions, viz. to make what is asserted of the concept into the content of the grammatical predicate. Consequently, one would expect that the reference of the grammatical subject would be the concept; but the concept as such cannot play this part, in view of its predicative nature; it must first be converted into an object, or, speaking more precisely, represented by an object. We designate this object by prefixing the words 'the concept': e.g., "The concept *man* is not empty." Here the first three words are to be regarded as a proper name.

And later on (p. 198): "In my way of speaking, expressions like 'the concept F' designate not concepts but objects."

Of course Frege has gone astray here: he does not clear himself of the charge of having made a concept into an object just by saying that 'the concept *man*' does not stand for a concept but for an object that 'represents' a concept; no more than a writer can escape the charge of vulgarity by a parenthetical "to use a vulgarism." But how then are we to get into the subject of predication a direct reference to what Frege calls a concept and Aquinas calls a form? I think the solution, the way to avoid the mistake of Platonism, is that an abstract noun (or noun-phrase) referring to the form can indeed occupy the place of the subject, but cannot be the whole of the subject; the form being signified, *in recto* as Aquinas would say, by an abstract noun, we must add a mention *in obliquo* of the individual whose form it is; 'the wisdom of Socrates' and 'the redness of Socrates' nose' give us designations of forms, the spurious proper names 'wisdom' and 'redness' do not.

We must not construe 'the wisdom of Socrates' as 'wisdom which Socrates possesses': apart from lapsing into the Platonic error of taking 'wisdom' as a singular term, we should run into notorious antinomies about the relation supposedly meant by 'possesses'. 'Of' in 'the wisdom of Socrates' does not signify a special relation, as in such phrases as 'the statue of Socrates' or 'the shield of Socrates'. The statue is *of* Socrates by being related to him in one way, the shield is *of* Socrates by being related to him in another way; but if we start saying "and the wisdom is *of* Socrates . . ." we have already gone wrong, for logically 'the wisdom of Socrates' does not split up into 'the wisdom' and 'of Socrates' (sc. 'that wisdom which is *of* Socrates') but into 'the wisdom of . . .' and 'Socrates'. What refers to a form is 'the wisdom of . . ', not the whole phrase 'the wisdom of Socrates'; 'the wisdom of . . .' needs to be completed with a name of something that has the form, just as the predicate ' . . . is wise', which also stands for this form, needs to be completed by a subject.

'Of' is a logically inseparable part of the sign 'the wisdom of . . .', indicating the need to put a name after this sign; and this need is what makes the sign suitable to express a form, since a form, as Aquinas says, is more properly termed *entis* than *ens* (Ia. q.45 art.4). The linguistic oddity of the division into 'the wisdom of . . .' and 'Socrates'—a division that cannot be made in Latin at all—is quite trivial and accidental; in Hebrew, for example, such a division would be perfectly natural, since 'the wisdom of Socrates' would be rendered by inflecting the word for 'wisdom' and leaving the name 'Socrates' uninflected.

It may be asked: How *can* a form be designated both by a logical predicate like '. . . is wise' *and* by an expression like 'the wisdom of . . .'? These sorts of expressions are certainly not interchangeable; but I think we can show that the difference between them is only *secundum modum significandi*, not *secundum rem significatam*; it relates to the way we are talking about a form, and makes no difference to which form we are talking about. When we want to mention a form for the sake of expressing the supposition that in a given individual that form is found, we refer to it by an expression which together with the name of that individual forms a proposition—i.e., by a logical predicate like 'is wise'. But when we want to talk directly about the form itself, to get a reference to the form into the subject-place in our proposition, then we need to refer to the form by an expression which, together with a reference *in obliquo* to that in which the form is found, will compose a complex that can replace a logical subject—e.g., the expression 'the wisdom of . . .'.

It admittedly looks queer that a form cannot be designated either (say) by 'redness' alone or by 'the redness of Socrates' nose', but only by 'the redness of . . .' (understood to be followed by some name or other). We may help our understanding by the analogous case of functions in mathematics: neither the isolated square-root sign nor (say) '$\sqrt{25}$' designates a function, but rather the circumstance that the square-root sign is followed by some numeral or other.

This comparison of forms to functions in mathematics seems to me very useful; it was suggested to me by Frege's assimilation of his *Begriffe* to mathematical functions. (Frege indeed held that *Begriffe are* a sort of functions, which can take only two values, the 'true' value and the 'false' value; I shall not try to explain here this part of his doctrine, and would emphasize that I am asserting no more than an analogy between forms and functions.) It may for instance help us to see how 'of' in 'the wisdom of Socrates' does not stand for a special relation of 'inherence in' or 'belonging to'. Somebody ignorant of mathematics might take 'the square root of 25' to mean 'that one among square roots which belongs to 25', and wonder how one number can 'belong' to another; but somebody who understands the term 'square root' can already understand 'square root of 25' and can see that a relation of 'belonging' does not come in. So also somebody who understands the term 'wisdom', and does not Platonically misunderstand it as a proper name, already understands the make-up of the phrase 'wisdom of Socrates' without needing to understand the mythical relation of inherence. The term 'wisdom', like the term 'square root', of itself demands a genitive to complete its sense.

Again, in the sense of the word 'form' that we have so far used, what the phrase 'the wisdom of Socrates' designates is not a form *simpliciter*, but can legitimately be said to be a form *of* Socrates, a form occurring in Socrates. This too can be elucidated by our mathematical analogy. Consider the square-root function: we cannot say that the number 5 is that function or any other function, but we can say that the number 5 is that function *of* the number 25. So also the wisdom of Socrates is not a form *simpliciter* but *is* a form *of* or *in* Socrates. What designates a form is not the whole phrase 'the wisdom of Socrates', but merely 'the wisdom of . . .', although without completion this latter phrase is senseless.

Now at this point I think Aquinas's terminology is defective. He emphatically rejects the Platonic error of taking 'wisdom' as the proper name of a form; he says, e.g., that when (pseudo-) Dionysius speaks of life *per se* and wisdom *per se*, we are not to take this authority to be meaning certain self-subsistent entities (*quasdam subsistentes res*) (Ia. q.44 art.3 ad 4 um). But he often uses the term 'form' for what is referred to by a phrase like '*sapientia Socratis*' ('the wisdom of Socrates'); whereas if we keep to the sense of 'form' that we have so far used, a sense that is also to be found in Aquinas, what designates a form is rather '*sapientia*' together with the genitive inflexion of the following noun. The syntax of Latin impedes clear statement of this point, and Aquinas could not, of course, use our mathematical analogy for elucidation.

I am here leaving myself open to the charge of developing a new doctrine of form and departing from Aquinas's own doctrine. But if we will not impute to Aquinas a slight and natural inexactness of language at this point, then his doctrine of form becomes mere inconsistency and nonsense. For 'the wisdom of *Socrates*' must designate something individual, something that is no more multipliable or expressible by a predicate than Socrates himself is; so if this is taken to be a typical designation of a form, the whole distinction between form and individual is undone. To keep our heads clear, we must distinguish two senses of 'form' in Aquinas—the form that is the reference of the predicate '. . . is wise' or of the phrase 'the wisdom of . . .', and the form that is the reference of a phrase like 'the wisdom of Socrates'. In the latter case I shall speak of individualized forms; individualized forms will then not be forms *simpliciter* (just as a number that is a certain function of another number is not a function *simpliciter*) and will always be referred to by the full style 'individualized forms'.

This distinction is needed in order to make Aquinas's doctrine of subsistent or separate forms logically intelligible. When Aquinas tells us that God is wisdom itself, *Deus est ipsa sapientia*, he is not meaning that God is that of which the noun 'wisdom' is a proper name; for the Platonists are wrong in thinking that there is such an object, and Aquinas says that they are wrong. But we *can* take it to mean that 'God' and 'the wisdom of God' both designate the same thing; and this interpretation does not make Aquinas guilty of the impossible and nonsensical attempt to bridge the distinction previously expounded between form and individual, or find something intermediate. For we can significantly say that 'God' and 'the wisdom of God' and 'the power of God' are three terms with the same reference; but 'the wisdom of . . .' and 'the power of . . .' have not the same reference, any more than the predicates 'wise' and 'powerful' have. *Non dicimus quod attributum potentiae sit attributum scientiae, licet dicamus quod scientia (Dei) sit potentia (Dei)* (Ia. q.32 art.3 ad 3 um).

This account, it may be argued, departs fatally from Aquinas's mind, in that it makes out that in 'the wisdom of God' and 'the power of God', 'the wisdom of' and 'the power of' differ in reference from the word 'God' and from one another; for this conflicts with Aquinas's teaching on the divine simplicity. But what *we* signify by 'the wisdom of' and 'the power of' is really distinct; otherwise 'the wisdom of Socrates' would coincide in reference with 'the power of Socrates'. On the other hand what we signify by 'the wisdom of' is not, and is not signified as being, a part or element of what we signify by 'the wisdom of God', i.e. (according to Aquinas), God himself. If one designation is part of another, it does not follow that the things designated are respectively part and whole. 'The square root of 25' is a complex designation having as parts the designations 'the square root of' and '25'; but it does not follow (as Frege oddly inferred) that there is some sense of 'part' in which we may suitably say that the number 5, which is the square root of 25, has two heterogeneous parts—the square-root function and the number 25. Again to get an analogy to the three designations 'God', 'the wisdom of God', and 'the power of God', the square and the cube are quite distinct functions, but '1' and 'the square of 1' and 'the cube of 1' all designate the same number, and there is no distinction even in thought between the 1 that is the square and the 1 that is the cube and the 1 that is squared and cubed.

The supposition that $x$ itself is that by (or in virtue of) which $x$ is $F$ is certainly not logically absurd on the face of it (as would be the supposition that $x$ was identical with the reference of the predicate '$F$', an individual with a form). It will be instructive to consider an example from modern philosophy in which the assertion of identity between $x$ and what makes $x$ to be $F$ might seem plausible, and to see why such identity must be here denied. The red-patch school of philosophy might well wish to say that a red patch in a sense-field neither is the red-patchiness of some other individual (of a *suppositum*) nor yet has any individualized forms distinct from itself. That in virtue of which the patch is red, that in virtue of which it is *so* big, that in virtue of which it is square, is nothing other than the patch itself, which is red, *so* big, and square.

But now let us observe our red square; after a short time it begins a gradual change, and the outer region of the square becomes green, while an inner region remains red and is circular in shape. Are we then to say 'The red was square and larger, and has become circular and smaller', or rather 'The square was all red and has become partly green'? Plainly we may say either—or rather *both*. But now the individual red and the individual square appear as distinct individual things, each with its own distinct persisting identity; there is no third individual, the red square; *rubrum et quadratum non est ens*. I do not mean, of course, that there cannot be a red square *object*; but then the persistent identity of this object will not consist in any simple sensible character like redness or squareness. It is because the philosophers' red square is supposed to have no characteristics except a few simple sensible ones that it falls to pieces under examination; for to each such character there answers a distinct individual reality, an individualized form—an individual extension, colour, shape, etc. and though these are united in one *suppositum x* as the redness of *x*, the squareness of *x*, etc., they are not all one thing, the red patch; the red patch has no identity of its own, *non est vere unum nec vere ens*.

These examples of individualized forms may be objectionable to some people as factitious philosophical examples. But a wave, for example, is an identifiable individual that can move locally (although Professor Prichard *knew* that it was nonsense to say so); and this is certainly an individualized form—it is that by which a certain body of water is in a certain shape over part of its surface.

## II

The expression 'that by which the individual *x* is (or: exists)' is senseless unless there is a sense in which 'is' or 'exists' is properly predicable of individuals. Now many modern philosophers would deny that there is such a sense: 'exists' is not a predicate. This maxim is often glibly and thoughtlessly used, but it has a serious use; it is an attempt to resolve the paradox of reference that arises over the denial of existence. For we *can* significantly and truly deny existence; indeed I should hold that there is no sense of 'exists' for which we do not get significant and true denials of existence. (Some philosophers have thought otherwise—that, for a certain sense of the verb 'to be', 'A is' or 'A's are' is a form of proposition that is always true; even dragons *are*, even round squares *are*, in this sense! But at any rate to a discussion of Aquinas this supposed sense is irrelevant; we may stick to the everyday senses of 'to be' or 'to

exist' for which existence *can* be truly denied.) How is such denial possible? It
might look as though 'A is not' or 'A does not exist' were never true; for if it
were, the subject-term 'A' would fail to have reference, and so no predication
would have been made at all, let alone a true predication.

We can get out of this difficulty by denying that in 'A is not' or 'A does not
exist' the verb 'is' or 'exists' is a logical predicate. For since 'subject' and 'predicate' are correlatives, this is tantamount to denying that the grammatical subject 'A' is a logical subject. And from this again it follows that the proposition
'A does not exist' is not really about what the subject 'A' ostensibly stands for;
so in asserting the proposition we do not fall into the absurdity of using 'A' as
though it stood for something and then in effect denying that it does so.

But though saying that 'exists' or 'is' is not a genuine logical predicate of individuals would thus resolve the paradox of non-existence, this does not prove
that it is not, sometimes at least, a genuine logical predicate; for the paradox
might be resoluble some other way. Moreover, it is not enough to say that in
'A does not exist' 'A' cannot be the genuine subject of predication, unless at the
same time we can bring out the real logical role of 'A' the real logical nature of
existential propositions.

I think it is a great mistake to treat all existential propositions as having the
same logical status. I am not here concerned with the familiar thesis that existence is an analogical notion—that questions of existence are different according to what it is whose existence is in question, a God, an historical character, an animal species, a sub-atomic particle . . . Quite apart from these
differences, we have to recognize three different kinds of existential proposition even about the same kind of things—e.g., about the existence of living
creatures. The difference perhaps comes out best when we take negative
propositions as our examples.

A.  There is no such thing as Cerberus; Cerberus does not exist, is not real.
B.  There is no such thing as a dragon; dragons do not exist.
C.  Joseph is not and Simeon is not.

The A proposition that I gave as an example might typically be used to
comfort a child who had been frightened by hearing Greek myths and thought
Cerberus would come and bite him. "Cerberus," we might say "doesn't exist (is
not real) like Rover." Here we are not pointing out any trait that Cerberus has
and Rover lacks; for it would be nonsense to speak of the trait of *being what
there is such a thing as*, and more nonsense to say that some things (e.g., Rover)
have this trait, while other things (e.g., Cerberus) lack it, and are thus things
that there is no such thing as. Logically our proposition is about a difference
not between two dogs, Cerberus and Rover, but between the uses of two words

'Cerberus' and 'Rover'. The word 'Rover' is seriously used to refer to something and does in fact so refer; the word 'Cerberus' is a term that we only make believe has reference.

Since 'Cerberus does not exist' and 'Rover does exist' have not (as they seem to have) the names of two dogs as their logical subjects since we are not here *using* 'Cerberus' and 'Rover' as names, but talking *about* their use, it is appropriate to say that in A propositions 'exists' or 'is real' is not a predicate, not even of the word 'Cerberus'. To show the real force of the parent's reassuring "Cerberus does not exist," and how it is about the word 'Cerberus', we cannot content ourselves with writing, "(The word) 'Cerberus' does not exist," but must completely recast the sentence, say as follows: "When I said 'Cerberus' in that story, I was only pretending to use it as a name."

As regards the B proposition 'there is no such thing as a dragon' or 'dragons do not exist', it is equally clear that this cannot be referring to an attribute of *being what there is such a thing as*, which cows have and dragons lack. But there is also a great difference between A and B propositions. In the A proposition we have an ostensible use of a proper name; in the B proposition we have a descriptive, predicable expression like 'cow' or 'dragon'—what Frege would have called a *Begriffswort* (concept-word).

The difference between A and B propositions may perhaps come out better if I shift to another pair of examples. A certain astronomer claimed to have identified an intra-Mercurian planet, which he christened 'Vulcan'. His claim was not substantiated; and a modern astronomer would accordingly say 'Vulcan did not exist' (an A proposition); he would also say, 'So far as we know, an intra-Mercurian planet does not exist' (a B proposition). The force of the A proposition is to deprecate the premature introduction of the term 'Vulcan' into astronomical discourse. But in the B proposition the astronomer does not deprecate the use of the term 'intra-Mercurian planet', but himself uses that term to make a scientific remark. He is not, however, using the term as a name, as a subject of predication, but as a logical predicate. 'There is no intra-Mercurian planet' means 'nothing at all is an intra-Mercurian planet'. (Similarly, the affirmative B proposition 'there is a hairless cat' means 'something or other is a hairless cat'.) Now the use of a logical predicate in general does not commit you to allowing that there is something it applies to; it does so commit you if you make an affirmative assertion with that as the predicate but not if, e.g., you use the predicate negatively or in the antecedent or consequent of a hypothetical. So saying "nothing whatever is an intra-Mercurian planet" does not commit you to allowing that there is after all such a planet.

The importance of B propositions is that the question whether there is *a* so-and-so, what Aquinas calls the question *an est?*, has to be answered with an affirmative or negative B proposition. Aquinas realized the logical peculiarity of

B propositions: that the B proposition 'an F exists' does not attribute actuality to an F, but F-ness to something or other; e.g., 'there is evil' does not mean 'evil has actual existence' but 'some things have defects' (Ia. q.48 art.2 ad 2 um).

And let us not think this is so because of some peculiarity of the term 'evil'; Aquinas speaks of the question *an est?* quite generally in the place I have cited, and says that the 'existence' involved in a true affirmative answer to it consists in the truth of an affirmative predication (*compositio*). This is exactly right, for 'an F exists' is true if and only if 'F' is truly predicable of something or other. Moreover, the same logical status is expressly ascribed to 'God exists', or 'there is a God' (Ia. q.3 art.4 ad 2 um); and Aquinas expressly denies that this proposition relates to what *he* calls God's *esse* or *actus essendi*. (This most important negative indication as to how we must understand the term *esse* has often been overlooked.) In 'God exists' we are not predicating something of God, but predicating the term 'God' itself; 'God exists' means 'something or other is God'. When we see this, we can steer our way safely through all the shoals of the seventeenth-century ontological argument. (Though it is commonly called by the same name, I think Anselm's argument is essentially different; I shall not here discuss it.)

It is important that for Aquinas 'God' is a descriptive, predicable term (*nomen naturae*—Frege's *Begriffswort*) and not a logically proper name. Only because of this can the question whether there is one God or many make sense; just as the question whether there is one sun or many makes sense only if 'sun' is used to mean 'heavenly body of such-and-such a nature', not if it is a proper name of *this* heavenly body (Ia. q.13 art.9). Only because of this can the heathen say his idol is God and the Christian contradict him and both be using 'God' in the same sense; if 'God' were a proper name, it would be a logically impossible, not a lying, wicked, act, to predicate it of sticks and stones (Ia. q.13 art.10).

This may seem to raise difficulties about another view of Aquinas I have discussed—that 'God' in the context of the phrases 'the power of God' and 'the wisdom of God' has the same reference with either of these phrases, namely God himself. If 'God' is a predicative expression, how can it significantly stand in place of a proper name like 'Socrates', after 'the wisdom of' or 'the power of'? I think it is enough to reply that 'God' in *such* contexts, or indeed in subject position before 'is wise' or 'is powerful', has the force of a definite description 'the one and only God'; whatever our theory of descriptions may be, it will have to yield the result that a definite description can significantly take the place of a proper name, as subject of a proposition or again after a phrase like 'the wisdom of'.

We now come on to C propositions like 'Joseph is not and Simeon is not'. It would be quite absurd to say that Jacob in uttering these words was not talking about Joseph and Simeon but about the use of their names. Of course he was talking about his sons; he was expressing a fear that something had happened to them, that they were dead. We have here a sense of 'is' or 'exists' that seems to me to be certainly a genuine predicate of individuals; the sense of 'exist' in which one says that an individual came to exist, still exists, no longer exists, etc.; the sense of 'to be' in which God says of himself "I am who *am*" (i.e., "I am he who *is*"), or in which Homer spoke of the Gods who ever are, *aien eontes*. Now why should one suspect that this cannot be a genuine predicate of individuals? The fact that in A and B propositions the verb 'exist' or 'be' is not such a genuine predicate tells us nothing about C propositions.

Moreover, we cannot argue that if the C proposition 'x is not' is true, then the subject term 'x' no longer has anything to refer to and therefore no predication has been made. As Wittgenstein says (*Philosophische Untersuchungen* I.§40): "That is to confound the reference (*Bedeutung*) of the name with the bearer of the name. When Mr. N. N. dies, we say that the bearer of the name dies, not that the reference dies. And it would be nonsensical to say that; for if the named ceased to have reference, it would make nonsense to say 'Mr. N. N. is dead.'" To put the same thing another way: The reference of a name admits of no time qualifications; names are tenseless. Octavian was not known as 'Augustus' till quite later in his career; but once the name was in established use with that reference, it could be used by anybody at any time, in relation to any stage of Octavian's career (e.g., in answering the question "Where was Augustus born?") and regardless of whether Octavian was alive or dead. So negative C propositions can raise no paradoxes of reference and in showing this we had no need to deny that in them 'is' or 'exists' is a genuine predicate.

Now it is *this* sense of 'is' or 'exists', the one found in C propositions, that is relevant to Aquinas's term *esse*. This interpretation, I maintain, alone makes coherent sense of all that Aquinas says about *esse*.

It is worth noticing that as regards living beings 'to be' (in the C sense) has the same reference as 'to live', *vivere viventibus est esse* (Ia. q.18 art.2). This may confirm us against sophistical attempts to show that the verb 'to be' in this sense is not a genuine predicate of individuals. "Poor Fred was alive and is dead"; how could one argue that this is not a genuine predication about poor Fred? And what difference does it make if we say instead, "Poor Fred *was*, and *is not*"?

Some people may not easily see the difference between 'God exists' (sense B) and 'God is' (sense C). But in the contradictories the difference is apparent. 'God is not' (sense C) would have to be construed like 'Joseph is not'; it would then suitably express the supposition that perhaps the world was made by an old superannuated God who has since died (a suggestion of Hume's). This is quite different from the atheist's 'there is no God' (sense B).

One would indeed wish to say that everlasting existence is part of the concept of a God; of Hume's senile creator one would wish to say that since he is dead now he never was God when he was alive. But saying this does not commit us to the fallacy of the Ontological Argument. It belongs to the concept of a phoenix that it should never die by accident and should ward off old age with a bath of flames at regular intervals; so a dead phoenix is a contradiction in terms. But this does not mean that there must be a live phoenix. If there is a God, then he lives for ever; but we cannot determine from this whether there is a God.

Existence in sense C is, according to Aquinas, always existence in respect of some form: *quodlibet esse est secundum formam aliquam* (Ia. q.5 art.5 ad 3 um). For it is in this sense of 'exist' that we say a thing goes on existing; and for a thing to continue to exist is for it to be the same X over a period of time, where 'X' represents some *Begriffswort*; and this in turn means the persistence in an individual of the form expressed by the predicable expression 'X'. Thus, a man continues to exist in that the baby, the youth, and the grown man are *the same man*; and this means the persistence in some individual of the form, *Begriff*, that answers to the *Begriffswort* 'man'.

### III

Having explained the construction of the phrase 'that by which . . .', and the relevant sense of 'is', we consider what is meant by phrases of the form 'that by which x is', 'x' being replaced by the name of an individual. Now it is the fundamental doctrine of Aquinas, repeatedly stated, that except when x is God, x is never identical with that by which x is. This doctrine is, I think, intelligible in the light of our previous enquiry; but it is a most surprising doctrine. Why should we, how can we, distinguish between an individualized form and that by which the individualized form *is*? e.g., between the redness of Socrates' nose and that by which the redness of Socrates' nose *is*, goes on existing? We find in Aquinas himself remarks which might suggest the view that *esse* is an inseparable and only conceptually distinct aspect of the individualized form itself. "*Esse* of itself goes with a form, for form is actuality" (*Esse autem per se convenit formae, quae est actus*) (Ia. q.75 art.6); "For any given thing, that *by which* it exists is its form" (*unumquodque formaliter est per formam suam*) (IIIa. q.2 art.5 ad 3 um).

All the same, I think there are good reasons for accepting the real distinction between an individualized form and the corresponding *esse*. The most important and most general reason is stated succinctly but clearly by Aquinas himself. If x is F and y is F, then in respect of F-ness x and y are so far alike; the F-ness of x will indeed be a different individualized form from the F-ness of y, but they will be, as F-nesses, alike. But when x is and y also *is*, the *esse* of x and the *esse* of *y* are in general different as such (Ia. q.3 art.5: *Tertio* . . .). Now this marks an un-bridgeable distinction between *esse* and any form F-ness whatsoever. And the distinction between the references of the expressions 'that by which—*is*' and 'that by which—is F' will not vanish even if the *esse* of God and (say) the wis-dom of God are identical; no more than 'the square of' and 'the cube of' have the same reference because 1 is both the square and the cube of 1.

A modern philosopher will often challenge philosophical assertions with the question: As opposed to what? This is a legitimate move; as Aquinas says, know-ing the truth of an assertion is tantamount to knowing the falsehood of its con-tradictory opposite (Ia. q.58 art.4 ad 2 um). Well then, as opposed to what does one say that in general the *esse* of *x* and the *esse* of *y* are as such distinct? In the fairy-tale, all the human members of the family and the family cat shared a sin-gle life, that is, a single *esse* (*vivere viventibus est esse*); and when the betrothed of the youngest daughter took a potshot at the cat, its death was the death of the whole family. In actual families, animality is common to all the members of the family, including the cat, but *esse* is not, and so killing the cat has no such conse-quence. So, although for a man or cat to go on existing is precisely the continued existence of his animality, that is, the persistence of a certain individualized form in continuously renewed matter: nevertheless we must recognize a real distinc-tion between his animality and his *esse*.

A second reason appeals to the nature of intensive magnitude. It may be that *x* is F and *y* is F, and that they have the same specific F-ness, but yet the F-ness of *x* is more intense than that of *y*. Moreover, the F-ness of *x* may be-come more or less intense; and increase of F-ness plainly resembles a thing's coming to be F, whereas a decrease of F-ness resembles a thing's altogether ceasing to be F. Now difference between *x* and *y* as regards intensity of F-ness is not difference precisely as regards F-ness (especially as we may suppose *x* and *y* to have the same specific F-ness); it is rather, I wish to say, difference as regards the existence of F-ness the F-ness of *x* exists more than the F-ness of *y*. So also a change in mere intensity is a change as regards existence; increase in the intensity of *x*'s F-ness resembles the coming to be of *x*'s F-ness, both being additions of existence; decrease in the intensity of *x*'s F-ness resembles the ceasing of *x*'s F-ness, both being subtractions of existence. Here again, there is a real distinction between the F-ness of *x* and the *esse* of this individ-ualized form; while the F-ness as such remains unchanged, its existence may vary in degree.

(I have deliberately stated this argument in a schematic way, in order to avoid irrelevant controversy about my choice as an example. It is not so easy as it looks to find an unexceptionable case of difference or change in mere in-tensity, without any difference or change in quality: Aquinas's favourite exam-ple, heat, would land us in many difficulties. So far as I can see, *sound* is a good example. A louder and a softer sound may be qualitatively identical; and a sudden increase of loudness resembles a sound's suddenly starting, a sudden decrease of loudness its suddenly stopping.)

A third reason is found in considering the nature of thought. How remarkable that if there can (logically) be an X, there can also be a thought of an X! What is this relation *being a thought of,* which can have anything whatsoever as its term—even non-existent things like dragons? And how can there be an activity whose whole nature consists in its having this relation to something to 'something' possibly non-existent?

Now Aquinas's account of thought denies that its nature consists wholly in relation to something outside itself. When Plato thinks of redness, what exists in Plato is not a certain *relation* to redness or red things, but *is* redness, is an individual occurrence of the very same form of which another individual occurrence is the redness of this rose. But how then is it that this rose is red but not Plato's mind? Because the *mode* of occurrence of redness—not the redness that occurs—is unlike; the redness in Plato's mind *is*, exists, in a different way (*esse intentionale*) from the redness in this rose (which has *esse naturale*). We thus understand the intimate connexion of thought and its object. There is, as Aquinas often says, *likeness* (*similitudo*) between them. We also now understand the odd-seeming fact that there can be a thought of anything that there can be. Existence makes no difference to, and can impose no restriction on, the nature of that which exists; if it is possible that there should be F-ness at all, then it is possible alike that there should be F-ness occurring with *esse naturale* (a real live cow, say) and that there should be F-ness occurring with *esse intentionale* (a thought of a cow). The whole basis of this account is that the individual F-ness is really distinct from its *esse, naturale* or *intentionale* as the case may be.

To get this doctrine of Aquinas's properly straightened out in our minds we must realize that Aquinas is not saying, e.g., that the cow in the meadow leads a double life and has another *esse* in my mind; or that I, when I think of the cow, become somehow identical with the cow. These kinds of talk (derived, I should guess, from taking too seriously the notorious trick expression 'in the mind') are expressly rejected by Aquinas. "A stone is *not* in the mind (*anima*), it is the likeness (*species*) of a stone that is there . . . the similitude of a thing thought of (*intellectae*) is a form in the understanding" (Ia. q.85 art.2). There is one individualized form in the stone, and another individualized form in the mind of the man who thinks of it; these individualized forms are both occurrences of the same form, but differ in their manner of *esse*; neither the stone nor its individualized form is to be found in my mind.

Even when one angel thinks of another, what is in the knower is an individualized form differing from the individualized form that is in (or rather, for Aquinas, is identical with) the angel who is known, although both are occurrences of the very same form. On Aquinas's view, the difference (say) between Michael's thought of Gabriel and Gabriel himself, like the difference between my thought of a cow and the cow in the meadow, consists in one and the same form's occurring in Michael (or me) with *esse intentionale*, in Gabriel (or the cow) with *esse naturale*; and this involves the existence of two individualized forms (Ia. q.56 art.2 ad 3 um). It should be noticed in regard to the last citation that the difference between *esse naturale* and *esse intentionale* can occur even when there is no question of matter; angels, for Aquinas, have no sort of matter in their make-up, but the difference still holds good in their case.

I have had to be brief and leave out many important topics: in particular, the difference between the nature or essence and the (substantial) form of a material thing; the sense in which the human soul is the 'form' of the human body; the conception of *materia prima*; the question whether angels are 'forms' (sc. individualized forms). Even so I could not make this chapter easy going, nor avoid what many people would call hair-splitting distinctions. But all serious philosophy *is* difficult; and, as for hair-splitting:

> A Hair perhaps divides the False and True,
> Yes; and a single Alif were the clue—
> Could you but find it—to the Treasure-house
> And peradventure to THE MASTER too.

## Note

This chapter was previously published as Peter Geach, "Form and Existence," in Peter Geach, *God and the Soul* (Routledge and Kegan Paul, London, 1969).

# 5

# Aquinas on What God Is Not

*Brian Davies*

THOMAS AQUINAS WAS VERY CONCERNED with the question "What is God?" And he thought that he had answers to this question. God, he says, is the beginning and end of all things, the Creator of a world which depends on him for its existence.[1] Among other things, Aquinas also holds that God is alive, perfect, good, eternal, omnipresent, omnipotent, and omniscient, that God is three persons sharing one nature, and that God became a human being so that humans might share in the life of God.[2] Yet in the writings of Aquinas we also find him holding that God is deeply mysterious. "The divine substance," he says, "surpasses every form that our intellect reaches. Thus we are unable to apprehend it by knowing what it is."[3] God, he maintains, "is greater than all we can say, greater than all we can know; and not merely does he transcend our language and our knowledge, but he is beyond the comprehension of every mind whatsoever, even of angelic minds, and beyond the being of every substance."[4] According to Aquinas: "The most perfect [state] to which we can attain in this life in our knowledge of God is that he transcends all that can be conceived by us, and that the naming of God through remotion (*per remotionem*) is most proper . . . The primary mode of naming God is through the negation of all things, since he is beyond all, and whatever is signified by any name whatsoever is less than that which God is."[5]

What does Aquinas mean when saying that we can speak truly of God even though we do not know what God is? One thing to stress is that when he denies that we know what God is he clearly does not intend to suggest that we can claim no knowledge of God at all. His meaning is that God is not an object in our universe with respect to which we can have what we would nowadays call a "scientific understanding." According to Aquinas, we know what something is (*quid est*) when we can single it out as part of the material world and define it. More precisely, we know what something is when we can locate it in terms of genus and species.[6] In saying that we cannot know what God is, therefore, he is chiefly denying that God belongs to a natural class and that God can be defined on this basis. Were he writing in English today he would not be saying "We do not know anything about God" or "We lack any knowledge of God."[7]

On the other hand, however, he does think that the nature of God defies our powers of understanding. He often says that an explicit human knowledge of God has to be derived from a process of inference making use of premises concerning the world as grasped by sensory experience. For Aquinas, we know God as accounting for or bringing about ourselves and our world. And this knowledge is limited. God, for Aquinas, transcends our attempts to picture or describe. So he thinks, for example, that it is equally appropriate to talk of God both in concrete terms and in abstract terms. In Aquinas's view, we cannot think of God as something with a nature shared by others. We cannot think of God as one of a class in a world of things. On Aquinas's account, God and God's nature are not, for us, distinguishable.[8] And hence, so he argues, while it makes sense to say such things as that "God is good" or "God is wise," it makes equal sense to say "God is goodness" or "God is wisdom." According to Aquinas, God is also the same as his existence. He is "subsistent existence" (*ipsum esse subsistens*).[9] Or, as Aquinas often puts it, God is entirely simple.

In effect, Aquinas's view is that the very logic of our language cannot capture God. We normally talk about, and understand, things by singling them out as subjects of statements and by saying what properties they have. Thus, for example, we say that Mary is tall and thin, or that the dog in the kitchen is black and weighs twenty pounds. For Aquinas, however, though we are forced to talk of God in a similar way because of the way our language works— though we are forced to say things like "God is good" or "God is wise"—that manner of putting things is also misleading. For, as Aquinas sees it, God is not something to be distinguished from what is ascribed to him. Mary might be good and Mary might be wise. But Mary is not goodness or wisdom. But, says Aquinas, having said that God is good or that God is wise, we must also allow that God cannot be distinguished from what is ascribable to him. So God is goodness, and God is wisdom, and the being of God is not something different from God himself.

When saying this kind of thing, Aquinas does not mean, as some have seemed to think, that statements like "God is good" and "God is wise" are synonymous.[10] But, so he thinks, what makes them true is the reality of God (i.e., God), which, so he says, is not to be thought of as something distinct from what can be affirmed of it. According to Aquinas, we can distinguish between what a word like "goodness" means and what is actually there in something that we call "good."[11] So there is a sense in which he thinks that we know what we are saying when we say, for example, that God is good. But he does not think that God is something we can single out and understand so as seriously to be able to say that we know what it is—even though he thinks that we can say, for example, "God is good." His conclusion, therefore, is that, though we can understand the meaning of the word "good" when saying that God is good, we cannot understand what God is. And he wants to say the same when it comes to anything which we might wish to affirm of God. We cannot know what any perfection ascribable to God is like as it exists in him. We can know what it is like for something to be a good human being or a good computer or a good meal. But God, says Aquinas, is not a good such-and-such. He is no kind of such-and-such. And he cannot be thought of as a perfect such-and-such regardless of the perfection in question.

In that case, however, can we know anything at all of God? People sometimes approach Aquinas on this question by focusing on what they call his "doctrine of analogy." They mean that Aquinas has something rightly called a "doctrine of analogy" which he viewed as a device for working out what we can know about God. And, though this idea has been rejected by some readers of Aquinas, it is not without merit.[12] For Aquinas certainly holds that we can make statements concerning God which we can know to be true. And in defending this position he invokes the notion of analogy. Take, for example, the first five articles of the famous Question 13 of the *Summa Theologiae*. Here Aquinas defends the following theses: (1) We can use words to talk of God; (2) Some of the words we use state what God is in himself; (3) We significantly speak of God while saying different things about him; and (4) We can apply certain words to God and to creatures analogously—i.e., neither univocally nor purely equivocally. Theses 1–3 are clearly intended by Aquinas as leading to 4, which he develops by providing what looks like a rule of thumb for speaking of God in a true and literal way. "Whatever is said both of God and creatures," Aquinas explains, "is said in virtue of the order that creatures have to God as to their source and cause in which all the perfections of things preexist transcendently." What does this mean? Article 3 of 1a,13 provides a clue: "God is known from the perfections that flow from him and are to be found in creatures yet which exist in him in a transcendent way." Aquinas thinks of effects as showing forth the nature of their cause.[13] An effect, for Aquinas, is somehow like its cause. So his view is that from God's effects we can know what God is since God is their cause. And that gives us what I just referred to as what looks like a "rule of thumb" offered by Aquinas for speaking truly of God. First take your creature. Then assume that it is like God since God is its Creator. Then speak accordingly of God.

This rule of thumb, however, might easily be used to defend what Aquinas would manifestly deny. Cats have fur. And God is the creator of cats. Does it follow that God is furry? Aquinas denies that God is anything material, and, since fur is pretty corporeal, we can expect him to deny that God is furry.[14] Yet he would not, I think, say that his "rule of thumb," as I call it, must therefore be simply abandoned. For it comes from him with a qualification.

An effect, for Aquinas, always resembles its cause.[15] But this, he thinks, need not mean that it looks like its cause or that it resembles it by being exactly like it.[16] Aquinas's idea is that a cause expresses itself in its effects and is therefore knowable from its effects. Suppose I stagger around and speak incoherently. You might wonder why I am doing this. Suppose you learn that I have just drunk a large amount of alcohol. You will say: "Oh, I see. Of course that explains it." But why? Aquinas would say that it is not at all surprising that the alcohol made me act as I did, because that is what alcohol characteristically does when drunk in large quantities by human beings. His line is that alcohol is something the effects of which show it forth. So he will say that my drunken state resembles alcohol since it shows forth the power of alcohol as it takes place in me. I cannot, when drunk, be described as looking like alcohol. But, so Aquinas thinks, I, when drunk, certainly exemplify what alcohol is when it works on me. In this sense, so he holds, I resemble it. When I am drunk, so Aquinas would say, I am alcohol in action. Alcohol being itself in me. Or, as Aquinas puts it: "What an agent does reflects what it is" (*omne agens agit sibi simile*).[17] Cashed with reference to God as Creator, this means that God shows himself in all of his effects even though we cannot say that, for example, God is furry. Just as alcohol can show itself in me without being inebriated, so, for Aquinas, God shows himself in his effects without being furry. And this is why we might agree with those who say that Aquinas has a doctrine of analogy which we can use as rule of thumb for saying what we know about God. The rule would be: "All of God's creatures show us what God is—somehow."

But how, for Aquinas, does the world give us knowledge of God as its cause? How does he think of his "rule" as helping us to a knowledge of God? Some have argued that this question is best answered in largely negative terms. In *Aquinas, God and Action*, for instance, David Burrell suggests that Aquinas is out to lay down "the universal (or logical) principles governing discourse about divine things rather than establishing a doctrine of God." Insofar as Aquinas has a doctrine of God, says Burrell, "it is a dreadfully austere one."[18] But other readers of Aquinas have not found him offering quite the austerity proposed by Burrell. Why not? Largely because of what Aquinas says about analogy. He maintains that one can use certain words of God and creatures in an analogical sense. And he seems to think that this fact allows us to speak of God in a literal way. Like 'univocal' and 'equivocal', 'analogical', for Aquinas, signifies a literal way of talking. 'New York is a city' and 'Paris is a city' give us univocal uses of 'city'; but both statements are literally true. 'Baseball players use bats' and 'Bats have wings' give us equivocal uses of 'bat'. But both statements here are also literally true. And, according to Aquinas, 'I have a good computer' and 'God is good' give us analogical uses of 'good' in two literally true statements. And, with this fact in mind, it is wrong, so some have stressed, to think of Aquinas along the lines suggested by authors like Burrell. If Aquinas holds that we can speak of God literally, then, so they reason, Aquinas has a positive doctrine of God.[19]

Yet how should we view analogy as it is invoked by Aquinas when talking of God? Commenting on the view that discourse concerning God is 'analogical', P. T. Geach observes: "It would be better to say that it turns out to be analogical: what happens, on Aquinas's view, is that we first call God 'wise'; then discover that 'the wisdom of God' is a designation of God himself, whereas the like does not hold of any other being whom we rightly call 'wise'; and thus reflecting upon this, we see that 'wise' cannot be applied to God in the same way as to other beings."[20] And Geach here is right. In the *Summa Theologiae* (as elsewhere) Aquinas only mentions analogy after he has explained why God must be spoken of in certain specific ways. 1a,13 follows a set of Questions in which Aquinas argues for the truth of a number of positive assertions concerning God. And most of 1a,13 looks as though it can be read as a general account of what Aquinas has been doing since 1a,1. To understand texts like 1a,13, then, we need to consider what has led up to them. And if we do that we shall see that Aquinas has a characteristic way of arriving at the sort of thing he says in texts like 1a,13.

He begins by trying to reject certain arguments for the conclusion that God exists. Is God's existence something one can deny only by failing to pay attention to a basic and undeniable deliverance of the intellect? Is there not a direct and explicit awareness of God present in all who care to reflect at all? Might "God exists" be as obviously true as the denial of what is clearly logically contradictory? Aquinas discusses such questions in a number of places, and his answer is always "No."[21] We can know that God exists, he thinks. But only by virtue of a certain kind of argument—an argument from effect to cause. In Aquinas's view, we do not have an understanding of what God is. So we cannot reason to God on the basis of any such understanding. But we can start with things of which we do have some understanding. From these, Aquinas thinks, we can argue to God as their cause.

Suppose, for example, that someone develops certain physical symptoms. We wonder what accounts for them. But we do not know that anything we understand (virus X, Y, or Z, for instance) has been around to account for them. In that case, we presume that the symptoms have a cause, and we do our best to construct an account of what this cause might be like. Here we are saying: "Given this, then there must be something which accounts for it. Now let us try to understand what this something must be like." According to Aquinas, we are saying just this when offering viable arguments for God's existence. In his view, any such argument must be one which starts with things of which we do have some knowledge and it must reason to God as less known but as accounting for them—as in the case of the famous "Five Ways."[22] Each "Way" begins with what, unlike God's nature, is clear to us. And they reason to a not-so-clear cause of this. They "do not presuppose any view of the nature of God, they simply begin with philosophical puzzles arising from features that we understand and take us to what we do not understand."[23] Or, as Aquinas himself writes: "When we argue from effect to cause, the effect must take the place of a definition of the cause in the proof that the cause exists; and especially so when the cause is God. For when proving anything to exist the central link is not what the thing is—we cannot even ask what it is until we know that it exists."[24]

Yet Aquinas does, in a sense, ask "What is God?" And he does, in a sense, have answers to the question. If we know that Fred is coughing up blood we assume that, as we often vaguely put it, something is causing this. Let us suppose that we cannot put our finger on the culprit or culprits. Most of us would then find ourselves saying that we shall have to settle for doing our best to talk about the offender or offenders in a roundabout kind of way. And that is how Aquinas proceeds as he develops what might be called his philosophical account of God's nature. In the interlude between 1a,2 and 1a,3 he writes: "Having recognized that a certain thing exists, we have still to investigate the way in which it exists, that we may come to understand what it is that exists." And much of the *Summa Theologiae* following that remark, and much that Aquinas writes in other works, can be read as an effort on his part to say what we are talking about when we say that God exists. The remark itself is immediately followed by another which seems to pull in a different direction. For, says Aquinas, "we cannot know what God is, but only what he is not" and must therefore "consider the ways in which God does not exist, rather than the ways in which he does." But we need to see what that statement means in the light of what Aquinas says generally.

One way of reading it would leave us taking Aquinas as holding that we can only say that God is not this, not that, not the other . . . *ad infinitum*. But that is clearly not his position if it is taken to mean that we can make no true affirmative predications concerning God. When Aquinas in the *Summa Theologiae* says that we must consider the ways in which God does not exist he goes on to offer a series of discussions designed to do just that. 1a,3 (*de Dei simplicate*) tells us what kinds of composition (*compositio*) *cannot* be attributed to

God. 1a,7 and 1a,9 tell us that God is limitless and unchangeable, i.e., *not* limited and *not* changeable. In 1a,4 and in 1a,11 Aquinas, in an apparently positive vein, argues that God is perfect and that God is one (*unus*). But here again he is telling us what God is not. As Geach observes: "A moment's thought shows that there is no such perfection as perfection: we cannot sensibly predicate 'perfect' unless we have in mind a perfect A, where 'A' stands in for a general term with some definite content."[25] And Aquinas does not suggest otherwise. God, he argues, is perfect not as having a particular perfection but as being wholly actual. As for "God is one," says Aquinas, the meaning is that God is not subject to multiplication, that there cannot be several Gods.[26] Yet Aquinas clearly holds that we can make true affirmative predications concerning God. And he explicitly denies that when we do so we are only saying what God is not. "Some," he writes, "have said that sentences like 'God is good', although they sound like affirmations, are in fact used to deny something of God rather than to assert anything."[27] But he rejects that position.[28]

So Aquinas thinks that "God is alive" has positive content, and he thinks the same of other assertions about God, ones which, in his view, we can know to be true.[29] And, though Aquinas continually stresses our ignorance when it comes to God, he also writes so as to suggest that he wants to shy away from the suggestion that we cannot know that certain statements with God as subject are true. Why so? Partly it is because he follows the Bible and the teaching of the Church, both of which provided him with apparently positive statements concerning God. But Aquinas also gives reasons for supposing that some positive statements about God are ones we can defend without appeal to Scripture and Church authority. Take, for example, "God is good." Why say that? Well, so Aquinas replies, it is a natural thing to say since the good is what is desirable and since God is the cause of the existence of everything other than himself and must therefore have in him all that things tend to in being good and in seeking their good.[30] Or again, what about "God is omnipresent" and "God is eternal"? Aquinas defends the first statement by arguing that, since God makes all places, he is in them all as making them to be.[31] The second statement is defensible, he argues, since anything eternal is wholly unchangeable and since God must be that if he is the source of the world of change.[32] Here, as in many other arguments he offers, Aquinas is holding that there are reasons for saying that God really is thus and so. Insofar as the reasons lead to their conclusions, he thinks, we have grounds for making various positive statements concerning God. In this sense, so he holds, we know what God is, and in this sense he employs what I have called his "rule of thumb." Affirmative predications concerning God are, in his view, wrung from us by argument.[33] Critics of belief in God have sometimes asked theists to prove in the abstract that statements about God are "coherent" or "meaningful" before ever considering why we might want to say that God is whatever we say that he is. And some theists have seemed to accept that proof like this ought to be supplied.[34] But a proof that **p** is true is proof that **p** is possibly true since it is proof that **p** is actually true. And much of Aquinas's thinking on the sense it makes to say "God is F," "God is G," etc. is inseparable from the reasons he thinks we have to speak in this way. And when Aquinas says that we can speak positively of God he intends us to understand that we can sometimes speak literally and not just figuratively. As we can see from texts like 1a,1,9, Aquinas certainly thinks that we can speak of God figuratively, that most Christian discourse will be figurative, and that speaking figuratively need not mean speaking falsely. But figurative statements about God can always, in his view, be rightly denied. I may say that God is a mighty fortress, but I may, Aquinas thinks, sensibly deny this by adding that God is not made of stone. Yet, so Aquinas also thinks, there are many things to be said of God which just cannot be sensibly and with reason denied. Hence, for example, it is, in his view, always false to say that it is not the case that God is good, omnipresent, and eternal. And, so he also thinks, statements like "God is good," "God is omnipresent," and "God is eternal" are wrung from us by argument, though they also come with the authority of Scripture and the Church.

But Aquinas also holds that other less positive things we need to say about God are equally wrung from us by argument. And here we return to what, in his view, cannot be said about God. God is nothing material. God is not an instance of a kind. God cannot be thought of as distinct from his "attributes" and his existence. God is entirely simple or non-composite. If Aquinas believes that there are reasons for saying that God is positively thus and so, he also maintains there are reasons for denying certain things about God. And all of his thinking here, together with what we have now seen concerning his general approach to knowledge of God, is clearly presupposed when he comes to write texts like 1a,13. Indeed, they form part of the argument of such texts. 1a,13,1 asks whether we can use any words to refer to God. Aquinas's reply notes that we can know of God through God's effects, but must also remember that God is simple. 1a,13,2 asks whether any of the words we use of God express something of what God is. Aquinas's answer to this question appeals to the fact that what we can know of God is derived from our knowledge that God is the cause of creatures. It then adds that, since God is the transcendent cause of all creatures, creatures fail to represent him adequately so that words like "good," when based on the goodness experienced in creatures and applied to God, signify "imperfectly."

Aquinas's use of the notion of analogy brings together all of these aspects of his teaching. We are not, he says, always equivocating when we apply certain terms to God and to creatures. We can argue for God's existence and we can argue for statements of the form "God is F." Here we use words which we apply when first talking of creatures, and we could not manage to do that if our use of the words as applied to God and creatures were purely equivocal.[35] On the other hand, so Aquinas also wants to say, "it is impossible to predicate anything univocally of God and creatures" since God, unlike creatures, is wholly simple. "Every effect that falls short of what is typical of the power of its cause," Aquinas argues, "represents it inadequately, for it is not the same kind of thing as the cause. Thus what exists simply and in a unified way in the cause will be divided up and take various different forms in such effects." And so, Aquinas adds, "the perfections which in creatures are many and various pre-exist in God as one."[36]

It has been argued that Aquinas cannot really mean what he says when he denies that a word can be applied to God and to a creature univocally since he clearly believes that God really is, for example, good, and since he does not think that calling God good is saying something entirely different from what is being said when calling a creature good.[37] And there is value in this sugges-tion if we construe "univocal" as meaning "not equivocal." There is value in the suggestion too if we draw a certain distinction between "meaning" and "sense." The word "good" does not "mean" something different when we refer to good beef, good spin-dryers, and good neighbours. We do not have special words meaning "good as beef," "good as a spin-dryer," and "good as a neigh-bour." One word serves for all. But we are not saying the same of all the things which we call "good" since, as we might say, we use the word with different senses—meaning that we put it to varying uses. And with this point in mind, and with an eye on Aquinas, we might suggest that "the whole point of ana-logical predication is that the meaning remains the same (univocal) but the *sense* is different."[38] But we must also bear in mind that Aquinas wants to deny that God belongs to any natural class. On his account, "God is F" and "Crea-ture X is F" are not attributing F-ness to each as F-ness may be attributed to each members of any natural class.

For Aquinas, God transcends the world of natural things, and attributes as-cribed to him are not just present in him somewhat differently from the way in which they are present in creatures said to have them. For, on Aquinas's ac-count, God, strictly speaking, does not have attributes. Simple and indistin-guishable from his "attributes," God, for Aquinas, has whatever it takes to bring it about that there are creatures with whatever attributes they have.[39] In his commentary on Aristotle's *Peri Hermeneias* he refers to God's will (not to be distinguished from God) as "existing outside the realm of existents, as a cause from which pours forth everything that exists in all its variant forms" (*extra ordinem entium existens, velut causa quaedam profundens totum ens et omnes eius differentias*).[40] In terms of this picture, God is not a substance with attributes distinguishable from itself and shareable, in different degrees, with other things.[41] God is the cause of all such substances. Since Aquinas thinks that these have their existence from God, and since he thinks that causes somehow contain their effects, he concludes that there is a likeness of creatures to God and that this can serve to justify much that we say of God. But this likeness, for Aquinas, is not that between members of a natural kind or even between members of different natural kinds.[42]

For this reason, Herbert McCabe is correct to note that "for St. Thomas, when we speak of God we do not know what we are talking about. We are simply taking language from the familiar context in which we understand it and using it to point beyond what we understand into the mystery that surrounds us and sustains the world we do partially understand."[43] For this reason also, Alexander Broadie is right to note that, although Aquinas denies that we can speak of God only by negations, and although he cites Maimonides as a major exponent of the thesis he is rejecting, there is still a striking similarity between the thinking of Aquinas and Maimonides when it comes to the "names of God."[44] Both insist that we do justice to God by denying that God is what creatures are. Aquinas looks for more than negative assertions concerning God.[45] But Maimonides concedes that terms implying imperfection cannot be fittingly used of God. So, on his view, not just anything said of God is acceptable. In his commentary on Book 1 of Peter Lombard's *Sentences* (Distinction 2,1,3), Aquinas, interestingly, tries to reconcile Maimonides (speaking negatively of God) and Dionysius and St Anselm (speaking positively of God). "It is clear," he suggests, "that neither view contradicts what the other wants to say, since the first people do not say that God is lacking in any mode of perfection, and the second do not say that there are in God any qualities or non-subsistent things."

At this point it might help if we focus on Aquinas's teaching that God is the source of the fact that things have being—or, as Aquinas puts it in Latin, that God is the source of the *esse* of things. As Aquinas often uses it, the word *esse* is best translated as if it were a kind of noun, literally as "the to be." Normally, though, when Aquinas uses *esse* in this sense, translators report him as talking about "being," which is also a perfectly respectable way of translating him. But we should not suppose that Aquinas thinks of *esse* as if it were an individual of some kind (as Mary is an individual woman, or Paul an individual man). Nor does Aquinas think that *esse* is a distinguishing property or quality of anything—like redness or being short-sighted. *Esse*, for Aquinas, is no independently existing thing. Nor is it anything that can enter into a description of what a thing is (in the language of Aquinas, it is not the name of a "form"). Yet it is, so he thinks, something very much to be reckoned with.

To try to understand what Aquinas is driving at here, we can start by noting that there is a difference between knowing what something is and knowing whether or not the thing actually exists. By this I mean that we can know what something is if we know the meaning of a word—the word "cat," say. But understanding the meaning of "cat" is different from knowing that there are any cats. You can see this if we change the example and talk, instead, about knowing what a unicorn is. We will not be puzzled if we read a story which features unicorns. We will not say "But the word 'unicorn' does not mean anything; 'unicorn' is a piece of gibberish." On the other hand, however, we will not suppose that there are any unicorns.

Now suppose that something actually turns up in the world which fits with what we mean when we use the word "unicorn." In that case, we can study it. And as a result of doing this, we might come to a deeper sense of what a unicorn is. We might develop a science of unicorns, just as we have developed a science of cats. We might come to know what a unicorn is in a way that goes beyond being able to make sense of stories with the word "unicorn" in them. We might come to know what a unicorn is in a way that goes beyond knowing the meaning of a word.[46]

Aquinas would put all this by saying that we might come to distinguish between *what* a thing is and *whether or not it is*. He would also say that, if a thing is, it has *esse*. Once again, I stress that Aquinas does not think of *esse* as a property or quality of anything. On his account, if a unicorn turned up so that we could produce a science of unicorns (an account of what unicorns are), we would not end up saying that as well as being like horses, say, they have *in addition* the characteristic of *esse*. But Aquinas does want to insist that genuine, breathing unicorns (genuine subjects of scientific investigation) would be different from what we might call "the meanings of words"—as when we observe that we can understand what "unicorn" means without believing that there are any unicorns. Or, as Aquinas would say, genuine, breathing unicorns would have *esse*—just as cats do.

But now suppose we ask how it comes about that there are cats. There are such things as cats. But how come that there are cats?

When we ask "How come?," the objects of our concern are fairly specifiable for the most part. We may, for example, wonder how it comes to be that some local phenomenon obtains. Why are there mountains to the east of Paris? Why is there a cat called Thor, who belongs to a Jesuit priest in New York (as there is) and who is called Thor since, according to his owner, he is "simply divine"?

Sometimes, however, the range of our inquiry may be wider. Someone might explain why there are mountains to the east of Paris. But we might then wonder why there should be *any mountains*, whether east of Paris or anywhere else. And we might wonder how there come to be *any cats*, whether in New York or anywhere else.

And if these questions are answered we might deepen the range of our inquiry. Mountains and cats are there for reasons to be documented and explored by physicists, geologists, chemists, astronomers, and so on. They will tell us how it comes to be, not that this and that individual is there, but why things of certain kinds are there. And in telling us this they will be invoking levels of explanation which run deeper and deeper.

In doing so, however, they will always presume a background of things, a world or universe in the light of which explanation is possible. The mountains east of Paris are explicable on geological and other grounds. Cats are explicable in genetic and other terms. And, if we ask why geology is possible and why genetics is possible, we shall again be looking for things of a kind behaving in certain ways.

But we might further deepen the level of our inquiry. For we might ask, not "What in the world accounts for this, that, or the other?," but "Why any world at all?" How come the whole familiar business of asking and answering "How come?"

The point to stress now is that this, for Aquinas, is a crucial question. For him, the question "How come any universe?" is a serious one to which there must be an answer. And he gives the name "God" to whatever the answer is. God, for Aquinas, is the reason why there is any universe at all. God, he says, is the source of the *esse* (and of the *essentia*) of things—the fact that they are more than the meanings of words.

Now (and this is what the last few paragraphs have been leading up to), Aquinas's views on *esse*, among other views he had, lead him to his conclusion that we cannot know what God is. How so? The answer Aquinas gives is that in speaking of whatever accounts for the fact that things have *esse* we must be careful not to attribute to it anything which cannot be true of whatever it is that accounts for there being any universe at all. For example, says Aquinas, we cannot suppose that God is part of the world of space and time. Nor can we suppose that God is subject to the limitations and changes which affect things spatial and temporal. So it will be nonsense to speak of God as literally being *here* as opposed to *there*, or as literally being *now* as opposed to *then*. And it will be nonsense to speak of God as something passing through successive states. And it will be even more nonsense to think of God as changing because other things have an effect on him. So it will be wrong to say that things in the world can modify God somehow. It will be wrong to say that they can, for instance, cause God to know things or cause God to undergo emotions. It will also, says Aquinas, be wrong to say that God has a character in any sense we can understand. Or, to put it another way, it will be wrong to assert that God is an individual—in the familiar sense of "individual" where to call something an individual is to think of it as a member of a class of which there could be more than one member, as something with a nature shared by others but different from that of things sharing natures of another kind. According to

Aquinas, to conceive of God as the reason why there is any universe at all is to conceive of God as the source of diversity and therefore as the source of there being classes with different members, classes containing things with characteristic activities and effects. In Aquinas's view, therefore, God cannot be thought of as something with a character which is shown by what it typically produces (as, say, alcohol can be thought of as a substance with a character which is shown by what it typically produces). If God is what accounts for there being any universe, then God accounts for there being anything we can single out as having a nature distinct from other things: God accounts for everything we can understand. But, so Aquinas thinks, something which accounts for everything we can understand cannot be thought of as having a character which is indicated by what it typically produces. Alcohol has a character shown by what it typically produces. But to see that this is so is also to be aware that it produces *these* effects and not *those*. Given his views about God as source of *esse*, however, Aquinas wants to say that God does not produce *these* effects and not *those*. God produces *esse*—the condition of us being able to describe things as truly being like *this* or like *that*.

In short, and as I mentioned earlier, Aquinas thinks that we cannot know what God is because we cannot have a science of whatever it is that accounts for there being any universe at all. "How come any universe at all?" is clearly not a scientific question. For it is asking how come that science itself is possible. And its answer cannot be anything which a scientist could investigate or analyze. Scientific questions concern objects or events which are part of the material universe. And answers to these questions refer us to other things of the same kind, to more objects or events which are part of the material universe. But the universe is not an object or event within itself. And whatever accounts for there being a universe cannot be this either. And that is what Aquinas wants to say. In asking how there comes to be any universe, we are raising what he would call the question of creation (because the notion that the universe is created is the notion that it is made to be). And, so he insists, to say that something is created is not to locate it in historical terms or in terms of things having effects within the universe (in terms, so we might say, of *transformers*). According to Aquinas, to call something created is to speak of it as derived, not because it has come from something equally derived, and not because it has come to be because something has been transformed. For Aquinas, to call something created is to speak of it as derived because its existence as such is derived. To view the universe as created, he thinks, is not to place it in a context of scientific causes. It is to see that there is a question to ask after science has done all the work it can possibly do. According to Aquinas, there is a puzzle concerning the fact that there is anything there to be identified and spoken about and explained in terms of scientific or transforming causes.

For this reason, and in spite of the way in which he thinks that we can speak truly and literally of God, authors like David Burrell have reason on their side as they tell us what Aquinas thinks of God. There is a serious austerity in his thinking and one can see why it might be said that he has no doctrine of God. One might even say that Aquinas may be called an "agnostic." He is not, of course, an agnostic in the usual, modern sense of the word. We normally think of an agnostic as someone who typically says something like "We do not know, and the universe is a mysterious riddle." And that is not quite what Aquinas wants to say. But he certainly wants to say something with a highly agnostic ring to it.

The late Victor White O. P. once tried to put what Aquinas wants to say in this form: "We do not know what the answer is, but we do know that there is a mystery behind it all which we do not know. And if there were not, there would not even be a riddle. This Unknown we call *God*. And if there were no God, there would be no universe to be mysterious, and nobody to be mystified."[47] A problem with this way of representing Aquinas's thinking is that it seems to make him saying (in modern everyday English) that God is wholly unknown and that we really have no idea at all what "God" means. And that is not quite his line. But his final position on our knowledge of God is decidedly agnostic, and White's paraphrase is, perhaps, more helpful than misleading in the long run. What Aquinas thinks about God may be compared with what we find at the end of Wittgenstein's *Tractatus Logico-Philosophicus*.[48] Here we read: "Not *how* the world is, is the mystical, but *that* it is."[49] For Wittgenstein, *how the world is* is a scientific matter with scientific answers. But, so he insists, even when the scientific answers are in, we are still left with the *thatness* of the world, the fact *that* it is. As Wittgenstein himself puts it: "We feel that even if *all possible* scientific questions be answered, the problems of life have still not been touched at all."[50] Aquinas seems to be saying something similar when he speaks of *esse* and creation. Unlike Wittgenstein, however, Aquinas sets himself to probe and to try to talk about the mystical. In a serious sense he does have a doctrine of God and his position is optimistic. But it is also highly modest.[51]

## Notes

This chapter was previously published as Brian Davies, "Aquinas on What God is Not" (*Revue Internationale de Philosophie* 52, 1998).

1. *Summa Theologiae*, 1a, Introduction to Q.2. Cf. 1a,1,3 ad 1; 1a,93,4 ad 1; 1a,45,1; *De Potentia*, VII,9.
2. Cf. *Summa Theologiae*, 1a,18; 1a,4; 1a,6; 1a,10; 1a,8; 1a,25; 1a,14; 1a,29; 2a2ae, 23,2 ad 1; 2a2ae,24,2.
3. *Summa contra Gentiles*, I,14.

4. Commentary on Dionysius's *Divine Names*, I,iii,77.

5. Commentary on Dionysius's *Divine Names*, I,iii,83–84.

6. Cf. Commentary on Peter Lombard's *Sentences*, I, d.37, q.3, a.3; *Sent.*, I, d.43, q.l, a.l; *Sent.*, IV,d.7,q.1.a.3.

7. Cf. G. E. M. Anscombe and P. T. Geach, *Three Philosophers* (Oxford, 1961), p. 117. Cf. also John F. Wippel, *Metaphysical Themes in Thomas Aquinas* (Washington, 1984), pp. 239f.

8. Cf. *Summa Theologiae*, 1a,3,3.

9. Cf. *Summa Theologiae*, 1a,3,3; *Summa contra Gentiles*, I,22; *De Potentia*, VII,2.

10. Cf. *Summa Theologiae*, 1a,13,4 and *Summa contra Gentiles*, I,35.

11. Aquinas understands what Frege would have called the distinction between "sense" and "reference." Cf. Gottlob Frege, *Collected Papers on Mathematics, Logic and Philosophy*, ed. Brian McGuiness (Oxford, 1984), pp. 157 ff. Cf. also Gerard J. Hughes, "Aquinas and the Limits of Agnosticism" in Gerard J. Hughes (ed.), *The Philosophical Assessment of Theology* (Tunbridge and Georgetown, 1987), pp. 42 ff.

12. For someone playing down the idea that Aquinas had a theory of analogy which he thought of as able to furnish us with knowledge of God, see Herbert McCabe O.P., Appendix 4 to Volume 3 of the Blackfriars edition of the *Summa Theologiae* (London and New York, 1964). According to McCabe, "much has been made of St. Thomas's alleged teaching on analogy. For him, analogy is not a way of getting to know about God, nor is it a theory of the structure of the universe, it is a comment on our use of certain words" (p. 106).

13. Cf. *Summa contra Gentiles*, I,29; I,49; II,16; II,21; II,46; III,21; *Summa Theologiae*, 1a,6,1; 91,2; 105,1 ad 1.

14. Cf. *Summa Theologiae*, 1a,3,1.

15. Aquinas distinguishes different senses of "cause." Here we are concerned with what he has in mind when speaking of what he calls an "efficient cause." But we have to remember that, for Aquinas, God is more than an efficient cause.

16. Cf. *Summa contra Gentiles*, I,29.

17. The thesis is repeated in many places by Aquinas. For some examples see *Summa contra Gentiles*, I,29; I,73; II,6; II,20. Aquinas's thinking here can be traced at least as far back as Aristotle. Cf. *Metaphysics*, 12.4. 1070b30 ff. It is helpfully expounded by Timothy McDermott in *Summa Theologiae: A Concise Translation* (London, 1989), pp. xxxiii–xxxiv.

18. David Burrell, *Aquinas, God and Action* (London and Henley, 1979), pp. 21 and 13. Cf. A. D. Sertillanges, *Les Grandes Thèses de la Philosophie Thomiste* (Paris, 1928), Ch. 3.

19. Cf. Patrick Sherry, "Analogy Today," *Philosophy* 51 (1976).

20. *Three Philosophers*, pp. 122 f.

21. Cf. *Summa Theologiae*, 1a,2,1; *Summa contra Gentiles*, I,10–11; *De Veritate*, X,12.

22. *Summa Theologiae*, 1a,2,3.

23. Herbert McCabe, "The Logic of Mysticism—I," in Martin Warner (ed.), *Religion and Philosophy* (Cambridge, 1992), p. 48.

24. *Summa Theologiae*, 1a,2,2 ad 2.

25. P. T. Geach, "The Meaning of 'God'—II," in Warner, op. cit., p. 86.

26. Cf. *Summa contra Gentiles*, I,42.

27. *Summa Theologiae,* 1a,13,2.

28. *Summa Theologiae,* 1a,13,2.

29. Having noted that Aquinas says that we must settle for knowing what God is not rather than what he is, Ralph McInerny reasonably observes that "this conviction scarcely reduces him to silence" and that one "might even find in the Summa a matter-of-factness in discussing things divine that seems presumptuous." See Ralph McInerny, *Being and Predication* (Washington, DC, 1986), p. 272.

30. Cf. *Summa Theologiae,* 1a,6,1; *Summa contra Gentiles,* I,13.

31. Cf. *Summa Theologiae,* 1a,8.

32. Cf. *Summa Theologiae,* 1a,10,2; *Summa contra Gentiles,* I,99.

33. For an essay exploring this line of thinking see C. J. F. Williams, "Existence and the Meaning of the Word 'God'," *The Downside Review* LXXVII (1958).

34. Cf. Richard Swinburne, *The Coherence of Theism* (Oxford, 1977).

35. Cf. *Summa Theologiae,* 1a,13,5.

36. *Summa Theologiae,* 1a,13,5.

37. Cf. Richard Swinburne, *The Coherence of Theism,* Ch. 4. Cf. also Patrick Sherry, op. cit.

38. Cyril Barrett, "The Logic of Mysticism—II," in Warner, op. cit., p. 66.

39. For a helpful critique of the view that talk about God and creatures as Aquinas thinks of God is sensibly construed as univocal, see Gerard Hughes, op. cit.

40. Book 1, lectio 14. Cf. *Summa Theologiae,* 1a,13,8 ad 2.

41. Cf. *Summa contra Gentiles,* I,25 and 26; *Summa Theologiae,* 1a,3,5.

42. Hence Aquinas argues that perfections "attributable" to God and creatures belong primarily to God and only secondarily to creatures. Cf. *Summa Theologiae,* 1a,13,3.

43. Herbert McCabe, "The Logic of Mysticism I," p. 58.

44. Alexander Broadie, "Maimonides and Aquinas on the Names of God," *Religious Studies* 23 (1987). Broadie usefully develops his reading of Maimonides and notes strong parallels between Aquinas and Maimonides in "Maimonides on the Great Tautology: Exodus 3,14," *Scottish Journal of Theology* 47 (1994).

45. *Summa Theologiae,* 1a,13,2.

46. Cf. Aquinas's Commentary on Aristotle's *Posterior Analytics* (*Comm. in II, Post Anal.* Cap. VII, Lect. 6): "Si non sit aliqua res cuius essentiam definitio significet nihil differt definitio a ratione exponente significationem alicuius nominis." That is: "If there is nothing to have its essence signified by a definition, then the definition is no different from the explanation of the meaning of a term."

47. Victor White O.P., *God the Unknown* (London, 1956), pp. 18 f.

48. Ludwig Wittgenstein, *Tractatus Logico-Philosophicus,* trans. C. K. Ogden (London, 1933). Cf. "Wittgenstein's Lecture on Ethics," *The Philosophical Review* LXXIV (1965).

49. *Tractatus,* 6.44.

50. *Tractatus,* 6.52.

51. For helpful comments on drafts of this paper I am indebted to Victor Austin, Alexander Broadie, Avery Dulles S.J., Denis Geraghty O.P., Norman Kretzmann, Herbert McCabe O.P., Timothy McDermott, James Sadowsky S.J., and Sara Penella.

# 6

# The Unity of Body and Soul

## Robert Pasnau

> Is there any principle in all of nature more mysterious than the union of
> soul with body: by which a supposed spiritual substance acquires such an
> influence over a material one, that the most refined thought is able to ac-
> tuate the grossest matter?

> Hume, *Enquiry Concerning the Human Understanding* VII.1

## I. The Failure of Nonreductive Theories

AFTER CONSIDERING THE SOUL IN ITS own right (*Summa Theologiae* Ia, 75), Aquinas turns to the relationship of soul and body. More specifically, he turns to "the soul's *union* with the body" (76pr). To say that soul and body are united (*unitur*) is simply to say that they make one (*unum*) thing. The first article of Q76 focuses on how this union is accomplished, taking for granted that soul and body do in fact make one thing. For several reasons, it is not surprising that Aquinas would take this much for granted. First, a human being certainly seems to be one thing, and Aquinas identifies a human being with the conjunction of soul and body (see Robert Pasnau, *Thomas Aquinas on Human Nature*, Cambridge: Cambridge University Press, 2002, §2.1). Second, a substance would seem to be a paradigmatic instance of a single, unified thing, and Aquinas holds that human beings count as complete substances, whereas their parts do not (see Pasnau 2002, §2.2).

On the other hand, there are numerous respects in which Q75 has made it more difficult, and less plausible, to hold that soul and body make one thing.

The six objections of 76.1 serve to remind the reader of these difficulties. First (obj. 1, 4, 5), Aquinas holds that the intellect operates without the body, and that therefore it has existence on its own, independent of the body (see Pasnau 2002, §2.2). Such independence in operation and existence makes it difficult to see how soul and body could constitute one thing. Also (obj. 2, 3), Aquinas believes that materiality is incompatible with intellectual cognition (Pasnau 2002, §2.2). It would seem, then, that the unity of body and soul would preclude intellect's activity. Finally (obj. 6), Aquinas holds that the soul is imperishable, whereas the body is not (75.6). But when one thing can exist independently of another, it seems difficult to hold that those two things are in fact one unified thing.

The difficulty of Aquinas's position becomes even more evident when we reflect on the sort of unity that he wants to ascribe to soul and body. The conclusion he wants is that "the intellective principle is united to the body as its form" (76.1c). Yet when one thinks about the nature of this hylomorphic relationship, it is hard to see how Aquinas will be able to reach such a conclusion, especially in light of Q75. Aristotle had remarked that "it is not necessary to ask whether the soul and its body are one, just as we do not ask about wax and its shape . . ." (*De Anima* II.1, 412b6–7). But clearly the wax and its shape will not be a workable model for Aquinas. The shape of the wax is far too dependent on that wax: it could not, for example, exist without the thing it gives shape to. So if Aquinas is to explain the unity of soul and body in hylomorphic terms, he will have to say quite a lot about how this relationship is to be understood. Prima facie, such an account seems poorly suited to his needs.

Among Aquinas's contemporaries, despite the pervasively Aristotelian atmosphere, there were those who doubted that the rational soul could be explained as the form of the body. Even Albert the Great, who was not just Aquinas's teacher but also a leader in the Aristotelian movement, wrote that the soul "is better spoken of as an actuality or perfection, rather than a form . . . A form, strictly speaking, according to natural philosophy, is that which has existence in matter and does not exist without it" (*Summa de Homine* 1.4.1 ad 6). Aquinas clearly has such worries in mind. He begins the long reply to 76.1 by recounting Aristotle's extended argument from *De Anima* II.2. But immediately after reciting this argument, Aquinas begins anew, in his own way, as if acknowledging that Aristotle's reasoning has not proved completely convincing to everyone:

> If someone wants to say that the intellective soul is not the form of the body, then it is incumbent on that person to find a way in which the action of intellectively cognizing is the action of a particular human being. For each one of us experiences that it is oneself who intellectively cognizes. (76.1c)

Aquinas issues a challenge: If the intellective soul is not the form of the body, then some other account needs to be given of what makes an episode of intellective cognition *mine* or *yours*. An account needs to be given, in short, of what unites each of us with our intellects. The leading premise here is that each one of us does engage in intellective cognition. Each of us "experiences" that such cognition is something we do. In the *De Anima* commentary he writes:

> it is clear that an individual human being has intellective cognition. If *that* is denied, then the person maintaining this view has no intellective cognition of anything and is not to be listened to. (*InDA* III.7.281–84)

The tone of the second sentence is derisive, but it makes a serious point. No one who did not engage in intellective cognition would be worth listening to—such a "person" could not even participate in the discussion.

What makes it the case that my intellectual activity really is *my* activity? That is, what makes it the case that my intellect really is *mine*? The most straightforward answer to these questions is Plato's: "a human being *is* the intellective soul" (76.1c). Aquinas has already rejected that possibility, in 75.4. Because I engage in sensation, and sensation requires the body, the body must be a part of me (see Pasnau 2002, §2.I). Conversely, because I engage in intellective cognition, and yet am not identical with my intellect, my intellect must be part of me; this is the only plausible way in which *I* could engage in intellective cognition. So I have a bodily part and an intellective part; to speak of them as parts of me entails that they are somehow unified, coming together as parts of a single thing, me:

> We can conclude, therefore, that the intellect by which Socrates cognizes is a part of Socrates, and consequently the intellect is somehow united to Socrates' body. (76.1c)

The problem of Q76 is to explain how intellect, and by extension the whole soul, is united to body. Aquinas believes not just that the form-matter relationship offers the *best* explanation of this unity, but that it offers the *only* workable explanation. The challenge he extends, then, is not to show that his Aristotelian account is wrong, but to offer a coherent alternative.

In 76.1, Aquinas focuses exclusively on those alternatives that would unify soul and body without entirely reducing them to one single thing. Standardly, such accounts are motivated by the background assumption of substance dualism. But Aquinas has in mind other possibilities as well, above all, the various forms of monopsychism that were influential in his day. Monopsychism is the thesis that human beings share a single intellect.

Although incredible sounding, such claims were in effect an alternative formulation of the thesis of divine illumination, a view which was taken very seriously by thirteenth-century Christians (see Pasnau 2002, §10.2). Monopsychism had its defenders in the Latin West, but was associated above all with Islamic philosophy: Averroes was taken to have held that human beings share a single possible intellect; he and Avicenna defended the view that human beings share a single agent intellect.

The goal of 76.1 is not to refute any of these theories directly. (See Pasnau 2002, §2.4 for why Aquinas would reject substance dualism. He attacks different versions of monopsychism in 76.2 and 79.5.) The goal is rather an indirect refutation, by way of establishing that no such nonreductive theory can account for the unity of soul and body. Regardless of whether the background theory is substance dualism, monopsychism, or something else, the nonreductivist will have to tell some kind of story about what it is that unifies soul and body. Some such accounts are so obviously unsatisfactory that Aquinas doesn't bother to mention them. One might, for instance, try to explain soul-body unity by the fact that soul and body are spatially connected (with one containing the other, or the two being contiguous). This will not work. If such local connections were sufficient for unity, then a fetus inside a woman would count as a part of her, and together they would make up a single living substance.

The focus of 76.1 is on the two leading medieval candidates to unify soul and body from within a nonreductive framework. These proposals are on the surface more plausible, but in the end they are no more successful. Each proposes to explain the unity of soul and body in terms of causal interrelations. The first account, attributed to Averroes, proposes uniting soul and body by a causal connection running from the body to the intellect. On this account the body and the soul are united in virtue of the fact that they share information about the world, in the form of phantasms:

> The Commentator . . . says that this union takes place through intelligible species. These species have two subjects, one the possible intellect, the other the phantasms that exist in corporeal organs. In this way, then, the possible intellect is connected to the body of one or another human being through an intelligible species. (76.1c)

This proposal can seem obscure and ill-motivated, particularly when understood in the context of Averroistic monopsychism. But despite its suspect origins, the underlying idea is a natural one. Surely it is reasonable to propose that body and intellect are a unified whole because intellect makes use of the body as a means of acquiring information. A hermit crab, in contrast, has no such connection with the shell that it takes up as its home. The shell protects the crab, but is not a conduit for information about the world. Thus we do not think of the shell as being part of the crab.

Despite the superficial plausibility of this proposal, Aquinas argues that such a causal connection is nowhere near sufficient. We might just as well say we are united with a wall, Aquinas remarks, since visual information passes from the wall into our eyes just as much as it passes from our eyes to our intellect.

> It is evident that we do not attribute the action of sight to a wall, just because that wall has the colors whose likenesses are in sight. For we do not say that the wall *sees*, but rather that it is *seen*. Therefore just because the species of phantasms are in the possible intellect, it does not follow that Socrates (in whom the phantasms exist) intellectively *cognizes*, but that he, or his phantasms, are intellectively *cognized*. (76.1c)

Socrates's phantasms pass from his body to his intellect, but we could say much the same about the colors that pass from the wall to Socrates's eyes. So this sort of causal connection does nothing to unify soul and body. At most it would show that the intellect cognizes the body, when in fact what is wanted is an account of how the intellect's cognitive activity could be the activity of the whole person.

The second alternative that Aquinas considers appeals to causality in the opposite direction:

> Now some want to say that the intellect is united to the body as its mover, with the result that from intellect and body one thing comes about, so that the action of intellect can be attributed to the whole. (76.1c)

On this proposal soul and body would be one thing because the soul moves the body; here 'move' should be understood quite broadly, so that it covers all kinds of causal impressions on the body. Again there is something attractive about this explanation of how soul and body are connected. At least part of our motivation for thinking of soul and body as unified does seem to be that the soul controls (parts of) the body. This was Plato's view of the soul-body relationship, or so Aquinas reports in 76.3c. This also seems to be a fair description of how some of Aquinas's contemporaries viewed the soul-body relationship. William of Auvergne (c. 1180–1249), for instance, held that the soul's presence in the body is required so as better to command and move the body (*De Anima* IV.35, 194–95; I.7, 72–73).

It seems evident that this sort of causal connection is not sufficient: the hermit crab moves its shell, even though that shell is no part of it. But it might at least seem that this account could supplement the first proposal, so that causal connections in both directions would account for the unity of soul and body. The wall is not part of me, because I exert no control over that wall's movements.

Even this joint account is not quite adequate, since I *could* move that wall if I went to sufficient trouble. But perhaps we could refine the account so as to rule out such occasional causal interactions. We might, first, specify that the mover-moved relationship be ongoing. If that were not enough, then we might add that the causal relationship be of a certain direct and unmediated kind.

---

### Platonism

When we rank the greatest philosophers of all time, the ancients get extra credit for having gone so far with so little help from their predecessors. How did Aristotle do it, with little more than Plato to guide him? How did Plato do it, almost from scratch? Obviously, medieval philosophers had more resources to draw upon. Still, we should marvel at how Aquinas managed to go so far with virtually no firsthand knowledge of Plato. And we can wonder just how much better he might have been, if he had known Plato's work firsthand.

In describing Plato's theory of soul, Aquinas is relying on *De Natura Hominis*, a work he believed to have been written by Gregory of Nyssa, but which was in fact written by the fourth-century Syrian Christian Nemesius of Emesa. Aquinas often acknowledges his dependence on this work for information about Plato (see, e.g., II *SENT* 1.2.4 ad 3).

Although Nemesius does not attribute to Plato specifically a mover-moved account of the soul-body relationship, he describes the account in a way that suggests as much:

Therefore Plato . . . did not hold that an animal is made up of soul and body, but that it is the soul using the body and (as it were) wearing the body. But this claim raises a problem: How can the soul be one with what it wears? For a shirt is not one with the person wearing it. (*De Natura Hominis*, chapter 3, pp. 51–52; see chapter 1, p. 5)

Is this Plato's view? The phrase 'soul using a body' is found at *Alcibiades* 129e, but it is not clear whether this dialogue was written by Plato. To make matters still worse, Nemesius himself does not seem to have had much direct knowledge of Plato's works. Still, fairness to Plato aside, the passage illustrates exactly what Aquinas takes to be wrong with Plato's view.

---

Yet even if these vague suggestions were developed, Aquinas would remain dissatisfied. At the most, he believes, the mover-moved relationship would establish for human beings the kind of unity that exists between me and my clothes (*SCG* II.57.1335). This seems right. No causal connection of the sort Aquinas considers seems able to explain why my body is a part of me but gloves, for example, would not be. The fundamental difficulty with the mover-moved account, then, is that it does not produce genuine, unqualified unity. This seems so self-evident to Aquinas that he simply announces, without argument, that on the mover-moved account "it follows that Socrates is not one thing absolutely [*unum simpliciter*]" (76.1c). Although 76.1 considers four different lines of argument against the mover-moved account, this lack of real unity is his fundamental complaint.

The notion of being *unum simpliciter* is central to Aquinas's thinking about human nature. To be *unum simpliciter* is contrasted with being one thing in some respect (*unum secundum quid*). Aquinas cites with approval a remark by Pseudo-Dionysius that any given group of things is one in some respect or other; Aquinas imposes strict criteria, however, on what can be *unum simpliciter*. First, merely being assembled or even joined together is not enough. This rules out, for instance, a pile of stones, and shows why mere spatial continuity does not make soul and body *unum simpliciter*. Second, it is also not enough to be assembled in some functional order. Aquinas denies that a house is *unum simpliciter*, for instance; it is one merely "by aggregation or composition" (*QDA* 10c).[1] Third, and most relevant for present purposes, being united as cause and effect does not make two things *unum simpliciter*. So, even if there is a sense in which soul and body are united by causal contact (see 75.1 ad 3), "things united by such contact are not *unum simpliciter*" (*SCG* II.57.1319).

Nonreductive attempts to unify soul and body will at best produce unity *secundum quid*. That in itself might not be a devastating objection: after all, the very point of nonreductive accounts is to insist that in a sense human beings are two things, not one. But Aquinas thinks that the failure to make human beings *unum simpliciter* has devastating consequences. The principle he relies on here and repeatedly restates is that "something is a being [*ens*] in just the way that it is one" (76.1c; see 76.3, 76.7). The intuitive idea is this. Not every gerrymandered compilation of things counts as a being. A forest or an army, for instance, is a being only in an attenuated sense, corresponding to the attenuated sense in which these collections can be considered one thing. Collections with even less of a claim to be one thing (the water from the lakes of all the states with Republican governors) can be considered a being even less. It is things that are *unum simpliciter*—an individual tree in a forest, an individual soldier in an army—that are beings in the fullest sense. Only beings of this sort are placed in a genus and species, are complete substances, and have actions attributed to them.[2] The *De Unitate Intellectus* spells this out in more detail:

> If you say that Socrates is not one thing *simpliciter*, but one thing in virtue of combining mover and moved, then many absurdities follow. First, since all things are one in the same way that they are a being, it follows that Socrates is not a being, and that he is not in a species or genus, and further, that he does not have any action, since an action belongs only to a being. (3.148–55 [223])

This last implication returns us to the commonsense premise on which 76.1 is based: "Each one of us experiences that it is oneself who intellectively cognizes." When something is not *unum simpliciter*, we tend to attribute its actions to a part of it, rather than to the whole. We attribute an action to an individual soldier, for instance, or to a platoon, rather than to the whole army—unless the whole army (or at least a substantial part) took part in the action (*InNE* I.1.78–95 [5]). We can conclude, therefore, that if Socrates were not *unum simpliciter*, it would be misleading at best to say that he intellectively cognizes. What would be more accurate is to say that some part of him, his intellect, is what intellectively cognizes: in that case, however, "intellect's action cannot be attributed to Socrates" (76.1c).

## II. The Unity of Substances

Aquinas takes the argument of the last section to rule out all the available non-Aristotelian options. He concludes:

> The only way that is left, then, is the way that Aristotle proposes: that this particular human being intellectively cognizes because the intellective principle is that person's form. (76.1c)

As is often the case in Ia, 75–89, this conclusion is something of an oversimplification, an inevitable result of *ST*'s ambition to be "concise and lucid" (Ia pr). Aquinas may have refuted some nonreductive theories, but he has not shown that the only theory left is hylomorphism. In particular, Aquinas has said nothing about another reductive strategy, reductive materialism. The expectation that he ought to consider this topic is not anachronistic; Aquinas knows (see Pasnau 2002, §1.2) that some ancient naturalists, rather than crudely eliminating the soul, considered theories on which the soul is a material property of the body. We will later see how Aquinas would reply to that sort of account.

Because he insists on the unity of soul and body, Aquinas commits himself to an account that is, in a very broad sense, reductive. The argument of the last section ruled out only some very implausible and extreme nonreductive theories: views on which the human intellect is a separate substance, and some (but perhaps not all) types of substance dualism. I now want to consider Aquinas's positive account of what unifies soul and body. I suggest that Aquinas's account of form and matter is reductive—meaning, roughly, that form and matter are not really distinct components of material beings (see Pasnau 2002, pp. 131ff.). This gives composite substances a kind of vertical unity. Here I want to consider how substances have a kind of horizontal unity among their various parts, in virtue of being actualized by a single substantial form. It is this kind of unity, in the terms of the previous section, that makes substances *unum simpliciter*.

It might seem as if the best points of entry into Aquinas's thinking about the unity of soul and body are the sorts of examples that Aristotle offers: for example, the wax and its impression (*De Anima* II 1, 412b6–7); the bronze of a statue and its shape (*Met.* VII 3, 1029a4–5); the material of an axe and its capacity to cut (*De Anima* II 1, 412b11–413a2). In fact, Aquinas believes that these are all misleading examples, because they all concern artifacts rather than genuine substances. With regard to the bronze statue, he remarks:

> [Aristotle] exemplifies this division through artifacts, in which the bronze is like the matter, the shape like "the form of the species" (i.e., it supplies the species) and the statue composed of these. Yet this example must certainly not be taken as a true instance of the relationship, but as a likeness, because shape and other artificial forms are accidents of various sorts, not substances. Still, in the case of artifacts the shape is related to the bronze much as the substantial form is related to the matter in the case of natural things. It is to that end that he uses this example, explaining the obscure through what is clear. (*InMet* VII.2.1277)

Artifacts are convenient illustrations of the hylomorphic theory of substance. It is easy to distinguish the shape of a statue from the bronze stuff out of which the statue is made, and Aristotle wants to use this clear case as an analogy for less obvious ones. But the example is merely analogous, Aquinas emphasizes, because a statue, qua statue, is an artifact, not a substance, and accordingly the shape of a statue is an accidental form, not a substantial one.

Despite the routine way in which Aristotle uses artifacts as examples, this point of disanalogy makes an enormous difference for Aquinas. To compare artifacts with natural substances is to mix things that have very different claims to being substances:

> Natural bodies are substances more than artificial ones are, because natural bodies are substances not only with respect to their matter, but also with respect to their form. (*InDA* II.1.157–58)

Aquinas does not absolutely deny that the statue is a substance, because the statue is composed of bronze and bronze is a substance (see below). Artificial bodies, then, are substances "with respect to their matter." But "with respect to their form" (qua form, to use the Latin expression more familiar to us than to Aquinas), the statue is not a substance, inasmuch as shape is an accidental form. In turn, because artifacts are not substances, they lack the unity that human beings and other natural substances have:

> Anything that is one in terms of substance is one thing *simpliciter* . . . A thing that is discrete [*diversa*] in terms of substance and one accidentally is discrete *simpliciter* and one in some respect [*secundum quid*]. (1a2ae 17.4c)

Artifacts are not entirely satisfactory, then, as a guide to Aquinas's thinking about the unity of soul and body. They are, in particular, poorly suited to explain the kind of unity that Aquinas associates with substances, the unity involved in being *unum simpliciter.*

Unfortunately, the last two paragraphs raise as many questions as they answer. If we are to understand Aquinas's position, it now seems, we will need to consider

(1) the difference between natural beings and artifacts;
(2) the difference between substantial and accidental forms;
(3) the reason why a substantial form has a special kind of unity with its matter, beyond the sort of unity an accidental form has with its subject.

Although (1) is an interesting question in its own right, I am going to pass it over in favor of the other two questions.[3] Regarding (2), we might initially say that a substantial form is a form in virtue of which a thing is the substance it is. And since "it is . . . impossible for something to be intermediary between substance and accident" (76.4 ad 4), we can say that all other forms are accidents. Here 'substance' means a complete substance, and a complete substance is that which "has the complete nature of some species" (75.2 ad 1; see Pasnau 2002, §2.2). *Bronze* is a substantial form, then, because that form specifies the species of the object—the object's essence—whereas the statue's shape is accidental. Likewise, *human* is a substantial form whereas *pale* and *musical* are accidental, because there is a human species, but no species of pale things. This gives us a rather thin account, however, because it presupposes a substantive and problematic distinction between species and nonspecies. Pursuing this line of thought would lead us to take up Aquinas's views about natural kinds, and why it gets us closer to the essence of things to classify in terms of *human* and *bronze* rather than *pale* and *human-shaped.*[4] Rather than move in that direction, I propose to see whether we can find another way of distinguishing substantial and accidental forms, independently of any determinations about natural kinds.

Often enough, Aquinas does propose another way of making this distinction. Substantial forms make a thing exist, he says, whereas accidental forms make a thing be such:

A substantial form differs from an accidental form in this respect: that an accidental form does not make a thing be *simpliciter*, but makes it be such. It is in this way that heat makes its subject not be *simpliciter*, but be hot . . . A substantial form, on the other hand, gives existence *simpliciter*. (76.4c)

This is how Aquinas defines substantial and accidental forms, and this definition is best understood in terms of examples. When copper and tin are fused into an alloy, something new comes about: bronze. The new substantial form, of bronze, makes something be. Because the tin and the copper cease to exist, we do not think of bronze as a modification of something else, but rather as something new coming into existence. In contrast, when that bronze is cast into a particular shape, nothing entirely new comes about. The bronze remains, merely taking on a new shape. That accidental form, the shape, makes the bronze be such. The same is true for body and soul. The human soul does not modify something that already exists, but brings a human being into existence. Before soul and body are joined, there is one thing (a fetus). Once they are joined, something new comes into existence, a human being. The old thing (the fetus) ceases to exist (see Pasnau 2002, §4.3).

This definition makes a fairly standard suggestion about how to distinguish substantial from accidental forms or properties: a substantial property is that which makes a thing be what it is, and without which that thing could not exist.[5] Accidents are properties that a thing could do without, and that may come and go while the substance remains. But this, too, is a rather thin account of substance, because it presupposes that we have a clear grasp of when we should claim that a thing has gone out of existence and when we should claim that it has merely changed. Also, it gives no further aid in analyzing what impels us to make such claims. (Why do we say that bronze is something new? Why do we say that the statue is not something new, but just the bronze with such a shape?) Moreover, the proposal does little to explain (3): why substantial forms should have a special kind of unity with their matter. The definition of 76.4c, then, offers little more than a glorified appeal to our intuitions, cloaked in theoretical terms.

Aquinas has something better to offer us, however. Whereas 76.4c offers a formal and rather unhelpful definition, 76.8c gives us a more meaningful analysis:

A substantial form perfects not only the whole, but each part. For since the whole is made up of its parts, a form of the whole that does not give existence to the individual parts of the body is a form that is a composition and ordering (the form of a house, for example), and such a form is accidental. The soul, on the other hand is a substantial form, and so it must be the form and actuality not only of the whole, but of each part.

This passage makes something more meaningful out of 76.4c by extending its scope. The criterion, we are now told, needs to be applied not only to the whole object, but to each part of the whole. This makes an enormous difference. If we ask whether something new comes into existence when we give bronze a shape or build a house out of wood and stone, it is not at all obvious how we should answer. Perhaps our intuitions point toward a negative reply, but here it is hard to distinguish intuitions from the force of habit, and it is tempting to think that our intuitions could stand being overhauled, if not revised wholesale, by a vigorous and thorough metaphysical analysis.

Aquinas proposes asking not only about the whole, but about each of the parts. When we cast a statue, or build a house, have we given existence to each of the individual parts? That is to say, does changing the shape of the bronze, or making walls out of bricks, make something new out of each of the parts? To these questions we can give a more confident negative reply. The individual parts of the bronze have been heated, molded, and cooled, but otherwise remain unchanged. The bricks and wood of the house have likewise been repositioned, but remain bricks and wood. So on this *extended criterion* (as I call it), neither house nor statue involves the imposition of a substantial form. Each provides merely "a composition and ordering."

One might attempt to resist this conclusion by charging that it rests on implicit and dubious assumptions about essences. If we think of the parts of the bronze statue as bronze, then certainly they remain after the statue has been destroyed. But what if we think of them as statue parts rather than as bronze? Similarly, the parts of the house remain once the house is destroyed, if we think of those parts as bricks and wood. But what if we think of them as house parts? The bricks remain, when the house has been torn down, but the chimney does not remain, and consequently neither do any of the chimney parts. We might say that this pile of bricks once was the chimney, but we cannot say that it is the chimney. And, since there is no chimney, we cannot say of any brick that it is part of the chimney. Characterized as a brick, then, it still exists. But characterized as a chimney part, it has ceased to exist. And what reason do we have for thinking that the first characterization is somehow closer to the real metaphysical truth?

The reply just made will seem successful only when the extended criterion is extended halfway. If we look only as far as chimneys and fireplaces, it may seem as if the parts go out of existence when the house does. Arguably, there can be no fireplace if the surrounding house has been torn down. To be a fireplace, we might say, requires being able to play a certain functional role. This case becomes harder to make if we descend to the level of the individual bricks, although perhaps here too we can think of the bricks as having a function. The case verges on the absurd, however, once we descend even farther, to ask about the constituent parts of each brick. Have the bits of clay that make up the brick changed in any way? Is there anything that would lead us to say that they have become something new, or changed their identity? At this level it seems absurd to appeal to function, as if the bits of clay become something different once they cease to be parts of a chimney. Aquinas's extended criterion derives its strength from the way it forces us to focus our attention on all parts of the substance-candidate. The criterion must be extended all the way down. As with any therapy, to stop the treatment halfway is to invite a relapse.

What about bronze? I have been assuming that what starts out as copper and tin becomes something new, not just as a whole but in each of its parts. This itself is an assumption that needs some defense (see **Molecules**, below). But there is a related question that needs addressing first: Is the whole lump of bronze a single substance, *unum simpliciter*, or is a lump of bronze more like a forest, a conglomeration of many substances? These questions have been obscured until now because the mass term 'bronze' is indeterminate among a single molecule, a larger lump, or even all the bronze in the world. Here too, however, the extended criterion supplies answers. A lump of bronze cannot be a substance, on this criterion, because the parts of that lump remain in existence even once the lump has been divided. Just as the bricks of a house remain bricks after the house has been destroyed, so, too, the individual molecules remain bronze after the lump has broken apart. If a piece of bronze counts as a substance, it will do so only at the microlevel: at the point at which that piece cannot be broken apart and still have bronze parts left over.[6]

As it turns out, then, the example of a bronze statue is doubly unsuitable for Aquinas as an example of the hylomorphic relationship. Not only is *statue* not a substantial form, but, moreover, the thing modified in an accidental way by *statue*, the lump of bronze, is not a substance at all, but a conglomeration more like a forest than like a proper substance. Generally, Aquinas's extended criterion seems to have the surprising implication that nonliving substances occur only at the microlevel. Anything larger is a mere aggregate.[7]

I turn in the next section to the case of living substances, and the unity of soul and body. But first we should dwell on the case of nonliving substances, and consider whether the extended criterion's surprising implications are consistent with Aquinas's overall ontology. My reading of Aquinas on this point is a controversial one; I am drawing conclusions about his metaphysics that go beyond what the texts explicitly say. One might suppose that, contrary to my view, it should be easy to find places where Aquinas characterizes nonliving mid-sized aggregates as substances. Yet the only passages of this sort I have been able to find are occasional offhand remarks that seem to bear little theoretical weight.[8] Moreover, his views about chemical structure are congenial to the extended criterion in several respects. First, he believes that bodies are not infinitely divisible:

> Although a body considered mathematically is infinitely divisible, a natural body is not infinitely divisible. For . . . in a natural body one finds a natural form, which requires a determinate quantity just as it requires other accidents. (*InPh* 1.9.66)

A natural body must be of a certain size, neither too large nor too small: if it goes beyond those limits, it will lose its form. Aquinas defines the *minimum* of a natural body as a body that "cannot be divided further without its being corrupted and then dissolved into the body containing it" (*InDSS* 17.200–3 [18.279]; see 14.221–26 [15.220]). Elsewhere he explains that water cannot be infinitely divided into more and more rarified parts: "the water could be so rarified that at that point it would not be water, but air or fire" (*QDP* 4.1 ad 5). So taking elemental water as our example, and applying the extended criterion, we can say that a body of water counts as a single substance if and only if it is not divisible into two discrete bodies of water—that is, if and only if there is not enough water there to constitute two (or more) *minima*. This does not mean that only the *minimum* of such a body counts as a substance. There might be the *minimum*, and a bit more besides. But if that further bit can be separated and can form a *minimum* of water on its own, then that body of water was not a single substance, but an aggregate of several substances. This is what 76.8c implies, in saying that "a substantial form perfects not only the whole, but each part . . ."

Of course it is not Aquinas's view that the only substances are the basic elements. Even among nonliving things, the basic elements can be combined to form complex substances, much in the way that modern chemistry tells us that elements can bond to form molecules or mix to form alloys. The difference between a mere aggregate and a complex substance is that the parts of the latter will lose properties they possess in isolation and take on new properties characteristic of the complex. Thus, "the form of a mixed body has an operation that is not caused by the elemental qualities" (76.1c). For Aquinas, salt and pepper is a mere mixture, because the bits of salt and pepper have the same function whether mixed or segregated. There is no interaction that produces something over and above the parts. On Aquinas's terminology, this sort of mere mixture counts as "an apparent mixture, one that occurs through minute [parts] being positioned next to one other" (76.4 ad 4). In the case of a complex substance, Aquinas speaks of "a true mixture, one that occurs throughout the whole" (ibid.). He devotes an entire treatise, *De Mixtione Elementorum*, to working out the details of this problem.[9]

Although Aquinas does not explicitly articulate the account I am proposing, he comes close in his *De Anima* commentary, when he explains why only living beings can be said to take nourishment, strictly speaking. That is not an obvious truth for Aquinas, because he holds that a thing is nourished when it "receives in its very self something that serves to maintain it" (II.9.135–36). On this criterion, it might seem that fire is nourished: one feeds a fire, after all, by adding more wood. Aquinas maintains that this is not a genuine case of feeding or nutrition, because strictly speaking the criterion is not satisfied. The original fire is not maintained when more wood is added, because the additional wood starts up a different fire.

This passage is relevant because it shows that fire does not have the requisite unity to satisfy the criterion:

> the whole fire that comes from many lit fires gathered together is not one fire *simpliciter*, but seems to be one due to aggregation, in the way that a heap of stones is one heap. (145–48)

In the case of fire, this is not surprising. But Aquinas goes on to reach a more general conclusion: that only living things have the requisite unity. Only in their case is "life maintained through food in the *same* part in which it was before . . . [E]ach one of their parts is both nourished and grows" (150–54). In contrast:

> This does not happen in things without souls; they seem to expand through addition. For it is not the case that what was there before expands, but that a different, greater whole gets established through the addition of something else. (154–57)

---

### Molecules

It would be an interesting and worthwhile project to apply Aquinas's extended criterion to modern chemistry. One might initially think it obvious that individual atoms will count as substances. But this is problematic in a number of ways. First, it is not clear that an isolated atom of, say, gold, genuinely counts as gold, given that it would lack most of the distinctive properties of gold. Peter Van Inwagen, *Material Beings*, Ithaca: Cornell University Presss, 1990, p. 17, quotes an expert who claims it takes sixteen or seventeen atoms to make gold. Also, atoms bound together as a molecule will make a single substance. Indeed, some definitions of 'molecule' appear to be virtually equivalent to Aquinas's extended criterion for substancehood:

A molecule is considered the smallest particle of any given kind of matter which, when taken alone, retains the properties of that kind of matter. ("Molecule," *Columbia Encyclopedia*, 2nd ed.)

A molecule of gold would be the smallest quantity of gold that retains the properties of gold (i.e., the essential properties, whatever they are). The same is true for

(*continued on next page*)

a compound, like salt. Sodium and chlorine, when joined in an ionic bound, are not separate substances, because together they take on a new set of properties, which they lose when separated.

A still harder case is bronze, a class of alloys most often composed of copper and tin. These atoms form crystals of regular shapes, and any given crystal is likely to have both copper and tin atoms. As an alloy, bronze has properties quite different from those of its component metals, and this is what makes it plausible to think of bronze as a distinct kind and a viable substance candidate. At the microscopic level, the atoms that alloy to make bronze mix in a random fashion, and can mix in varying proportions. (Such variability is what distinguishes alloys from compounds.) This opens the door to problems of vagueness. When is there enough tin for there to be bronze, and when too much tin? When is copper pure enough to be pure copper? See Rogers (1964), p. 51: "Actually, a metal almost always contains measurable amounts of other elements even after energetic efforts have been made to eliminate them."

Things without souls do not meet the criterion for nutrition because the stuff that is added does not form a part of the original substance. Genuine nutrition does involve the addition of new material, food, but this food becomes part of the original substance. When fire is added to fire, in contrast, there is mere aggregation without true unity. The original substance is not maintained, but instead "a different, greater whole gets established" (as above). Aquinas believes that this is true for all nonliving things, and so he concludes that "only ensouled things truly grow" (152–53). Applying this same logic to stones, we would have to say that liquifying and then cooling some sort of rocky material so as to form a larger stone does just that: it produces a "different, greater whole." Stones cannot grow, because they lack the requisite unity. In general, adding material to anything nonliving produces mere aggregation. The moral is that living things are the only aggregates that are unified substances.

### III. Body and Soul as a Unified Substance

Artifacts do not count as substances, no matter how highly organized. Lumps do not count as substances, even if those lumps are homogeneous assemblages of a single kind of substance. In general, nonliving things seem to be substances only at the microlevel. All of this is the natural consequence of a claim we saw Aquinas make in section 1: that simply being joined together is not sufficient for being *unum simpliciter*. But this line of thought does not lead Aquinas, in Leibnizian fashion, to reject all but the most simple substances. He accepts that elements can mix to form complex substances. Among these mixed substances, the most complex by far are living things. Here the constituent parts depend for their existence on the survival of the living organism. So whereas bronze is a substance only at the atomic level, a whole human being counts as a substance, as does a whole tree.[10]

How exactly do living things satisfy the extended criterion for substancehood offered in the previous section? How is it, in other words, that a soul "perfects not only the whole, but each part" (76.8c)? Aquinas's reasoning crucially depends on an application of Aristotelian homonymy: that the parts of a human being exist only for as long as the human being exists. A corpse is not a human body, and so too for all of the parts of that corpse:

> Just as one does not speak of an animal and a human being once the soul has left—unless equivocally, in the way we say that an animal has been painted or sculpted—so too for the hand and eye, or flesh and bones, as the Philosopher says. An indication of this is that no part of the body has its proper function once the soul has left, whereas anything that retains its species retains the operation belonging to that species. (76.8c)

It is not evident from our ordinary ways of talking that this invocation of homonymy is correct. Socrates, for instance, immediately after deploring the effects of careless speech, is made to remark in the *Phaedo* that "it is only my body that you are burying . . ." (115e). But Aristotle, and Aquinas following him, hold that such claims are equivocal, and that neither my body nor any of its parts survives death (see, e.g., *Meteor.* IV 12, 389b31–390a19, and Christopher Shields, *Order in Multiplicity: Homonymy in the Philosophy of Aristotle*, Oxford: Clarendon Press, 1999, chapter 5). If that is right, then the soul passes the extended criterion of 76.8c. It follows, then, that the soul is a substantial form and a human being a substance.

As usual, Aquinas is not content merely to make an appeal to Aristotle's authority. Such arguments from authority, he remarks near the outset of *ST* (1.8 ad 2), are "the weakest" of all arguments. In the above passage he goes on to give an argument for such homonymy, pointing to the fact that the body's parts do not maintain their function after death. This line of argument explicitly acknowledges something assumed several times in the last section about how we should apply the extended criterion: in asking whether a form gives existence to all of the parts, and whether those parts cease to exist when the form ceases to exist, we should focus on the function of the parts. This claim is consistent with several arguments offered by Aquinas. He establishes that the body is part of a human being because the body is required for essential human functions (see Pasnau 2002, §2.1). He also establishes the rational soul's subsistence on the basis of its capacity for continued operation (see Pasnau 2002, §2.2). Both of these arguments are based on the principle that "any given thing is identified with what carries out the operations of that thing" (75.4). Existence, then, depends on the capacity for ongoing function. At death the body ceases to exist; this is true insofar as it ceases to function:

> Damage to the heart destroys the soul's operation in all of the body's parts. *As a result* it destroys the existence of these parts, which was maintained by the soul's operation. (I *SENT* 8.5.3 ad 3)

The hands and eyes of a corpse cannot be identified with the hands and eyes of the formerly living body, because they have lost the capacity to carry out their former operations. Although the point is most clear in cases where the part's function is obviously lost, Aquinas maintains this claim generally, down to the least part of the body: "not only does the animal not remain, but also no part of the animal remains" (*InGC* I.15.108). It is easier to miss this point, he acknowledges, in the case of flesh and bones. But these parts remain no more than does a hand or an arm—even if "in these [latter] cases the soul's operations are more evident" (ibid.). Flesh and bones had a function as well, and that function has now equally been lost.

If the human soul is to satisfy Aquinas's extended criterion, then Aristotelian homonymy must hold for every part of the body, even for very small pieces of bone and flesh. This may seem implausible, for the same reason it seemed that tiny pieces of brick remain in existence when the house goes out of existence. But there is an important disanalogy here, which Aquinas can exploit in insisting that human beings are substances in a way that houses are not. Tear down a brick house and the parts of the brick remain unchanged. With respect to how the parts of the brick are functioning and what they are doing, nothing has changed. (They are, of course, no longer parts of a house. But that is a mere Cambridge change, not a real change to the brick itself.) Matters are quite different for the parts of a living body even for parts that remain within the body for a very short time. Consider an example of Peter van Inwagen's: a carbon atom that passes into and out of the body within a few minutes. The atom enters the digestive system as sugar, moves into and through the bloodstream, is oxidized (in the process producing energy), and is finally exhaled as part of a carbon dioxide molecule. At each step this atom is acting (or being acted on) in ways that are characteristic of living organisms. The atom is, in van Inwagen's words, "caught up in the life of an organism" (1990, p. 94). It starts out as sugar, it ends up as carbon dioxide. In between, the carbon atom should be described as part of a human being rather than simply as carbon. Its identity is subsumed by that of the whole organism. Again, this makes for a contrast with the case of a house. The clay bricks remain clay, regardless of whether they compose a house or lie scattered on the ground. And, again, Aquinas's criterion for making these distinctions is the function of the material. It is the complex interrelatedness of living organisms that gives them their special kind of unity.

Not all living things are equally complex, and in some cases this lack of complexity poses a prima facie difficulty for the extended criterion. Aquinas identifies two such cases in his *De Anima* commentary:

- the case of a slip from a plant, which will survive if replanted;
- the case of a worm from which a cut-off piece can survive.[11]

These cases pose a challenge to the extended criterion; they suggest that not all living things are substances, insofar as their souls do not meet Aquinas's test for being a substantial form.

Such cases do not give us reason to abandon the extended criterion; they are in fact the proverbial exceptions that prove the rule, by pointing the way toward a clearer understanding of the extended criterion. Take the case of a plant. With care and skill, a cutting can be made to survive on its own. But the operation does take care and skill: a piece of plant cut off at random and left untended will almost certainly not survive. The parts of the plant display a mutual dependence that aggregates display not at all, or at best very slightly. It is precisely this mutual dependence that is characteristic of substances. So the case of a cutting from a plant, in virtue of the difficulty involved in this operation, in fact helps to confirm the distinction between substances and mere aggregates.

Here one might raise a further worry. If mutual dependence comes in degrees, then what justifies Aquinas in drawing a hard and fast distinction between substantial and accidental forms, or between substances and nonsubstances? Perhaps human beings, plants, and bronze lumps should be viewed on a continuum, with human beings highly organized, worms moderately organized, and bronze lumps barely organized. A bronze lump could be regarded as a weakly unified substance, or it could be regarded as a highly unified aggregate. The difference wouldn't amount to much—which would explain why Aquinas is never very concerned about fixing his terminology in this area.

Although this suggestion is plausible, it fails to do justice to the insight expressed by the extended criterion. The whole force of the doctrine of substantial forms comes from there being a dramatic divide in the natural world between the organizational unity of substances and the lack of such unity in aggregates. The case of a worm illustrates this point. A cut-off piece may survive for some time, but not just any cut-off piece will do. One has to cut off enough of the worm, and one cannot repeat the process too many times. A worm chopped into twenty pieces is simply a bloody mess. So the case of a worm, on its face problematic for Aquinas, in fact helps to illustrate the metaphysical divide between substances and nonsubstances. A mid-sized piece of bronze entirely lacks the kind of mutual dependence that one finds even in a worm. Although it is not infinitely divisible, for all practical purposes bronze can be divided without end. For this reason, it is simply not plausible to put a bronze lump on the same continuum as living things.

---

### Ecosystems

Just as aggregates of simple substances can appear to have the unity of genuine substances, so can aggregates of living things. Consider a rainforest, where the highly specialized species of life depend on one another for their existence. Laura Landen ("Of Forests and Trees, Wholes and Parts," *Proceedings of the American Catholic Philosophical Association* 69, 1995, pp. 81–89) develops this example in the context of Aquinas's theory, and remarks of such interdependent species that "without the forest, they would not be what they are; indeed, they would not be" (p. 83). In light of Aquinas's extended criterion for substancehood, such interdependence seems to entail that the rainforest is itself a substance. Surely that is not right.

The mistake is in supposing that exotic plants and animals literally cannot survive outside the rainforest. Perhaps it could be true of the occasional species that we do not know how to keep it alive outside its native habitat. But by and large the parts of a rainforest can exist outside of that environment, in a simulated rainforest. So, strictly speaking, the parts of a rainforest are not interdependent in the way the parts of a substance are. Still, one might wonder: Is this so different from taking a cutting from a plant? Zookeepers take elaborate measures to keep their animals alive. Gardeners do the same with their cuttings. The difference is that while a plant may have a few branches that can survive apart, an ecosystem can be split up into millions of parts. Each insect could be shipped in a different direction, each clump of dirt scattered, each plant dug up and delivered somewhere else. The rainforest would no longer exist, of course, but its parts would. This is the hallmark of a mere aggregate.

---

We might imagine a species of worm that could be divided into twenty pieces, or even a hundred pieces, each piece still alive. Such a worm would be much more like bronze, and in such a case we might speak not of having a worm, but of having worm—that is, we might use 'worm' as a mass term. If worms were like that then we would have to acknowledge that the distinction between substance and nonsubstance is not as clear-cut as Aquinas supposes. But although we might imagine such a living organism, I wonder whether we would be imagining a coherent possibility. I doubt whether anything divisible in the way that a bronze lump is could actually be considered living. If it were considered living, I doubt whether it could be considered a *single* living substance. Moreover, even if such a creature is possible, this shows only that Aquinas's metaphysics does not hold as a matter of conceptual necessity. There *might* be worlds where no meaningful distinction could be drawn in Aquinas's terms between substances and aggregates. But ours is not that world. In this world, there is such a distinction. Aquinas's ontology of substance is not a necessary and a priori truth about reality, but neither is it based on mere convention or linguistic fact. It captures fundamental features of the natural world as it is. The following passage summarizes the argument:

> (a) For since the body of a human being, or of any other animal, is a kind of natural whole, it will be called one from the fact that it has one form perfecting it—and not just as an aggregate or composite, as with a house and other such things. (b) Thus every part of a human being and an animal must receive its existence and its species from the soul as its proper form. (c) And thus the Philosopher says that once the soul has left, neither the eye nor the flesh nor any other part remains, except equivocally. (*QDA* 10c)

Aquinas's reasoning runs as follows:

(a) Living things are unified in a distinctive way; their unity is greater than that of artifacts and nonliving aggregates. (I am extrapolating. The passage speaks only of animals, not of all living things, and does not explicitly say that natural aggregates like rocks fall in with houses. But these points seem implicit.)

(b) The reason living things have this special sort of unity is that "every part . . . must receive its existence and its species" from its substantial form. That is, living things meet the test I have been calling the extended criterion.

(c) The rationale for thinking that living things meet this test is an application of Aristotelian homonymy: without the substantial forms, each and every part goes out of existence.

This account explains the difference between substantial and accidental forms, and explains why the soul is a substantial form. Also, as promised at the start of the previous section, it explains why a substantial form has a special kind of unity with its matter. An object is unified to the extent it is undivided: "A thing is related to unity in proportion to its being related to undividedness . . . That which is undivided *simpliciter* is said to be one thing *simpliciter*" (I *SENT* 24.1.1c). More precisely, "a being is said to be one thing when it is indivisible or undivided" (*InMet* X.3.1974). The second formulation is more precise because it is indivisibility, rather than being in fact undivided, that characterizes the union of substantial forms with their matter. It is not obvious why we should say an accident is *divided* from its subject. But accidents are *divisible* from their subjects insofar as an accident may come and go while the subject remains. In contrast, the substantial form is indivisible from the matter it actualizes, in the sense that if that form is destroyed, the substance as a whole is destroyed, as is each of its individual parts. Because substantial forms are thus inseparable from their matter, they make up one thing with their matter, *unum simpliciter.*

Aquinas conceives of indivisibility from the perspective of the parts, not from the perspective of the whole. This makes a crucial difference. If we look at a human being and ask whether the body is separable from the whole person, it looks as if the answer is yes. We can lose legs and arms, organs and tissue without the person's being destroyed. Moreover, we lose and gain cells on a constant basis: liver cells are replaced within five days (van Inwagen 1990, p. 94). From this perspective, it looks as if the body is eminently separable from the whole person. Aquinas looks from the opposite perspective. Rather than focusing on whether the whole survives without some part, he asks whether the parts can survive without the whole. In the case of a living substance, they cannot. The cells of the liver cease to exist when they pass out of the body. They no longer function as they once did, contributing in a certain way to a living organism. From the perspective of the parts, then, the substance is an indivisible whole. From this perspective, living substances appear to have a unity fundamentally different from that of nonliving aggregates.

This account has much to offer. It is highly plausible to suppose that the unity of a living substance is qualitatively different from the unity of objects that can be dissolved and divided without destroying their parts. It is perhaps surprising to find Aquinas committed to the view that these other objects are not substances at all, and that substances are found in nonliving objects only at the atomic level. Yet once one sees the sort of unity he claims for living substances, one should be struck by the absence of that unity in mere artifacts and aggregates. In denying that artifacts and aggregates possess this sort of unity, the unity of substances, Aquinas is not denying that such things are real or that they exist. Houses and statues exist, and so do forests, beaches, and pints of strawberries. But all of these objects have a weaker claim to be single, individual things.

This conception of soul as substantial form also sheds light on Aquinas's puzzling claim that the soul, like all forms, exists as a whole in every part of the matter that it actualizes. In 76.8, Aquinas defends this doctrine with regard to the soul. Elsewhere he makes it clear that the doctrine holds more generally: "it is apparent in the case of every form that it is whole in the whole and whole in each part" (*SCG* II.72.1485). Aquinas thinks there is nothing at all puzzling about this aspect of form. The form of whiteness, he explains (*SCG* II.72.1485), covers the whole surface of a white object, and that form is whole in each part—inasmuch as each part is equally white. In much the same way, the soul of a living being exists in every part, because every part is alive, and (as we have seen) to say that a body has soul is simply to say that it has life.[12] If some are confused on this question, it shows simply that they have the wrong conception of soul. Thus, after explaining how soul is present throughout the body, he adds:

> Neither is this difficult to grasp for someone who understands that the soul is not indivisible as a point is, and not something nonbodily joined to something bodily in the way that bodies are joined to one another. (*SCG* II.71.1485)

In his *Sentences* commentary he makes the point even more clearly. Speaking of those who took the soul to have a determinate location in the body, he writes:

> The cause of this view was that in two respects they had the wrong picture [*falsa imaginatio*]. First, they pictured soul's being in the body as if in a place, as if it were only its mover and not its form, as a sailor is in a ship. Second, they pictured the soul's simplicity being like that of a point, as if it were something indivisible that has an indivisible location. Each of these assumptions is ridiculous. (I *SENT* 8.5.3c)

If it seems odd to think of the soul as spread throughout the body, this indicates that one has the wrong picture of what soul is. Soul is not a mysterious nonextended force, located at some central point within the body and moving the body as one would move a puppet. Soul exists throughout our body, giving it life.

---

#### Simplex, Multiplex

The *sed contra* to 76.8 quotes Augustine in defense of the doctrine that "in any one body, the soul is whole in the whole body, and whole in each part of it" (*De Trinitate* VI.vi.8). Augustine had introduced this claim to help illustrate how God can be at the same time "simple and multiple." Aquinas accepts this suggestion wholeheartedly, and even extends the claim to all forms. But others weren't so sure. John Buridan (1295–1358) would accept the claim in the case of soul, but he writes that such a thing "is truly miraculous and supernatural" (*De Anima* II.9). How, he wonders, could something be nonextended and yet exist throughout the body? In effect, Buridan accepts Augustine's illustrative analogy but dismisses its explanatory value.

---

This account has one final advantage: it explains the unity of soul and body in a way that allows for the human soul's peculiar autonomy relative to the body. Indivisibility is analyzed in one direction: the substance and its parts cannot exist without the form, but it remains possible for the form to exist without the substance. This leaves room for Aquinas to reply to the seemingly insurmountable objections of 76.1 (described at the start of this chapter). First, it is entirely consistent for the rational soul to be united with the body and yet be able to operate and exist independently of the body (ad 1, 4, 5). Second, the soul can be united to the body without itself becoming material (ad 2, 3). Third, the soul's immortality does not stand in the way of soul and body's being *unum simpliciter* (ad 6). Even though the soul can exist without the body, the body remains inseparable from the soul, in that it cannot exist without the soul. So despite being part of a unified material substance, the soul preserves the autonomy necessary for immortality and abstract thought.

## IV. Reductive Materialism

We have now seen the failure of certain nonreductive accounts and the kind of unity supplied by Aquinas's own type of hylomorphism. A question that remains is whether another sort of reductive account might work at least as well. For modern philosophers, the obvious candidate is some sort of reductive materialism.

The ancient naturalists, Aquinas tells us, "said that the only things that exist are bodies, and that what is not a body is nothing. And, in keeping with this doctrine, they said that the soul is a body" (75.1c). As elsewhere, Aquinas is suppressing interesting details for the sake of the concision and lucidity that is his announced goal (1a pr). Not all of the ancients held that the soul is a body; some, in particular, Empedocles, proposed that soul is the harmonious composition of various material parts. Aquinas was well aware of these other views; he discusses them in detail in his commentary on *De Anima* I. A complete treatment of non-Aristotelian attempts to unify soul and body would have to deal with such accounts, but *ST* does not aspire to completeness, and 76.1 is already the longest article in the Treatise. So in order to understand Aquinas's views we need to look elsewhere.

The fact that some ancient naturalists attempted to define soul in terms of harmony illustrates that the ancients, even as understood by Aquinas, were not so hopelessly crude and misguided as to reject all talk of forms, properties, and states. In addition to their elemental bodies (fire, water, etc.), the ancients recognized the existence of forms such as color, shape, and position (see Pasnau 2002, §1.2). Soul, on this harmony account, would be another such form, existing for as long as the various components of the body exist in a harmonious or well-balanced state. There is something plausible about the theory, Aquinas admits, because it seems that the soul remains with the body for as long as the body retains its harmonious composition.

Moreover, as soon as that harmony is lost, the soul seems to disappear. It is tempting to infer, then, that the soul just is the body's harmonious composition. Still, Aquinas argues that the inference is fallacious: harmony is not the soul but the proper bodily disposition for the soul (*InDA* I.9.196–212). This sort of bodily disposition is essential to a body's being ensouled (see Pasnau 2002, §12.4) but cannot be identified with the soul.

Why not? Aquinas's answer to this question grows out of the status that harmony has as a form. The ancients identified their basic material principles as the enduring substances that exist through change (see Pasnau 2002, §1.4). Added onto these substances were various forms:

> Matter, which they said was the substance of a thing, endures through every change. Its states, however, are changed: the form, and all the things that are added onto the matter's substance. (*InMet* I.4.74)

These added-on forms are accidents; they come and go while the substance remains. On the ancient theory, harmony would be one such added-on form, and therefore to identify the soul with harmony is to make the soul an accidental form. Aquinas argues that it is absurd to treat the soul as an accidental feature of a living thing (*InDA* I.9.65–69). On this ancient account, a substance could remain in existence while the substance goes from living to dead or vice versa. The soul-as-harmony theory treats *being alive* as a property much like *living in Philadelphia*, as if dying is no more substantive a change than leaving town. This is of course implausible: dying seems to be no mere accidental change, but to represent a fundamental change in a thing's nature. If an argument is even needed here, we have seen how Aquinas would invoke Aristotelian homonymy: a living body has existence only in virtue of its soul, and goes out of existence when separated from that soul (§3.1). In maintaining that all things can be given a fundamental explanation in terms of matter, the ancients were forced to treat as accidents attributes such as *having life* that manifestly are not accidents.

Aquinas often quotes Aristotle's remark that "for living things, living is existing" (*De Anima* II 4, 415b13). The point is that living and existing are not wholly distinct attributes of a living being. Living just is the mode in which living things have existence, and so it is absurd to give a different explanation for each, and to treat living as an accidental quality that might come and go while the substance remains in existence. The soul does not merely make the body be of a certain kind, the living kind; the soul also gives a body its very existence. "Soul itself forms the body that fits it; it does not take up one already prepared" (*InDA* I.8.358–59). On Aquinas's account, the soul gives a living substance both existence and life, because to give a substance life just is one way of bringing it into existence.

Aquinas thinks this mistake about the soul is symptomatic of the ancients'
most general failing: their inability to distinguish natural substances from artifacts, or substantial forms from accidental ones. The heart of their problem
was that they held a mistaken theory of matter:

> The ancient natural philosophers, not able to reach all the way to prime matter . . . ,
> claimed that some sensible body was the prime matter of all things—fire, air, or
> water. And in this way it followed that all forms would come to matter as it [al-
> ready] actually existed, as occurs in the case of artificial things. (For the form of
> a knife comes to iron when it already actually exists.) And so they held a view
> about natural forms that was just like their view about artificial forms. (*InPh*
> II.2.149)

The ancients failed to recognize prime matter, preferring instead to take certain bodies as their basic elements (see Pasnau 2002, §1.4). But because the
ancients described these bodies as actually existing—as having their actuality
built into them—it follows that any further forms must be accidents. For it is
true by definition that accidental forms are ones that do not bring existence to
their subject, but rather inhere in substances that *already* exist (77.6c; *De Principiis* 1.20–35 [339]). A craftsman does not, in making a knife, bring into existence a new substance. Instead, the artist takes the substance, the iron, and
gives it a new accidental form, a shape. For the ancients, the only substances
were their basic substances. They were therefore compelled to treat complex
substances, even plants and animals, as if they were artifacts.

On the ancient account, therefore, all forms would be accidental forms. As
a result, nothing would ever be generated anew, or thoroughly corrupted; all
change would be modification, since their basic substances (air, water, etc.)
endure through all change. Aquinas believes that from this failure we can
come to grasp the proper relationship of form and matter. Indeed, "substantial generation and corruption are the starting-points for one's coming to
grasp prime matter" (*InMet* VIII.1.1689). When one sees what is required for
genuine coming-into-existence and going-out-of-existence, one sees what
prime matter must be like:

> All those who hold that the first subject is some sort of body, such as air and
> water, claim that generation is the same as alteration. On the basis of this rea-
> soning, then, it is clear how *we* must reach an understanding of prime matter.
> (Ibid.; see *InGC* I.1.5)

We, Aquinas tells us, must understand prime matter as something that exists
only insofar as it is actualized through a substantial form. Because the ancients
were wrong about prime matter, identifying it with something actually exis-
tent in its own right, they ended up thinking of generation and corruption as

mere accidental changes. On their view substances never go out of existence, and new substances never come into existence.

Of all the ancient theories of soul, the harmony theory "most seemed to approach formal causes." In actual fact, however, "the ancient philosophers never took up formal causes, only material ones" (*InDA* I.5.25–28). The harmony theory represents movement in the right direction, Aquinas thinks, because at least it identifies soul with a form rather than with a body. But even here the ancients were not arguing in terms of formal causes, because they failed to understand the nature of substantial forms. Aquinas thinks that the only tenable theory of human nature is one that explains human beings in terms of the union of substantial form with matter. Given his theory of substance, and the way he thinks a human being is one thing *simpliciter*, he has reason to conclude that "the only way that is left, then, is the way that Aristotle proposes . . ." (76.1c). Only the hylomorphic theory has seemed able to give human beings the sort of unity required of a genuine substance.[13]

Aquinas's quarrel is not with materialism in general. Except for the special case of intellectual substances (see Pasnau 2002, §2.2), Aquinas is himself a kind of materialist (see Pasnau 2002, §2.3). But he finds reductive materialism objectionable insofar as it eliminates forms from playing even an explanatory role. The ancients did not entirely eliminate forms, but they failed to develop a theory of forms adequate to account for substantial change and unity.

It is perhaps not obvious how this critique of ancient materialism should be extended to cover modern versions of materialism. So let us shift to the beginnings of modern philosophy, and to Francis Bacon's programmatic denunciation of Aristotelianism:

> Matter rather than forms should be the object of our attention, its configurations and changes of configuration, and simple action, and law of action or motion; for forms are figments of the human mind. (*New Organon* I.51)

This is far cruder than anything we have seen from the medieval or ancient period; if Aquinas had had Bacon in front of him, he wouldn't have needed to portray the ancient materialists in caricature. Bacon tells us to give up on form, and to focus on configuration, as if that were not itself a paradigmatic kind of form. In fairness, Bacon no doubt intends to attack forms of a more abstruse sort, above all, substantial forms. And in light of the dismal decline of philosophy during the so-called Renaissance, it is easy to feel some degree of sympathy with Bacon's complaint. In fact, he proposes quite a reasonable test: "Wherefore, as in religion we are warned to show our faith by works, so in philosophy by the same rule the system should be judged of by its fruits" (1.73). Even by Bacon's own standards, however, we can now point to the fruits of an analysis in terms of substantial forms. Bacon wanted philosophers to focus their efforts on explaining the natural world; Aquinas uses substantial forms to do just that. On his analysis, the distinction between substance and nonsubstance corresponds to a genuine and important distinction among natural entities. The theory of substantial forms gives us a way—Aquinas believes the only way—to explain the nature of that difference, and to explain why some objects have a distinct kind of unity that warrants their being described as substances.

Still, what does this have to do with philosophy today? Reductive materialism, in suggesting that all things ultimately reduce to material explanations, seems committed to supposing that even the study of living organisms can ultimately be cashed out in terms of microlevel material events. It is now very common among philosophers of science to deny that this is so: a real understanding of biology, for instance, is said to show such reduction to be impossible even in principle (see, e.g., John Dupré, *The Disorder of Things: Metaphysical Foundations of the Disunity of Science*, Cambridge, MA: Harvard University Press, 1993).

Although Aquinas never shows much interest in empirical science, he gets this sort of antireductionism out of his metaphysics. To understand what is special about living organisms—their coherence and endurance over time, the complex behavior they exhibit—one cannot look simply at their constituent material parts. The theory of substantial forms attempts to shift the focus of analysis to a higher level, where an organism can be studied not as a collection of discrete parts but as a single, unified substance.

In this light, it becomes clear that the soul is more than just a placeholder for whatever it is that gives life to living things (see Pasnau 2002, §1.1). Moreover, though Aquinas devotes the remainder of the *Summa Theologiae*'s Treatise on Human Nature (QQ77–89) to analyzing the human soul's various powers and operations, the conclusions he establishes here show that the soul is more than just a collection of powers carrying out the various operations of life. Beyond these discrete functions of nutrition, sensation, and intellection, the soul has the more basic function of accounting for the unity of a living organism.

## Notes

This chapter was previously published as Robert Pasnau, "The Unity of Body and Soul" (chapter 3 of Robert Pasnau, *Thomas Aquinas on Human Nature*, Cambridge University Press, Cambridge, 2002). Reprinted with the permission of Cambridge University Press.

1. For Pseudo-Dionysius, see *De Div. Nom.* XIII.2, cited at 1a2ae 17.4c. On mere assembly as insufficient for real unity, see *SCG* I.18.141, 1a2ae 17.4c, *InMet* VIII.3.1725; on ordered assembly, see 76.8c, *SCG* IV.35.3731.

With respect to ordered assembly, and specifically the case of a house, it is interesting that Aquinas repeatedly says something quite different in his Aristotelian commentaries. See, in particular, *InMet* VII.17.1672–74, where a house is claimed to be *unum simpliciter*. (See also *InNE* I.1.78–95 [5].) In these passages Aquinas seems to be adapting himself to Aristotle's way of speaking; as we will see, Aquinas standardly denies that artifacts can be *unum simpliciter*.

Aristotle, in contrast, is not concerned (or merely not so careful?) to distinguish artifacts from (what Aquinas would regard as) genuine substances. Indeed John Ackrill ("Aristotle's Definitions of Psyche," *Proceedings of the Aristotelian Society* 73, 1972–73, pp. 119–33) seems to think that Aristotle's account holds together only in the case of certain artifacts (pp. 132–33). Montgomery Furth ("Transtemporal Stability in Aristotelian Substances," *Journal of Philosophy* 75, 1978, pp. 624–46), on the other hand, remarks that "it is both unfortunate and puzzling that Aristotle's *Metaphysics* discussions of material substance are oriented so obsessively around artefactual study objects" (p. 646). In his later book, Furth comes to a reading of Aristotle much like the reading I propose for Aquinas (Pasnau 2002, §§1.2 and 3.1), concluding that for Aristotle living things are the only full-fledged substances (*Substance, Form and Psyche: An Aristotelian Metaphysics*, Cambridge: Cambridge University Press, 1988, pp. 181–84). But Furth suggests that Aristotle's notion of substance admits of degrees. This is not a suggestion I embrace for Aquinas.

2. See 1a2ae 17.4c, *InMet* X.1.1931. As Pasnau 2002 §2.2 shows a complete substance is that which is the member of a species (75.2 ad 1). The link between being *unum simpliciter* and being a substance becomes more clear in §1.2. For further discussion of the relationship between being and being one (*ens* and *unum*), see Aertsen (*Medieval Philosophy and the Transcendentals: The Case of Thomas Aquinas*, Leiden: Brill, 1996), chapter 5. One remote source for Aquinas's view is Boethius's claim that "everything that exists, insofar as it exists, is one" (3a 17.1sc, referring to *Contra Eutychen*, chapter 4, p. 94).

3. Aquinas is committed to the view that all artifacts are nonsubstances with respect to their form. (See, e.g., *InDA* II.1.157–58, as quoted in main text, and also *QQ* 11.6 ad 3, *De Principiis* 1.74–81 [342].) So we might try defining an artifact as a substance (or substances) that has been purposefully altered by a change to one or more of that substance's accidental forms. Or, if 'purposefully' seems too broad in light of Aquinas's across-the-board teleology (see Pasnau 2002, §§6.2 and 7.1), we might instead require that the alteration come from an external principle (following *InMet* IX.6.1837). See Pasnau 2002, §4.1 for how *natural* generation requires an *internal* principle.

One might suppose that simply being man-made is at least a sufficient condition for being an artifact. (Cf. the definition proposed by Bernard Wuellner [*A Dictionary of Scholastic Philosophy*, Milwaukee: Bruce Publishing, 1966]: "an object, or an order among objects made by human art or transitive work.") But it seems that Aquinas should not accept this because (for reasons that will become clear) his account of substance leaves open the possibility that human beings might make substances—that is, might bring into existence a new substantial form. Cloning might be an example of this. An even clearer example would be our constructing from scratch a new living organism. What is known as the Minimal Genome

Project is presently attempting to determine the minimal configuration of genes required for a living substance, "an advance that could ultimately allow scientists to design and create living organisms completely from scratch" (*Washington Post*, Dec. 10, 1999, A8).

But if we can make substances, then Aquinas might want to reconsider his claim that artifacts as such are not substances. For he might want to agree that being man-made is a sufficient condition for being an artifact. In that case he might have to concede that their nonsubstantiality was a contingent feature of the state of technology in the thirteenth century.

4. See *InDA* II.2.32–36: "an accidental form, which is not in the genus of substance, does not pertain to the essence or quiddity of its subject . . . But a substantial form does belong to the essence or quiddity of its subject." This line of thought would quickly lead to the problematic sort of Aristotelian essentialism that Willard Van Orman Quine ("Reference and Modality" in *From a Logical Point of View*, 2nd ed., New York: Harper and Row, 1963) characterized as "adopting an invidious attitude toward certain ways of uniquely specifying x . . . and favoring other ways . . . as somehow better revealing the 'essence' of the object" (p. 155). See Richard Cartwright ("Some Remarks on Essentialism," *Journal of Philosophy* 65, 1968, pp. 615–26) and David Wiggins (*Sameness and Substance*, Cambridge, MA: Harvard University Press, 1980), pp. 130–31.

Aquinas doesn't regard this as a dead-end project, however, because he believes the essence of a substance is determined by the subject's end, its final cause.

5. Wiggins (1980) picks up on the second part of this characterization: "According to whether 'x is no longer f' entails 'x is no longer,' the concept that the predicate stands for is in my usage a *substance concept*" (p. 64). Also Baruch Brody (*Abortion and the Sanctity of Human Life: A Philosophical View*, Cambridge, MA: MIT Press, 1975), p. 97: "If, before a change, there was an object *o* with a property *P*, then the change is what we can call an alteration (as against a substantial change) if *o* continues to exist after the change though it no longer possesses *P*. On the other hand, the change is a substantial change if, after its occurrence, *o* no longer exists."

A properly Aristotelian notion of essences imposes a further condition, that the property describe what the thing is, its quiddity.

6. One might claim that I have shown only that bronze is not a substance *qua* lump. True, when the lump breaks apart, the parts remain as they were. But all that shows (one might say) is that *lump* is not a substantial form.

The example shows more than that, as becomes clear once it is set out in a way that makes no assumptions about what the substantial form in question is. Take some mid-sized bronze substance candidate. Now, destroy that substance candidate by freezing and then shattering it, so that what was a mid-sized piece of bronze is now many tiny shards of bronze. It is evident (1) that the substance candidate no longer exists (which would entail the loss of its substantial form); and (2) that the pieces of that substance candidate remain in existence. Therefore, a mid-sized piece of bronze does not meet Aquinas's extended criterion for substancehood.

7. Quite aside from the problematic chemical nature of bronze, the example of a statue is more complex than I have indicated, and the interested reader should see the

discussions in *QQ* 11.6 ad 3 and IV *SENT* 44.1.1.2 ad 4. In each of these passages, Aquinas explains that artifacts like a statue are substances with respect to their matter, but not with respect to their form. So what happens when a statue is destroyed and then reproduced? According to each passage, the statue does not remain the same relative to its form: this is because numerically the same form cannot be destroyed and then brought back to existence. (Hence personal immortality requires the survival of the soul. But in another sense—relative to its matter—the statue is the same. In fact, Aquinas claims that the statue remains the same substance. So its substantial form must remain the same. But how can this be, given that this collection of bronze stuff has been destroyed? Conceivably, Aquinas assumes that even after the statue is destroyed, the bronze holds together as a clump, and that this (*being a clump?*) is somehow its substantial form. Yet what seems far more plausible, both philosophically and exegetically, is that the individual molecules of bronze are what retain their substantial forms. So when those molecules are brought back together as a statue, there is no substantial change. "When considered as a substance, a statue rebuilt from the same matter is numerically the same" (IV *SENT* 44.1.1.2. ad 4). The substance remains the same, in the sense that the myriad bronze substances that once made up a statue do so again. *Their* forms are never lost.

8. Here I am indebted to Eleonore Stump, who has tried her best to talk me out of this view. In comments on this material for an American Philosophical Association colloquium, Stump has proposed a series of texts that seem problematic. Closest to home, she points out that 76.4 ad 4 speaks of the substantial form of a stone. (An even clearer passage on stone as a substance is *CT* 211.20–29 [410].) But it is not clear that Aquinas always uses the term 'stone' (*lapis*) as we do, as referring to rock clumps of a certain smallish size. At least in some contexts, though admittedly not in all, *lapis* might serve as a mass term for Aquinas, like bronze. And if *lapis* can work as a mass term, then to call it a substance shows nothing about how much or little *lapis* might constitute a single substance.

Moreover, if stumped, I have a fallback position, in that I am not really concerned to show that Aquinas *never* speaks of substance in a way that is incompatible with the extended criterion. The term 'substance' is a broad one, used in many ways in many contexts, and Aquinas is not always careful to use terms in their strictest technical sense. What I want to insist on is that (1) the account of 76.8 has the implications I have identified; (2) the account is consistent with the general contours of Aquinas's thinking about artifacts and natural substances; (3) if (and only if) we take this account seriously, we can understand how it is that soul and body are unified; (4) the account yields the further dividend of an interesting and sophisticated ontology.

9. Another interesting discussion in this context is 3a 2.1, where Aquinas develops his account of how two natures, one human and one divine, were united in Christ. They could not have been united as one nature, Aquinas argues, because there are only three possible ways for that to occur: (1) as a mere aggregate; (2) as a mixture; (3) as incomplete parts of a form-matter composite. None of these possibilities make sense for the Incarnation. For our purposes, however, what is interesting is that a lump of bronze or a piece of stone can fall only into category (1). Not into (2): Aquinas is explicit here that the parts of a mixture undergo a change in species when they are mixed

together. Not into (3), because such parts are incomplete. See also *SCG* IV.35.3731–32, where Aquinas gives much the same taxonomy.

10. The comparison between Aquinas and Leibniz is instructive. Leibniz's ultimate considered position, as expressed in a letter to de Volder from 1703, is that "there can be nothing real in nature but simple substances and the aggregates that result from them" (Leibniz, *Philosophical Essays*, tr. R. Ariew and D. Garber, Indianapolis: Hackett, 1989). But sometimes Leibniz expresses more sympathy for the view that at least some extended things can be substances. He writes to Arnauld (July 14, 1686)

> If the body is a substance and not a simple phenomenon like the rainbow, nor an entity united by accident or by aggregation like a heap of stones, it cannot consist of extension, and one must necessarily conceive there something that one calls substantial form, and that corresponds in some way to the soul. (R. C. Sleight, *Leibniz and Arnaud: A Commentary on Their Correspondence*, New Haven: Yale University Press, 1990, p. 103)

Sometimes, in fact, Leibniz seems inclined to hold that the only extended substances are living substances: "perfect unity must be reserved for bodies that are animated, or endowed with primitive entelechies" (*New Essays* 3.6.42). For one effort to sort through Leibniz's complex and varying positions, see Sleight (1990), chapters 5 and 6.

11. See *InDA* II.4.33–89, re. *De Anima* II 2, 413b15–24. Although Aquinas is not considering these as potential counterexamples to the extended criterion, the context in which they arise is intimately related to the concerns of this chapter. Aristotle had presented these cases as evidence for the thesis that the soul exists throughout the body. Correspondingly, Aquinas says that in these cases a part of the soul separates with the bodily part. The cutoff branch or worm part can survive precisely because it takes a part of the soul with it (cf. 76.3c, *InDA* I.14.107–34).

12. There is a further question of how the soul can be *whole* in each part. After all, not all of the soul's capacities are present in each part: we can see, for instance, only through the eyes. Aquinas explicitly addresses this issue in 76.8c, and solves it by invoking his distinction between the soul's essence and its capacities (see Pasnau 2002, §5.2). The soul's essence is whole in each part of the body. Its capacities, in contrast, are generally located by the relevant organs. And some capacities are not bodily at all (76.8 ad 4).

13. Aristotelian hylomorphism is "the only way that is left"—but at this point I mean it to be an open question as to whether the proper form of hylomorphism embraces a single substantial form (Aquinas's view) or a plurality of substantial forms (the standard view). Either way, the ancient harmony theory is unacceptable because it didn't recognize harmony as a substantial form at all. If harmony were treated as a substantial form, then it might be something like the scholastic *forma corporeitatis*, which authors like Scotus treated as one among several substantial forms. The present arguments have no bearing on that kind of account.

# 7

# The Nature of the Intellect

*Anthony Kenny*

A QUINAS'S TREATMENT OF THE MIND in the *Summa Theologiae* begins properly with Ia 79, a long question with thirteen articles with the title "On the Intellectual Powers."

Before discussing the question, we need to say something about the translation of the crucial terms of the discussion. Aquinas's *intellectus* is fairly enough translated by the English word 'intellect': as we shall see, it is the capacity for understanding and thought, for the kind of thinking which differentiates humans from animals; the kind of thinking which finds expression especially in language, that is in the meaningful use of words and the assignment of truth-values to sentences. But English does not have a handy verb 'to intellege' to cover the various activities of the intellect, as the Latin has in *intelligere*. To correspond to the Latin verb one is sometimes obliged to resort to circumlocutions, rendering *actu intelligere*, for example, as 'exercise intellectual activity'. An alternative would be to use the English word 'understanding', in what is now a rather old-fashioned sense, to correspond to the name of the faculty, *intellectus*, and to use the verb 'understand' to correspond to the verb *intelligere*. In favour of this is the fact that the English word 'understand' can be used very widely to report, at one extreme, profound grasp of scientific theory ('only seven people have ever really understood special relativity') and, at the other, possession of fragments of gossip ('I understand there is to be a Cabinet reshuffle before autumn'). But 'understand' is, on balance, an unsatisfactory translation for *intelligere* because it always suggests something dispositional rather than episodic, an ability rather than the exercise of the ability; whereas *intelligere* covers both latent understanding and current conscious thought. When Aquinas has occasion to distinguish the two he often uses *actu intelligere* for the second: in such cases the expression is often better translated 'think' than 'understand'.

In the first article we are told that the intellect is a power of the soul. It is not identical with the soul; the soul has other powers too, such as the senses and the powers of nutrition (*ad* 3). But because the intellectual power is the most important of the powers of the soul, the intellectual soul itself is sometimes called the intellect.

What is the relationship between the intellect and the mind? Do we have here two words for the same thing? Following Augustine, Aquinas thinks of the mind as consisting not just of intellect, but of intellect plus will. The intellect is a power of apprehension, the will is a power of appetition; that is to say, understanding is an exercise of the intellect, love is an exercise of the will (2 and *ad* 2). Not all appetition is mental; there is also the animal appetition of hunger, thirst, lust; what is special about the will is that it is the power to want objects grasped by the understanding; it is a power of the mind: it is the power for intellectual appetition.

What is it that *has* the power which is the intellect? Aquinas is prepared to call it a power *of the soul*. This is because (as he has explained earlier, *S* 1,77,5) he regards thought as an activity which has no bodily organ. Because the activity does not involve the body, he goes on to say that the power, which is the source of the activity, must belong to the soul. But of course ultimately what the activity and the power belong to is the *person* who is performing the activity and whose soul and intellect are in question. Hence Aquinas says that in creatures the intellect is a power of the person thinking.[1]

If the intellect is a power, is it an active or passive power? Is it a power to act on something, or is it a power to suffer change? Aquinas's answer is that it is both. First he discusses the sense in which the intellect is a passive power. In thinking and coming to understand we undergo change[2]: that is to say, we start our lives in a purely potential state, with our intellect like a blank sheet with nothing written on it, and gradually we acquire understanding and our mind fills with thoughts. It would be possible to imagine beings who did not have to acquire the ability to think in the slow and toilsome way in which children have to be brought to the understanding of language. We might imagine creatures who were born with the ability to speak in the same way as we are born with the ability to hear. Aquinas believed that the heavenly angels provided an example of understanding which was exempt from the slow progress characteristic of human beings. They are throughout their existence in full possession of everything they will ever know. But human understanding is something very different, and so the human intellect is a passive power, a power to undergo change which needs to be acted upon by many factors if it is to realize its potentiality (*S* 1,79,2c).

The intellect considered as a passive power, the potentiality to receive thoughts of all kinds, is called by Aquinas, after Aristotle, the *intellectus possibilis* or receptive intellect (*S* 1,79,2 *ad* 2). It is contrasted with the *intellectus agens*, or agent intellect, which was described by Aristotle in the third book of his *De Anima* and which is discussed by Aquinas in the third article of question seventy-nine. If the function of the receptive intellect is as it were to provide room for thoughts, the function of the agent intellect is to provide furniture for that room, that is to create objects of thought. The material objects of the physical world are not, Aquinas believed, in themselves fit objects of thought; they are not, in his terminology, actually thinkable, *actu intelligibilia*. A Platonic Idea, something universal, intangible, unchanging and unique, might well be a suitable object of thought: but are there any such things as Platonic Ideas? To explain the function of the agent intellect, Aquinas gives the reader a brief lesson in ancient Greek philosophy.

> According to Plato's theory, there was no need for an agent intellect to make things actually thinkable . . . Plato thought that the forms of natural things existed apart without matter and were therefore thinkable: because what makes something actually thinkable is its being non-material. These he called *species* or Ideas. Corporeal matter, he thought, takes the forms it does by sharing in these, so that individuals by this sharing belong in their natural kinds and species; and it is by sharing in them that our intellect takes the forms it does of knowledge of the different kinds and species.
>
> But Aristotle did not believe that the forms of natural things had an existence independent of matter; and forms which do exist in matter are not actually thinkable. It followed that the natures or forms of the visible and tangible objects we think of would not be, on their own, actually thinkable. But nothing passes from potentiality to actuality except by something already actual, as sense-perception is actuated by something which is already perceptible. So it was necessary to postulate a power belonging to the intellect, to create actually thinkable objects by abstracting ideas (*species*) from their material conditions. That is why we need to postulate an agent intellect. (*S* 1,79,3)[3]

Plato's theory of Ideas, at least as Aquinas understood it, went like this. We see in the world around us many different dogs, each separate from the others, each living its own individual life. In addition to all these individual dogs, there is an Ideal Dog, which is identical with none of them, but to which they all owe their title to the name 'dog'. The Ideal Dog may also be called the Form of Dog; unlike individual dogs, it is not in space and time, it has no parts, and does not change, and it is not perceptible to the senses; it has no properties other than that of being a dog; it is The Dog, the whole Dog, and nothing but the Dog. Ordinary individual dogs, like Fido, Bounce and Stigger, owe to The

Dog the fact that they too are dogs: it is by imitating the Ideal Dog, or sharing in the Form of Dog, that they are dogs.

What goes for dogs goes also for cats, and humans, and beds, and circles: in general, wherever several things are F, this will be because they participate in or imitate a single Form of F or Ideal F. By postulating these Forms or Ideas, Plato sought to explain, among other things, why many different things can all be called by the same name, and how the mind can have universal and un-changing knowledge about continually changing individuals.

In another passage (*S* 1,84,1) Aquinas explains how Plato was led to this po-sition. The early Greek philosophers, he says, believed that the world con-tained only material things, constantly changing, about which no certainty was possible. What is in constant flux cannot be grasped with certainty, be-cause it slips away before the mind can grasp it; as Heraclitus said, you cannot step into the same river water twice.

> Plato, to save the fact that we can have certain intellectual knowledge of the truth, posited, in addition to ordinary bodily things, another class of things free of mat-ter and change, which he called *species* or ideas. It was by participation in these that all particular tangible objects get called 'man' or 'horse' or whatever. Accordingly, Plato held that definitions, and scientific truths, and all other things pertaining to the operation of the intellect, are not about ordinary tangible bodies, but about those immaterial things in another world. Thus the soul's thinking would not be about the material things around us, but about their immaterial ideas.[4]

Aristotle and Aquinas maintained that there were no such things as immate-rial Ideas, and believed that Plato's method of accounting for universal knowl-edge led to absurdity. If the Ideas are immaterial and unchanging, and all knowledge is of Ideas, then there can be no knowledge of matter and change. That would rule out natural science, and any form of explanation which in-volves material or variable causes. It is ridiculous, Aquinas said, when seeking information about things plain to view, to bring in strange intermediaries of a totally different order. If there were any such things as Ideas, knowledge of them would not help us in any way in making judgments about the things we see around us (*S* 1,84,1c).

Aquinas and Aristotle were prepared to go along with Plato to the extent that they would agree that what made Fido a dog was a form—the form of doggi-ness or caninity, or what you will—but they denied that there was any such form existing apart from matter. Fido's dogginess exists in Fido, Bounce's dog-giness exists in Bounce, and Stigger's in Stigger. Fido, Bounce and Stigger are all material objects in our familiar world, and in the real world the only forms to be found are individualized forms like the dogginess of Stigger. There is not, in the world, any dogginess which is not the dogginess of some particular dog.

How, then, are we to account for the properties of our thinking about dogs? We can think about dogs without thinking of any particular dog; but there is no such thing as a dog which is no particular dog. When we think a general thought about dogs, the object of our thought is, we might say, the universal dog. It is the universal dog which is the actually thinkable dog, the dog *actu intelligibile*. But if Plato is wrong there is not, in heaven or earth, any such thing as the universal dog. Plato's mistake is the attempt to locate in the extra-mental world entities whose only home can be in the mind.

> Plato was misled because, believing that like can only be known by like, he thought that the form of what is known is necessarily in the knower exactly as it is in the known. He noted that the form of an object of thought in the intellect is universal, immaterial, and invariant . . . Thus he concluded that the things thought of must exist independently in an immaterial and invariant manner. But this is unnecessary. (*S* 1,84,1c)[5]

How then do we explain the mind's capacity to have general thoughts about dogs, when the only dogs there are to think about are all individual? The answer given by Aristotle and Aquinas is that the universal dog, the actually thinkable dog, is the creation of the agent intellect. "It was necessary to postulate a power belonging to the intellect, to create actually thinkable objects by abstracting ideas (*species*) from their material conditions. That is why we need to postulate an agent intellect" (*S* 1,84,1c).

Here it is necessary to say something about the word *species*. In the passages we have discussed it was first used as an expression for Platonic Forms, synonymous with the Latin word 'Idea'. But Aquinas goes on to use it in the exposition of his own theory. 'Intelligible species' are the acquired mental dispositions which are expressed, manifested, in intellectual activity: the concepts which are employed in the use of words, the beliefs which are expressed by the use of sentences. My grasp of the meaning of the English word 'rain' is one kind of species; my belief that red night skies precede fine days is another kind of species.

The most natural English word to cover both concepts and beliefs is 'idea', and in many contexts 'idea' makes an unproblematic equivalent for 'species', and I will use it as such. If the English word is dangerously ambiguous, that is all to the good, since the Latin word is ambiguous in closely parallel ways.

Ideas may be ideas *of* or ideas *that*: the idea of gold, the idea that the world is about to end. Similarly, species may correspond either to the understanding of individual words, or to affirmation and negation (*S* 1–2,55,1). Summarizing, we might say that ideas comprise both concepts and beliefs.

Aquinas expounds the Aristotelian theory of the agent intellect by means of a comparison between sense and intellect. Colours are perceptible by the sense of sight; but in the dark, colours are only potentially, not actually, perceptible. (In the daylight, they are actually perceptible, but they are not necessarily actually perceived—perhaps no one is looking at them.) The sense of vision is only actuated—the colours are only seen—when light is present to render them actually perceptible (1,79,3 *ad* 2).

Similarly, according to Aquinas, substances in the physical world are in themselves only potentially thinkable, because they are individual and thought is universal. To make potentially thinkable objects into actually thinkable objects, we need an intellectual analogue of light in the visible world. And it is this intellectual analogue of light which is the agent intellect. One can think of the agent intellect as like the lantern a miner carries in his helmet, casting the light of intelligibility upon the objects a human being encounters in his progress through the mysterious world.

What can we say about the agent intellect apart from this metaphorical description? First of all, it is an ability, or capacity, belonging to individual thinkers. For Aquinas, it is a natural endowment which each human being has; it is not—as it was for some other medieval Aristotelians—a supernatural agent acting on human beings from outside in some mysterious way (*S* 1,79,4).

The agent intellect is the power which humans, unlike other animals, have of acquiring abstract information from sense experience. Animals with senses like ours perceive the same material objects as we do, but they lack the ability to talk about them, to think abstract thoughts about them, to acquire scientific knowledge about them. The species-specific ability which they lack is the agent intellect.

It helps to understand the kind of thing that Aquinas meant by 'agent intellect' if we consider human beings' ability to acquire language. Human beings are not born knowing any language; but it has been argued by the linguist Noam Chomsky that it is impossible to explain the rapidity with which children acquire the grammar of a language from the finite and fragmentary utterances of their parents unless we postulate a species-specific innate language-learning ability.

Even though Chomsky's innate language-learning capacity has to be an ability of a very general kind if it is to explain the learning of all the many diverse natural languages, it is not quite the same as Aquinas's agent intellect. While Chomsky, in talking about innate abilities, has in mind particularly the ability to master the internal structure of language, Aquinas is more interested in semantics than in syntax or grammar; he is concerned above all with the mind's capacity to understand meaning. Again the agent intellect, as we shall see, has functions which are broader than those of Chomsky's species-specific capacity.

Nonetheless, for Aquinas the intellect is something very much akin to the ability to master language. For the intellect is a capacity, the capacity to think, and capacities are specified by their exercises: that is to say, in order to understand what the capacity to *f* is, one must know what *f*-ing is. So to understand what the intellect is, we have to examine what its activities are; and according to Aquinas the various activities of the intellect may all be defined in terms of the use of language.

Following Aristotle, Aquinas maintained that intellectual operations could be divided into two types: the understanding of simple ideas (*intelligentia indivisibilium*) on the one hand, and affirmation and negation (*compositio et divisio*[6]) on the other. Both of these operations of the mind are defined by means of their expression in language. The understanding of simple ideas corresponds, roughly, to the mastery of individual words; affirmation and denial find utterance in affirmative and negative sentences.

Here is a typical passage where Aquinas makes his distinction between the two kinds of intellectual activity:

> There are, as Aristotle says in the *De Anima*, two kinds of activity of our intellect. One consists in forming simple essences, such as what a man is or what an animal is: in this activity, considered in itself, neither truth nor falsehood is to be found any more than in non-complex utterances. The other consists in putting together and taking apart, by affirming and denying: in this truth and falsehood are to be found, just as in the complex utterance which is its expression. (*V* 14,1)[7]

The way in which the distinction between these two types of thought is linked with the difference between the use of individual words and the construction of sentences is brought out when Aquinas explains how any act of thought can be regarded as the production of an inner word or sentence:

> The 'word' of our intellect . . . is that which is the terminus of our intellectual operation: it is the thought itself, which is called an intellectual conception; which may be either a conception which can be expressed by a non-complex utterance, as when the intellect forms the essences of things, or a conception expressible by a complex utterance, as when the intellect makes affirmative or negative judgments (*componit et dividit*). (*V* 4,2c)[8]

The two types of thought are distinguished by Aquinas with reference to the presence or lack of complexity. There are other types of complex thought beside the actual making of affirmative and negative judgments. Consider any proposition you like: let us take as examples 'Inflation leads to unemployment' or 'Angels have no bodies'. With respect to a proposition such as these, a judgment, affirmative or negative, may be made or withheld; if made, it may be made truly or falsely, with or without hesitation, on the basis of argument or on grounds of self-evidence. According to various combinations of these possibilities, the making or withholding of the judgment will be an instance of doubt, opinion, belief, knowledge or understanding.

Thus, one may refrain from making a judgment because of lack of evidence on either side, or because of the apparent equality of reasons pro and con. If one does make a judgment, it may be made on the basis of the alleged self-evidence of a proposition, or be the result of a more or less prolonged train of reasoning. Judgment may be tentative and hesitant, or firm and unquestioning. Aquinas classifies exercises of the intellectual powers on the basis of these different possibilities: the withholding of judgment is doubt (*dubitatio*); tentative assent, allowing for the possibility of error, is opinion (*opinio*); unquestioning assent to a truth on the basis of self-evidence is understanding (*intellectus*); giving a truth unquestioning assent on the basis of reasons is scientific knowledge (*scientia*); unquestioning assent where there are no compelling reasons for the truth of the proposition is belief or faith (*fides, credere*). Forming or holding a belief, accepting an opinion, coming to a conclusion, and seeing a self-evident truth are all instances of *compositio et divisio*; all have in common that they are intellectual acts or states expressible by the utterance of sentences.

There is, then, a very close relationship between thought and words, between the operation of the intellect and the use of language. But it is important not to overstate this relationship. Aquinas believed that any judgment which can be made can be expressed by a sentence (*V* 2,4). It does not follow from this, nor does Aquinas maintain, that every judgment which is made *is* put into words, either publicly or in the privacy of the imagination. Again, even though every thought is expressible in language, only a small minority of thoughts are *about* language. The capacity of the intellect is not exhausted when language has been acquired.

The understanding of simples is related to the entertaining of judgments as the use of individual words is related to the construction of sentences. An example of the understanding of simples would be the knowledge of what gold is—knowledge of the *quid est* of gold. Such knowledge can be exercised in judgments about gold, and without some such knowledge no judgment about gold would be possible. Some such judgments, such as 'gold is valuable' or 'gold is yellow', require no great understanding of the nature of gold; they presuppose little more than an awareness of what the word 'gold' means. A chemist, on the other hand, knows in a much richer way what gold is. Not only can she list many more of the properties of gold, but she can relate and present those properties in a systematic way, linking them, for instance, with gold's atomic number and its place in the periodic table of the elements. The chemist's account of gold would seem to approximate to the ideal described by St. Thomas as knowledge of the quiddity or essence of a material substance (for example, *S* 1,3,3 and 4,17,3).

However, Aquinas's account of the first operation of the intellect is not as easy to follow as his theory of judgment. The word (*verbum*) which results from the understanding of simples is not a judgment but a definition or *quidditas* (*V* 1,3c). Aquinas appears to use *quidditas* in two different ways and to give two correspondingly different accounts of the intellect's first operation.

In many places St. Thomas observes that one can know what a word 'A' means without knowing the quiddity or essence of A. We know, for instance, what the word 'God' means, but we do not and cannot know God's essence (for example, *S* 1,2,2 *ad* 2). Learning the meaning of a word and acquiring a scientific mastery of the essence of a substance are both exercises of the intellect; but the grasp of essences is understanding *par excellence*. In the case of the understanding of simples no less than in compounding and dividing, we meet a distinction between a broad and a narrow sense of 'understand'. In the broad sense, the acquisition and application of any concept, the formation and expression of any belief count as exercises of the understanding; in the narrow sense, understanding is restricted to insight into essences and the intuition of self-evident truths.

Once language has been acquired, the thinker is in a position to use language to learn about the world—to think thoughts, make judgments, acquire knowledge and build up science about everything under the sun. This means, in Aquinas's terms, that the receptive intellect of an individual will be stocked with ideas about many things other than language. But what of the agent intellect? That is only one part of the intellect: is it a part which can be identified with the ability to master language? The identification here would be much less misleading; but here too there are qualifications to be made. For Aquinas the operation of the agent intellect is not the same as the acquisition of the mastery of a word: it is rather a prerequisite for it, the general ability to abstract ideas from the material conditions of the natural world. Chomsky, at least at one time, appeared to believe that there is a human language faculty which is distinct from the kind of general intelligence which a human, or an extra-terrestrial mind, might use in general computational activity. Aquinas's agent intellect, though like Chomsky's language faculty peculiar to the human species, would be involved no less in the acquisition of arithmetical concepts than in gaining mastery of syntax. Finally, as we shall see later, not every mastery of a word which a person would acquire in the course of learning a language like English would count, for Aquinas, as an instance of the abstractive activity characteristic of the agent intellect.

With these qualifications, however, it is helpful to think of the agent intellect as being in essence the species-specific power which enables human beings to acquire and use language in their transactions with the world which we perceive around us. As has been said, an animal with the same senses as ours perceives and deals with the same material objects as we do; but he cannot have intellectual thoughts about them, such as a scientific understanding of their nature, because he lacks the light cast by the agent intellect. On the other hand, for Aquinas, a being with an agent intellect but without the senses that we share with animals would be equally impotent to think even the most abstract and intellectual thoughts. In answer to an objection that if the agent and receptive intellect are both parts of the same soul, everyone will be able to understand everything whenever they want, he says this:

> If the agent intellect stood to the receptive intellect in the relationship in which an active object stands to a power, as a visible object does to the sense of sight, then it would indeed follow that we would immediately understand everything, since the agent intellect is what makes everything intelligible. But it is not itself the object of thought, but is rather that which makes actually thinkable objects; and for that we need not only the presence of the agent intellect, but the presence of sense experience (*phantasmata*), and sensory powers in good condition, and practice in operation; because understanding one thing leads to understanding others, and we pass from terms to propositions, and from premises to conclusions. (*S* 1,79,4,3)[9]

The human mind has the ability not just to acquire concepts and beliefs, but to retain them. Aquinas, having introduced the agent intellect as the mind's concept-acquiring faculty, turns to consider memory, as the mind's capacity for retaining concepts and beliefs. He asks whether the memory is part of the intellect, and in reply he is led to make a number of distinctions.

Most of what we know comes only rarely before our minds. When I talk, whether aloud or in my head, I use only a tiny sample of my active vocabulary; when I listen or read, likewise, I draw on only a fraction of my passive vocabulary. We all know many facts, important or trivial, which we hardly ever call to mind or have brought back to our attention. We think of all these things as being somehow stored in our minds; and one of the things we mean by 'memory' is simply the ability to store ideas in this way. Memory in this sense, Aquinas says, is part of the intellect: it is identical with the receptive intellect, which, according to Aristotle, is the storehouse of ideas (*S* 1,79,6; 7 *sed* c).

Though the picture of the mind as a storehouse is a familiar one, we may well find it difficult to give an account of what is the literal reality which lies behind the picture. Avicenna denied that ideas could remain in the mind unthought of. We might speak without difficulty of things being stored in the brain; but how can things be stored in the mind? To be in the mind is simply to be an object of thought; so how can something still be in the mind when it is no longer being thought of? He concluded that when we reuse a concept, or recall a belief, we must go through the same process as when we first mastered the concept or acquired the belief.

Aquinas disagreed. There is an obvious difference between learning something for the first time, which may take effort and calls for the appropriate environment, and making use of a skill already mastered, or bringing to mind a fact already known. Against the Aristotelians who agreed with Avicenna, he quoted the authority of Aristotle:

> In *De Anima* III he says that when the receptive intellect "becomes identical with each thing as a knower, it is said to be actualized; and this comes about when it is capable of acting on its own. But even then it is in potentiality, though not in the same way as before learning or discovering." For the receptive intellect is said to become things when it receives the ideas of them. Having received the ideas of thinkable objects, it has the power to think of them at will, but it does not follow that it is always doing so. It is still in a manner in potentiality, though not as it was before first understanding; it is the kind of potentiality which a person has to bring to actual attention a piece of knowledge which is habitual. (*S* 1,79,6)[10]

In other places, Aquinas, followed by later scholastics, codified the different kinds of actuality and potentiality. A human baby, not yet having learned language, is in a state of remote potentiality with regard to the use of language: he has a capacity for language learning which animals lack, but he is not yet able to use language as an adult can. An adult who has learned English, even if he is not at this moment speaking English, is in a state of actuality in comparison with the child's potentiality: this was called 'first actuality' (*S* 1,79,10). But a state of first actuality is still itself a potentiality: the knowledge of English is the ability to speak English and understand it when spoken to. This first actuality can be called a *habitus* or disposition; it is something halfway between potentiality and full-blooded actuality (*S* 1,79,6 *ad* 3). The latter, the 'second actuality', is the actual speaking or understanding of English: particular activities and events which are exercises of the ability which is the first actuality (*S* 1,79,10).

Once I have learned English and still remember it, I am in this state of first actuality. Abiding intellectual abilities of this kind constitute one form of memory, and as Aquinas says, this kind of memory is not anything distinct from the power of the intellect itself. A power to acquire concepts and beliefs without the power to retain them would be something quite different from the human intellect; indeed, it is difficult to make sense of such a power, since a concept is itself an enduring understanding, and a belief is an abiding mental state, not a transitory mental episode.

But 'memory' does not mean only the retention of acquired knowledge. I remember the twelve-times table in the sense that I have learned it and not forgotten it. But when I say that I remember being taken to the seaside at the age of 3, I do not mean simply that I have learned, and not forgotten, that I was taken to the seaside at the age of 3. The remembrance of a childhood visit to the seaside is not, according to Aquinas, something which is purely intellectual. Thus, he states the following argument against the thesis that memory is part of the intellect:

> Memory is of past things. But the past is referred to by reference to a definite time. Memory therefore is a way of knowing things in reference to a definite time, which is to say that it knows things by reference to here and now. But such knowledge is the province of the senses, not of intellect. So memory belongs not to the intellectual part of the soul, but to the same part as the senses. (*S* 1,79,6,2)[11]

Aquinas accepts the conclusion that if a memory is a memory of a past object, considered as past, then it is not an operation of the intellect, which is concerned with what is universal and timeless, but an operation of that part of the soul, like sense-perception, which is concerned with what is particular and temporal.

> Pastness can be considered in relation to the object known, or to the knowing itself. These two things go together in the case of sense-perception, which is acquaintance with an object through a modification brought about by a sensory quality which is present. Hence by one and the same act an animal remembers a past sensing of something and a sensing of something past. It is not the same with the intellectual part: pastness is irrelevant to something when it is considered as an object of thought.[12]

This is because an idea such as the idea of *dog* is something which abstracts from particular times and places, but is concerned only with what makes a dog a dog. The word 'dog' applies equally well to all dogs, past, present or future. The object we know when we have mastered the word 'dog' is something to which any particular time is irrelevant. But if we distinguish, as Aquinas does, between the object known and the knowing itself, then matters are different. Any actual case of thinking about a dog will be a thought thought by a particular individual at a particular time:

> Our intellect's thinking is a particular act, occurring at one or other particular time, so that a man is said to think now or yesterday or tomorrow. This does not conflict with the nature of intellect . . . just as the intellect thinks about itself, even though it is itself a particular individual, so it thinks of its own thinking, which is an individual act which is either past present or future.[13]

This means, Aquinas says, that despite what he said earlier, there is in the intellect a kind of knowledge of what is past, as past: namely the knowledge which the intellect has of its own past acts. This seems surprising. Surely my memory that when I was 7 I learned Pythagoras's theorem is just as individual and particular a memory as my memory that when I was 3 I had a bucket and spade. So why does Aquinas want to make a distinction between the two? In fact, I do not think Aquinas is referring to memories of particular intellectual exploits in the past. What he has in mind is something different, along the following lines. If I know that whales are mammals, and call this knowledge to mind, then in the very act of such recall I know that this is something I have already known previously. (If I were in any doubt about this, my thought that whales are mammals would not really be a case of knowledge.) It is the awareness that one's knowledge of language, or of universal truths, is not something novel but something habitual that constitutes the element of pastness in intellectual memory.

Having discussed the relationship between intellect and memory, Aquinas goes on in the eighth and ninth articles of question seventy-nine to discuss the relationship between intellect and reason. Reason seems to be a peculiarly human faculty, since man is standardly defined as a rational animal. Is it the same faculty as the intellect, or something different (*S* 1,79,8,3 and *ad* 3)?

Aquinas's answer is simple:

> Reason and intellect cannot be different powers in human beings. This is clearly seen if one considers the activities of both. Understanding is an immediate grasp of an intellectual truth. Reasoning is passing from the understanding of one thing to the understanding of another thing in order to reach knowledge of intellectual truth . . . So reasoning is to understanding as motion is to rest, or getting to having.[14]

The simplicity is a little deceptive: Aquinas has suddenly changed the focus of the noun 'intellect' and of the corresponding Latin verb *intelligere*, here translated 'understand'. Hitherto he has been talking of the intellect in the very general sense of the capacity for thought, and the verb *intelligere* has corresponded to the verb 'think'. Now he moves to a narrow sense of *intelligere* which means to grasp self-evident truths, and talks of the intellect as the power of such immediate understanding rather than of thought in general. "Human reasoning," he says, "when engaged in inquiry or discovery, starts from truths immediately understood, namely first principles." Reasoning and understanding, therefore, are two stages of a single process, and hence are activities of one and the same faculty.

Aquinas's text here can mislead in two ways, one trivial and one important. The switch of sense just mentioned, once it is pointed out, does not affect the argument. For understanding in the narrow sense of the grasp of self-evident principles is indeed an activity of the intellect in the broad sense. The power to grasp these principles is indeed, for Aquinas, the fundamental endowment of the intellect; that is why it is called *intellectus* in the strictest sense. The process of inferring conclusions from premises, which is the kind of reasoning which Aquinas here has in mind, is likewise a crucially important activity of the intellect. Aquinas is quite right to say that these are two parts of a single ability, two exercises of the same faculty.

What is seriously misleading is the suggestion that human intellectual knowledge can be laid out in an axiomatic system with self-evident propositions as axioms and the whole of science as a set of theorems from these axioms. Aquinas seems to have believed that every truth which is capable of being strictly known is a conclusion which can be reached by syllogistic reasoning from self-evident premises. There are some propositions which have only to be understood in order to command assent; such are the law of non-contradiction and other similar primary principles: the grasp of these is called *habitus principiorum*. There are other propositions which are proved from these by deduction; the grasp of those is called *habitus scientiae* (S 1,79,9c).

Aquinas nowhere gives a list of the self-evident principles which are the premises of all scientific knowledge, nor does he try, like Spinoza, to exhibit his own philosophical theses as conclusions from self-evident axioms. But he tells us that the findings of any scientific discipline constitute an ordered set of theorems in a deductive system whose axioms are either theorems of a higher science or the self-evident principles themselves. Thus, for instance, a conclusion of the science of optics may be derived from an axiom of optics which is itself a theorem of geometry (S 1,79,9c).

In the ancient world and in the Middle Ages Euclidean geometry appeared to be the paradigm of ordered knowledge, a paradigm to which, in due course, all scientific disciplines could be made to conform. We now know that even Euclidean geometry does not rest on self-evident axioms. But much more importantly, the axiomatic model of science quite misrepresents the relationship of scientific conclusions to the reasons for believing them to be true. The relation between even the best-established hypothesis and the evidence which confirms it is quite different from that between theorem and axiom in a formal abstract system. And even in the a priori sciences of logic and mathematics, Aquinas exaggerates the part played by syllogistic reasoning; syllogistic is only a small part of the predicate calculus, and there are areas, such as the logic of relations, which are beyond the reach of the medieval theory of syllogism.

Elsewhere in Aquinas we shall encounter elements which show that this model—derived from Aristotle's *Posterior Analytics*—is not the only one which he uses to represent the operation of scientific inquiry. But it is well for the reader of the *Summa* to be put on guard, at an early stage, against the damaging effect which this inappropriate model can have on Aquinas's exploration of the faculties of the mind.

## Notes

This chapter was previously published as Anthony Kenny, "The Nature of the Intellect" (chapter 4 of Anthony Kenny, *Aquinas on Mind*, Routledge, London and New York, 1993).

1. In . . . creaturis intellectualibus intellectus est quaedam potentia intelligentis.

2. Because of the overtones of the Latin word *pati*, from which the notion of passive power is derived, Aquinas has to make rather heavy weather of the fact that the kind of change involved does not involve any actual *suffering* for the intellect.

3. Secundum opinionem Platonis, nulla necessitas erat ponere intellectum agentem ad faciendum intelligibilia in actu; sed forte ad praebendum lumen intelligibile intelligenti, ut infra dicetur. Posuit enim Plato formas rerum naturalium sine materia subsistere, et per consequens eas intelligibiles esse: quia ex hoc est aliquid intelligibile actu, quod est immateriale. Et huiusmodi vocabat species, sive ideas, ex quarum participatione dicebat etiam materiam corporalem formari, ad hoc quod individua naturaliter constituerentur in propriis generibus et speciebus; et intellectus nostros, ad hoc quod de generibus et speciebus rerum scientiam haberent.

Sed quia Aristoteles non posuit formas rerurn naturalium subsistere sine materia; formae autem in materia existentes non sunt intelligibiles actu: sequebatur quod naturae seu formae rerum sensibilium, quas intelligimus, non essent intetigibiles actu. Nihil autem reducitur de potentia in actum, nisi per aliquod ens actu: sicut sensus fit in actu per sensibile in actu. Oportebat igitur ponere aliquam virtutem ex parte intellectus, quae faceret intelligibilia in actu, per abstractionem specierum a conditionibus materialibus. Et haec est necessitas ponendi intellectum agentem.

4. Plato, ut posset salvare certam cognitionem veritatis a nobis per intellectum haberi, posuit praeter ista corporalia aliud genus entium a materia et motu separatum, quod nominabat species sive ideas, per quarum participationem unumquodque istorum singularium et sensibilium dicitur vel homo vel equus vel aliquid huiusmodi. Sic ergo dicebat scientias et definitiones et quidquid ad actum intellectus pertinent, non referri ad ista corpora sensibilia:, sed ad illa immaterialia et separata; ut sic anima non intelligat ista corporalia, sed intelligat horum corporalium species separatas.

5. Videtur autem in hoc Plato deviasse a veritate, quia, cum aestimaret omnem cognitionem per modum alicuius similitudinis esse, credidit quod forma cogniti ex necessitate sit in cognoscente eo modo quo est in cognito. Consideravit autem quod forma rei intellectae est in intellectu universaliter et immaterialiter et immobiliter: quod ex ipsa operatione intellectus apparet, qui intelligit universaliter et per modum necessitatis cuiusdam; modus enim actionis est secundum modum formae agentis. Et

ideo existimavit quod oporteret res intellectas hoc modo in seipsis subsistere, scilicet immaterialiter et immobiliter. Hoc autem necessarium non est.

6. *Compositio et divisio* means literally: putting together and taking apart. An instance of a *compositio* would be the judgment 'arsenic is poisonous'; an instance of a *divisio* would be 'arsenic is not poisonous'. By 'putting together' Aquinas does not mean the putting together of the words 'arsenic' and 'poisonous'; this is something which occurs in both the positive and the negative sentences. He calls the positive sentence a putting together because it states that arsenic and poisonousness are as it were put together in reality, and the negative sentence a taking apart because it states that arsenic and poisonousness are as it were far apart from each other in reality. Aquinas explains this in the Commentary on Aristotle's *Peri Hermeneias*, 1,3,26.

7. Intellectus enim nostri, secundum Philosophum in lib. de Anima, duplex est operatio. Una qua format simplices rerum quidditates; ut quid est homo, vel quid est animal: in qua quidem operatione non invenitur verum per se nec falsum, sicut nec in vocibus incomplexis. Alia operatio intellectus est secundum quam componit et dividit, affirmando et negando: et in hac iam invenitur verum et falsum, sicut et in voce complexa, quae est eius signum.

8. Verbum intellectus nostri, secundum cuius similitudinem loqui possumus de verbo in divinis, est id ad quod operatio intellectus nostri terminatur, quod est ipsum intellectum, quod dicitur conceptio intellectus; sive sit conceptio significabilis per vocem incomplexam, ut accidit quando intellectus format quidditates rerum; sive per vocem complexam, quod accidit quando intellectus componit et dividit.

9. Si intellectus agens compararetur ad intellectum possibilem ut obiectum agens ad potentiam, sicut visibile in actu ad visum, sequeretur quod statim omnia intelligeremus, cum intellectus agens sit quo est omnia facere. Nunc autem non se habet ut obiectum, sed ut faciens obiecta in actu: ad quod requiritur, praeter praesentiam intellectus agentis, praesentia phantasmatum, et bona dispositio virum sensitivarum, et exercitium in huiusmodi opere; quia per unum intellectum fiunt etiam alia intellecta, sicut per terminos propositiones, et per prima principia conclusiones.

10. Dicit enim in III de Anima, quod, cum intellectus possibilis sic fiat singula ut sciens, dicitur qui secundum actum; et quod hoc accidit cum possit operari per seipsum. Est quidem igitur et tunc potentia quodammodo; non tamen similiter ut ante addiscere aut invenire. Dicitur autem intellectus possibilis fieri singula, secundum quod recipit species singulorum. Ex hoc ergo quod recepit species intelligibilium, habet quod potest operari cum voluerit, non autem quod semper operetur; quia et tunc est quodammodo in potentia, licet aliter quam ante intelligere; eo scilicet modo quo sciens in habitu est in potentia ad considerandum in actu.

11. Memoria praeteritorum est. Sed praeteritum dicitur secundum aliquod determinatum tempus. Memoria igitur est cognoscitiva alicuius sub determinato tempore; quod est cognoscere aliquid sub hic et nunc. Hoc autem non est intellectus sed sensus. Memoria igitur non est in parte intellectiva, sed solum in parte sensitiva.

12. Praeteritio potest ad duo referri: scilicet ad obiectum quod cognoscitur; et ad cognitionis actum. Quae quidem duo simul coniunguntur in parte sensitiva, quae est apprehensiva alicuius per hoc quod immutatur a praesenti sensibili: unde simul animal memoratur se prius sensisse in praeterito, et se sensisse quoddam praeteritum

sensibile. Sed quantum ad partem intellectivam pertinet, praeteritio accidit, et non per se convenit, ex parte obiecti intellectus.

13. Intelligere animae nostrae est quidam particularis actus, in hoc vel in illo tempore existens, secundum quod dicitur homo intelligere nunc vel heri vel cras. Et hoc non repugnat intellectualitati . . . sicut intelligit seipsum intellectus, quamvis ipse sit quidam singularis intellectus, ita intelligit suum intelligere, quod est singularis actus vel in praeterito vel in praesenti vel in futuro existens.

14. Ratio et intellectus in homine non possunt esse diversae potentiae. Quod manifeste cognoscitur, si utriusque actus consideretur. Intelligere enim est simpliciter veritatem intelligibilem apprehendere. Ratiocinari autem est procedere de uno intellecto ad aliud, ad veritatem intelligibilem cognoscendam . . . Patet ergo quod ratiocinari comparatur ad intelligere sicut moveri ad quiescere, vel acquirere ad habere.

# 8

# The Immortality of the Soul

*Herbert McCabe*

I HAVE BEEN ASKED TO PRESENT once more the traditional Thomist argument that the soul must be immortal because by the soul we think and understand. I intend simply to restate the argument which St. Thomas develops in *Q. D. de Anima* a.14, and in Ia, 75, 2 and 6.

First I should like to make it clear that the argument with which I am dealing is intended to be a demonstration; that is, it is intended to make it quite certain that the soul is immortal. I should not be surprised to find that the argument is full of unsuspected flaws, but I should be very surprised to find that it rendered the immortality of the soul probable or highly likely. Someone of proper modesty might say, "I find this argument entirely convincing, but I have been wrong so many times before; for this reason I only find it very probable that the soul is immortal." My point is that there cannot be an argument to show that it is probable that the soul is immortal. I shall not argue this point: I only mention it because one sometimes hears people saying that no argument for the immortality of the soul can be absolutely convincing. I think that such an argument cannot claim to be anything less.

First of all, then, why do we speak of a soul at all?

We say that Fido sees and barks and wags his tail and so on. He sees with his eyes and without them he cannot see. Nevertheless, when we want to find out whether Fido sees or not we do not simply examine his eyes. We know that termites cannot see, not because we have examined their eyes but because they behave in exactly the same way in the dark as in the light, etc. To find out whether an animal sees we look at its whole behaviour, we look at what it does with its feet as well as what it does with its eyes. But Fido won't go blind if you injure his feet, whereas he may well go blind if you injure his eyes. The whole animal is concerned in seeing, but the eyes specially. The other parts of the body have no special task in seeing; there are all kinds of things that they might do to show that seeing is going on, but the eye has a special task. What the eye does is only seeing if this special task plays some part in the whole behaviour of the animal. An eye cannot see by itself, even if it goes through the motions, just as a leg cannot walk by itself. What sees is Fido with his eyes.

We say that Fido has a soul and is not simply a collection of instruments because we say that these instruments are doing certain jobs—seeing, swallowing, walking, etc.—and what they are doing would not be these jobs unless the tasks they performed were parts of the behaviour of the whole animal. To talk about the activities of a thing as seeing, or eating, etc., in fact to talk about its behaviour at all, is to talk about it as having a soul, or it is to talk of it as though it had a soul (e.g., we sometimes talk about machines as if they grasped and swallowed and detected and rejected, and this is to talk of them as if they had souls).

When Fido is dead he no longer *behaves*, things go on but they are no longer behaviour. Perhaps we could stimulate any of the organs of the body so that it did the same things as it did in life, but we would not call this seeing or sneezing or walking just because there is no general response of the whole animal. When Fido dies he is not *altered* in some way. It is not that something is true of him now which was not true of him before: but a whole way of talking about him has become inappropriate. He has been replaced by something or else some things which have to be spoken about in a different way. We cannot say that the group of chemicals which is Fido's corpse have stopped barking or are blind. It is true that until the chemical changes are well advanced we still do use animal language; we speak of his head and legs and tail, but this is simply to speak of the corpse as though it were an animal (cf. the machines) and the words are used, as Aristotle says, equivocally.

All this is to say that Fido's death is, in traditional terms, a *substantial change*. To lose the soul is to lose the substantial form and not just an accidental form, it is to perish and not just to be altered. The substantial form is that in virtue of which the thing is what it is (e.g., that in virtue of which Fido is a dog) and hence that in virtue of which the thing is at all. For Fido to cease to be a living dog is for him to cease to be at all.

Having buried Fido let us turn to George. George, like Fido, is an animal, and in his case, too, we speak of a soul. What makes his eyes genuine eyes that *see*, and makes his legs genuine legs that *walk*, is his soul. It is his soul that makes his body what it is. But the soul of George is not simply a matter of his having genuine bodily organs. Of course it is by his soul that George sees and walks, but it is also by his soul that he does some other things which are not bodily activities, notably understanding. I know it sounds scandalous to suggest that understanding is an operation that can be placed beside or alongside bodily activity, but this seems to me no more inevitably misleading than to say that George both sees and walks. Certainly seeing is not an operation in the sense that walking is and, of course, understanding is an operation in yet another sense. The general modern practice seems to be to restrict the word "operation" to bodily or physical processes. I think this arises because of a strong emphasis on the difference between what St. Thomas would call transient and immanent activity. This is all to the good, but while most philosophers would agree in warning us not to be misled by treating seeing or thinking as an operation in the sense that running or pushing is an operation, there seems to be no generally agreed advice on how we *are* to talk about seeing and thinking. Until a new terminology appears we shall have to be content with the old one.

The conclusion that George performs by his soul activities which are not bodily activities will be taken to show that the soul of George is subsistent. And this will be taken to show that the doctrine that his soul does not perish is not a trivial doctrine, as it might appear at first sight. For as we shall see there is a *trivial* sense in which the soul of Fido, or the number 2, cannot perish. To say that some things can and others cannot perish is, of course, to lay claim to a theory of perishing, and at the risk of being very tedious I must say something briefly about this.

A thing cannot simply *be* in the vague. It has to be something. For an elephant to be is not for it to have a common property called being or existence; it is for it to be an elephant. And if it is to cease to be, it must be by its ceasing to be an elephant.

Each thing, says St. Thomas, has existence according to its own form, hence existence and form cannot be separated.

Where there is form there is existence. Things cease to be by ceasing to be this kind of thing; that is, they cease to be by losing the form in virtue of which they are what they are. The kind of change in which they perish is a change in which their form is replaced by another form, and for this to happen is for a new thing to come into existence.

When we say that something, e.g., a dog, can perish, we are saying both that it is (a dog) and that it is capable of becoming an indefinite variety of other things. That in virtue of which it is a dog we call its *form*. That in virtue of which it is capable of being something other than it is we call its *matter*. To have this capacity just is to be perishable.

Perhaps I ought to say here, to avoid misunderstanding, that there is a sense in which absolutely anything which is not God is capable of not being. Even a "necessary being," which is imperishable in the sense that it cannot substantially change into something else, is capable of not existing in the sense that its existence is *received* from God. I am here concerned simply to show that the soul cannot perish.

Now since matter and form are the terms in which we analyse perishing, it seems clear that we cannot sensibly talk of either matter or form themselves perishing. It is as though I should say "We shorten this pole by making it less than a yard long; now how do we shorten a yard itself?" The difficulty about shortening a yard is not that it is peculiarly tough, but that it has not got any length to decrease. A yard, unlike a yard-stick, is not 36 inches long, it is 36 inches. It is therefore trivial to say that a yard cannot be shortened: it is crazy to speak of a yard being 36 inches long and hence equally crazy to speak of its being or becoming less than 35 inches long. In the same way it seems trivial to say that a form cannot perish. It clearly is trivial in the case of a form which is simply that in virtue of which something is; but it would not be trivial in the case of a form which itself existed.

At first sight we might be inclined to think that to say a form exists is like saying that a yard is 36 inches long; it is one of the things we may not do with language.

Thus St. Thomas says: "Existence is not taken away from anything that has it except by taking its form from it; hence if what has existence is the form it-self, it is impossible that existence should be taken from it."

And this certainly looks like saying: "Wetness is not taken from anything that has it except by taking water from it; hence if what has wetness is the water itself, it is impossible that wetness should be taken from it."

In this second case we do not say that whereas other things can be dried with phosphorus pentoxide or towels, water has a special logical resistance to such methods and remains immutably wet; we say that water can only be called wet in the special sense that it makes other things wet.

Similarly in the first case we do not say that whereas most things can be de-stroyed by massacre or fire or atomic fission, forms have a queer logical dura-bility that resists all attack; we say that forms only exist in the pickwickian sense that they are that in virtue of which other things exist. Philosophers have often said that just as words like "wet" and "36 inches long" have a restricted field of application, so "exists" can only be used of certain kinds of things; some of them, for example, have thought that "God exists" can only mean "God is what makes sensible things exist."

Metaphysical objections can be dealt with as they are brought up; for the moment let me remind you of what St. Thomas is saying when he says that "this form exists." St. Thomas simply says that man has an operation by his soul which is not an operation of the body and that therefore his soul itself subsists. The subsistence of the soul has no more *content* than that. If St. Thomas had argued that the body has also operations which are not operations of the soul, he would have held, as, e.g., Descartes seems to have done, that man is two substances, a soul and a body. This, of course, he constantly denies.

There are two points to be made clear here. The first is that St. Thomas did not think that the soul is immortal because it is immaterial. He held that the soul of Fido is immaterial and that the number 2 is immaterial. His argument is not simply that the soul is not material but that it subsists immaterially inasmuch as it operates immaterially. The second point is that he does not make what would ordinarily be called a psychological search to find this operation of the soul. We are not going to be presented by introspection with an activity of the mind which is commonly overlooked. We shall not in the end be able to see ourselves think, except in the sense that it is perfectly easy to see ourselves or other people thinking. We shall simply be concerned to see what is involved in saying that we understand something. We shall not be able to tease much out of this but we shall find that whatever understanding means, it *at least* means a nonbodily operation.

St. Thomas illustrates his argument with the aid of medieval physiology. The eye, he says, can see all colours just because the pupil of the eye has no colour itself. The same point can, I think, be made with coloured spectacles. A man who wears blue spectacles does not simply see things differently from a man with colourless spectacles; he sees *less* because he cannot distinguish between white and pale blue. If we are told that a man can distinguish all the colours then we can be sure that his spectacles are themselves colourless and invisible. Now St. Thomas says: by his mind a man can understand the natures of all corporeal things and therefore it cannot itself possess the nature of any corporeal thing. To understand, therefore, is not the function of any corporeal thing.

In St. Thomas's view one can possess a nature, say the nature of a dog, naturally—this would be *to be* a dog; or one can possess it intentionally or intelligibly—this would be *to know* the nature. He argues that one could not possess *every* bodily nature intentionally if one possessed *any* bodily nature naturally. The mind must be beyond any particular bodily nature because it stands over, transcends, them all.

Now it sounds arbitrary to say that understanding a nature means possessing it, even if we qualify the possessing by saying "only intentionally, of course." But here we ought to notice how little "possession" or "having" means here: it is just the word we use with "nature": George *possesses* or *has* the nature of George.

What is being said is that, for example, the nature which is the meaning of the word "cow" having *esse naturale* constitutes that cow a cow and not, e.g., a horse, and having *esse intentionale* in my mind constitutes my understanding the understanding of the meaning of "cow" rather than, say, of "horse."

This doctrine will be totally misunderstood if it is not recognized that it is intended to be *obvious*. It is not a description of a process by which we understand, if there is any such process. It is a platitude; it says "What I have in mind when I know the nature of a cow is the nature of a cow and nothing else." Now in case someone says "But if the nature you have in your mind is that of a cow, surely your mind must be a cow—for to have the nature of an X simply means to be an X," St. Thomas merely replies that to understand the nature of a cow is to have this nature precisely *without* being a cow, and this is what is made clear by saying that one has the nature in mind. To have it in mind doesn't mean anything except that you have the nature without being the thing whose nature it is. And this he calls "having the nature intentionally."

The mind, for St. Thomas, just is the locus of intentional being.

Suppose someone thought of the mind as a place or as an instrument, like the retina of the eye, or the nose. And suppose he said: I understand what a cow is because I have a representation or picture of a cow in my mind. This picture is what makes him able to distinguish between what a cow is and what a horse is. The picture by which he understands what a cow is differs from the picture by which he understands what a horse is in ways exactly corresponding to the differences between horses and cows. Now one of the characteristic things about a picture is that it is first of all something in its own right—a piece of canvas or wood—and then it resembles something. Now it is just the things that the picture has in its own right that must be forbidden to the picture in the mind. If it were a picture on wood, it would not serve to distinguish a cow from a cow painted on wood; if it were made of cast iron it would not help to tell a cow from a cast iron lawn-cow. There is no *mental stuff* that the picture could be made of—it must have everything the cow has and nothing else. It cannot *resemble* a cow because anything except the sheer resemblance will be an alien element like wood or cast iron. It must be simply everything that a cow has and nothing else. And what is this except to be the nature of the cow?

I have said a lot about the act of understanding, but this might seem a puzzling notion. Where is such an act to be found? What, for instance, connects a calculation on a bit of paper with an act of understanding, if there is such an act?

To answer this question we may digress for a moment. St. Thomas connects understanding with knowing what a thing is, with knowing the *quod quid est* of a thing. To know the *quod quid est* of a thing means knowing the kind of questions which can be asked and which cannot be asked about it.

This sense of the question "What is it?" is answered by trying to give a definition and the purpose of a definition is to give some account of the field of discourse to which the thing belongs, to know the definition is to know how to talk appropriately about the thing. It follows from this that the question "What is it?" is the one question which can never be inappropriate; there are indeed ways of answering the question which will be inappropriate—it would be wrong to expect an account of the ways in which we should talk about something of which we cannot talk because we do not understand it.

This sense of the question "What is it?" is not simply one important sense amongst others. There are innumerable ways in which the question may be asked, but in all these cases the question is asked because we have lost touch with the speaker. We have not understood something which we suppose him to understand. We may merely have lost touch physically as when we do not hear him and we say "What"—meaning "please repeat that," or we may fear that we may have not got the right nuance of meaning in one of his words, or we may be simply at a loss. Now I suggest that the fundamental sense of "What is it?" has to do with the fundamental way in which we lose touch with, or come to grips with, a speaker. We ask this question when there is danger of complete cross-purposes, when we are in danger of talking different languages. We need to know the answer to this sense of the question "What is it?" lest the things that the speaker says should sound like "The square root of aluminium is . . ." To be told the answer is to be told how to talk about the thing under discussion and how not to talk about it.

Now to return to the question where the understanding comes in. The understanding comes into the calculation in so far as the calculation is an exercise of this knowing how to talk about something. It is this that characterises it as a *sum*. It is not an element in what goes on which makes the difference between a mechanical and a human calculation. To say that would be like saying that the one element which distinguished a man from a very life-like statue was his humanity. It is a queer thing to ask for the one important difference which will enable you to distinguish between a man thinking and a machine. You might not be able to distinguish between them under some circumstances and in some respects, but this is just because the calculating machine is intended to be an imitation of man, just as a statue is an imitation of man.

## Note

This chapter was previously published as Herbert McCabe, "The Immortality of the Soul." A paper read to a symposium at Spode House, Staffordshire, UK. It is printed in Anthony Kenny, ed., *Aquinas: A Collection of Critical Essays* (University of Notre Dame Press, Notre Dame, IN, 1976).

# 9

# Aquinas's Account of Freedom: Intellect and Will

*Eleonore Stump*

## I. Introduction

IT IS DIFFICULT TO DEVELOP A comprehensive and satisfactory account of Aquinas's views of the nature of human freedom.

For one thing, contemporary discussions of free will tend to belong to an older, non-Thomistic tradition of thought about the topic. In this tradition, human freedom is a property of just one component of human mental faculties, namely, the will; and freedom consists in an agent's ability to will autonomously in general and independently of the intellect in particular. The influence of this tradition persists in contemporary discussion, both for libertarians and for their opponents, with the result that Aquinas's account tends to be interpreted by its lights. Consequently, the lineaments of his theory are obscured. For Aquinas, freedom with regard to willing is a property primarily of a human being, not of some particular component of a human being. Furthermore, the will is not independent of the intellect. On the contrary, the dynamic interactions of intellect and will yield freedom as an emergent property or a systems-level feature.

Another reason why interpreting Aquinas's account is difficult is that he gives a complicated analysis of the several acts of will he takes to be associated with a free bodily action. Scholars sometimes pick out a subset of these acts or even just one of them as if for Aquinas freedom of the will were lodged in that sort of act of will alone. So, for example it is sometimes said that Aquinas has a particularly full treatment of free will in *De Malo* q.6 because in that text he discusses at length *liberum arbitrium*.[1] But there is something anachronistic about trying to identify *liberum arbitrium* with free will in our sense[2]; volitions characterized by *liberum arbitrium* are associated with Aquinas with only one sort of voluntary act, namely, the sort he calls *electio*. *De Malo* q.6 is therefore not about freedom of the will as a whole but only about one of the acts of will, namely, *electio*, in which such freedom is exemplified. (In order to avoid confusion, I will leave both '*liberum arbitrium*' and '*electio*' untranslated and let their meanings emerge from a consideration of Aquinas's views).

For these reasons, to understand Aquinas's account of human freedom, I will focus on his account of the nature of intellect and will, the interactions between them, and the emergence of freedom from their interaction. With that background, I will look in detail at Aquinas's theory of freedom, in particular at his views of human ability to do otherwise and the relation of that ability to freedom. Finally, I will consider what answer can be given to a taxonomic question: Is Aquinas's theory a compatibilist account, as is sometimes claimed, or is it a libertarian theory; and if it is a libertarian theory, what species of libertarianism is it?

Because of his views of divine grace and its effect on the will, we cannot be entirely clear about Aquinas's theory of freedom without also understanding his account of grace.[3] But this is a large subject, which needs a careful treatment of its own. Furthermore, it is Aquinas's firm conviction, reiterated in many passages, that God moves the will only in accord with its nature, and not against it. According to Aquinas himself, then, his account of grace should not alter the conclusions we reach about his theory of the nature of the will, independently considered. This chapter will therefore consider Aquinas's account of the will apart from his views of grace.


## II. Intellect and Will

Contemporary philosophers tend to operate with a conception of the will as the mind's steering-wheel, neutral in its own right but able to direct other parts of the person. Aquinas's conception is different. He takes the will to be not a neutral faculty, but a bent or inclination. The will, he says in the *Summa Theologiae* (hereafter *ST*), is a hunger, an appetite, for goodness.[4] By 'goodness' in this connection Aquinas means goodness in general, not this or that specific good thing; that is, the will is an inclination for what is good, where the phrase 'what is good' is used attributively and not referentially.

By itself the will makes no determinations of goodness; apprehending or judging things as good is the business of the intellect. The intellect presents to the will as good certain things or actions under certain descriptions in particular circumstances, and the will wills them because it is an appetite for the good and they are presented to it as good. For this reason, the intellect is said to move the will not as an efficient cause but as a final cause, because its presenting something as good moves the will as an end moves an appetite.[5] This is one reason for calling the will a 'moved mover' (as Aquinas notes that Aristotle does), because, in moving what is under its control, the will is moved by an object intellectively apprehended as good, or an "intellectively cognized appetible,"[6] as Aquinas puts it.

Understood in this way, the will can be seen as part of a larger scheme. Because all things are created by a good God who wills what is good for his creatures, all things are created with an inclination of their own to the good, but of very different sorts. Some, like plants or even inanimate things, have a built-in inclination to the good apart from any cognition of the good. Aquinas sometimes calls this inclination a natural appetite. (The sort of thing he has in mind is exemplified by plants naturally turning toward sunlight.) Higher up the ladder of being are animals of certain sorts which are naturally inclined to the good but with some (sensory) cognition.[7] They can cognize particular goods, although they lack the ability to reflect on them or to think of them as good. Inclination dependent on limited cognition of this sort Aquinas calls 'sensory appetite'. Higher still are human beings whose inclination to the good is dependent on intellect, which allows them not only to cognize particular goods but to think about them reflectively as good. This inclination is rational appetite, and it is what Aquinas takes the will to be.[8] So close is the association between intellect and will for Aquinas that he often speaks of the will as being in the intellect,[9] and he thinks that anything which has intellect must also have will.[10]

Understood as rational appetite, the will is the primary mover of all the powers of the soul (including itself) except the nutritive powers,[11] and it is also the efficient cause of motion of the body. Most important for our purposes, the will exercises some degree of efficient causality over the intellect. In some circumstances, it can command the intellect directly to adopt or to reject a particular belief.[12] It can also move the intellect by directing it to attend to some things and to neglect others,[13] or even to stop thinking about something altogether. So, for example, while you are reading a magazine, you come across an advertisement asking for money for children, with an emotionally powerful picture of a starving child. Your intellect recognizes that if you look at the ad for very long, you are likely to succumb to its emotional force. Intellect sees the goodness of contributing to the charity, but it also recognizes that if you give money to this charity, you won't have it for the new computer you have been coveting. Your desire for the new computer is strong and influences intellect to rank saving money for the computer as best for you now. In consequence of the finding on intellect's part, and with this influence from the passions, will directs intellect to stop thinking about the charity, and (after a further interaction of intellect and will) you turn the page of your magazine.

As this example shows, in addition to control over intellect by will, the passions—sorrow, fury, fear, greed, etc.—can also influence the intellect, because in the grip of such a passion, something will seem good to a person which might not seem good to her otherwise.[14] The intellect, however, typically isn't compelled by the passions in any way;[15] it can resist them, for example, by being aware of the passion and correcting for its effects on judgment, as one does when one leaves a letter written in anger until the next morning rather than mailing it right away. Furthermore, the passions are themselves theoretically subject to the will. In other animals, Aquinas says, motion follows directly from the sensitive appetite's positive or negative reaction. In human beings, however, the sensitive appetite awaits the act of the will, which is the superior appetite. The lower appetite, Aquinas thinks, isn't by itself sufficient to cause movement in other powers unless the higher appetite, the will, permits that movement.[16] That is why, for example, human beings can go on hunger strikes and stay on them to the point of starvation.

I raise the subject of the relation of the passions to intellect and will, however, only to put it to one side. Although Aquinas has many interesting things to say about the moral psychology of the passions, his account of the intellect and will and the freedom that emerges from their interaction is more than enough for our focus here. I will therefore introduce the passions into the discussion only when it is necessary to do so in order to understand what Aquinas has to say about intellect and will.

Just as the will can affect the intellect in various ways, so the intellect can move the will (as a final, not an efficient, cause) in more than one way. The will can be moved to will as distinct from not willing—the "exercise" of its act; or it can be moved to will this rather than that particular thing—the "specification" of its act.[17]

There is nothing in this life that invariably and ineluctably moves every human will to the exercise of its act, because it is always in a person's power to refuse to think of the thing at issue.[18] Since will wills something only in case intellect presents it as some sort of good, the fact that will can command intellect to stop thinking about something means that will can, indirectly, turn itself off, at least with regard to a particular action or issue. This is only a limited ability on the part of the will, however, since the apprehensions of the intellect can occur without any preceding act of will and so in some cases may force the issue back on the agent's attention. That is why, for example, the prisoner who wants not to think about what is happening next door where other prisoners are being tortured will find that their screams make him recur to what he wants to stop thinking about.[19]

As far as the specification of its act is concerned, there is no object, other than happiness in this life and God in the next, which by its nature necessarily moves every human will to want *that*.[20] Because God has created the will as a hunger for the good, every human will by nature desires the good. And whatever is good to such a degree and in such a way that a person cannot help but see it as good, the will of that person wills by natural necessity. One's own happiness is of this sort,[21] and so a person necessarily wills happiness.[22] But even things which have a necessary connection to happiness aren't willed necessarily unless the willer is cognizant of their necessary connection to happiness.[23] Except for happiness and things so obviously connected with it that their connection is overwhelming and indubitable, it is not the case that every human will is in general determined to one thing because of its relation to the intellect. On Aquinas's account, the will wills only what the intellect presents at that time as good under some description. Acts of will, then, are for something apprehended or cognized as good at a particular time in particular circumstances, as distinct from something which is good considered unconditionally or abstractly. Besides happiness and the vision of God, all other things are such that they can in principle be considered good under some descriptions and not good under others, so that there is nothing about them which must constrain the will of any agent always to want them. So, for example, the further acquisition of money can be considered good under some descriptions in some circumstances—e.g., the means of sending the children to school—and not good under others—e.g., wages from an immoral and disgusting job.

Finally, the will can move itself in more than one way. It can move itself indirectly by commanding intellect to stop thinking about something, as we've just seen. It can also move itself indirectly because in virtue of willing a certain end it moves itself to will the means to that end. That is, the will wills a certain means because it wills a particular end and because intellect presents that means as best for attaining that end.

But a more direct control over itself is possible for the will, too. All the higher powers of the soul, Aquinas holds, are able to act on themselves.[24] So, for example, intellect is able to cognize itself.[25] By the same token, the will can will to will.[26] In fact, Aquinas confronts a problem that has troubled some contemporary hierarchal accounts of the will, namely, that there may be an infinite regress of higher-order willings. I can will that I will something, and I can also will that I will that I will something, and so on, apparently *ad infinitum*. But in such an apparently infinite series, the will is not actually taking ever-higher orders of volition as its object. At some point, Aquinas thinks,[27] the apparently higher-order volitions collapse, and the object of the will is just whatever action was at issue at the beginning of the series of volitions.

If intellect does present something to the will as good, then, because the will is an appetite for the good, the will wills it—unless will directs intellect to reconsider, to direct its attention to something else, or to stop considering the matter at hand. Will's doing such things, of course, is a result of intellect's presenting such actions on the part of the will as good, and that act of intellect may itself be a result of previous acts on the part of the will directing the attention of the intellect. On Aquinas's view, every act of willing is preceded by some apprehension on the part of the intellect, but not every apprehension on the part of the intellect need be preceded by an act of will.[28]

It is apparent, then, that on Aquinas's account, the will is part of a dynamic feedback system composed primarily of the will and the intellect, but also including the passions. The interaction between will and intellect is so close and the acts of the two powers so intertwined that Aquinas often finds it difficult to draw the line between them. So, for example, he says that

> it happens sometimes that there is an act of the will in which something of the [preceding] act of reason remains . . . and, *vice versa*, there is [sometimes] an act of reason in which something of the [preceding] act of will remains.[29]

That is why it sometimes looks as if, for Aquinas, will engages in acts of apprehension and intellect engages in acts of willing.

If we remember this part of Aquinas's account and also take seriously his identification of the will as a hunger or appetite, we will be less likely to identify the will on his account as nothing more than a toggle switch with three positions: accept, reject, and off. Aquinas's account of the will is more complicated than such an identification implies. Because it is an appetite, the will can have dispositions, so that it can be more or less readily inclined to want something; it can will something with more or less strength.[30] It can give specific commands to body parts. And under the pull of the passions, for example, it can influence what intellect presents to it as good by selectively directing the attention of the intellect.

For this reason, too, although Aquinas's account of the will assigns a large role to intellect, he isn't committed to seeing immoral actions simply as instances of mistakes in deliberation, since intellect's deliberations are in many cases dependent on the will's influence. In cases of incontinence, where the intellect seems to be representing something as good which the will isn't willing, Aquinas would say that the intellect, influenced by the will, is in fact being moved by opposed desires to represent the thing in question as both good (under one description) and not good (under a different description), so that the intellect is double-minded.[31] In the last analysis, what the intellect of the incontinent person represents as the best alternative in *these* circumstances at *this* time isn't what the agent takes to be good considered unconditionally or in the abstract.

Cases of incontinence illustrate the further complicating fact that intellect need not present one simple, unified result to will. Sometimes an agent is entirely of one mind about something, and what intellect presents to will is one unified message that a particular thing is good. But what is no doubt also often the case is that an agent's intellect is not entirely unified. The doctor has recommended x-raying the agent's head to check for a sinus infection. On the one hand, the agent's intellect may recognize, the doctor is an expert in her field, and her advice for that reason should be followed. On the other hand, the intellect may be aware that even low-level x-rays are carcinogenic, and the intellect may wonder whether the doctor's ordering the x-ray reflects her concern to avoid malpractice lawsuits rather than her own view about what is necessary for the health of her patient.

Furthermore, the influence of the passions may also complicate the case. It might be that a patient's intellect supposes some medical tests are in fact medically required, but his passions might recoil strongly from the tests. In that case, his aversion may influence the intellect to give a divided verdict: on the one hand, it would be good to undergo the tests, because they are important for health; on the other hand, it would be bad to undergo the tests because they are painful or disgusting. In such cases, there may be considerable interaction among intellect, will, and passions, until, in consequence of such iterated interaction, one side or another of the divided intellect becomes strong enough to override the other. This is a process familiar enough to anyone who has had to talk himself into doing something he originally feared or disliked.

### III. The Relation of Freedom to Intellect and Will

One of the perplexing things about the preceding analysis of the relation of intellect to will is that it isn't immediately apparent in what sense the will is free.

It is helpful in this connection to notice that Aquinas recognizes a distinction between freedom of action and freedom of willing.[32] He acknowledges, for example, that we can lose our freedom of action while retaining our freedom with regard to willing. Even when the will itself is not compelled or coerced in any way, he says, the members of the body can be impeded by some external cause so that they don't follow the command of the will.[33] While an agent might still be free with regard to his willing in such a case, he wouldn't be free with regard to his actions, which in the case envisaged are at least in part under some control other than his own. In order for an agent to have freedom of action, then, it isn't sufficient that his will be free in its willing of that action. It must also be the case that there is no external impediment to the action of the relevant body parts and that those parts are themselves functioning normally.

Consequently, freedom of action is not a property of just one component of a human being. Rather, it is a property of a whole system, comprised at least of the will and the members of the body. It emerges when the will is freely commanding a certain sort of movement and when the relevant bodily parts are functioning normally and are not kept by any cause external to the agent from being under the will's control.

It is helpful to see this feature of freedom in action, because it points us in the right direction for Aquinas's account of free will: for Aquinas, freedom with regard to willing is also a feature of a whole system.

In explaining what constitutes a distinctly human action, Aquinas puts the point this way. What differentiates human beings from non-rational animals is that a human being is master of his acts, in virtue of having intellect and will. Consequently, no freedom with regard to willing remains for a person who, through madness, for example, has lost the use of his intellectual faculties.[34] Aquinas makes the same point another way by saying that the root of freedom is in the will as subject but in the reason as the cause.[35] That is, the property of freedom inheres in the will, which is the subject for the property, but it does so because of the intellect; will's relations to and interactions with the intellect are the source of the freedom in the will. Freedom with regard to willing, then, is not characteristic either of the will or of the intellect alone.[36] Like freedom of action, freedom with regard to willing emerges from the functioning of a system, in this case the system comprised of intellect and will.

Furthermore, Aquinas says that an agent is master of his acts or has his acts in his own power insofar as they are voluntary, and that it is a person's voluntary acts which make him subject to praise or blame.[37] But, in his view, whatever is voluntary requires an act of the intellect as well as an act of the will.[38] Seconding a view of Damascene's, Aquinas calls a voluntary act "an act that is a rational operation."[39] In fact, Aquinas holds that because the will has the relation it has to the intellect, all the acts of the will are voluntary, whether they are simple acts of will (such as willing an end) or are commands to some other power which the will controls (such as willing to move one's arm).[40] Finally, in Aquinas's view, anything that takes away an agent's use of her intellectual faculties also takes away the voluntariness of her action.[41]

A voluntary act is thus a special case of being moved by an intrinsic principle.[42] Whatever is moved by an intrinsic principle in such a way that it acts for an end which it cognizes as an end has within itself the principle of its action. Some creatures act with a limited cognition of the end for which they are acting, so that their acts are voluntary but in a limited sort of way. The acts of young children and some animals are voluntary in this way. Normal adult human beings can have a full cognition of their ends, and so they can have complete voluntariness with regard to their acts.[43]

By the same token, and perhaps as a consequence of the same thought about the voluntary, Aquinas thinks that anything external to the agent which acted coercively on the agent's will would thereby destroy voluntariness. That the voluntary movement of the will be from an extrinsic principle, Aquinas says, is impossible.[44] This is not an empirical claim but a conceptual one. For something to be an act of will, it has to stem from an intrinsic source, in particular the will as informed by the intellect. So, Aquinas says:

> An act of the will is nothing other than an inclination which proceeds from an interior cognizing principle . . . but what is compelled or violent is from an extrinsic principle.[45]

If something extrinsic to the agent were to act on the will with efficient causation, then the tie of the will to the intellect, from which acts of will get their voluntary character, would be broken, and so the act of the will wouldn't be voluntary—or to put it more nearly as Aquinas seems to think of it, in such a case it wouldn't be a real act of the will at all.

We might wonder here why Aquinas wouldn't grant that an act of will could be voluntary even if it were caused by an extrinsic principle, provided that the extrinsic principle produced its effects by operating directly on the agent's intellect and only thereby, indirectly, on the agent's will. Aquinas considers something like this question himself when he asks whether Satan could bring it about that a human being sin.[46] Aquinas subscribes to the demon-possession theory of mental illness, so he supposes that Satan can causally determine a human intellect (to one degree or another) by possessing it. But this is to destroy it as a human intellect; an insane person has lost his reason. At any rate, if some external agent S has taken over entirely the intellect of some human H, then the intellect that is operative in that human person is S's and not H's. In that case, what the will operative in H wills might be voluntary, but it would count as S's will, not H's, since the intellect that informs the willing is S's. In this case, there can be an extrinsic principle S which operates on the intellect of some other agent H, but the operation of the extrinsic principle won't give us an act of will that can count as H's.

On the other hand, if we were to imagine Satan (or the evil neurosurgeon) invading H's intellect only partially, for example, by producing a thought or a train of thoughts, H's intellect will then examine that thought or set of thoughts and evaluate it, retaining or rejecting it according as it seems right to H to do so. In that case, however, the voluntary acts of will which may result will stem from the reflections of H's intellect, not S's. Here again, then, we will not have a case in which a voluntary act of will on H's part is causally determined by an extrinsic principle S, operating through H's intellect.

So, worries about grace aside, it should by now be clear that Aquinas is not a compatibilist. The causal chain resulting in any voluntary act on an agent's part has to originate in the system of the agent's own intellect and will. If it originates in some cause external to the agent which acts with efficient causation on the agent's will, what results will not be an act of will at all. And if it takes over the agent's intellect which in turn determines the content of the agent's will, what results will not be an act of *the agent's* will. So while extrinsic principles may influence human volition, as, for example, we sometimes do when we persuade one another by arguments, causes external to an agent cannot effect a voluntary act of will on that agent's part, either directly or indirectly.

If Aquinas isn't a compatibilist, what sort of incompatibilist is he? It seems clear that he must be a libertarian. And yet, although the outlines of Aquinas's theory of human freedom are now somewhat clearer, it still isn't obvious in what sense the will—or the system of will and intellect—is supposed to be free. No doubt, part of what gives rise to this perplexity is the presupposition, common enough in discussions of free will, that libertarian free will includes or even just consists in the ability to do otherwise.[47] But in what sense is it possible for the will, or the will-and-intellect, to do otherwise on Aquinas's view?

## IV. *Liberum Arbitrium* and the Ability to Do Otherwise

Aquinas's account of a person's ability to will otherwise typically occurs in connection with his discussion of *liberum arbitrium*, and it is because of what Aquinas says about this that he is supposed by many scholars to see human freedom just as a function of the will's ability to do otherwise.

It is true that Aquinas makes a strong connection between *liberum arbitrium* and the ability to do otherwise. In fact, although '*liberum arbitrium*' means 'free *judgment*', Aquinas sometimes sounds if *liberum arbitrium* is just the power of the *will* to do otherwise than it does. For example, he says, "whoever has *liberum arbitrium* has it in his power to will or not to will, to do or not to do."[48]

Nonetheless, it is a mistake to suppose that '*liberum arbitrium*' is Aquinas's term for the freedom of the will in general. In fact, he explicitly associates *liberum arbitrium* with only one of the acts of will needed to produce a bodily movement in a free human action, namely, the act of will which is *electio*. So, for example, he says, "*liberum arbitrium* is that in accordance with which we have *electio*."[49] And in another place, he says, with regard to intellective appetite, will and *liberum arbitrium*—which is nothing but the power of *electio*—are related just as intellect and reason are related with regard to intellective cognition . . . Now the act of *electio* is to desire something for the sake of obtaining something else, so that, strictly speaking, it has to do with means to an end . . . Therefore, it is clear that will is related to the power of *electio*—that is, to *liberum arbitrium*—just as intellect is related to reason.[50]

Elsewhere he associated the act of *liberum arbitrium* just with the selection of a means to an end,[51] which is *electio*.

So although, on Aquinas's account, *liberum arbitrium* involves being able to do otherwise, it is not identical to freedom of the will in general, but instead picks out just the power of the will manifested in the act Aquinas calls *electio*.

Now *electio* is the will's assenting to the means which the intellect has apprehended as best for the end wanted by the willer.[52] It is therefore a very specific sort of act of will. Furthermore, not every free action has an act of *electio* in the series of acts of will and intellect producing such an action. When the intellect finds only *one* acceptable means to an end, then the act of *electio* collapses into the act of consent[53]—an act of will which is *not* associated with *liberum arbitrium*—precisely because there aren't alternatives available for intellect and will to rank-order.[54]

In addition, even understood narrowly as confined to the power of the will producing *electio*, *liberum arbitrium* isn't a property of the will alone. It can be understood as a property of the will only insofar as the will itself is understood to be the *rational* appetite and to have a close tie to the intellect. In some places Aquinas speaks of *liberum arbitrium* as if it were in fact a power of both the will and the intellect. When he is asking whether God has *liberum arbitrium*, one of the objections he raises begins with the uncontested remark that "*liberum arbitrium* is a faculty of reason and of will."[55]

Elsewhere he says:

> *liberum arbitrium* should be considered on the basis of *electio*. But both the cognitive power and the appetitive power contribute something to *electio*. From the cognitive power we need counsel, by which we determine what is to be preferred to what, and from the appetitive power we need the desire to accept what counsel has determined.[56]

That is why, he goes on to say, Aristotle supposed we ought to assign *electio* either to the "appetitive intellect" or to the "intellective appetite," phrases meant to indicate the intertwining of intellect and will in *liberum arbitrium*. (Of this pair, Aquinas opts for "intellective appetite"—the will understood as preceded by certain acts of intellect—as the more appropriate candidate for the faculty to which *liberum arbitrium* is to be assigned.) Although he thinks that if we take *liberum arbitrium* to be a faculty rather than one of the powers of a faculty, then it is just the will itself, he emphasizes that *liberum arbitrium* is the will understood as interwoven with and dependent on intellect.[57]

Finally, that will has the ability to do otherwise even in acts of *electio* does not stem from the fact that the will may simply choose not to follow intellect,[58] or may act in some other way as a homunculus independent of intellect. It concerns instead the relations between intellect and will. Insofar as the will has control over itself, this is mediated by the intellect. It is also limited, since there are intellective apprehensions which are not preceded by or dependent upon acts of will. Will may not always succeed, for example, in getting intellect to stop thinking about something, because something in the environment causes the thought to recur repeatedly in the intellect, as in the case described above of the prisoner who wants not to think about what his hearing keeps calling to his mind, namely, the torture of his fellow prisoners. But, within a limited range, will can be effective at controlling intellect, for example, by being able in some circumstances to redirect the attention of the intellect, and in that way the will can also have indirect control over itself.

Of course, the will's directing intellect in any of these ways will depend on intellect's presenting will's doing so as good in these circumstances. That is why a human agent's control over her own actions is a function of intellect and will and is an emergent power or property, resulting from the dynamic interaction between intellect and will, rather than a static power localized in the structure of one particular faculty. Given the nature of Aquinas's account of freedom, it makes more sense to attribute freedom to a human being with regard to willing or acting than to take freedom as a property of one particular component, whether will or intellect.

### V. Freedom and the Will's Ability to Do Otherwise

Aquinas supposes that human beings have control over their own actions and that this control is manifest, perhaps even specifically evinced, in certain acts of *electio* involving the ability to do otherwise. It is also important to recognize that for Aquinas the powers that give a human being control over her actions aren't themselves grounded in an ability to do otherwise. What produces such control is the nature of human intellect and will and their interaction. As long as these are functioning normally (and that, as we have seen, precludes will's being causally determined by anything outside the willer), an agent has control over her actions and freedom with respect to her willing and acting, even if she cannot do otherwise.

Some sign of this attitude on Aquinas's part can be found in what he says about the limits of *liberum arbitrium*. Something can be outside the power of *liberum arbitrium* in two ways. First, it can exceed the efficacy of the motive powers. For example, flying by flapping one's arms is not within the power of human *liberum arbitrium*, because flying exceeds human powers of movement. Secondly, and this is the important point for our purposes, acts which we do under the sudden impetus of some passion, such as wrath or concupiscence, are outside the power of *liberum arbitrium* because they occur quickly, before reason can deliberate about them. An agent may be able to avoid letting passion have such effects by paying careful attention; but an agent cannot always be paying careful attention. In unguarded moments, such passions can arise without the process of reason, even tacit reason, necessary to choice; and the agent in acting on such a passion is consequently unable to do otherwise on that occasion. If Aquinas supposed that *liberum arbitrium* were identical to free will or if he thought that the ability to do otherwise were essential to free will, he should go on to say here that such acts aren't sinful or blameworthy in any respect since they occur unfreely. What he in fact says is that they are sinful, but constitute only venial sins since their suddenness and their taking us by surprise provide us with some excuse.[59]

In *De Malo* (*QDM*) Aquinas argues at length that it is heretical to suppose that the will is moved of necessity to will whatever it wills, because such a supposition undermines all attributions of praise and blame, removes the impetus to deliberation, exhortation and precept, and so on. But in that very question he also grants that the will sometimes wills what it wills of necessity. This happens when what is willed is so altogether good that intellect can't find any description under which to present it as not good—as in the case of happiness. But it also happens in other sorts of cases, as when intellect establishes very clearly that one course of action is in every respect superior to any other available.[60] So Aquinas ends his discussion of this point with the conclusion that although the will is sometimes moved of necessity, it isn't always so moved.

What Aquinas means us to understand here, we might suppose, is that what the will wills is free only when the will is not moved of necessity. But such an interpretation would be a mistake. In arguing that the will does will some things of necessity, Aquinas explains that there are two relevant sorts of necessity. One is the necessity of coercion, which would occur if some cause outside the agent causally produced in the will a volition for some particular thing.[61] This, Aquinas says, is incompatible with freedom. (In fact, as we saw earlier, there can be no such coercion of will for Aquinas, because he thinks that it is conceptually impossible for any necessity of this sort to operate on the will.) But there is also the necessity of natural inclination. This is the sort by which the will wills, for example, things whose goodness is overwhelmingly apparent to the agent. Necessity of this sort, according to Aquinas, is not repugnant to the will and doesn't take away its freedom.[62] Siding with Augustine, he says,

"Freedom . . . is opposed to the necessity of coercion, but not to the necessity of natural inclination."[63]

That is why Aquinas thinks that there can be freedom of will on the part of the redeemed in heaven who no longer have the ability to will evil.[64] Their inability to will anything but the good stems not from any extrinsic coercion being exercised on their wills but rather from the clear view their intellects have on the nature of the good:

> Where there is no defect in apprehending and comparing, there can be no volition for evil with regard to those things which are ordered to the end, as is clear in the case of the blessed.[65]

Their intellects can no longer find descriptions under which to present as good things that are really evil. And so, although the blessed cannot will evil, they nonetheless will freely whatever they will.

Elsewhere Aquinas contrasts the necessity of coercion with the necessity of the end. When someone is compelled by an extrinsic cause in such a way that he cannot do otherwise than he does, this is the necessity of coercion, and it is altogether repugnant to the will. But necessity of the end is different. It arises, for example, when the end desired can be attained in only one way, as when crossing the sea requires using a ship. This is in no way repugnant to the will, on Aquinas's view. But, Aquinas concludes, the necessity of natural inclination is similar in the relevant respects to necessity of the end, and so necessity of natural inclination is also not repugnant to the will. For this reason as well as others, he maintains that "natural necessity doesn't take away the freedom of the will."[66]

Clearly, then, Aquinas doesn't suppose that human freedom even as regards willing consists in or depends on the ability to do otherwise. Aquinas would consequently reject what is called the Principle of Alternative Possibilities (PAP). PAP has many different formulations, but they all share this claim:

> (PAP) A person has free will with regard to (or is morally responsible for) doing an action A only if he could have done otherwise than A.[67]

Aquinas would reject this principle not only for bodily actions but even for acts of will.

Many contemporary philosophers also argue that PAP is false. A standard strategy for showing that PAP isn't necessary for free will is what has come to be known as a Frankfurt-style counterexample.[68] In such an example, a person P does an action A in circumstances that incline most people to conclude that P is doing A freely, but (in the example) there is some mechanism that would have operated to bring it about that P would have done A if P had not done A by himself. In the actual sequence of events presented in the counterexample, however, the mechanism does not operate, and P does do A by himself. So the counterexample is designed to make us think that P does A freely in the actual sequence of events although it is not the case that P could have done otherwise than A.[69] Frankfurt-style counterexamples can be constructed either for bodily actions such as leaving a room or for mental actions such as deciding to leave a room.

Some libertarians defend PAP by arguing strenuously against Frankfurt-style counterexamples.[70] But Aquinas would presumably find such counterexamples to PAP acceptable. In the actual sequence of events, P's doing A is *not* brought about by any cause extrinsic to P, and nothing in the counterexample keeps us from supposing that it is only P's own intellect and will which are responsible for P's doing A.

These reasons for the rejection of PAP don't have the implication that libertarian free will is never accompanied by alternative possibilities. On the contrary, as we have seen, Aquinas emphasizes human ability to do otherwise, for example in his account of *liberum arbitrium*. It may in fact be true on his view that in most cases in which an agent acts with free will, the agent can do otherwise. The ability to do otherwise would then be what medieval logic calls "an associated accident," a non-essential property that accompanies its subject much or even all of the time. Nonetheless, as I have argued, on Aquinas's account human freedom with regard to willing isn't to be identified with the ability to do otherwise; it is possible for an agent to act freely even when she can't act otherwise than she does.

Even where there are alternative possibilities available, on Aquinas's account of the will's relations to intellect they will be open to the agent only because she can be in a different intellective state from the one she is in fact in. For Aquinas, alternative possibilities for the will are dependant on alternative possibilities for the intellect; it is not possible for the determination of the intellect to be doing A is what is good now and for the will (with that determination of the intellect still in place) to will not to do A. But it may nonetheless be possible for the will to will not to do A because it may be possible for the agent's intellect to recalculate and to rescind the determination that doing A is good now.

## VI. Aquinas among the Libertarians

Although standard Frankfurt-style counterexamples are commonly thought to show that alternative possibilities aren't necessary for freedom, there are also analogues to Frankfurt-style counterexamples which show that alternative possibilities aren't sufficient for freedom either.

Consider, for example, Robert Heinlein's *The Puppetmasters*. In that story, an alien race of intelligent creatures wants to conquer the earth. Part of the alien plan for invasion includes a covert operation in which individual aliens take over particular human beings without being detected. When an alien "master" takes over a human being, the human being (say, Sam) has within himself not only his own consciousness but the master's as well. Since it is crucial to the alien plan that their taking over human beings be undetected in the early stages of the invasion, they're careful to make the behavior of people like Sam correspond to the behavior Sam would normally have engaged in had he not been infected with the alien. So when, under the control of the alien, Sam does some action A, it is also true that if there had been some reason sufficient for Sam in his uninfected state to do not-A, the alien would have brought it about that Sam in his infected state did not-A. In that case, then, there is a possible world in which Sam does otherwise than A. Sam has the ability to do otherwise, then; nonetheless, Sam isn't free with respect to his doing A.

In the standard Frankfurt-style counterexamples, the absence of alternative possibilities doesn't preclude an agent's acting on his own unimpeded intellect and will in the actual sequence of events. In the analogue counterexamples, the presence of an alternative possibility doesn't stem from any ability that the agent's own intellect and will have in the actual sequence. What the standard and analogue counterexamples together show, I think, is the correctness of Aquinas's position. In order to determine whether or not an agent is free, it is important to determine whether the intellect and will on which he acts are his own, not whether alternative possibilities are present or absent for him. For Aquinas, human freedom depends on human cognitive capacities and on the connection of the will to those capacities. Consequently, as long as human acts of will originate in those faculties, those acts count as voluntary and free, even if the agent couldn't have done otherwise in the circumstances or the act of will is necessitated by natural inclinations of intellect and will.

So Aquinas holds a view which is libertarian in some sense. It maintains that human beings have free will and that free will is incompatible with causal determinism. Nonetheless, this is a position that will strike some libertarians as highly unsatisfactory. For some medieval libertarians (and for some contemporaries), an act of will is free only in case the agent could have performed a different act of will in exactly the same set of circumstances with exactly the same set of beliefs and desires.[71] For such libertarians, the alternative possibilities available to the will need to be available to the will simultaneously, with the agent in the same state of mind. On this way of thinking about free will, to be free, the will needs to be unconstrained not only by causal influences outside the agent; it needs to be unconstrained even by the agent's intellect. On Aquinas's view, however, it isn't possible for the will to be unconstrained by the intellect, and what is necessary for freedom is that an agent's will not be causally determined by anything outside the agent. For Aquinas, there is an alternative possibility open to the will only in virtue of the fact that it is possible for the intellect to be in a different state.

Such different intuitions about what is needed for free will are reminiscent of medieval debates about the nature of the autonomy of a free will. Some Franciscans tended to suppose that a *free* will had to be independent of the intellect as well as of all external causal influence.[72] Aquinas thought that the will is free just because of its connection with the intellect. For my purposes here, what is most important to see in this dispute is the nature of Aquinas's position within the genus of libertarian theories of free will. One can hold an incompatiblilist theory of free will, as Aquinas does, without accepting the principle of alternative possibilities; one can maintain that the will is free in a way incompatible with causal determinism without espousing the Franciscan version of libertarianism. What exactly to call Aquinas's position is not clear. It seems to me that it is a species of libertarianism, but one which grounds libertarian freedom in an agent's acting on his own intellect and will, and not in the alternative possibilities open to the agent.[73]

## Notes

This chapter was previously published as Eleonore Stump, "Aquinas's Account of Freedom: Intellect and Will" (*The Monist* 80, no 4, October 1997). Copyright © 1980, *THE MONIST: An International Quarterly Journal of General Philosophical Inquiry*, Peru, Illinois, U.S.A. 61354. Reprinted by permission.

1. See, for example, Klaus Riesenhuber, "The Bases and Meaning of Freedom in Thomas Aquinas," *Proceedings of the American Catholic Philosophical Association* 48 (1974), 99–111, esp. p. 101.

2. Cf. J. Korolec, "Free Will and Free Choice" in the *Cambridge History of Later Medieval Philosophy* (ed. Norman Kretzmann, Anthony Kenny, Jan Pinborg, associate editor Eleonore Stump [Cambridge University Press, 1981]), p. 630; David Gallagher, "Thomas Aquinas on the Will as Rational Appetite," *Journal of the History of Philosophy* 29 (1991), p. 570, n. 26; and Daniel Westberg, "Did Aquinas Change His Mind About the Will?" *The Thomist* 58 (1994), 41–60.

3. Cf. David Burrell, *Freedom and Creation in Three Traditions* (Notre Dame, IN: University of Notre Dame Press, 1993), and Brian Davies, *The Thought of Thomas Aquinas* (Oxford: Clarendon Press, 1992), pp. 174–78.

4. *ST* I–II q.10 a.1 and I q.82 a.1.

5. *ST* I q.82 a.4.

6. *ST* q.59 a.1 obj.3.

7. For a discussion of sensory cognition, see my paper "Aquinas on the Mechanisms of Cognition: Sense and Phantasia," forthcoming in *The Copenhagen School of Medieval Philosophy*, ed. Sten Ebbesen.

8. See, for example, *ST* I q.59 a.1 corpus. See also *ST* I q.83 a.1, I–II q.6 a.1, and *De Veritate* (*QDV*) q.xxiv a.1.

9. See, e.g., the reference to Aristotle in *ST* I q.59 a.1 obj.1.

10. See, e.g., *ST* I q.19 a.1 corpus.

11. See, e.g., *ST* I–II q.9 a.1, *ST* I q.82 a.4, and *ST* I–II q.17 a.1.

12. Although faith is divinely infused, according to Aquinas, he also seems to suppose that faith results from such an action of the will on the intellect. See, for example, *QDV* q.14 a.3 reply, ad 2, and ad 10. I have defended Aquinas's view that will can act on intellect in this way in "Intellectual Virtues: Wisdom and the Will to Believe" in *Aquinas's Moral Theory*, ed. Scott MacDonald and Eleonore Stump, Cornell University Press, forthcoming.

13. See *ST* I–II q.17 a.1 and a.6.

14. *ST* I–II q.9 a.2.

15. *ST* I q.81 a.3 and I–II q.10 a.3.

16. *ST* I q.81 a.3.

17. Cf. *ST* I–II q.9 a.1.

18. Cf. *De Malo* (*QDM*) q.6 a.1, where Aquinas says that even as regards happiness, the exercise of the will is not necessary since a person can always will on a particular occasion not to think about happiness.

19. For the way in which intellect makes use of sensory cognition to apprehend particulars, see my paper "Aquinas on the Mechanisms of Intellective Cognition," *Révue internationale de philosophie,* forthcoming.

20. See *ST* I q.82 a.2.

21. The ultimate good *simpliciter* is God, on Aquinas's account. Hence the sight of God in the beatific vision also moves the will necessarily.

22. *ST* I q.82 a.1.

23. *ST* I q.82 a.2.

24. *QDV* q.22 a.12.

25. There is something misleading about talk of intellect's cognizing or will's willing. Aquinas says, "We *can* say that the soul understands, in the same way that we can say that the eye sees; but it would be more appropriate to say that *a human being* understands *by means of* the soul." (*ST* I q.75 a.2 ad 2).

26. For Aquinas's general view that all acts of will must be preceded by an act of intellect, see, for example, *ST* I q.82 a.4 ad 3.

27. *ST* I–II q.1 a.4, esp. obj.3 and ad 3.

28. *ST* I q.82 a.4; *QDV* q.22 a.12. Cf. also *QDM* q.6 a.1.

29. *ST* I–II q.17 a.1.

30. *ST* I–II q.50 a.5, I–II q.52 a.1, and I–II q.66 a.1.

31. Cf., e.g., *ST* I–II q.17 a.2 and a.5 ad 1.

32. This distinction is related to the distinction between external and internal actions. For a helpful discussion of this distinction, see David Gallagher, "Aquinas on Moral Action: Interior and Exterior Acts," *Proceedings of the American Catholic Philosophical Association* 64 (1990), 118–29.

33. See, for example, *ST* I–II q.6 a.4 and *QDV* q.24 a.1 ad 1. Cf. also *QDM* q.6 a.1 ad 22, where Aquinas says, "he who does what he does not want [to do] does not have free action, but he can have free will."

34. *ST* I–II q.10 a.3.

35. *ST* I–II q.17 a.1 ad 2.

36. Aquinas's position here is like his position as regards perception and intellection. The proper sense organ for sight is the eye, and yet, Aquinas thinks, it is a human being who sees, not the eye, and a similar point could be made about intellective cognition. See, for example, *ST* I q.75 a.2 ad 2.

37. *ST* I–II q.6 a.2 and q.17 a.5.

38. *ST* I–II q.6 a.3 ad 3.

39. *ST* I–II q.6 a.1 sc.

40. *ST* I–II q.6 proemium.

41. *ST* I–II q.6 a.7 ad 3.

42. *ST* I–II q.6 a.1 corpus.

43. *ST* I–II q.6 a.2.

44. *ST* I–II q.9 a.6. The exception to this claim about extrinsic principles is God, who can be an extrinsic cause without removing voluntariness since he is the extrinsic cause creating the will with its inclinations and its connections to the intellect. (See, for example, *ST* I q.105 a.4 ad 2.)

45. *ST* I–II q.6 a.4.

46. *ST* I–II q.80 a.3. See also, for example, *QDV* q.24 a.2 where he says, "If the judgment of the cognitive [faculty] is not in a person's power but is determined extrinsically (*aliunde*), then the appetite will not be in his power either, and consequently neither will [his] motion or activity."

47. I discuss the relationship of libertarianism and the ability to do otherwise at some length in "Libertarianism and the Principle of Alternate Possibilities," ed. Jeff Jordan and Daniel Howard-Snyder. *Faith, Freedom, and Rationality: Philosophy of Religion Today* (Rowman & Littlefield, 1996), pp. 73–88.

48. *ST* I q.83 a.1 obj.2. See also *ST* I q.83 a.3 where Aquinas says, "we are said to have *liberum arbitrium* when we can receive one and reject another."

49. *ST* I q.83 a.3 sc.

50. *ST* I q.83 a.4.

51. *QDV* q.24 a.6.

52. See, for example, *ST* I–II q.13.

53. See, for example, *ST* I–II q.15 a.3 ad 3.

54. See also in *NE* III.v [434] where Aquinas says that the genus of *electio* is the voluntary; on his view, although "every [act of] *electio* is something voluntary, *electio* and the voluntary are not altogether the same, but voluntary is in more [acts than *electio* is]." One reason for insisting that *electio* is not identical to the voluntary is this: [436] "Those things which we do quickly we say are voluntary, because their source is in us, but they are not said [to be done] with *electio*, because they don't arise from deliberation."

55. *ST* I q.19 a.10 obj.2.

56. *ST* I q.83 a.3.

57. *ST* I q.83 a.4.

58. Cf. *QDM* q.16 a.2 where Aquinas says, "evil cannot arise in an appetite in virtue of appetite's being discordant with the apprehension it follows."

59. *QDV* q.24 a.12.

60. *QDM* q.6 a.1.

61. God's grace does operate on the will with causal efficacy, but Aquinas's account of grace is complicated and it isn't at all clear that the operations of grace constitute an exception to his claim here.

62. *QDV* q.22 a.5; see also *QDV* q.24 a.10 obj.5 and ad 5.

63. *QDV* q.22 a.5 ad 3 in contrarium.

64. See, for example, *QDM* q.16 a.5, where Aquinas says that there is not state in which human beings lack *liberum arbitrium*.

65. *QDV* a.22 a.6.

66. *ST* I q.82 a.1 corpus and ad 1.

67. For different versions of (PAP) and an assessment of their strengths and weaknesses, see, for example, Thomas Flint, "Compatibilism and the Argument from Unavoidability," *Journal of Philosophy* 84 (1987), 423–40.

68. See, for example, Harry Frankfurt, "Alternate Possibilities and Moral Responsibility," *Journal of Philosophy* 66 (1969), 829–39.

69. See my discussion in "Intellect, Will, and Alternate Possibilities," reprinted in John Martin Fischer and Mark Ravizza, *Perspectives on Moral Responsibility* (Ithaca, NY: Cornell University Press, 1993), pp. 237–62.

70. See, for example, David Widerker, "Libertarian Freedom and the Avoidability of Decisions," *Faith and Philosophy* 12 (1995), 113–18, and "Libertarianism and Frankfurt's Attack on the Principle of Alternative Possibilities," *The Philosophical Review* 104 (1995), 247–61.

71. For the medieval position in question, see Bonnie Kent, *Virtues of the Will: The Transformation of Ethics in the Late Thirteenth Century* (Washington, DC: The Catholic University of America Press, 1995), esp. chapters 3 and 4.

72. For an example of a Franciscan position of the sort opposed to Aquinas's, see, for example, *John Duns Scotus. Contingency and Freedom. Lectura I 39*, tr. A. Vos Jaczn, H. Veldhuis, A. H. Looman-Graaskamp, E. Dekker, and N. W. den Bok (Dordrecht: Kluwer Publishing Co., 1994), The New Synthese Historical Library, vol. 42, pp. 116–17.

73. I am grateful to the faculty and students at the Thomas Institute in Cologne and to William Alston, David Burrell, Brian Leftow, and Timothy O'Connor for helpful comments on earlier drafts of this paper. I am especially indebted to Norman Kretzmann for many very useful comments and suggestions.

# 10

# Habits and Virtues

*Bonnie Kent*

M ODERN READERS SOMETIMES SEE IN THE scholastic practice of citing "authorities" an excessive concern with tradition, or an aversion to original thinking, or both. In interpreting the *Summa Theologiae*, this is a serious, though natural, mistake. In fact, Thomas operates very much like a host laboring to produce congenial, fruitful conversation among guests deeply at odds with each other. Like all good hosts, he conceals how hard he must work to ensure that conflicts are defused and the party goes well. Sometimes Thomas repeats, approvingly, the words of an authority while giving them a meaning rather different from what the author intended. (One would need a knowledge of the history of ethics independent of the "history" offered by the *Summa* to recognize such distortions.) Sometimes he sounds as if he agrees wholeheartedly when he actually agrees only with significant reservations. And sometimes his reservations become clear only later in the *Summa*, so that his earlier statements appear, retrospectively, in an altogether different light.

### Second Nature

Thanks to this triumph of diplomacy, the whole project of synthesizing the chaotic array of Greek, Hellenistic, Muslim, and Christian sources into a single, coherent theory of virtue appears far less demanding than it actually was. In explaining the *Summa*'s account of habits and virtues, I shall accordingly try to provide enough historical background to compensate for Thomas's finesse. To

appreciate his own innovations, one needs some sense of the serious philosophical problems he actually faced and worked to solve.

When Aristotle places virtue in the metaphysical genus of *habit* (or *hexis*),
he runs true to form for classical ethics. Philosophers of antiquity were much
impressed by the many years of learning and practice necessary to become a
thoroughly admirable human specimen. While they all emphasized the intellectual prerequisite of "practical wisdom" (Greek: *phronesis*; Latin: *prudentia*),
they also emphasized the long conditioning, habituation, and sheer practice
necessary to produce excellent moral character. Hence Aristotle's definition of
moral virtue: "a *hexis* concerned with choice, lying in a mean relative to us,
this being determined by a rational principle and in the way in which the man
of practical wisdom would determine it."[1]

The Greek *hexis* was translated into Latin as *habitus* and thence into English
as "habit." The English word tends to mislead insofar as habit can signify for
English speakers any routine performance, however trivial or mechanical—
tugging at one's necktie, for example, or wincing at the scream of a police siren.
A *hexis* or *habitus*, in contrast, is a durable characteristic of the agent inclining
to certain kinds of actions and emotional reactions, not the actions and reactions themselves. Acquired over time, habits grow to be "second nature" for the
individual. Aristotle himself appeals to this factor in distinguishing habits from
other qualities he labels mere "conditions":

> A habit (*hexis*) differs from a condition in being more stable and lasting longer.
> Such are the branches of knowledge and the virtues . . . It is what are easily
> changed and quickly changing that we call conditions, e.g., hotness and chill and
> sickness and health and the like. For a man is in a certain condition by dint of
> these, yet he changes quickly from being hot to cold and from being healthy to
> being sick. Similarly with the rest of the conditions, unless indeed even one of
> these were eventually to become through length of time part of a man's nature
> and irremediable or exceedingly hard to change—and then one would perhaps
> call this a habit.[2]

The idea of virtue as a habit and habit itself as a second nature was a commonplace for the Romans as well as the Greeks. There was, however, some di-
vergence in terminology. When commenting on Aristotle's works Latin authors
tended to use the word *habitus* for the Greek *hexis*—an etymologically sound
translation, as Thomas points out, because both words have their root in the
verb "to have" (Ia IIae, q. 49, a. 1). On the other hand, when writing without
any special reference to Aristotle, Latin authors commonly spoke of "custom"
or "usage" (*consuetudo*) rather than habit (*habitus*) as "another nature" or a
"second nature."[3] Despite their differences, both words can indeed signify those
characteristics which become natural and enduring through long practice,

thereby making the individual, in one way or another, the person she is: a brilliant mathematician, a brave soldier, or a faithful wife, and likewise, negatively, a mathematical moron, a contemptible coward, or a despicable cheat.

The arcane topic of translation deserves mention on two grounds. First, Augustine gave serious thought to the process of habituation, spoke of habits in many of his works, but typically used the word "custom" (*consuetudo*), not *habitus*. Second, although he was well aware that classical philosophers described moral virtue as the product of habituation, as a second nature we create through our own activities, Augustine himself insisted that all true virtues are forms of charity: the love of God that God alone can give. What good is the learning and practice so prized by the ancients when genuine virtue requires a radical, divinely produced change in values? According to Augustine, apparent virtues in pagans are actually hidden vices. Even when pagan virtues are sought for their own sake, those attaining them are inflated by pride in their own characters.[4] As Augustine regarded charity as the root of all virtues, so he regarded pride as the root of all sins. He thus saw habit not as the genus of virtue but closer to the enemy of virtue—so many chains forged by our own wills, making it all the harder for us to love most what most deserves to be loved.[5]

Indeed, Augustine lived to regret having reproduced in one of his works Cicero's famous definition of virtue as "a habit of the soul conforming to the mode of nature and of reason" (*animi habitus naturae modo atque rationi consentaneus*).[6] As Augustine's works were copied and circulated, so, too, was this definition, leading him finally to complain that it was *Cicero's* definition, not his own, and that he included it at the request of others.[7] What, then, should we make of Thomas's decision to define virtue as a habit (Ia IIae, q. 55, a. 4)? Does it represent a rejection, however tactful, of Augustine's teachings? To answer the question, we need to understand exactly what Thomas means by a habit.

## Rethinking Habits

In the section of the *Summa* known as "the treatise on habits" (Ia IIae, qq. 49–54), Thomas draws so heavily on Aristotle and his commentators that he seems at first glance to be following ancient thought quite closely. Like Aristotle, Aquinas places habits in the category of quality, where they are distinguished from other qualities by both their durability and their tendency to dispose the possessor well or badly (Ia IIae, q. 49, aa. 1–2). As he explains that habits are, by their very nature, principles of action (Ia IIae, q. 49, a. 3), Thomas appears to be continuing in the Aristotelian vein, but already a strangely un-Aristotelian idea has crept in. Citing a commentary by Averroes on Aristotle's *De Anima*, Thomas declares that "a habit is that whereby we act when we *will*" (Ia IIae, q. 49, a. 3).[8] He quotes this dictum again and again, not only in the *Summa Theologiae* but also in other works, from his youthful commentary on the *Sentences* onward, despite the fact that Aristotle himself claimed no such relationship between habit and will.[9] When Thomas proceeds to argue that certain habits are infused in us by God, it becomes all the more evident that ancient philosophy has been left behind (Ia IIae, q. 51, a. 4). Our second natures need not be generated naturally and gradually, through our own long practice (Ia IIae, q. 52).[10]

At the time, the notion of divinely produced habits would not have raised eyebrows. Theologians as early as the twelfth century had stretched the ancient concept of habit wide enough to include dispositions produced directly by God, not only in adult converts but even in newborn babies, through the sacrament of baptism.[11] In endorsing the view that certain habits are God-given, Thomas explains:

> There are some habits by which man is disposed to an end exceeding the capacity (*facultas*) of human nature, which is the ultimate and perfect happiness of man, as was said above; and since habits should be in proportion to that to which man is disposed by them, for this reason it is necessary that habits disposing one to such an end likewise exceed the capacity of human nature. Hence, such habits can never exist in man except by divine infusion, as is the case for all virtues of grace.[12] (Ia IIae, q. 51, a. 4)

Aristotle linked all virtues to happiness in this life; Augustine linked them all to happiness in the afterlife. Thomas himself argues that humankind has as ends *both* kinds of happiness and so needs *two* kinds of virtue: divinely infused as well as naturally acquired (Ia IIae, q. 51, a. 4).[13] Notice, though, that our need for God-given virtues would be a reason for positing God-given habits only if all virtues should be taken as habits, which will not be argued until later.

Where Aristotle speaks now one way, now another, Thomas consistently teaches that only qualities of the soul, not qualities of the body—such as beauty or health—can be habits *simpliciter* (Ia IIae, q. 50, a. 1). Habits arise from actions of a power capable of exercise in one way or another, not determined by its very nature to operate as it does. When the body digests food, it does so strictly as a matter of nature; hence, it neither needs nor acquires some digestive habit. In contrast, when the body is moved by the soul—in pitching a baseball, for example—it can indeed acquire a habit, albeit merely a habit in the secondary sense.

Imagine a major-league player who has learned to pitch with impressive accuracy, speed, and control. According to Thomas, the pitcher owes his motor skills more to the soul than the body, for the body engages in the long hours of practice necessary to develop such skills only because the soul commands it to do so. The habit of skillful pitching, then, belongs to the soul without qualification (*simpliciter*) and to the body only in an extended sense. The skillful movements of the body, caused by its disposition to function in a skillful way, should be seen mainly as residual effects of the soul's control.

Consider now how well or ill this conception of a habit jibes with our own intuitions. Even if we grant Thomas the point about major-league pitchers, we ourselves might still be inclined to regard animals as much better examples of habituation than human beings. As the star pitcher learns to throw the ball, so the cat learns to run expectantly to its dish when it hears someone open the cupboard where the cat's food is stored. When shown a baseball, the pitcher does not automatically seize and throw it: his behavior in sporting goods stores differs strikingly from his behavior on the mound. In contrast, the mere opening of the cupboard might well send the cat running to its dish even when mealtime is hours away and its food, disappointingly, has never appeared at any other time. Should we not then consider the cat, rather than the major-league pitcher, the true "creature of habit"?

Thomas defends the opposite position: that human beings can acquire habits properly so-called, but animals cannot (Ia IIae, q. 50, a. 3, ad 2). Of course, animals can be trained through a combination of punishment and reward. We can modify their behavior by cashing in on their natural instincts. Yet Thomas believes that even the best-trained animals always act from instinct. Hence he claims that the dispositions they acquire fall short of the essential character (*ratio*) of a habit as regards "the use of the will." Unlike human beings, animals do not have the power to exercise a habit or not, "which seems to belong to the very *ratio* of habit."[14]

For Thomas, then, habits in the strict sense are never the product of bodily constitution, mere "animal" instinct, upbringing, or some combination. Nor can they ever compel us to act or react as we do. On the contrary, Thomas argues that we can always refuse to act in accordance with our habits and can even choose to act against our habits. Where Aristotle repeatedly suggests that the truly virtuous are beyond danger of degeneration, just as the truly vicious are beyond hope of improvement, Thomas has no such confidence.[15] Habits make it harder, but never impossible, for the virtuous among us to degenerate and the vicious among us to improve (Ia IIae, q. 53, aa. 1–3; Ia IIae, q. 63, a. 2).

Among the powers of the human soul, some are better suited than others to developing habits, just as people are better suited than animals. Insofar as a power acts from natural instinct, it cannot acquire habits in the strict sense. Thomas accordingly sees more room for habits in the sensory *appetite*, the seat of emotions, than in powers of sensory *apprehension* such as memory and imagination (Ia IIae, q. 50, a. 3, ad 3). In downgrading the latter powers he appeals to their connection with the body, the force of sheer repetition in conditioning them to operate in certain ways, how they tend to influence, instead of being influenced by, our intellectual judgment of the particular situation in which we find ourselves, and just how far removed they are from the control of the will (Ia IIae, q. 56, a. 5, ad 1). Here we see the influence of Aristotle's psychology, but perhaps Thomas also recalls Augustine's agony at the inability to control his own memory and the tempting images it produced.[16] Dreams of what we believed we long ago stopped wanting, what we would now never seek in our waking lives, might be taken as evidence of the deeply uncontrollable aspect of imagination and memory.

The *Summa* uses the saying of Averroes—that a habit is that whereby we act when we *will*—to support an even more radical claim: from the essential character (*ratio*) of a habit alone, it is plain that a habit is *principally* related to the will (Ia IIae, q. 50, a. 5).[17] To say the least, this represents a substantial departure from Aristotle's teachings. Aristotle holds people responsible for actions proceeding from passion or non-rational appetite even when the agent acts against her own choice, her own reasoned and settled conception of the good. No single power of the soul is even the indirect source of all moral actions. Thomas, however, regards the will as just such a source.[18] In his view, human beings are blamed for tantrums, fits of gluttony, and other such actions because we never act from passion without the consent of our wills. Animals cannot fairly be blamed for apparently similar behavior because they lack the power of will. They are not, as are human beings, "masters" of their own actions. Although reason might at first appear more important, the will receives increasing attention as the *Prima Secundae* unfolds.


## The Definition of Virtue


The *Summa*'s discussion of human virtue as a habit, an "operative" habit, and a good habit (Ia IIae, q. 55, aa. 1–3) should be seen not only in relation to the preceding treatise on habits but also in relation to the definition of virtue that immediately follows (Ia IIae, q. 55, aa. 1–3) For the topic is initially *human* virtue, a restriction Thomas stresses (for example, Ia IIae, q. 55, a. 3), and yet the definition is not restricted to human virtue. Why, one wonders, does the adjective "human" drop out?

The aim cannot be to make the definition wide enough to accommodate the virtues of animals, for animals are unable to develop habits in the strict sense, much less virtues. Instead, Thomas wants his definition to cover both the human virtues acquired through our own natural resources and the superhuman virtues Christians have through God's grace. Aristotle, he believes, had some valuable insights in the first area. Thus the division between moral and intellectual virtues provided by the *Nicomachean Ethics* can be considered adequate for human virtues (*virtutes humanas*). But as Aristotle failed to consider faith, hope, and charity, those virtues of human beings (*virtutes hominis*) that surpass our nature and make us participants in God's grace, his definition of virtue proves myopic (Ia IIae, q. 58, a. 3, ad 3).

The definition of virtue chosen for discussion accordingly comes not from the *Nicomachean Ethics* but from Peter Lombard's *Sentences*, the standard theological textbook of the day: "Virtue is a good quality of the mind, by which we live rightly, of which no one makes bad use, which God works in us without us" (Ia IIae, q. 55, a. 4).[19] Recognizing that the textbook definition was pieced together from the words of Augustine, Thomas expresses firm approval: "It should be said that this definition embraces perfectly the whole essential character (*ratio*) of virtue. For the complete essential character of anything is gathered from all of its causes. The preceding definition, however, comprehends all the causes of virtue" (Ia IIae, q. 55, a. 4).[20] The article continues by discussing the formal, material, final, and efficient causes of virtue, along with some apparently modest suggestions for revision.

In discussing virtue's formal component, for example, Thomas proposes to substitute "habit" (*habitus*) for "quality" in order to make the definition "more appropriate." He gives no justification other than a perfunctory allusion to Aristotle's categories. Remember, though, that Thomas has already stretched the ancient concept of habit to cover God-given dispositions and described all habits as principally related to the will. In the next question of the *Summa* he also takes pains to distinguish his own position from Cicero's (Ia IIae, q. 56, a. 5). Granted, there are certain habits acquired in the mode of nature, from mere repetition or frequent usage (*consuetudo*). The natural effects of such brute repetition cannot be denied; we commonly see them in our powers of memory and imagination. Yet Thomas denies that these are habits in the strict sense. Even if they were, he adds, they could not be called "virtues." In a similar vein, he argues that the Latin "moral" can signify either *mos* as custom (*consuetudo*) or *mos* as an inclination that has become quasi-natural for the individual (Ia IIae, q. 58, a. 1). When we speak of "moral virtue," moral has the second meaning, so that one should not imagine some essential connection between moral virtue and custom.

Thomas's distinction between habit and custom seems rather strained—and, from the perspective of ancient philosophy, hopelessly misguided. Augustine, however, would probably have appreciated Thomas's efforts. Why should Augustine object to defining virtue as a habit when the concept of habit itself has undergone such a significant change? At the same time, Augustine might reasonably wonder about the reasons for this conceptual revisionism. What advantages could there be to describing even God-given virtues as "habits"?[21]

To answer this question, it helps to move beyond the *Prima Secundae* to Thomas's criticisms of Peter Lombard's teachings on charity (IIa IIae, q. 23, a. 2). Suppose that charity, as Peter had suggested, is not something created in the human soul. Suppose that human acts of charity come not from some divinely infused habit but rather from the soul's being moved directly by the Holy Spirit. No doubt Peter was trying to flag the unique excellence of charity, but to Thomas's mind, his position is still "ridiculous."[22] If charity is not something created in the soul—if it is not a habit inclining the human agent to act from the love of God, not a "second nature," albeit divinely produced, so that acts of charity continue to run counter to the individual's inclinations—how could such acts ever be done easily, promptly, and with pleasure? How could acts of charity even be considered "voluntary"? If the person experiences no internal alteration but instead is moved by God to act contrary to her nature, how is she any more the cause of her own behavior than a rock is the cause of its own "behavior" when God snatches it from its natural descent toward the sewer and sends it shooting toward the heavens? In sum, Thomas does have his reasons for wanting all virtues, including the infused, classified as habits.

Only when he turns to the efficient cause of virtue does Thomas venture a clear criticism of the Augustinian definition: God is the efficient cause of infused virtue, to which the definition applies. Thus it says, "which God works in us without us." If this phrase were omitted, the remaining definition would be common to all virtues, both acquired and infused (Ia IIae, q. 55, a. 4).[23] In other words, the textbook formula suffices for God-given virtues but lacks sufficient generality to cover the full range of virtues—a serious philosophical objection to its adequacy as a definition. Thomas never mentions that the narrowness of the definition was no mere oversight. Because Augustine himself regarded all the "virtues" of pagans as vices in disguise, he had no reason to seek a definition of virtue encompassing them.

Thomas's more generous assessment of non-Christians was common among scholastic theologians. Just the standard distinction between "acquired" and "infused" virtues suggests that genuine virtues can indeed be developed without God's grace. To understand why this departure from Augustine's teachings proves less than revolutionary when seen from the perspective of the *Summa* as a whole, we need to consider the place that naturally acquired virtues actually occupy.

## Virtues in a Relative Sense

Soon after defining virtue, Thomas argues that a virtue without qualification can belong only to the will or some other power of the soul insofar as it is moved by the will (Ia IIae, q. 56, a. 3). Intellectual habits such as science and art must therefore be considered virtues in only a relative sense (*secundum quid*). The aim here is to distinguish virtues that make one a good mathematician, painter, or auto mechanic, or good relative to some other specific role, from virtues that make one an all around good human being. Most habits of intellect fall in the first category, as evidenced by their potential for abuse. Consider, for example, how knowledge and skills acquired in medical school could go to make both an excellent doctor and a talented, undetected murderer. An ambitious toxicologist might use her expertise to develop antidotes for previously untreatable poisons; then again, she might use it to dispatch rivals for research funding by adding to their morning coffee little-known toxins from Amazonian jungles. While her intellectual virtues give her capacities for action not to be found in most people, she needs moral virtues to ensure that her capacities are put to good use.

When he turns to a more specific discussion of intellectual virtues, Thomas again reminds us that such habits make the mind function well, but they do not ensure that the person puts his mind to good use (Ia IIae, q. 57, a. 1). As virtues of the speculative mind wisdom, science, and understanding enable us to grasp the truth. Art, a virtue of the practical mind, gives us skill in making things. Yet none of these intellectual virtues has any necessary relationship to a good will or well-ordered emotions. The most brilliant theorist might well have a streak of cruelty or a short temper; so, too, might the most expert craftsman (Ia IIae, q. 57, aa. 3–5). Prudence, a habit of the practical intellect, is the sole intellectual virtue inseparable from moral virtue and hence from good moral character. Following Aristotle, Thomas argues that no one can have justice, courage, or any other moral virtue without prudence, nor can one have prudence without the moral virtues (Ia IIae, q. 58, aa. 4–5).

As philosophical readers continue with the *Prima Secundae*, they will probably take an interest in the differences between moral and intellectual virtues, differences between the moral virtues themselves, the connection between prudence and moral virtue, and other topics addressed in the *Nicomachean Ethics*. But Aristotle's influence should not be overestimated, for the *Summa* posits a whole species of moral and intellectual virtues with the same names as virtues discussed by Aristotle (prudence, justice, temperance, and so on), but which are infused by God along with the theological virtues of faith, hope, and charity. When Thomas refers to moral and intellectual virtues, he might therefore be referring either to naturally acquired virtues or to virtues that Christians possess due to God's grace. Should one focus on the division between acquired and infused virtues instead of the division between moral and intellectual virtues, the rest of the *Prima Secundae* looks rather different.

In discussing the cardinal virtues, for example, Thomas considers the assertion of Macrobius that they belong to four different genera: "political, purifying, purified, and exemplary" (Ia IIae, q. 61, a. 5).[24] Far from dismissing the suggestion that there are very different kinds of prudence, justice, and so on—not only different species but possibly different genera—Thomas supports it. He distinguishes sharply between virtues suited to our natural status as "political animals," disposing us to behave well in the social interactions characteristic of the present life, and the purifying virtues of persons striving for a likeness to God. The purifying virtues lie between the exemplary virtues, which truly belong to God alone, and the political virtues:

> Prudence of this kind, by contemplating the divine, scorns all the things of this world and directs all its thoughts to divine truths; temperance sets aside what the body requires, insofar as nature allows; courage prevents the soul from being terrified about losing the body as it approaches heavenly things; and justice lies in the consent of the whole soul to the way thus proposed.[25] (Ia IIae, q. 61, a. 5)

In a related article of his *Disputed Questions on the Cardinal Virtues,* Thomas adds that the political virtues fall short of the true essential character (*ratio*) of virtue. As moral inclinations without prudence fall short, so too, from a wider perspective, do moral virtues acquired together with prudence. Unless directed to God through charity, naturally acquired (alias "political") virtues are deficient in the truly essential character of virtue. The purifying virtues, by contrast, infused by God together with charity, are unqualifiedly perfect and make a person's actions good without qualification.[26]

The *Prima Secundae* moves more slowly. Having briefly sketched a distinction between the different species of cardinal virtues (political, purifying, and so on), Thomas turns to the three theological virtues: faith, hope, and charity (Ia IIae, q. 62). These are the sole virtues that have God as their object. Because they enable us to share in the divine nature and direct us to a happiness unattainable in the present life, we cannot acquire them through our own resources; we can have them only through the grace of God.

Thomas follows St. Paul in praising charity or love as the greatest of the theological virtues (Ia IIae, q. 62, a. 4; 1 Cor 13:13). Although God infuses all three virtues together, one can still discern a conceptual order. Through faith, we believe what God has revealed of Himself and of the future life; through hope, we come to love Him as the source of our own happiness; but only through charity can we love Him as an end in Himself—as the supreme good, deserving of more love than any other, not merely as good for *us.* The love characteristic of hope is the love of desire; charity alone produces the genuine love of friendship. The crucial difference in motivation explains why Thomas describes charity as the "mother," "root," and "form" of all the virtues, even going so far as to declare that faith and hope are not virtues properly so called in the absence of charity (Ia IIae, q. 62, a. 4; Ia IIae, q. 65, a. 4; Ia IIae, q. 66, a. 6).

Readers must wait until the next question, concerning the causes of virtue, to learn more about the prudence and moral virtues given by God. Thomas argues first that we need these infused virtues to attain the complete happiness of the afterlife, then that they differ not merely in degree of perfection but in kind (*species*) from virtues acquired naturally (Ia IIae, q. 63, aa. 3–4). The difference in kind derives partly from the different goods to which the virtues are ordered. While naturally acquired moral virtues make people well suited to the human affairs and earthly happiness that concern all—because we are all human—infused moral virtues make people well suited to the life Christians must live because they are Christians: persons belonging to the household of God, with love of God as the highest good, faith in God's word, and hope for the happiness of the afterlife. The difference in perceived goods and related motivations dictates different standards of conduct. This is Thomas's second reason for regarding naturally acquired and infused moral virtues as different species. For instance, while human reason alone establishes that people should not eat or drink in ways harmful to body or mind, the higher rule of divine law requires more in the way of abstinence (Ia IIae, q. 63, a. 4).

The next question (Ia IIae, q. 64), about how virtues observe a mean, only appears to shift the focus away from God-given virtues and narrow it to naturally acquired virtues. As Thomas previously transformed Aristotle's concept of virtue as a habit, he now transforms Aristotle's doctrine of the mean, so that it applies not only to naturally acquired virtues but also to infused moral virtues (Ia IIae, q. 64, a. 1, ad 3; a. 4). Thus he lays the groundwork for the next, crucial discussion of how various virtues are connected with each other (Ia IIae, q. 65).

At first, Thomas seems to follow Aristotle in arguing that nobody can have a perfect moral virtue without prudence, nor can somebody have prudence without perfection in all the moral virtues.[27] Of course, one can have what people call "temperance" without what people call "courage" and vice versa. We often praise the "courage" of soldiers who habitually drink to excess, the "temperance" of abstemious but spineless neighbors, and so on. The character traits in question can indeed exist independently of each other; we might even regard them as imperfect virtues. But strictly speaking, they are only inclinations to certain kinds of actions or emotional responses that people have by native temperament, or frequent repetition or usage (*ex naturali complexione vel ex aliqua consuetudine*). Strictly speaking, someone who behaves well in one aspect of human life but not in another acquires a habit. Such a habit, however, will lack the essential character of a *virtue* unless accompanied by prudence (Ia IIae, q. 65, a. 1).

The argument that no proper moral virtue can exist without prudence makes more sense if one recalls that a virtue cannot be put to bad use. The ability to face danger, in its own right, would go just as well to make a daring bank robber as an admirable war hero. A person needs prudence to judge correctly which dangers would be *good* to face. As moral virtue requires prudence, so, too, prudence requires moral virtue. A fearful person, with an excessive desire for safety, will naturally tend to judge too dangerous by half situations that it would actually be good to face. Someone's sense of justice cannot consistently govern her actions if she often lacks the courage to do the right thing.

To this point, Aristotle would have been nodding supportively. However, the very next article of the *Prima Secundae* reapplies the distinction between perfect and imperfect virtues along lines undreamed of by Aristotle. Thomas argues that the moral virtues people acquire through their own natural resources can exist without charity, as was the case in many pagans. These virtues, however, are intrinsically imperfect—virtues merely in a relative sense. Only the moral virtues infused by God along with charity "perfectly and truly have the essential character (*ratio*) of virtue," and therefore deserve to be called virtues without qualification (Ia IIae, q. 65, a. 2).[28] As no one can have the naturally acquired moral virtues without naturally acquired prudence, so no one can have the distinctively Christian (infused) moral virtues without the God-given theological virtue of charity.

Note that the naturally acquired moral virtues, which enable one to attain the imperfect happiness possible in human society in this life, are unified by the intellectual virtue of prudence, just as Aristotle claimed. In contrast, what Thomas considers the only perfect, unqualified moral virtues are those unified by charity, a virtue of the will given by God. Again, the connection is reciprocal: we cannot have the infused moral virtues without charity, nor can we have charity without the infused moral virtues (Ia IIae, q. 65, aa. 2–3). At the same time, Thomas sees no essential connection between the infused virtues and the naturally acquired virtues. Christians might accordingly be well directed to the happiness of the afterlife and yet lacking in those virtues that enable a person to be happy in the ordinary human society of the present life. The virtues discussed by Aristotle, however useful to us now, are unnecessary for attaining our ultimate end of happiness in the company of God. Indeed, when Thomas argues in q. 65, a. 3, that "all the moral virtues are infused together with charity,"[29] he seems to have forgotten the kind of moral virtues discussed in the first article. The conversation has turned, by stages, so much away from Aristotle that the ancient conception of virtues as naturally acquired habits now represents an exception to the increasingly Christian "rule."

The series of moves just sketched should help to explain why the *Summa* can be better understood as a conversation continuing over the course of many evenings than as the straightforward textbook discussion modern readers might expect. Naturally acquired habits described as perfect, unqualified virtues by comparison with habits unrelated to a good will and uninformed by prudence gradually emerge as imperfect virtues and virtues only in a relative sense by comparison with God-given habits. Scholastics would have been better able to appreciate the finesse of Thomas's gradual shift of focus and less likely to be confused by it.[30]

The connection of the virtues represents another case where positions apparently endorsed earlier in the *Summa* are modified later. In Question 65, Thomas writes approvingly of Aristotle's claim that one cannot have prudence without having *all* the moral virtues. He seems to make an exception only for the large-scale virtues of magnificence and magnanimity, arguing that someone might have acquired all the other moral virtues and yet have lacked the opportunity to acquire these special ones. On the other hand, a person who already has the virtue of generosity (*liberalitas*) *would* acquire the virtue of magnificence, and with very little effort, if he ever came into a large sum of money; so, generally speaking, all the moral virtues are connected (Ia IIae, q. 65 a. 1, ad 1). In Question 66, however, we find that generosity properly belongs to the same class of virtues as magnificence and magnanimity, so that the connection of the moral virtues must be reconsidered. Here Thomas distinguishes between the four principal or cardinal virtues and various secondary virtues, which merely serve to enhance these four. Generosity belongs to the second group. Thus, Thomas argues, a person cannot have the virtue of generosity without justice. (If I do not have a stable disposition to understand and give people what I owe them, how would I have a stable disposition to give them more than I owe?) In contrast, a person might indeed have the virtue of justice without generosity (Ia IIae, q. 66, a. 4, ad 1). In the *Secunda Secundae*, Thomas explains that the virtue of justice might eventually be enhanced by the related virtue of generosity, but generosity is only a "potential" part of justice, not a species of justice or an "integral" part of it (IIa IIae, q. 117, a. 5). By distinguishing between the cardinal virtues and various secondary virtues potentially related to the cardinals, a distinction that figures prominently in the *Secunda Secundae*, Thomas respects the common intuition that certain virtues are simply more essential than others to good moral character. Patristic writings often award the cardinal virtues this special status; the *Nicomachean Ethics* does not. However marginalized the virtues discussed by Aristotle might become as the *Prima Secundae* proceeds, Thomas never declares that Christians alone have genuine virtues. He continues to insist that persons of different faiths, even of no faith at all, be given moral credit where credit is due:

> True unqualified virtue is that which directs one to mankind's principal good . . . and understood in this way, no true virtue can exist without charity. But if virtue is understood in relation to some particular end, something can be called a virtue without charity, insofar as it is directed to some particular good. However, if that particular good is not a true good, but merely apparent, the virtue related to this good will not be a true virtue but merely a false likeness of virtue, as the prudence of the greedy is not a true virtue . . . Yet if that particular good actually is a true good, such as the preservation of the community or the like, it will indeed be a true virtue, although imperfect unless it is referred to the final and perfect good.[31] (IIa IIae, q. 23, a. 7)

Thomas's account of God-given prudence and moral virtues nonetheless raises problems. Why does he posit this separate species of virtue? Other scholastics faulted him for multiplying virtues beyond necessity; only his most loyal followers defended him. Many of today's Thomists likewise regard the positing of infused moral virtues as a mistake by an otherwise brilliant philosopher-theologian.[32] Of course, no moral theorist posits more virtues than he himself deems necessary. The key, then, is understanding the explanatory value that Thomas believes infused prudence and moral virtues offer.

### Complexities of Christian Life

We already know that Thomas endorses two ends of humankind: the limited happiness attainable in human society through our own natural resources, and the perfect happiness of the afterlife attainable by Christians with God's grace. The virtues discussed by Aristotle prove generally adequate with regard to the first kind of happiness. Were there no greater happiness possible, and no higher measure than human reason, the *Nicomachean Ethics* would be a fine guide to the moral life. As it is, Christians must regard the work as seriously flawed, not only in its ignorance of supernatural happiness and the God-given virtues ordered to it, but also as a guide to the moral life here and now. Those motivated by charity, who have faith in God and hope for happiness after death, must respect the rule of divine law governing their conduct. What Christians regard as reasonable—such as laypeople's observance of the Church's fasting regulations, or more poignantly, a life of religious poverty and complete sexual abstinence—could therefore look unreasonably ascetical to a non-Christian.

Note that someone who regards the Christian life as a matter of beliefs, hopes, and motivations, with no observable effect on behavior other than prayer and church attendance, would not be acutely concerned about the influence of faith on people's everyday lives. Christianity would be mostly a private relationship between the individual conscience and God—chiefly a matter of one's heart and mind, so that one's everyday behavior might be hard to distinguish from the behavior of non-Christians. Thomas, however, expects Christianity to have a significant influence on people's day-to-day conduct. In describing (for example) infused temperance as different in kind from acquired temperance, he at once acknowledges and counters likely objections to the way Christians live. A pagan who chose to avoid all sexual activity might appropriately be suspected of finding sex repugnant, or of trying to awe others with his powers of self-control, or otherwise running to an extreme instead of observing the mean; however, for Christians, Thomas argues, with their own distinctive ends and motivations, reason will dictate a mean more exacting than that revealed by natural reason unaided by grace (Ia IIae, q. 63, a. 4; Ia IIae, q. 64, a. 1, ad 3; Ia IIae, q. 65, a. 3). What would be prudent for a Christian might thus appear, and even be, imprudent for a non-Christian.[33]

At the same time, Thomas has a healthy respect for human nature and the happiness attainable through people's natural resources in human society. His steadfast defense of pagan virtues as genuine virtues attests to this. But in insisting on the two ends of humankind, he sees more at stake than the moral credit that Christians should award non-Christians. The earthly happiness of Christians themselves deserves attention. Thomas firmly resists any attempt to reduce life to some dreary waiting room on the train route to heaven—as if its value were purely instrumental to salvation, or as if the loves, friendships, and work Christians enjoy here and now were so many false goods. Purely human goods are still genuine goods, for Christians no less than other people.

How does this bear on the positing of infused prudence and moral virtues? While Thomas believes that only the infused virtues are necessary for happiness in the afterlife, he also believes that people need the acquired virtues to be happy in the ordinary human society of this life.[34] Infused prudence does not enable one to deliberate well about everything under the sun, but only about things related to salvation.[35] People must learn from experience how to succeed in business, deploy troops in combat, and exercise judgment in other worldly affairs. Having as one's ultimate end the complete happiness possible only in the presence of God does not prevent one from regarding the happiness of this life as an intrinsic good. A good can be loved both for its own sake and for the sake of God, as an end in itself and yet as subordinate to a higher end (Ia IIae, q. 70, a. 1, ad 2). Book I of the *Nicomachean Ethics* explains how ends are architectonically ordered, with some as ends in their own right and yet subordinate to further ends. To deny that some good is the *ultimate* end is not necessarily to assert that it has, like a tetanus shot, merely instrumental value. Putting the Aristotelian lesson to theological use, Thomas envisions what might be described as the sanctification of a Christian's everyday life in human society.

In Thomas's view, the virtue of charity, which has God as its object and enables people to act from the love of God, exceeds every other virtue. As Aristotle was correct to praise the intellect as the power of the soul most crucial to attaining earthly happiness, so Augustine was correct to praise the will as the power most crucial to deserving eternal happiness. Because God far surpasses what the human intellect can comprehend, the love of God—a virtue of the will—is more essential to living as a Christian than any virtue of the intellect.[36] While this does not mean that all actions by non-Christians are sinful, it does mean that they cannot be "meritorious," that is, reckoned by God as deserving of reward in the afterlife (Ia IIae, q. 62, a. 4; IIa IIae, q. 10, a. 4). People are capable of merit only if they have, through God's grace, the end and motivations provided by the theological virtues. Those with the virtue of charity might nonetheless develop the natural virtues and exercise them both for their intrinsic worth and for the sake of God. When they do, Thomas says, the acts of these naturally acquired virtues are meritorious.[37] Thus a Christian's daily conduct in selling cars, caring for patients, or teaching philosophy, and likewise, her routine behavior with family and friends, can express both her love for strictly human goods *and* her love for God.

To put it crudely, Thomas does not regard God as some jealous lover who insists that people care for no one but Him and for no happiness other than the happiness they could have in His presence. God Himself gave human beings bodies and emotions; God Himself made human beings social (political) animals, inclined by their very nature to seek happiness in the company of others of their kind. Heaven itself should not be regarded as some eternal tête-à-tête with God. Like Augustine, Thomas describes heaven as a community (or city), where Christians enjoy not only the company of God but also the company of the saints.

Thomas's efforts to legitimate both pagan virtues and Christian concern for worldly happiness are carefully balanced with efforts to avoid giving the erroneous impression that various Christian saints were morally inferior to ancient sages. Recall the words of St. Paul in Romans 7: "I delight in the law of God in my inmost self, but I see in my members another law at war with the law of my mind." Also consider Augustine's description of temperance: "What is the activity of virtue here but a perpetual war with vices?—not external vices but internal, not alien but clearly our very own—a war waged especially by what is called *sôphrosynê* in Greek and *temperantia* in Latin which bridles our fleshly lusts lest they drag our will to consent to crimes of every sort."[38]

In fact, what Aristotle calls temperance (*sôphrosynê*) produces harmony between the possessor's emotions and rational judgment. The temperate person no longer need struggle to resist temptation because he no longer feels tempted to do anything bad. While Aristotle recognizes that some people have emotions that they must perpetually work to control, he labels this state of character "continence" (*enkrateia*) and distinguishes it from virtue.[39] Should we conclude, then, that saints praised as a virtue what ancient philosophers judged second-rate—or worse, that Augustine and Paul were themselves second-rate in moral character?

Thomas's discussion of merit alone should help to answer the question. But he has at least two more answers. First, the saints, with infused virtues, judge themselves by *higher* standards than pagans. Because they measure themselves by the rule of divine law, they inevitably see more shortcomings in themselves.[40] Second, naturally acquired, infused moral virtues have different effects on one's emotions. Like Aristotle, Thomas holds that virtues acquired naturally, through long practice, work to eliminate contrary emotions. In time the agent feels much less troubled by his emotions and comes to find virtuous actions pleasant. Infused moral virtues, Thomas explains, can indeed have such an effect (that they *can* is important), but they might not have it immediately. Christians can continue to feel internal conflict and have difficulty in exercising the virtues given by God (Ia IIae, q. 65, a. 3, ad 23).[41] Infused moral virtues nonetheless provide a Christian with the strength to lead a good life (emotionally tumultuous or not) and keep her from feeling distress (*tristitia*). Should anyone object that virtues are supposed to make the possessor find virtuous actions uniformly enjoyable, Thomas reminds us that even Aristotle defended a more qualified position.[42]

Many of Thomas's contemporaries believed it sufficient to posit only naturally acquired virtues and the three theological virtues of faith, hope, and charity.[43] In contrast to Augustine, they acknowledged naturally acquired habits as genuine (albeit limited) virtues in pagans; in support of Augustine, they suggested that Christians do not have such virtues—because any virtues naturally acquired by Christians are redirected to the end of charity (in effect, "supernaturalized") through divine infusion of the theological virtues. I have already presented various reasons why Thomas declined to adopt this view. The one point that remains to be considered is his concern for a fine-grained analysis of moral actions.

According to Thomas, we should distinguish between the love of God produced by charity and actions of other virtues performed for the sake of God.

For example, when a Christian abstains from food, drink, or sex, she might well do so for the sake of God; but having God as the final cause of such actions does not prevent them from being acts of temperance. Of course, the same acts "elicited" by the virtue of temperance may be "commanded" by the virtue of charity. Perfection in charity may also be needed extrinsically for perfection in temperance. Nevertheless, Thomas wants us to be precise in describing the moral actions of Christians. Should one blur the distinctions among formal, final, and material causes; between intrinsic and extrinsic perfections of virtues, one runs the risk of having distinct virtues collapse into just so many different aspects of charity.[44] A plurality of virtues, related and interdependent, but each with its specific goods, would become essentially one and the same virtue.

More precise descriptions of actions represent a gain in moral analysis. While the general lesson was learned by studying Aristotle, who suggests that illicit sexual intercourse for the sake of money be considered less an act of intemperance than an act of greed, Thomas uses it to distinguish between different virtuous actions by Christians.[45] Lenten fasting for the sake of God remains "materially" an act of temperance, so that Christian acts of abstinence should never be conflated with Christian acts of charity. Confuse declining to eat meat with loving God, and one still has some way to go toward understanding charity's unique status as the foundation, form, and "mother" of all virtues.

## Notes

This chapter was previously published as Bonnie Kent, "Habits and Virtues," in Stephen J. Pope, ed., *The Ethics of Aquinas* (Georgetown University Press, Washington, DC, 2002). Reprinted with permission from Georgetown University Press.

1. Arist. *Eth. Nic.* 1106b36–1107a2.

2. Arist. *Cat.* 8b28–9a4. See also *Eth. Nic.* 1100b2, 1105a34–35, 1152a29–33.

3. A few examples: Cic. *De Finibus Bonorum et Malorum*, 5.25; Macrob. *Sat.* 7.9; August. *De Civ. D.* 12.3.

4. See, for example, August. *De Civ. D.* 21.16.

5. For an excellent study of Augustine's treatment of *consuetudo* see John Prendiville, "The Development of the Idea of Habit in the Thought of Saint Augustine," *Traditio* 28 (1972): 29–99. For present purposes, the reader might simply recall that Augustine's famous *Confessions* bears eloquent testimony to the negative role of habituation, both in delaying his own conversion ("Lord, give me chastity and continence, but not yet") and in tormenting him with what he regarded as sinful yearnings even after his baptism. Consider, for example, *Conf.* 10.30: "Assuredly you command that I contain myself from 'the lust of the flesh, the lust of the eyes, and the pride of

life' [1 Jn 2:16]. You commanded me also to abstain from fornication, and in the matter of marriage, you advised me a better course, though you allowed me a lesser good. And since you gave me the power, it was done, even before I became a dispenser of your sacrament. Yet there still live in my memory images of those things of which I have already spoken so much which my long habit (*consuetudo*) has fixed there. When I am awake they beset me, though with no great power, but in sleep they not only seem pleasant but even to the point of consent and the likeness of the act itself."

6. August. *Div. Quaest.* 1. 31; Cic. *Inv. Rhet.* 2.53.

7. August. *Retract.* 1.25.

8. "Et Commentator dicit in 3. de Anima, quod habitus est, quo quis agit cum voluerit." See below, n. 17.

9. A few examples: *In III Sent.*, d. 23, q. 1 (Moos, 696–718), and d. 34, q. 3 (Moos, 1157–68); *In III Ethicorum.*, lect. 6 (Leonine, 135–39); *De Virt. in Comm.*, q. un., a. 1 (Marietti, 707–10).

10. In ST Ia IIae, q. 52, where he discusses the growth of habits, Thomas returns to speaking chiefly of naturally acquired habits. Although the change of focus might prove rather disorienting for the reader, Thomas does indicate that the special case of virtuous habits will be considered later: "Quomodo autem circa virtutes se habeat, infra dicetur"; "Quomodo autem se habeat circa virtutes, infra dicetur" (q. 52, aa. 1–2).

11. On important developments during this period see Cary Nederman, "Nature, Ethics, and the Doctrine of 'Habitus': Aristotelian Moral Psychology in the Twelfth Century," *Traditio* 45 (1989–1990): 87–110, and Marcia Colish, "*Habitus* Revisited: A Reply to Cary Nederman," *Traditio* 48 (1993): 77–92.

12. "Aliqui habitus sunt quibus homo bene disponitur ad finem excedentem facultatem humanae naturae, qui est ultima et perfecta hominis beatitudo, ut supra dictum est [Ia IIae, q. 5, a. 5]. Et quia habitus oportet esse proportionatos ei ad quod homo disponitur secundum ipsos, ideo necesse est quod etiam habitus ad huiusmodi finem disponentes, excedant facultatem humanae naturae. Unde tales habitus nunquam possunt homini inesse nisi ex infusione divina: sicut est de omnibus gratuitis virtutibus."

13. For some examples, see ST Ia IIae, q. 3, a. 6; Ia, IIae, q. 4, aa. 5–6; Ia, IIae, q. 62, a. 1; Ia, IIae, q. 63, a. 3.

14. On the face of it, the *Summa* describes animals as so many appetite-driven robots, incapable of calculation, self-assertion, or much of the behavior that people routinely attribute to their cats and dogs. This is a mistake; it might be better to say that Thomas simply believes animals act "on principle." Sadly, limitations of space preclude further discussion of this topic.

15. Arist. *Eth. Nic.* 1100b35–1101a8, 1146a9–11, 1150b32–34.

16. See above, n. 5.

17. It seems no small irony that Thomas should cast Averroes as his authority for the doctrine that habits, by their very nature, are principally related to the will. In the passage Thomas cites repeatedly, Averroes's actual contention is that a habit is that whereby one may *understand* (versus the more general "act") *quando voluerit*, which should perhaps be translated as "when one wants" or "when one wishes" rather than as "when one wills," given that Thomas's own conception of the will is just as alien to

Averroes as it is to Aristotle. Commenting on Aristotle's account of the intellect, Averroes is only pointing out that understanding, an intellectual "habit," frees the agent from dependence on external aid or stimulation. See Averroes, *In Aristotelis De Anima, Lib. III*, n. 18 [re 430a15–16]: "Et oportet addere in sermone: secundum quod facit ipsum intelligere omne ex se et quando voluerit. Haec enim est diffinitio habitus, scilicet ut habens habitum intelligat per ipsum illud quod est sibi proprium ex se et quando voluerit, absque quod indigeat in hoc aliquo extrinseco."

18. *In III Ethicorum*, lect. 4 (Leonine, 129–30). For further discussion of the difference between Thomas and Aristotle on this topic see Charles Kahn, "Discovering the Will: From Aristotle to Augustine," in *The Question of "Eclecticism": Studies in Later Greek Philosophy*, ed. John Dillon and A. A. Long (Berkeley: University of California Press, 1988), 234–59, esp. 239–45, and my *Virtues of the Will: The Transformation of Ethics in the Late Thirteenth Century* (Washington, DC: Catholic University of America Press, 1995), 156–74, esp. 171–74.

19. "Virtus est bona qualitas mentis, qua recte vivitur, qua nullus male utitur, quam Deus in nobis sine nobis operatur." Cf. Peter Lombard, *Sententiae in IV Libris Distinctae*, d. 27, chap. 1, d. 27, q. 5 (ed. Ignatius Brady [Rome: Editiones Collegii S. Bonaventurae ad Claras Aquas Grottaferrata, 1971], 480): "Virtus est, ut ait Augustinus, bona qualitas mentis, qua recte vivitur et qua nullus male utitur, quam Deus solus in homine operatur."

20. "Dicendum quod ista definitio perfecte complectitur totam rationem virtutis. Perfecta enim ratio uniuscuiusque rei colligitur ex omnibus causis eius. Comprehendit autem praedicta definitio omnes causas virtutis." In a disputation on the same topic Thomas was more straightforward, mentioning the chief problem with the definition at the outset. See *De Virt. in Comm.*, q. un., a. 2: "Dicendum quod ista definitio complectitur definitionem virtutis, etiam si ultima particula omittatur; et convenit omni virtuti humanae" (Marietti, 710–14).

21. Note that gifts of the Holy Spirit are likewise classified as habits (Ia IIae, q. 68, a. 3).

22. *De Caritate*, q. un., a. 1 (Marietti, 753–57); cf. IIa IIae, q. 23, a. 2. The withering term of dismissal, "ridiculous," appears in the disputed questions but not in the *Summa Theologiae*. This is only one of many cases where the "host" of the *Summa*, a textbook written for beginning theology students, proves somewhat less diplomatic when debating with peers.

23. "Causa autem efficiens virtutis infusae, de qua definitio datur, Deus est. Propter quod dicitur, 'quam Deus in nobis sine nobis operatur.' Quae quidem particula si auferatur, reliquum definitionis erit commune omnibus virtutibus, et acquisitis et infusis."

24. *In Somnium Scipionis*, a commentary by Macrobius on Cicero's *Dream of Scipio*, represents a Neoplatonic influence on Aquinas's moral thought now widely ignored. Thomas cites Macrobius repeatedly in the *Secunda Secundae*, just as he often cites Cicero himself.

25. "Ita scilicet quod prudentia omnia mundana divinorum contemplatione despiciat, omnemque animae cogitationem in divina sola dirigat; temperantia vero relinquat, inquantum natura patitur, quae corporis usus requirit; fortitudinis autem est ut

anima non terreatur propter excessum a corpore, et accessum ad superna; iustitia vero est ut tota anima consentiat ad huius propositi viam."

26. *De Virt. Card.*, q. un., a. 2: "Secundus autem gradus virtutum est illarum quae attingunt rationem rectam, non tamen attingunt ad ipsum Deum per caritatem. Hae quidem aliqualiter sunt perfectae per comparationem ad bonum humanum, non tamen sunt simpliciter perfectae, quia non attingunt ad primam regulam, quae est ultimus finis, ut Augustinus dicit *contra Iulianum*. Unde et deficiunt a vera ratione virtutis; sicut et moralis inclinationes absque prudentia deficiunt a vera ratione virtutis. Tertius gradus est virtutum simpliciter perfectarum, quae sunt simul cum caritate; hae enim virtutes faciunt actum hominis simpliciter bonum, quasi attingentem usque ad ultimum finem ... Oportet igitur quod similiter cum caritate infundantur habituales formae expedite producentes actus ad quos caritas inclinat. Inclinat autem caritas ad omnes actus virtutum, quia cum sit circa finem ultimum, importat omnes actus virtutum" (Marietti, 818–819).

27. Arist. *Eth. Nic.* 1144b36.

28. "perfecte et vere habent rationem virtutis."

29. "cum caritate simul infunduntur omnes virtutes morales."

30. For example, while modern readers of the *Summa* might assume that Thomas's discussion of how virtues endure in the afterlife applies to naturally acquired as well as infused moral virtues, he states explicitly in another work that he is referring only to infused virtues. See also ST Ia IIae, q. 67, a. 1; *De Virt. Card.*, q. 1, a. 4 (Marietti, 825–28).

31. "Virtus vera simpliciter est illa, quae ordinat ad principale bonum hominis ... ; et sic nulla vera virtus potest esse sine caritate: sed si accipiatur virtus, secundum quod est in ordine ad aliquem finem particularem, sic potest aliqua virtus dici sine caritate, inquantum ordinatur ad aliquod particulare bonum: sed si illud particulare bonum non sit verum bonum, sed apparens, virtus etiam quae est in ordine ad hoc bonum, non erit vera virtus, sed falsa similitudo virtutis: sicut non est vera virtus avarorum prudentia ... Si vero illud bonum particulare sit verum bonum, puta conservatio civitatis, vel aliquid huiusmodi, erit quidem vera virtus, sed imperfecta, nisi referatur ad finale, et perfectum bonum."

32. For admirably candid reservations, see Odon Lottin, *Principles de Morale*, vol.2 (Louvain: Éditions de l'Abbaye du Mont César, 1947), 213–25. Twentieth-century authors are usually more prone to reveal their doubts about infused moral virtues by mentioning this aspect of Thomas's ethics only in passing or even altogether ignoring it. The policy of silence is especially pronounced among philosophical authors who seek to abstract Thomas's moral philosophy from his moral theology and treat it independently. I think it safe to say that Thomas would have frowned upon this practice.

33. See *De Virt. in Comm.*, q. un., a. 13, ad 6, where Thomas argues that Christian poverty and virginity are means of reason, not to be confused with the pagan vice of insensibility (Marietti, 750).

34. *De Virt. in Comm.*, q. un., a. 1, ad 11: "Dicendum quod ad utrasque operationes habitu indigemus; ad naturales quidem tribus rationibus superius positis [in corp. art.]; ad meritorius autem insuper, ad naturalis potentia elevetur ad id quod est supra naturam ex habitu infuso. Nec hoc removetur ex hoc quod Deus in nobis operatur;

quia ita agit in nobis, quod et nobis agimus; unde habitu indigemus, quo sufficienter agere possimus" (Marietti, 710).

35. *De Virt. Card.*, q. un., a. 2, ad. 3 (Marietti, 819).

36. *De Caritate*, q. un., a. 3, ad 13 (Marietti, 762).

37. *De Virt. in Comm.*, q. un., a. 10, ad 4 (Marietti, 736).

38. August. *De Civ. D.*, 19.4.

39. Arist. *Eth. Nic.* 1145a35–36.

40. For discussion of this point see Norman Kretzmann, "Warring against the Law of My Mind: Aquinas on Romans 7," in *Philosophy and the Christian Faith*, ed. T. Morris (Notre Dame, IN: University of Notre Dame Press, 1988), 172–95.

41. My explanation of this point draws on Thomas's *De Virt. in Comm.*, q. un., a. 10, ad 14–15.

42. Arist. *Eth. Nic.* 1117b9–19.

43. Both Henry of Ghent and Godfrey of Fontaines, leading secular masters at Paris in the last quarter of the thirteenth century, argued at length against positing infused moral virtues. For helpful selections from their works, as well as from works by other masters critical of Thomas on this issue, see Odon Lottin, "Les vertus morales infuses pendant la seconde moitié du XIIIe siècle," in Lottin, *Psychologie et morale aux XIIe et XIIIe siècles*, vol.3, pt. 2 (Louvain-Gembloux, 1949), 487–534. See also Duns Scotus, *Ordinatio* III, suppl. dist. 36, in *Duns Scotus on the Will and Morality*, ed. Allan Wolter (Washington, DC: Catholic University of America Press,1986), 414–17; and especially the strong criticism by Thomas's fellow Dominican, Durand of St. Pourçain, in *Durandi a Sancto Porciano in Setentias Theologicas Petri Lombardi Commentarium*, III, dist. 33, q. 6 (Lyons, 1587), 613–14.

44. For discussion of these distinctions see *De Caritate*, q. un., aa. 3, 5 (Marietti, 760–62, 765–66).

45. Arist. *Eth. Nic.* 113024–26.

# 11

# Natural Law: Incommensurable Readings

*Fergus Kerr*

THOMISM IS "ONE PROMINENT FORM OF natural law theory," according to Jeffrey Stout: like many other theories, such as those of Calvin, Hooker, Locke and Pufendorf, it depends on the idea of a divine lawgiver, which makes it of limited use in pluralistic society. Vernon Bourke, on the other hand, contends that the term "natural law" should be abandoned altogether in connection with Thomas Aquinas: whatever he meant, it is nothing to do with what modern theories talk about; we should speak of his ethics of right reason.[1]

## Standard Accounts

The classical study of the idea of natural law in the development of Western European thought, by A. P. d'Entrèves, remains fairly widely in use as a textbook in university courses in jurisprudence and political philosophy. It is an excellent book. Thomas Aquinas is more cited than any other author. His great *Summae* "contain the most complete statement of that ideal of a thorough Christianization of life which inspired medieval Catholicism and which found its highest artistic achievement in the Divine Comedy of Dante."

As an Italian and a Catholic and a great scholar (one-time professor of Italian literature in the University of Oxford), d'Entrèves plainly had no post-Reformation qualms about reason and faith, nature and grace, working in harmony. He rejoices that "the Protestant Hooker" continued the tradition; the Thomist notion of natural law, paradoxically enough he thinks, lies at the basis of Anglicanism and thus also of "the English way of life."[2]

However all that may be, his account of Thomas's view cannot be faulted, as far as it goes. He regards natural law as the basis of morality, in Thomas's conception. He pays no attention to the place of virtue. He does, however, insist strongly on the metaphysical foundation of Aquinas's natural law doctrine, seeing this as supposing the world to be governed by divine providence. Thus, d'Entrèves would have agreed with Stout: Thomas's natural law doctrine is theologically grounded; but not with Bourke's shifting of emphasis from natural law theory to virtue ethics.

The standard account by a philosopher in the analytic tradition, D. J. O'Connor, certainly assumes that Thomas's moral philosophy is dominated by the concept of natural law.[3] What Thomas has to say relates to many practical questions, such as sexual conduct, and, on the other hand, more theoretically, to whether or not judgements of value can be deduced from accounts of empirical fact. From the outset, according to O'Connor, we can set aside Thomas's religious beliefs. His work is of great philosophical interest, comparable with that of Aristotle, Hume and Spinoza. Indeed, in a time when influential moral philosophers have abandoned objective theories of ethics, Thomas's work is of all the more interest. Moreover, it would be superficial to regard his work as mere Christianization of Aristotle; on the contrary, there is profound change of emphasis, and much alteration of detail. The important point is that, while the concept of natural law has a long history, there is no single theory; the common core is that in some sense or other the basic principles of morals and legislation are objective, accessible to reason and based on human nature. The doctrine of natural inclinations is very important—a set of dispositions or tendencies to act and react that we have in virtue of our nature.

The difficulties O'Connor sees include the following. Thomas is so unclear about which of the natural law precepts are primary and which are secondary, and, anyway, allows so much variability at the level of detailed choices, that his position seems little different from any other relativism. Moreover, his notions of nature and of reason seem ambiguous and even vague. Perhaps he sets his standards too high. If we regard knowledge as tentative, experimental, corrigible, and so on, as we surely should, then we cannot but find his ideas about how much we know about human nature much too certain.

The great difficulty with the appeal to natural law in Christian ethics, according to Michael Keeling, is that it becomes "almost inevitably, the preserve of ecclesiastical authority."[4]

Keeling characterizes the basic principle of natural law ethics as follows: despite the ways in which human beings keep failing to do so, "anyone who accepted the discipline of rational thought could both see what the world was meant to be and follow through the moral indications which arose from that

fact." Thomas Aquinas put this principle into the form that has been fundamental in modern as well as medieval "Catholic understanding of the moral
world." For all the damage done to human nature by sin, it remains possible
to see from the creaturely order as it exists the moral end which it was intended to serve. Certainly, "the divine revelation of Holy Scripture" is required
for "the fullest knowledge of God," "nevertheless the 'natural law', the law
given in nature when we perceive the ultimate purposes there, still provided a
sufficient moral basis for daily human existence."

As Keeling rightly says, natural law ethics, as in Thomas Aquinas, does not generate "widely agreed detailed rules in terms of human moral life." True, "many
ethical precepts would find acceptance among human beings generally"—yet
others, "such as the control of contraception or possibly of abortion," are "a matter of controversy, even among Christians." The "temptation," to which the teaching authorities in the Roman Catholic Church have persistently yielded, has been
to press the theory into far too great detail and, worse, to make the definition of
'natural law' an 'act of authority'. In the encyclical letter *Humanae Vitae* (1968),
Pope Paul VI declared authoritatively that the content of the natural law is a matter for the Magisterium to define. With *Veritatis Splendor* (1993), Pope John Paul
II has made it impossible for the concept of natural law even to be discussed between Catholics and Protestants.

Keeling seeks to "define mandates for the whole of humanity," starting from
a "Protestant Christian theological basis." He is clearly happier with Protestants like Joseph Fletcher than with Karl Barth or Dietrich Bonhoeffer. He
contends that natural law, far from being "the discovery of a plan and even less
the discovery of a set of rules for putting a plan into effect" is "a dance"—"As
the Greek fathers said, life is a *perichoresis*, a dance of the universe led by
Christ the Lord of Creation, towards a fulfilment that is not yet seen."[5]

However that may be, it is significant that a Christian moralist, long experienced in ecumenical and inter-faith dialogue, believes that the very idea of
natural law has been appropriated by the Roman Catholic Church, or anyway
by the Vatican, in such a way that it is now a useless concept in any conceiv-
able attempt to work out basic principles of a morality which adherents of
various religious traditions would endorse.

## Non-standard Accounts

There are other philosophical and theological accounts, probably much less
familiar. Howard Mounce, for example, questions whether Thomas's conception of natural law is quite what is often assumed: "Some have taken him to
mean that moral principles can be verified as one might verify the law of

gravity"—that is, "by appealing to facts that can be appreciated even by people who otherwise have no sense of good and evil," in much the same way as people who have no sense of the possibility of religion are thought to be able to argue usefully about facts about the world (change, contingency, etc.).[6]

That is not what Thomas meant, Mounce says. For Thomas, "moral reasoning depends on principles which do not themselves depend on reasoning but are given us by nature." There is nothing mysterious or metaphysical about this.

Why do we think murder is wrong, Mounce asks: we can easily think of reasons, but it turns out on further reflection that none of the reasons we might cite is any more certain and fundamental than our original conviction that murder is wrong. We might say that murder is wrong because it has bad social effects—but then, when there are no such consequences, we should have to find a different reason. It might be held, on the other hand, that murdering certain persons would have good social effects: that might lead into further debate about the rights and wrongs of assassinating tyrants, and so on. As the 20 July 1944 plot to kill Hitler is enough to show, even assassination in such circumstances confronted the conspirators with a terrible moral dilemma. Partly, no doubt, as officers, they had a problem about breaking their oath of allegiance to the head of state. Also, however, they shrank from an act of homicide which, if successful, was likely to have good political results. This is not surprising. We think there is something wrong with murder, independently of whatever results it might have. The reasoning that might come into the question begins after, not before, some act is regarded as murder. Our reaction to murder is an example of what Thomas means by saying that we have moral principles which are not founded on reasoning but are given us by nature.

For Thomas, moral reasoning is cogent only to the extent that it is framed and informed by principles that are given to us by our nature. We know the difference between right and wrong not because we have discovered it by reasoning but because it is given us as a natural disposition, "a natural way of reacting to good and evil when they appear," as Mounce says.

If this seems too mysterious we need to consider what the alternative might be. If our belief that some action is right or wrong rests on reasoning, we certainly move far from what Thomas and (before him) Aristotle held. For Thomas it is part of our being created to the image and likeness of God that we have these natural dispositions which provide the principles upon which our moral reasoning can begin to work.

Given that by nature we are drawn to the good and inclined to resist evil, we have a 'natural law' which then requires us to reason, in particular cases. Of course we have to reason; our natural reactions will not do it all. For Thomas, as for common sense, there is something given to us and something that we have to do ourselves.

Moreover, again as Mounce notes, it is mistaken to think that for Thomas natural law enables us to have solutions to every moral problem—he thought, on the contrary, that no such clear-cut solutions were available in most cases.

In short, we always have to work at moral problems. With our practical reason we have "a natural participation in the eternal law"—"according to certain general principles"—but "not as regards the particular determinations of individual cases."

Obviously, the idea of there being a basis for morality in human nature has plausibility, perhaps a certain unavoidability, in common sense. Without some appeal to the notion that moral behaviour is governed to some extent by an understanding of human nature as (again to some extent) given and shared, what else is there for us but the option between the idea that we human beings create whatever moral values there are or the idea that we simply have to submit to the 'divine command' ethics disclosed by revelation to some Christians? In other words, what else is natural law ethics but an attempt to find middle ground between the doctrine that 'it's right because we judge it so' and 'it's right because God tells me so'? Essentially, whatever the various developments of the idea and their eventual incompatibility, the point of invoking natural law is to maintain a space between what human beings may reason their way into regarding as allowable and what those who speak in the name of God would permit.

At least since the Nuremberg trials, with their charge of "crimes against humanity," jurisprudential thinking has moved away from legal positivism (Justinian: "What pleases the prince has the force of law") towards natural law ethics. It comes, of course, in several varieties. In an explicitly Thomist tradition we should note the work of Jacques Maritain.[7]

Among recent theological accounts one of the most interesting we owe to Oliver O'Donovan.[8] Despite "points of strong sympathy" between his exposition of the moral significance of created order and "the more realist versions of Natural Law theory," he wants to avoid using the "classic term" because of the ambiguity that he sees in attributing universality not only to being but to knowledge. He regrets that in the great theological attack on the idea of natural law spearheaded by Karl Barth there was confusion between epistemological and ontological issues, such that some aspects of the doctrine of creation (like "ordinances") fell under suspicion, leaving a very thin basis for moral deliberation—nothing but the divine command. This was not helped by his subordinating the doctrine of creation ontologically to Christology, leading to "disturbing results in a series of frankly Apollinarian Christological conceptions."[9] Barth lays so much emphasis on the unity of divine and human natures in the person of the Word incarnate that he effectively denies the presence of a human mind or soul. Human nature as a whole, and particularly human rationality and moral development, are so marginalized as not to be included in what is redeemed. Over against that view, we need to see that creation and redemption has each its ontological and epistemological dimension: the created order and natural knowledge; the new creation and revelation in Christ. Thus, the epistemological programme required for natural ethics, in the sense of an ethics known to everyone, is very high— even impossibly so—but O'Donovan refuses to conclude there is no ontological ground for an ethics of nature, meaning by this an objective order to which the moral life can respond. If we were to take that line, we should have to say that any certainty we may have about the order which God has created depends solely upon God's own disclosure of himself and of his works. For O'Donovan, it is only in the sphere of divine revelation that we can see the natural order as it really is and so overcome the epistemological barrier to an ethic that conforms to natural law. But nature thus understood involves all human beings and cultures, not excluding a certain "natural knowledge" which is also part of our created endowment—a position very close, as he says, to what Thomas maintained.

The appeal to the natural law tradition in some form is motivated, obviously, by horror at the abuse of law by so many states. If justice is determined by what the state decrees, as the abandonment of traditional belief in something normative beyond positive law seems to involve, it is not surprising that we should want to return to the principle that the law is always finally subject to what 'natural justice' requires.

Environmental issues, as well as state despotism, invite renewed reflection on the natural law tradition. One of the finest recent retrievals of natural law ethics, and particularly of Thomas Aquinas's version, is provided by Michael S. Northcott, in the context of working out a theological ethics adequate to respect for our physical environment. Thomas's version develops from the natural law ethics to be found in the Hebrew prophets and Paul. It offers "the strongest conceptual base within the Christian tradition for an ecological ethic." It remains particularly strong in English culture (Shakespeare, Hooker, Hopkins, C. S. Lewis). On the other hand, it is diminished in the "humanocentric" conception of natural law in modern papal ethics—which (Northcott contends) fails to maintain the "deep understanding of the moral significance of created order" in the "pre-modern natural law tradition."[10]

Russell Hittinger, among the most persuasive of Catholic exponents of the natural law tradition, deplores the way that natural law, in much modern Roman Catholic discussion, is regarded as functioning independently of the eternal law in the mind of God: "what began for the Christian theologians as a doctrine explaining how the human mind participates in a higher order of law is turning into its opposite."[11] For over a century, he says, papal encyclicals have overlooked the theological background as they declared a great number of activities contrary to nature and reason, such as (his list) dueling, Communism, divorce, contraception, Freemasonry, in vitro fertilization and contract theories of the origin of political sovereignty. This, as he says, is not to mention "the bevy of rights and entitlements that have been declared to be owed to persons under the rubric of justice *ex ipsa natura rei*, by the very nature of the thing." The problem is not the judgements about the rightness or otherwise of this or that activity, he insists, but the impression that these encyclicals so often create that "on any vexed issue the minds of the faithful and the gentiles [i.e., non-Christians] can be adequately directed to appeal to elementary principles of natural law." The fact is that "trimming arguments" to fit what everyone is supposed to know irrespective of what they believe about God, and buttressing this with appeals to papal authority, "would eventually yield diminishing and disappointing results, not only for the gentiles but also for the faithful—especially the moral theologians." While theologians once upheld the dependence of the moral order on divine providence, Hittinger maintains, there is now a generation of Catholic moralists who have come to think that the rudiments of the moral order ought to be discussed without any reference to divine government, or, for that matter, to "created nature." Careful to note that this is not a result of the reforms of the Second Vatican Council, Hittinger cites Servais Pinckaers in support of his claim that natural law theory had been disembedded from moral theology, and moral theology from the rest of theology, long before that, in the standard exposition in seminary textbooks and suchlike.[12] Thomas's theology was greatly respected but in practice his account of natural law was extracted from its theological context and deprived of its vital connections with beatitude and virtue as well as with the Law of Moses and the New Law. In short, the precepts of the natural law were represented as what every human being is supposed to know by nature, while at the same time being the pronouncements of church authority ("Cartesian minds somehow under church discipline").

## Thomas on Natural Law

When we turn to Thomas, in particular to the *Summa Theologiae* and the most widely read text, the first surprise, as with the arguments for the existence of the first cause, is that there is only a single question about natural law (ST 1–2. 94), in the middle of 19 (90–108), in which three deal with human law, eight with the Mosaic law, and three with the New Law of the Gospel. This one question has received an inordinate amount of attention and, abstracted from its context, as it usually is, may be rather misleadingly expounded. Treating the treatise on law, let alone the single question on natural law, in isolation from the rest of the *secunda pars* is plainly to get things out of proportion.

One of the most interesting recent discussions is the "narrative understanding of Thomistic natural law" offered by Pamela M. Hall.[13] Her first point is that reading the questions on law in the *Summa Theologiae* on their own, without attending to how interwoven they are with the rest, only results in distortion. Her project goes well beyond trying to get Thomas right— which is all that need concern us here.

As Hall notes, discussing several very different commentators, Thomas's natural law is customarily identified with a set of commands and prohibitions, with a set of rules. Some interpret natural law on analogy with human law. For Thomas, however, natural law is linked, time and time again, in the relevant questions in the *Summa Theologiae*, with eternal law: the law by which God governs the entire cosmos. That means, as Hall says, that we need to go back to Thomas's discussion of the nature of divine providence (ST 1–2. 90).

Goodness is found in creatures not only in their "substance" but also insofar as they are ordered to their "ultimate end, which is divine goodness." Rational creatures "direct themselves to an end . . . through free will, because they can take counsel and they can choose." Since God is the first cause of freedom on the part of creatures as secondary causes, "human providence is contained under the providence of God as a particular cause under a universal cause."

At this point Thomas does not describe how human providence actually works in relation to divine providence. The *secunda pars* is his massive account of how human beings, with minds and wills, direct themselves in decisions of ethical significance and, in doing so, are drawn towards (or away from) God. As Thomas says in the prologue, he will consider human beings on analogy with God, since they are like God, precisely in regard to mind and will.

Thomas starts with an inquiry into the human end, for which no natural good or set of goods can ever suffice (ST 1–2. 1–5). Nothing but God, as known and loved in the beatific vision, can fully satisfy the human desire for truth and the good. Thomas then considers will (6–17), the criteria for good and bad action (18–21) and the emotions (22–48). Following Aristotle, he wants to resolve the issue of the *telos* of human life; then he brings in the concept of voluntariness, incorporating remarks about the passions. He proceeds to consider the virtues, both natural and theological (49–70). Characterizing the only completely and radically fulfilling *telos* for human beings as participation in God's beatitude already moves a long way from Aristotle; but the lengthy discussion of sin and its kinds, degrees and effects (71–89) departs absolutely from anything that the *Nicomachean Ethics* could have envisaged or included. It is immediately after this that Thomas opens his consideration of law (90–114). That is to say: what Thomas has to say about law, including natural law, follows upon what he says about sin. His consideration of law is part of his consideration of the "exterior principle" moving us to good, namely, God, who "instructs us through law and helps us through grace" (ST 1–2. 90 prologue).

Setting law against grace and vice versa would, of course, have seemed unintelligible to Thomas. Law is regarded as a form of instruction, education, intellectual formation; grace is clearly something much more practical and holistic. In principle, Thomas should be able to say a good deal about law, natural and human, without bringing in the Christian economy of salvation, and indeed many read him as doing precisely that; but, as Hall among others insists, the fact is that he does not do so here. On the contrary, human and natural law, as well as divine law, are located firmly in the context of divine providence.

Law (*lex*) is something rational (*aliquid rationis*) directed to the common good by those who are responsible for the community, and adequately promulgated. Thomas distinguishes four kinds of law: eternal law, natural law, human law, and divine law. Natural, human, and divine law, working together, are how eternal law is realized and manifested in and for human beings. This is how divine providence works in the case of human beings, these free and rational creatures who are, as it happens, lamentably prone to sin.

"Granted that the world is ruled by divine providence," as Thomas assumes we believe, "the whole community of the universe (*tota communitas universi*) is governed by God's mind (*ratione divina*)." For Thomas, at least on the face of it, there is no place for talking about natural law outside the context of this belief in the sovereignty of God.

More than this, he appeals implicitly to the doctrine of divine simplicity: in our case, rulers have an end outside themselves, to which their legislation is subordinate; but "the end or *telos* of divine government is God himself, and his law is nothing other than himself." The *telos* of the universe is to be found in the subsistent goodness of God himself (1.103.2).

For Thomas, it seems, even the Mosaic Law and the Law of the Gospel, let alone natural and human law, are located in the context of eternal law: namely, God himself. Once again, everything in Christian doctrine is related back to God (ST 1.1.7). As the space devoted to them indicates, the Mosaic Law and the New Law are the phenomena at the forefront of theological attention. But neither may be discussed, Thomas thinks, except in the light of the eternal law which is nothing other than God himself, nothing other than the divine light in which the blessed see God.

Granted that "everything in the world is subject to divine providence and so is regulated and measured by eternal law," it follows that "everything participates in some way (*aliqualiter*) in eternal law, namely by its impact on them giving them tendencies (*inclinationes*) to their own proper acts and ends." The kind of creature that we human beings are "is subject to divine providence in (so to speak) a more excellent way, inasmuch as it even becomes a sharer in providence, providing for itself and for others" (*in quantum et ipsa fit providentiae particeps, sibi ipsi et aliis providens*). Thomas redescribes this: "there is in us a participating in the eternal reason, by our having a natural inclination to our due activity and end." And this "participation in eternal law that is to be found in rational creatures" is what Thomas calls "natural law."

Moreover, this is what the Psalmist means, in one of Thomas's favourite mantra-like texts: "The light of thy countenance, Lord, is signed upon us" (*Signatum est super nos lumen vultus tui*)—"as if the light of natural reason by which we discern what is good and what is evil is nothing other than an impression of the divine light in us."

Thus it is clear, Thomas concludes, that "natural law is nothing other than the sharing in the eternal law in the case of rational creatures."

In short, Thomas's concept of natural law is thoroughly theological, and his appeal is to Scripture (Romans 2:14; Psalm 4: 6), not to philosophical authorities or considerations.

One thesis Thomas discusses is to the effect that natural law for human beings is superfluous: the eternal law surely suffices for the government of the human race. He rejects this line of thought: it would work very well if natural law were something quite separate from eternal law but that is just what he refuses to accept: natural law is "participation in eternal law, in some sense" (*quaedam participatio ejus*). Of course this is not the point that he is making; but it is plain that he would not endorse the idea of a natural law ethics which is autonomous and independent of theological considerations. There may well be room for a theology-free ethics, drawing even on Thomas's distinction between nature and grace; but it seems not to be envisaged here.

Time and again, the eternal law is identified with God himself. Everything created by God is subject to the eternal law but it makes no sense to say that anything divine is either subject to the eternal law or otherwise: "all that is attributed to the divine essence or nature does not fall under the eternal law, in reality they are the eternal law" (1–2.93.4). God and the eternal law are identical. "The Son of God," meaning the second person of the divine Trinity, "is not subject to the eternal law but rather is himself the eternal law" (93.4). The *ratio* of divine providence is the eternal law (93.5).

Turning more specifically to ourselves, Thomas maintains that we all have "some notion of the eternal law" and secondly we all have within us some bent (*inclinatio*) towards what is consonant with the eternal law (93.6).

It might seem that no one recognizes the eternal law but God himself (93.2). On the contrary, citing Augustine's claim that "a notion of the eternal law is imprinted on us," Thomas concedes that no one except God and the blessed who see God face to face can recognize the eternal law as it is in itself (its being identical with God himself), yet there are degrees of dawning of its light. For that matter, again following Augustine, "any knowledge of truth is, so to speak, a ray and share in the eternal law which is the unchangeable truth"; but, more specifically, since everyone has knowledge of truth, *aliqualiter*, we all know the common principles of the natural law, more or less.

Citing Aristotle—"we are adapted by nature to receive virtues"—Thomas insists that we have a natural instinct for virtue (*inclinatio naturalis ad virtutem*), which may indeed be "spoilt by a vicious habit," just as our natural knowledge of good is "darkened by the passions and habits of sin" (93.6).

It may be noted, however, that, for Thomas at least, "sin never takes away the entire good of [human] nature" (93.6). There always remains a certain *inclinatio ad agendum ea quae sunt legis aeternae*.

The same point is repeated, this time explicitly referring to the natural law: as regards the commonest principles of the natural law, recognized by everyone, the natural law "can never be deleted from the human heart" (94.6). We may be prevented from doing the right thing in this or that particular instance, for example by lust or some other passion. As regards the less commonly recognized principles (not that Thomas spells out what these are at all adequately), he allows that they may indeed be "deleted from the human heart," "either by evil counsel or by perverse customs and corrupt habits." Robbery is not counted as sin among some people; sins against nature are not always recognized as such. (It looks as if these are secondary principles of the natural law.)

It is perfectly possible that legislators have passed wrongful enactments against secondary precepts of the natural law. Here, clearly, for Thomas, legislation may, at least in some instances, run against the requirements of natural justice. Unfortunately, he does not provide examples, either real or imagined, such as we should need to take the discussion any further.

Though Thomas sometimes speaks of "precepts" it is more usual for him to refer to "inclinations": something between psychology and ontology, somewhere on the range between instincts and existential orientations. When he considers the "content," or the "extent," of "the order of the precepts of the natural law" he equates it with the "order of the natural inclinations"—the instincts and ontological orientations of the human creature (94.2). These turn out to be, first, "the tendency towards the good of the nature which we share with all other beings"—to preserve our lives; secondly, at the level of the life we share with other animals—"nature has taught all animals to mate, to bring up their young, and suchlike"; and thirdly, as rational animals, we have a natural inclination to know the truth about God and to live in community, which means that "it is a matter of the natural law that we have an inclination, for instance, to avoid ignorance, not to offend those with whom one ought to live amicably, and other such related matters."

We might be tempted to identify divine law with eternal law. In Thomas's usage, however, divine law means the Old Law and the New Law: the whole body of Mosaic legislation, not merely the Decalogue, but including the moral, liturgical, legal and political requirements and prescriptions (ST 1–2. 98–105), and the New Law (106–114, shading into the Gospel).[14] At least in terms of space, he has much more to say about Torah and Gospel than about Natural Law. In fact, as has been clear at least since Chenu pointed it out to students of Aquinas, the growing importance of the Old Testament for Thomas's theology cannot be over-estimated.[15] Partly, no doubt, since the Cathars rejected the Old Testament, mainstream theologians were prompted to study it more assiduously. Mainly, of course, since the Bible was read as a whole, and the Christian dispensation was constantly interpreted as the fulfilment of the Covenant, the Law of Moses, the Prophets and the Wisdom books, Thomas was only an heir to a long tradition of typological exegesis.[16]

As regards the Mosaic Law, Thomas has little to say in his Commentary on the *Sentences* (1256); the massive treatment in the *Summa Theologiae* is new, and due no doubt to his study of the *Summa* of the Franciscan Alexander of Hales, posthumously completed about 1260 by two of his students.[17]

In sum, in the *Summa Theologiae*, Thomas presents the natural law in the context of Torah and the New Law of the Holy Spirit, in the wider context of an account of the virtues (theological and cardinal) as the moral agent's journey to face-to-face vision with God, all framed by the presupposition that the natural law is a participation in the eternal law which is identical with God himself.

## Ethical Naturalism

So it seems, on the face of it. Nevertheless, the thesis that Thomas's doctrine of natural law is completely separable from Christian theology remains an option, capably expounded and defended by Anthony J. Lisska.[18]

Lisska provides an excellent overview of recent interest in Aristotelian ethics, starting with Anscombe's "Modern Moral Philosophy" and MacIntyre's *After Virtue*. He links natural law ethics with contemporary jurisprudence and philosophy of law. He expounds the reconstruction of natural law ethics by John Finnis, Germain Grisez and Joseph Boyle, continuing with Henry Veatch's objections to their "revisionist Thomism" (objections he clearly endorses).[19] He has a substantial discussion of human rights and natural law, including the work of Maritain. Throughout, however, taking a hint from a paper by Columba Ryan, Lisska contends that natural law is not something either in the human heart or in the mind of God but a philosophical concept offering an answer to the question of what makes laws possible at all: "It is the ontological foundation in human nature which explains the possibility of a moral theory and of lawmaking in the first place." Roughly speaking, Ryan asked the Kantian question: what is necessary theoretically in order to make lawmaking possible? And Thomas, as Lisska reads him, comes back with an Aristotelian response: the possibility of lawmaking is grounded in a theory of human nature.[20]

Far from being based on Christian theology, so Lisska maintains, Thomas's natural law ethics is a version of ethical naturalism, based on a revision of Aristotle's metaphysical account of human nature. Citing Ryan again, suggesting that "human nature, upon which the whole fabric of the natural law is based, may change and develop," Lisska likes the implied emphasis on the contingent nature of moral decision making: as moral agents, we may have to confront radically new situations in which "conclusions earlier drawn [from the general principles of natural law] may, in the changed circumstances, have no further application, or only a modified application."

This seems a considerable distance from the ecclesiastical appropriation of the doctrine feared by Michael Keeling, for example. On the other hand, significantly, the concept of divine providence is not listed in Lisska's index. He constantly glosses the eternal law as a quasi-Platonic set of archetypes, analogous to the Forms, which are found as the divine ideas in God's mind. He seems not to attach much importance to the texts where Thomas identifies eternal law with God, not just with archetypes. For Lisska, Thomas argues for a "humanist" account of moral theory, which is based upon reason alone.

## Back to Theology

According to John Bowlin, in another excellent book, we must not ignore the theological background. Far from being an attempt to provide a morality common to all human beings, a perfectly worthy venture, Thomas was out to provide an exegetical principle for discerning those elements of Torah still incumbent upon Christians.[21]

When we read Thomas it must be in awareness of his otherness, Bowlin contends. For example, he argues that doubts about our most basic moral obligations should not motivate our philosophical inquiry into the character of the moral life. We do not need to be told, by philosophers or anyone else, what our most basic obligations are. It would be insulting to be told how they are justified. We should regard with suspicion anyone whose scepticism about the rightness or wrongness of certain courses of action needed to be supported by moral theories. Perhaps we might not be able to say much about the basis of the obligations that we recognize, but that would not prevent us from thinking that there are some things we should do, others we should never do. Basic obligations aside, of course we rapidly disagree in the specifics, nor should that surprise us. Thomas, at any rate, is not offering to remove basic doubt about good and evil in human action, or to guide conduct in the particular. He is trying to educate Christians who by definition have an untroubled belief in moral realism, and who are to be pastors, hearing confessions, providing spiritual advice, and so on. What he offers is an account of why it is difficult to know what is right and wrong in particular circumstances because of what we are like and what the hindrances and helps are: the moral life, as he says (ST 1–2. 6). If we assume that doubts about obligation motivate our interest in moral philosophy and in natural law ethics, we are surely only looking for security, Bowlin thinks. When the basic inclinations which Thomas describes are turned into the specific prescriptions and prohibitions of our common human nature, then our access to the content of moral obligation in the concrete may seem to be freed from dispute—but are Thomas's considerations intended to dispel basic doubts about what we are to do? According to Bowlin, Thomas is not out to secure us against moral scepticism (an entirely modern project), nor on the other hand does he think his natural law considerations provide an adequate basis for moral guidance. On the contrary, the rest of the *secunda pars*, or rather the *secunda pars* as a whole, shows why a moral agent relying only on natural law—on what we all regard as basically required (no doubt about that, Bowlin thinks) finds it so difficult to make moral decisions, or to appreciate what decision making involves, or to understand what it is to be good in the first place.

Bowlin reminds us of how the *secunda pars* unrolls. God made us for beatitude, that is to say, for the perfect activity of our highest or deepest powers, with the assistance of "law," analogously understood, inscribed as "inclinations" in our nature as rational creatures, partly translatable into legislation by the political community, revealed as Torah and Gospel, in the historical economy of salvation, with the deiforming virtues of faith, hope, and charity, and the cardinal virtues—all badly disrupted in our sin-prone condition.

As Thomas remarked, in his last recorded notes on natural law:

> Now although God in creating man gave him this law of nature, the devil oversowed another law in man, namely the law of concupiscence . . . Since then the law of nature was destroyed by concupiscence, man needed to be brought back

to works of virtue, and to be drawn away from vice: for which purpose he needed the written law.[22]

That sounds somewhat less than ethical naturalism grounded on human reason. But the conflicting interpretations continue to flourish, at an unprecedentedly high level of philosophical rigour and sophistication.

It is tempting to agree with Servais Pinckaers, however, that abstracting Thomas's questions on natural law from those on the Old Law and the New Law, and from the questions on beatitude and virtue, produces nothing but confusion, and that, whatever happened after his day, he never saw natural law as functioning independently of the eternal law which is nothing other than the creator. But it would be premature to opt for one interpretation rather than one of the many others, in what is currently perhaps the most contested topic in Thomas's work.

One might even be tempted to go back to the finest study of Thomas's theology of law, untranslated into English, by the Protestant scholar, Ulrich Kühn. He places himself in a line of distinguished Protestant studies of aspects of Thomas's theology: H. Lyttkens on analogy (1953), Per-Erik Persson on the relationship between faith and reason (1957), Thomas Bonhoeffer on the doctrine of God (1961), and H. Vorster comparing Thomas and Luther on the concept of freedom (1965).[23] He notes that, although the literature created the impression that neo-Thomism was the only way of reading Thomas, indeed as if not just Cajetan but Thomas himself took a stand against Luther, Thomas nevertheless "belongs among the fathers of Protestant theology," and "deserves to be listened to as a pre-Reformation theologian, not as a voice in the chorus of post-Tridentine theology."

Kühn welcomes the work of Catholic scholars, naming S. Pfürtner, Otto Hermann Pesch, E. H. Schillebeeckx, B. Decker and G. Söhngen, as showing that, from within Thomist scholarship itself, Thomas was being freed from the anti-Reformation apologetics which he thinks distorted received neo-Thomist interpretations.

His own study begins with a remark by Heinrich Maria Christmann, in 1958, regretting that Thomas had been pictured for so long more as a philosopher than a theologian—agreeing, then, explicitly with Chenu's insistence, in 1950, that he is more a theologian than a philosopher. He takes us back to Gilson's Aberdeen Gifford Lectures, and insists that Thomas's theology has to be read as the fructification of contemplative study: the teaching of a saint, theologian, mystic. This "new picture of Thomas" is largely an achievement of French theology, culminating in the sidelining of neo-Thomism prior to Vatican II—indeed this "new Thomas-understanding" was an element in the "revolution" of Vatican II, so Kühn thinks.

Kühn traces the history of the idea of natural law through Thomas's work. In the Commentary on the *Sentences* and on Matthew, he shows, law is treated in the light of the virtue of Christ. In the *Summa contra Gentiles* and in the *Compendium Theologiae* law is treated in the light of God as creator. In the *Summa Theologiae*, by contrast, law is discussed neither in Christology nor in *de Deo creatore*, but in the context of the theology of the moral agent as *imago Dei* returning to God; law is the exterior principle that moves the human being to do well, ultimately to attain beatitude in the communion of saints. Law is oriented to beatitude. Natural law is a kind of reflection of the eternal law—requiring to be taken up into the Mosaic Law, oriented then towards the promise of salvation; and then to be taken into the New Law, in which the believer is instructed by the teaching of Christ interiorized by the Spirit received in the sacraments, the inward grace that allows us to keep the Law and thus attain the righteousness. The essence of what Thomas means is that the New Law is an interior law of God giving himself freely in love to human beings who respond to God's will in complete "autonomy"—Thomas needs both the metaphysical and the Old Testament.

Whatever Luther feared, Thomas's theology was not entirely subjugated by pagan philosophy. Kühn explains the difference between Thomas and Luther as follows.[24] For Luther sinners become friends of God not only by receiving the divine gift of charity but by the light of the Cross. That we are righteous is something that transcends us: "righteousness is extrinsic to us" (*justitia extra nos posita*). Thomas, obviously, does not deny that the transcendence of Christ is righteousness; but he certainly denies that our being justified is nothing other than Christ's righteousness. There is a sense in which we are ourselves actually justified: righteousness is intrinsic to us, so to speak. For Luther, however, "all our righteousness is to be sought *extra nos*." In practice, so Kühn argues, the absence of this "*extra nos*" in Thomas's theology means that his appeal to the image of God is not in the end controlled as it should be by explicit trust in the mercy of God revealed in Christ's Passion. This does not mean that Christ has no place in Thomas's understanding of the relationship between the righteous and God. On the contrary, Kühn contends, the friendship between the righteous and God rests in nothing other than the grace given through Christ's Passion. Thomas's personal faith is certainly centred on Christ crucified; but his theology, Kühn holds, is not a *theologia crucis*, Cross-centred, as Luther's is.[25]

In short, when Thomas reaches the question of natural law, it is long after he has put in place his theology of beatitude and virtue; he takes natural law to be self-evidently participation in divine providence and always already requiring deeper instruction by the Law of Moses and by "the Law of the Gospel," as he calls it, "the grace of the Holy Spirit given inwardly" (1–2.106.1–2). But, for Kühn, Thomas's discussion is not explicitly Christological enough.

## Notes

This chapter was previously published as Fergus Kerr, "Natural Law: Incommensurable Readings" (chapter 6 of Fergus Kerr, *After Aquinas*, Blackwell, Oxford, 2002).

1. Jeffrey Stout, "Truth, Natural Law, and Ethical Theory," in *Natural Law Theory: Contemporary Essays*, edited by Robert P. George (Oxford: Clarendon Press, 1992): 71–102, an excellent essay in a first-rate collection, with chapters by Joseph Boyle, Robert P. George, and Russell Hittinger on natural law, practical reasoning, and morality, as well as on natural law and legal theory by Neil MacCormick, John Finnis, Jeremy Waldron and Michael S. Moore, natural law, justice, and rights by Hadley Arkes and Lloyd L. Weinreb, and on legal formalism by Joseph Raz and Ernest J. Weinrib; Vernon Bourke, "Is Thomas Aquinas a Natural Law Ethicist?" *The Monist* 58 (1974): 66.

2. A. P. d'Entrèves, *Natural Law: An Introduction to Legal Philosophy* (London: Hutchinson, 1951, revised 1970): 42, 49; whether Hooker had this much importance, or was even much read, before John Keble brought out his edition of the Works in 1836, is debatable; for more on the continuity of Anglicanism with the pre-Reformed Church see d'Entrèves, *The Medieval Contribution to Political Thought: Thomas Aquinas, Marsilius of Padua, Richard Hooker* (London: Oxford University Press, 1939).

3. D. J. O'Connor, *Aquinas and Natural Law* (London: Macmillan, 1967); out of print, not listed in recent bibliographies, but still much consulted in philosophy department libraries, no doubt in the absence of anything else as lucid and short.

4. Michael Keeling, *The Mandate of Heaven: The Divine Command and the Natural Order* (Edinburgh: T. and T. Clark, 1995): 17.

5. Ibid, p. 203. Whether the Greek Fathers understood *perichoresis* in the Trinity as dancing depends on conflating an omega and an omicron.

6. H. O. Mounce in Brian Davies (ed.), *Philosophy of Religion: A Guide to the Subject* (London: Cassell, 1998): 270ff.

7. Jacques Maritain, *The Rights of Man and Natural Law* (London: Bles, 1944), *The Person and the Common Good* (London: Bles, 1947), *Man and the State* (Chicago: University of Chicago Press, 1951).

8. Oliver O'Donovan, *Resurrection and Moral Order: An Outline for Evangelical Ethics*, 2nd edn. (Leicester: Apollo, 1994): 87.

9. Apollinarius (c.310–c.390) denied that Christ had a human mind or soul; the view that Barth's doctrine of Christ's divinity diminishes his humanity to this extent seems rather implausible.

10. Michael S. Northcott, *The Environment and Christian Ethics* (Cambridge: Cambridge University Press): 135.

11. R. Hittinger, "Natural Law and Catholic Moral Theology" in *A Preserving Grace: Protestants, Catholics, and Natural Law*, edited by Michael Cromartie (Washington, DC: William B. Eerdmans, 1997): 1–30, quotations in text pp. 11–12, 16.

12. Servais Pinckaers, *The Sources of Christian Ethics* (Washington, DC: Catholic University of America Press, 1995).

13. Pamela M. Hall, *Narrative and the Natural Law: An Interpretation of Thomistic Ethics* (Notre Dame, IN: University of Notre Dame Press, 1994).

14. Thomas's discussion of law in the *Summa Theologiae*, as J. Tonneau, "The Teaching of the Thomist Tract on Law," *The Thomist* 34 (1970): 11–83, demonstrates, is pervaded by biblical allusions: even in 1–2.90–97 there are 64 references to Scripture, compared with 48 to Aristotle and 35 to Augustine; in 90–108 there are 724 to Scripture, 96 to Aristotle, 87 to Augustine, 5 to Denys; the references are especially to Deuteronomy, Psalms, the Wisdom books, Isaiah, Ezechiel, Hosea, Job, Jeremiah; and, of course, as Tonneau notes, when Thomas writes of "reason" (*ratio*), he thinks implicitly of *logos* with the divine *Logos* in the background, and not of "reason" as philosophers think of it since the Enlightenment; the whole discussion is conducted as polemic with Pelagianism; and the questions on grace should not be treated as a complete treatise *de gratia*; they contain very little about illumination, adoption and divinization.

15. M. D. Chenu, "L'Ancien Testament dans la théologie médiévale," in his splendid collection *La Théologie au douzième siècle* (Paris: Vrin, 1957), covering the twelfth-century Renaissance, the discovery of nature and history, Platonism, the work of Boethius, symbolism and allegory, the "evangelical revival," the entry of Greek patristic theology, etc., by far the best introduction to the background to Thomas Aquinas's thought, partly translated as *Nature, Man, and Society in the Twelfth Century: Essays on New Theological Perspectives in the Latin West* (Chicago: University of Chicago Press, 1968, reprinted Toronto: University of Toronto Press, 1997).

16. The best book here is W. G. B. M. Valkenberg, *"Did Not Our Hearts Burn?": Place and Function of Holy Scripture in the Theology of St. Thomas Aquinas* (Utrecht: Thomas Institute, 1990).

17. See Beryl Smalley, "William of Auvergne, John of La Rochelle and St. Thomas Aquinas on the Old Law," in *St. Thomas Aquinas: Commemorative Studies*, edited by A. A. Maurer, vol. 2 (Toronto: Pontifical Institute of Medieval Studies, 1974): 11–71; her pioneering book *The Study of the Bible in the Middle Ages* (Oxford: Oxford University Press, 1940), remains indispensable.

18. Anthony J. Lisska, *Aquinas's Theory of Natural Law: An Analytic Reconstruction* (Oxford: Clarendon Press, 1996).

19. Ibid., pp. 167–68. Lisska sides with Henry Veatch in his criticism of the "Cartesianism" that distorts the "revisionist Thomism" represented by the work of John Finnis, Germain Grisez, and others: one more version of Thomism, much contested, and regrettably much too large a subject to be discussed here.

20. Lisska, *Aquinas's Theory*, p. 81. Columba Ryan, "The Traditional Concept of Natural Law," in *Light on the Natural Law*, edited by Illtud Evans (London: Burns & Oates, 1965).

21. John Bowlin, *Contingency and Fortune in Aquinas's Ethics* (Cambridge: Cambridge University Press, 1999).

22. Thomas Aquinas, *Collationes in Decem Praeceptis*, edited with introduction and notes by J. P. Torrell, *Revue des Sciences Philosophiques et Théologiques* 69 (1985): 5–40, 227–63.

23. Ulrich Kühn, *Via Caritatis: Theologie des Gesetzes bei Thomas von Aquin* (Göttingen: Vandenhoeck & Ruprecht, 1965); Hampus Lyttkens, *The Analogy Between God and the World: An Investigation of its Background and Interpretation of Its Use by Thomas of Aquino* (Uppsala: Lundequistka Bokhandeln, 1953); Per-Erik Persson, *Sacra Doctrina: Reason and Revelation in Aquinas* (Oxford: Blackwell, 1970; Swedish original 1957); Thomas Bonhoeffer, *Die Gotteslehre des Thomas von Aquin also Sprachproblem* (Tubingen: Mohr, 1961); Hans Vorster, *Das Freiheitsverständnis bei Thomas von Aquin und Martin Luther* (Gottingen: Vandenhoeck & Ruprecht, 1965).

24. Kühn, *Via Caritatis*, pp. 30–43, 252–58.

25. On Luther and natural law see Antti Raunio, "Natural Law and Faith: The Forgotten Foundations of Ethics in Luther's Theology," in *Union with Christ: The New Finnish Interpretation of Luther*, edited by Carl E. Braaten and Robert W. Jenson (Grand Rapids, MI: Eerdmans, 1998): 96–124.

# Suggested Readings

---

## A. Primary Sources

The critical edition of Aquinas's works is currently being published by the Leonine Commission, established in 1880. This contains the best available Latin text of the *Summa Theologiae*. To date there are only two complete English translations of the *Summa*: the Blackfriars one (London: Eyre and Spottiswoode; New York: McGraw-Hill Book Company, 1964–1980) and *St. Thomas Aquinas: "Summa Theologica,"* translated by the Fathers of the English Dominican Province (originally published by Burns, Oates, and Washbourne in London in 1911 and now available from Christian Classics, Westminster, MD, 1981). This translation is also freely available on the Internet at www.gocart.org/summa.html. Note also that there are currently available some single volumes offering translations of various sections of the *Summa Theologiae*. Examples include: *God and Creation*, trans. William Baumgarth and Richard J. Regan (Scranton, PA: University of Scranton Press, 1994); *The Treatise on Human Nature: "Summa Theologiae" Ia 75–89*, trans. Robert Pasnau (Indianapolis: Hackett Publishing Company, Inc., 2002); *Virtue: Way to Happiness*, trans. Richard J. Regan (Scranton, PA: University of Scranton Press, 1999); *Aquinas: Treatise on Law*, trans. Richard J. Regan (Indianapolis: Hackett Publishing Company, Inc., 2000). See also Timothy McDermott, ed., *St. Thomas Aquinas: "Summa Theologiae": A Concise Translation* (London: Eyre and Spottiswoode, 1989) and *Aquinas: A Summary of Philosophy*, ed. and trans. Richard J. Regan (Indianapolis: Hackett Publishing Company, Inc., 2003).

## B. Secondary Sources

### 1. Books

Jan Aertsen, *Nature and Creature: Thomas Aquinas's Way of Thought* (Leiden: E. J. Brill, 1988).

G. E. M. Anscombe and P. T. Geach, *Three Philosophers* (Oxford: Basil Blackwell, 1961).

David Burrell, *Aquinas, God and Action* (Notre Dame, IN: University of Notre Dame Press, 1979).

M. D. Chenu, *St. Thomas D'Aquin et la théologie* (Paris: Éditions du Seuil, 1959).

M. D. Chenu, *Toward Understanding Saint Thomas*, trans. A. M. Landry and D. Hughes (Chicago: Henry Regnery Company, 1964).

F. C. Copleston, *Aquinas* (Harmondsworth: Penguin Books, 1955).

Brian Davies, *The Thought of Thomas Aquinas* (Oxford: Clarendon Press, 1992).

Brian Davies, *Aquinas* (London and New York: Continuum, 2002).

Brian Davies, ed., *Thomas Aquinas: Contemporary Philosophical Perspectives* (New York: Oxford University Press, 2002).

James C. Doig, *Aquinas on Metaphysics* (The Hague: Martinus Nijhoff, 1972).

James C. Doig, *Aquinas's Philosophical Commentary on the "Ethics"* (Dordrecht, Boston, and London: Kluwer Academic Publishers, 2001).

Leo J. Elders, *The Philosophical Theology of St. Thomas Aquinas* (Leiden: E. J. Brill, 1990).

John Finnis, *Aquinas* (Oxford: Oxford University Press, 1998).

Thomas Gilby, *The Political Thought of Thomas Aquinas* (Chicago: University of Chicago Press, 1958).

Etienne Gilson, *The Christian Philosophy of St. Thomas Aquinas* (London: Victor Gollanz Ltd., 1961).

W. J. Hankey, *God in Himself: Aquinas's Doctrine of God as Expounded in the "Summa Theologiae"* (Oxford: Oxford University Press, 1987).

R. J. Henle, *Saint Thomas and Platonism* (The Hague: Martinus Nijhoff, 1956).

Thomas S. Hibbs, *Dialectic and Narrative in Aquinas* (Notre Dame, IN: University of Notre Dame Press, 1995).

John Inglis, *On Aquinas* (Belmont, CA: Wadsworth, 2002).

John Jenkins, *Knowledge and Faith in Thomas Aquinas* (Cambridge: Cambridge University Press, 1997).

Anthony Kenny, *The Five Ways* (London: Routledge and Kegan Paul, 1969).

Anthony Kenny, ed., *Aquinas: A Collection of Critical Essays* (London and Melbourne: Macmillan, 1969).

Anthony Kenny, *Aquinas* (Oxford: Oxford University Press, 1980).

Anthony Kenny, *Aquinas on Mind* (London and New York: Routledge, 1993).

Anthony Kenny, *Aquinas on Being* (Oxford: Clarendon Press, 2002).

Norman Kretzmann, *The Metaphysics of Theism* (Oxford: Clarendon Press, 1997).

Norman Kretzmann, *The Metaphysics of Creation* (Oxford: Clarendon Press, 1999).

Norman Kretzmann and Eleonore Stump, eds., *The Cambridge Companion to Aquinas* (Cambridge: Cambridge University Press, 1993).

Anthony J. Lisska, *Aquinas's Theory of Natural Law: An Analytic Reconstruction* (Oxford: Clarendon Press, 1996).

C. F. J. Martin, *Thomas Aquinas: God and Explanations* (Edinburgh: Edinburgh University Press, 1997).

Ralph McInerny, *St. Thomas Aquinas* (Notre Dame, IN and London: University of Notre Dame Press, 1982).

Ralph McInerny, *Ethica Thomistica: The Moral Philosophy of Thomas Aquinas* (Washington, DC: The Catholic University of America Press, 1982).

Robert Pasnau, *Thomas Aquinas on Human Nature* (Cambridge: Cambridge University Press, 2002).

Robert Pasnau and Christopher Shields, *The Philosophy of Aquinas* (Boulder, CO: Westview Press, 2004).

Per Erik Person, *Sacra Doctrina: Reason and Revelation in Aquinas* (Oxford: Basil Blackwell, 1970).

R. W. Schmidt, *The Domain of Logic according to Saint Thomas Aquinas* (The Hague: Martinus Nijhoff, 1966).

Eleonore Stump, *Aquinas* (London and New York: Routledge, 2003).

Jean-Pierre Torrell, OP, *Saint Thomas Aquinas: The Person and His Work* (Washington, DC: The Catholic University of America Press, 1996).

Jean-Pierre Torrell, OP, *Saint Thomas Aquinas: Spiritual Master* (Washington, DC: The Catholic University of America Press, 2003).

John F. Wippel, *Metaphysical Themes in Thomas Aquinas* (Washington, DC: The Catholic University of America Press, 1984).

John F. Wippel, *The Metaphysical Thought of Thomas Aquinas* (Washington, DC: The Catholic University of America Press, 2000).

## 2. Articles

Jan A. Aertsen, "The Convertibility of Being and Good in St. Thomas Aquinas," *The New Scholasticism* 59 (1985).

Jan A. Aertsen, "The Philosophical Importance of the Doctrine of the Transcendentals in Thomas Aquinas," *Revue Internationale de Philosophie* 52 (1998).

E. J. Ashworth, "Signification and Modes of Signifying in Thirteenth Century Logic: A Preface to Aquinas on Analogy," *Medieval Philosophy and Theology* I (1991).

E. J. Ashworth, "Analogy and Equivocation in Thirteenth-Century Logic: Aquinas in Context," *Medieval Studies* 54 (1992).

Patterson Brown, "St. Thomas: Doctrine of Necessary Being," *The Philosophical Review* LXXIII (1964).

W. N. Clarke, "What Is Most and Least Relevant in the Metaphysics of St. Thomas Today?" *International Philosophical Quarterly* 14 (1974).

Brian Davies, "Classical Theism and the Doctrine of Divine Simplicity," in *Language, Meaning and God*, ed. Brian Davies,(London: Geoffrey Chapman, 1987).

Alan Donagan, "Thomas Aquinas on Human Action," in *The Cambridge History of Later Medieval Philosophy*, ed. N. Kretzmann, A. Kenny, and J. Pinborg (Cambridge: Cambridge University Press, 1982).

Robert J. Fogelin, "A Reading of Aquinas's Five Ways," *American Philosophical Quarterly* 27 (1990).

John J. Haldane, "Aquinas on Sense-Perception," *The Philosophical Review* 92 (1983).

Mark Jordan, "The Intelligibility of the World and the Divine Ideas in Aquinas," *The Review of Metaphysics* 38 (1984).

Bonnie Kent, "Transitory Vice: Thomas Aquinas on Incontinence," *Journal of the History of Philosophy* 27 (1989).

Fergus Kerr, "Aquinas After Marion," *New Blackfriars* 76 (1995).

Gyula Klima, "The Semantic Principles underlying Saint Thomas Aquinas's Metaphysics of Being," *Medieval Philosophy and Theology* 5 (1996).

Kenneth J. Konyndyk, "Aquinas on Faith and Science," *Faith and Philosophy* 12 (1995).

Norman Kretzmann, "Goodness, Knowledge, and Indeterminancy in the Philosophy of St. Thomas Aquinas," *Journal of Philosophy* LXXX (1983).

Scott MacDonald, "Aquinas's Libertarian Account of Free Choice," *Revue Internationale de Philosophie* 52 (1998).

Scott MacDonald, "Practical Reasoning and Reasons-Explanations: Aquinas's Account of Reason's Role in Action," in *Aquinas's Moral Theory: Essays in Honor of Norman Kretzmann*, ed. Scott MacDonald and Eleonore Stump (Ithaca, NY, and London: Cornell University Press, 1999).

Herbert McCabe, "The Logic of Mysticism," in *Religion and Philosophy*, ed. Martin Warner, (Royal Institute of Philosophy Supplement 31 (Cambridge: Cambridge University Press, 1992).

Robert Pasnau, "Aquinas on Thought's Linguistic Nature," *The Monist* 80 (1997).

Hilary Putnam, "Thoughts Addressed to an Analytical Thomist," *The Monist* 80 (1997).

# About the Editor and Contributors

Leonard E. Boyle was born in 1923 and died in 1999. For many years he was a professor in the Pontifical Institute of Medieval Studies at Toronto. He also taught at the Center for Medieval Studies at the University of Toronto. He subsequently became Prefect of the Vatican Library. He is the author of *Medieval Latin Paleography* (1984).

Brian Davies is professor of philosophy at Fordham University. His books include *The Thought of Thomas Aquinas* (1992), *Aquinas* (2002), and *An Introduction to the Philosophy of Religion* (3rd ed., 2004). He is editor of *Thomas Aquinas: Contemporary Philosophical Perspectives* (2002). With G. R. Evans, he is coeditor of *Anselm of Canterbury: The Major Works* (1998). With Brian Leftow, he is coeditor of *The Cambridge Companion to Anselm* (2004).

Peter Geach is one of the most distinguished living British philosophers. His writings are numerous. Especially famous are: *Mental Acts* (1957), *God and the Soul* (1969), *The Virtues* (1977), and *Reference and Generality* (3rd ed., 1980). Many of his articles appear in *Logic Matters* (1972).

Anthony Kenny has taught for many years at Oxford University and has been master of Balliol College, and warden of Rhodes House, Oxford. A prolific writer, whose published works include volumes on Aristotle, Descartes, and Wittgenstein, Kenny has also written books on Aquinas. These are: *The Five Ways* (1969), *Aquinas* (1980), *Aquinas on Mind* (1993), and *Aquinas on Being* (2002).

**Bonnie Kent** teaches philosophy at the University of California, Irvine. She is the author of *Virtues of the Will: The Transformation of Ethics in the Late Thirteenth Century* (1995).

**Fergus Kerr** was regent of Blackfriars Hall, Oxford University, until 2004. Currently editor of *New Blackfriars*, he is the author of *Theology After Wittgenstein* (1986) and *After Aquinas* (2002).

**Herbert McCabe** was born in 1926. He died in 2001. For much of his life he taught at Oxford, though he also lectured widely in the United Kingdom and the United States. For a number of years he edited the journal *New Blackfriars*. His books include *Law, Love and Language* (1968) and *God Matters* (1987). Three posthumously published volumes of his writings have appeared: *God Still Matters* (2002), *God, Christ and Us* (2003), and *The Good Life* (2005).

**Robert Pasnau** teaches philosophy at the University of Colorado, Boulder. He is the author of *Thomas Aquinas on Human Nature* (2002). His annotated translation of Aquinas's commentary on Aristotle's *De Anima* appeared in 1999. He has a translation and commentary on *Summa Theologiae* Ia, 75–89 (2002). Together with Christopher Shields, he is the author of *The Philosophy of Aquinas* (2004).

**Eleonore Stump** is the Robert J. Henle Professor of Philosophy at Saint Louis University. She is the author of *Dialectic and its Place in the Development of Medieval Logic* (1980) and *Aquinas* (2003). Also the author of many published articles, she is, with Norman Kretzmann, coeditor of *The Cambridge Companion to Aquinas* (1993) and *The Cambridge Companion to Augustine* (2001).

**Victor White** was born in 1902 and died in 1960. He was an associate of C. G. Jung, who said that he hoped that White "would carry on the magnum opus." White also taught for the English Dominican Province. He specialized in Thomistic thinking and modern psychology. The author of many published articles, he also wrote *God and the Unconscious* (1952) and *God the Unknown* (1956).

**John Wippel** is professor of philosophy at the Catholic University of America, Washington, DC. The author of many articles, he has also written *The Metaphysical Thought of Godfrey of Fontaines* (1981), *Metaphysical Themes in Thomas Aquinas* (1984), *Thomas Aquinas and the Divine Ideas* (1993), and *The Metaphysical Thought of Thomas Aquinas* (2000).